DRAGON EGG

A PRACTICAL GUIDE TO INNOVATION

DR GORDON HART

Copyright © 2020 Dr Gordon Hart

All rights reserved.

ISBN: 9798672432205

CONTENTS

1. Introduction 5
2. About this book 7
3. Philosophical and historical foundations 13
4. Frameworks 25
5. Case study: Employing a familiar framework. 45
6. Problems 55
7. Case study: A problem arises. 75
8. Customer discovery describes the problem 85
9. Case study: A cry for help is eventually heard. 115
10. Solutions 121
11. Case study: Solving the problem. 213
12. Innovation 221
13. Case study: A necessary innovation. 237
14. Workshops 243
15. Case study: Storms, norms, performs. 295
16. Presentation 307
17. Case study: A bold proposal. 331
18. Letting go. 337
19. Case study: Letting go. 353
20. The last word 359
21. The 76 standard solutions 361
22. Works Cited 369

1. INTRODUCTION

Problem solving is demanding. At its heart is a contradiction.

To solve a problem well requires a wild and creative chaos to accumulate a mass of potential solutions. The mind must be free to roam far and wide in search of a valuable problem and to discover all of its potential solutions. Each problem and every solution must be turned this way and that. Each viewed from every angle. Observed up close and then seen from afar. You may face a common problem that now demands a new solution. You may face a new problem that has never before been explored. To solve either may demand an enthusiasm for adopting an unusual perspective and a readiness to propose a course that no other would adopt.

To solve a problem well also demands a conscientious attention to detail to identify the very heart of each problem and the fitness of each potential solution. Each solution must be exercised, contrasted and compared to its siblings to determine which will win the race to resolve the problem. Problem solving demands a firm, formal framework into which each solution must be pinned, classified, catalogued and labelled with care.

Perhaps you can exhibit both a creative chaos and a conscientious attention to each detail simultaneously. Alternatively, perhaps you must collaborate with others who possess the skills that you lack. In either case, to solve a difficult problem well will demand a careful negotiation. The two strategies required to solve a problem will exhibit quite contrary behaviours that can repel one another with disdain for the other's lack of vision or lack of rigour.

For thousands of years Humans have faced a cruel and unforgiving universe in which life may be cut short by a multitude of terrible fates, from starvation and disease to sharp teeth and grasping claws that crouch in the dark. We have also learned that this cruel and unforgiving world is our only source of all that sustains us. A bountiful cornucopia. A paradise. An Eden, if only we can learn how to separate those rewards that sustain life from punishments that are cruel and final.

Humans have solved difficult problems for thousands of years, and have learned how to reconcile these two problem-solving spirits. In the moral of an ancient tale, the creative soul of a hot-headed young hero is tempered by the cool head of experience by the tale's end. In the procedures of modern science, we learn how a creative chaos can be captured in a test tube by a conscientious attention to detail. Humans have evolved to solve problems and have learned how to reconcile these warring siblings.

This book describes how.

2. ABOUT THIS BOOK

I am a Rocket Scientist, and it was not until I attempted to explain how I design rockets did I realise that I also needed to know why this knowledge worked. This is harder than it sounds. A thorough understanding of developmental psychology, comparative mythology, religion and philosophy is rather beyond my areas of expertise. Little did I know that I'd need at least a rudimentary understanding of these topics to complete this task.

After all, we act things out before we understand them. A young child may not be able to articulate the rules of a game despite being quite capable of playing this game with confidence. As we grow into adulthood knowledge is framed and understood in a hierarchy. At the bottom is play, then narrative, which is captured in drama, embedded into culture through myth, codified into rules through religion and ultimately analysed and understood by the philosophers. Despite the support offered by this framework upon which knowledge is hung, I knew how to solve problems long before I knew how I knew.

This text started as a simple bibliography. The development of new concepts in commercial rocket science requires an understanding of formal science and technology to be mixed with an ability to scan the technology horizon and predict an uncertain future. With so many unknowns to juggle, a reliable predictive skill demands negotiation between a good technical understanding and a strong intuition to fill the inevitable gaps. To achieve this feat of prophecy requires some tools, and these tools are to be found within this bibliography - an assembly of sources that I have found useful over the years to help me to divine the future.

I offer this short library to new colleagues to help them find their feet when they join the innovation team within which I work. It's not required reading, but it seems to help. It seems insufficient to offer new employees this reading list without explaining why this particular set of texts would offer a useful primer on our working practices. I must not only explain how to solve problems but must also explain why these particular working practices offer the predictive power that we need.

To write a *How To...* book based upon this bibliography would offer a poor facsimile of these excellent source materials. To offer a step by step guide on how to solve problems would offer an anthology of fragments drawn from selected sources which, after a little reading, you can assemble for yourself from these source texts.

Alternatively, I elected to explain why you might wish to invest the considerable time and effort it may take to work through this reading list. Throughout this material the reader is directed to these texts for a comprehensive understanding of these methods. Assembling a philosophy of problem solving and concept development is out of my particular reach, but perhaps I can offer a few fragments of its *Tao*[1].

'Who's the book for?'. I was only a few pages into this text when a friend, a professional writer, asked this reasonable question. The answer was clear. At the time of this conversation the intended readership of this text exhibited a grand total of one. Me. I could solve tricky problems well, but I needed to understand why I knew what I knew and why it worked.

My career has drawn me away from the formal system design of engineering structures and the practical application of scientific principles to realise these designs. The more experience I gained in the design of engineered solutions, the more I wanted to work ever earlier in the design process. I needed to witness and manipulate that first spark of inspiration that transforms a simple observation into a business winning innovation.

My early attempts to decorate the back of envelopes with designs for the future followed every cliché in the book. After all, action movies often require a technological or scientific creative genius to construct the hero's *Deus ex Machina* that will save the day. A clever car with an oil slick and smoke screen. A convenient hack into an impregnable computer system. A watch, with a trick. All are fashioned by an eccentric boffin who is ever ready to produce some outlandish innovation at a moment's notice. You too can design the future, but are a million dreams all it's going to take? Is a little more passion and a little luck all that you need, and the coveted job title of crazy boffin is all yours?

Unlike the movies, if you play the eccentric boffin in real life it is likely that no one will listen to you. Pulling innovation out of your creative psyche and expecting anyone to value it requires a screenplay that demands that they do. The reality of innovation is quite different,

---

[1] A Chinese word signifying 'way', 'path', 'route', 'road' or sometimes more loosely 'doctrine', 'principle' or 'holistic science'. Within the context of traditional Chinese philosophy and religion, Tao is the natural order of the universe whose character human intuition must discern to realize the potential for individual wisdom. This intuitive knowing of 'life' cannot be grasped as just a concept but is known through actual living experience of one's everyday being. Wikipedia.

particularly if you work in a large and established corporation. It has taken years with the support of talented colleges to marshal this creative chaos into a framework that is rational, explainable and, above all, convincing. I needed to write it all down. Get it straight. Observe it all on one grand vista.

It didn't take long to realise that others may be trapped by this cliché. If you are attempting to innovate your way to becoming the next Major Boothroyd or a Lucius Fox with the enthusiasm and creativity that the role demands, then I apologize to the reader for not considering you from the start. I assume that you are a person who needs to solve problems, and solve them well. The problems that you wish to solve may never have been encountered before. Alternatively, the problems that you face are long standing and familiar, but now demand a new approach. In both cases you may now be motivated to offer more innovative solutions. You are not familiar with the techniques and tools of problem solving, and you may be new to a role that demands an innovative approach. Alternatively, you may be familiar with innovation but find your current approach isn't offering the outcomes that you need. Hopefully this text can offer some small inspiration to help you to move forward.

In this book I cast my net across multiple techniques of problem solving, but do not sink a hook as deeply as a specialist text. I reference the sources that have guided me over the years, and encourage the reader to dive more deeply into specific areas of problem solving through these texts. This particular book can be treated as a *primer*. In this primer I introduce the topic of problem solving, describe how problems are identified and articulated, and offer methods to solve these problems. Finally, I explain how these solutions can be articulated back to those who suffer the problem that you may have solved.

This book is not about business modelling, because I don't think that I'm particularly entrepreneurial. I leave the business modelling to the experts, but do ask them a fundamental question. In *The Startup Way* [1] Eric Reis observes that entrepreneurs can be found anywhere that people are doing the honourable and often unheralded labour of testing a novel idea, creating a better way to work, or serving new customers by extending a product or service into new markets. But where did that novel idea come from?

In *The Four Steps to the Epiphany* [2] Steve Blank explains that being a great entrepreneur means finding the path through the fog, confusion and myriad of choices confronted when discovering new customers and new products. To do that, you need vision and a process. How does one first glimpse that vision?

In *Value Proposition Design: How to Create Products and Services Customers Want* [3] Alexander Osterwalder offers visual tools to help us connect a detailed description of our customer to the gains that our proposed product or service may offer and to the pains that this offering may resolve. This connection may be clear, but how is the leap from an understanding of the customer to a valuable product achieved? How can we bridge the gap between the customer's needs and the product that will serve those needs? Can we bridge this gap using tools that consistently and predictably create multiple potential solutions?

An individual is often described as an innovator if they exhibit a talent for entrepreneurial success. The innovator is often imagined as a bold, creative entrepreneur. The focussed, driven, hardworking nucleus of a new enterprise in possession of all the creativity and drive required to construct a viable and successful business. A visionary that is well rewarded for delivering a valuable product to a grateful customer.

An individual may also be recognised as an innovator if they exhibit the chaotically creative talent required to understand and resolve intractable problems. A problem solving mind so bursting with ideas that it can barely keep up with its own output.

The greatest share of attention often seems to rest front of house, in the limelight, with the entrepreneur. My contribution does not focus upon the diligent work of business building, but upon the discovery of that elusive great idea that connects the customer to a valuable product. This role is not entrepreneurial at its core. This activity is better described as *diagnostic*. Imagine a medical drama that portrays an unfortunate patient with a rare and unidentified condition brought before the skilled but flawed doctor. The patient is scrutinised by the belligerent intellect of this medical genius. Inspiration will strike. Diagnosis is made. Obscure cure proscribed. The patient is then hurried away to the tender care of those doctors and nurses who must engage in the unseen labour of saving the patient's life. This diagnostic role is better illustrated with the detective skills of Sherlock Holmes rather than the business acumen of the world's current crop of Rockstar Entrepreneurs.

Despite this distinction between the entrepreneurial and the diagnostic, to establish the true cause of a customer's problems and crafting potential solutions is intimately linked to the task of business building. Both characters are open to new ideas and are creative in their output. Like entrepreneurship, the diagnostic role takes place within that extreme uncertainty of new customers, new problems, and new products. There are many excellent works on business building to choose from and I doubt that I can add much value to this large and well researched field. Consequently, in this text I will focus upon my own diagnostic role.

Furthermore, much of my problem-solving career has taken place within the structure of large and well-established organisations. This can be both a blessing and a curse. The biggest blessing that I enjoy is working within the security of a well understood, established and successful business model. I usually know who the customer is and the organisation will have a successful and well understood product line to serve that customer.

The biggest curse is this very same business model. It may constrain me from investigating outside the established business boundaries. If a customer is well understood and supports the business well, then it can be difficult to find support in the search for valuable opportunities faced by a new customer with new problems. If an organisation enjoys a well understood product line that evolves in predictable steps year on year, it can be hard to gain support for radical or revolutionary solutions. I will attempt to explain how to innovate within an established model, but will not delve too deeply into how that existing business model may be structured.

The works of Reis focus upon the efforts of an innovator to found a new business, or recognises that a leader within an established organisation may demand a different approach. At both ends of this spectrum of scale and success these texts often seem to have already secured the authority to transform the organisation as required.

Injecting more innovative thinking into an established organisation is not automatically associated with the authority to make changes to that organisation. In fact, significant structural changes may only be authorised after you can demonstrate that a new approach will bear fruit. You may not yet possess endorsement from any significant authority within your organisation to make any changes. You must attempt to adopt new working practises, find new customers and propose radical new product lines between the cracks of the existing structure. You will be judged not on the value of the processes you adopt but on the results of your work. You may in good faith attempt to spot valuable new problems and solutions before your competition. Enthusiasts for this role must recognise that the disruptive voice is not often treated as a safe pair of hands, ripe for promotion.

Reis observes that great ideas sometimes appear in unexpected places. If you labour in one of these unexpected places, then this book is for you. If you don't have support for your ideas from the executive board, if you are not yet authorised nor resourced to engage in a program of innovation, if you only have your own resources to turn to in your effort to conjure up these unexpected ideas, if you aspire to be a start-up founder but have not yet had that killer idea, if you work beneath an unremarkable rock at the bottom of a deep corporate ocean and are only as valuable as your last unexpected idea, if the President of the United States is unlikely to sweep into the room and press his entire executive power behind you and your idea, then this book is for you. Under these meagre circumstances your ideas must be very good if they are to attract any attention at all.

I have invested much of my working life trying to understand what problems are and how to identify the most valuable. I have attempted to understand how one might solve problems quickly and efficiently whilst surviving the austerity of innovation. This is why I have tried to learn what innovations are, and why they seem to matter so much. This is why I have worked hard to understand where good ideas come from, and how we can increase the likelihood of encountering a really, *really* good one. Can we predict the future better than the competition? Can we learn how to frequently and reliably diagnose the customer's problem and offer an effective resolution?

If I was presented with the most intractable problem in the whole world, could I solve it? With a long enough lever, perhaps I could move the Earth itself. This book describes my efforts to find that lever.

3. PHILOSOPHICAL AND HISTORICAL FOUNDATIONS

Where do ideas come from? Can we grab them from the air? This was the question asked late one night by a taxi driver as I returned home from yet another long and distant meeting. I've had some of the most interesting conversations in taxis over the years, and the drivers are likely to ask about my day. In this instance I was presented with this question to which I felt I could offer some sort of answer. *Where do ideas come from?* The driver had asked his question late in the journey, after we had reached my destination. I stopped to think, half way out of the taxi. As a rational scientist and engineer my reply was not an answer that I would ever have expected to offer. *If metaphorically grabbing ideas out of the air means that you have better ideas, then why not? So, yes, ideas do indeed fly around our heads for us to pluck whenever life presents us with a difficult problem.* The driver seemed happy with this answer and we parted ways into the night.

If you browse the shelves of any bookshop you are likely to find many texts on this topic. Innovation seems to be a growth industry, particularly for the authors of books on the subject. However, the best place to start any journey is at the beginning. In my effort to understand how I might improve my own problem-solving skills I was keen to find the foundation stones of the topic. How far back in time must I journey to find the source material for the field of innovation? I was surprised to learn that my ultimate destination in this quest was the dawn of recorded history. In hindsight, this was obvious.

When building a start-up, an innovative approach may be a very good idea indeed. Everything seems to be innovation with start-ups, and the relevant texts offer all the support that you need [4] [5] [3]. *Who is the customer? What do they want? What is their problem? How are we going to solve this? How are we going to structure the business?* Everything may be up for grabs, and the best solution may be the solution you grab with both hands.

Within the corporate world I have struggled to understand the contradictory reactions I provoke in my efforts to offer innovative solutions to new, difficult and important problems. The corporate structure can simultaneously encourage innovation and recoil at a successful result. *Innovate, but not too much. Find the game changers, but don't change to a game that we don't know how to play. Think outside the box, but keep your arms and legs inside the vehicle at all times. Be* revolutionary, but follow trends. Make omelettes, but don't break any eggs. Stray off the beaten track, but do stay on the map. Be disruptive, but don't rock the boat.

The obvious solution is to compromise. Trade away a new truth to retain enough of the old order. This is unsatisfactory and leaves me with a feeling of a job incomplete. I don't enjoy adopting the style of innovation but without any of its substance. The busy-work of *innovation theatre* does not offer the satisfying pay-off of a hard problem well solved. The pay-off one receives from a difficult problem solved with an elegant solution can be extremely satisfying. I don't like to be short changed.

If you are inclined towards an innovative approach, take pride in your work and don't appreciate the motivations that drive a more conservative approach, you may react in all the wrong ways. You may attempt to do the opposite of what people are telling you. You may attempt to sweep away the old to bring in the new. If that doesn't work then perhaps a little more passion may tip the scales in your favour? If passion does not provoke the desired response then perhaps you could find a means to force the issue? In a well-established corporate environment, all of this sound and fury is definitely a very bad idea.

If you are gripped by an innovative fervour then you may be a little blind to this and search for answers in all the wrong places. I too have suffered this affliction. After a number of years receiving mixed messages, I began a journey to understand how good ideas are formed, how we can bring them to life and ultimately find the source of these mixed messages. This was the beginning of my journey back to the wellspring of innovation.

I am a rocket scientist, so understanding the development process of these aerospace marvels of the 20th Century is straightforward. To understand the motivations and methods of the iron and steam wonders of the industrial revolution is also familiar territory. The mechanisms that drove a character such as von Braun, Tesla or Brunel are easy to appreciate as they seem little different from my own.

As I work back in history to discover the foundations upon which these innovators built their creative skills my understanding becomes a little murkier. The form, function and purpose of many medieval war machines are straightforward to understand, but the innovative steps someone must have taken to invent the cannon are less clear. How did they come up with the idea at all? What steps led up to the cannon? What understanding of natural principles was available to the medieval engineer? What did they copy? What contemporary inventions were similarly pneumatic? What feature of nature were they imitating? When the first cannons were built, how did they know the cannon would not burst? Calculation? Experimentation? Rules of thumb? Trial and error? Long experience? When they did inevitably explode, why did they spend any time and effort building another? I can imagine how I might invent a cannon from my modern perspective. The true inventor lived well before the scientific method became a primary means through which an innovator might observe, record and understand the physical world.

How many different versions of the cannon existed before innovators settled upon the familiar thick metal tube with a large hole at one end and a tiny hole at the other? Cursory research might suggest some evolution from the rocket. Turn the rocket around to create the fire lance. Fill that lance with shrapnel to create a rudimentary shotgun. Then grow the size of the whole system from there, as these things tend to grow. I won't speculate further as these are mere guesses. Suffice to say, I would love to have been a fly on the wall at each step of that innovative journey, but am sure would only be left with a question. What intermediate steps led to the medieval rocket? I guess historians know.

Capra's *The Tao of Physics* offered me a clue to a potentially innovative approach by the pre-scientific mind [6]. Capra attempts to reconcile the modern discoveries of Physics with Humankind's understanding of the universe described in religion, spirituality and antiquity. I can't pretend to understand much of the high energy physics nor any of the religion. I am a mere engineer, a life-long atheist, and never assembled the background required to understand either well. I persevered all the same, and did manage to extract one small but firm and useful lesson. I don't *have* to describe the universe using the scientific structure that has framed my whole life. Who knew? A subjective metaphor may suffice if it helps to progress my understanding, even if it may not literally describe the objective truth.

This was both a revelation and no real surprise. After all, in my own efforts to provoke others to innovate I have learned that an emotive narrative can unblock an innovative impasse. I will digress with an example that has stuck with me for many years.

The problem at hand considered a military objective. Prevent the opposition from employing a bridge to cross a river. The solutions offered by a team of young, highly intelligent and recently graduated engineers are listed, as follows,

- Blow up the bridge.

We spent some time exploring this problem, but every solution offered by the group boiled down to this singular idea. Blow up the bridge. This was a team of young engineers hoping to impress. It was no surprise that they were keen to remain within the company's remit and employ our products to their most effective use. Furthermore, they all had a professional credibility to build and to maintain, so were not going to step too far out of the box. I, on the other hand, feel no such constraint.

We needed more than this singular idea if we were to describe the problem as fully explored and our solution as optimal. I needed to provoke the team to consider more radical options. More specifically, I needed to offer the group *permission* to pursue more radical options. Despite the corporate setting, I took drastic action. Raising my hands into claws I let out a weak roar and hobbled, Jurassic-like, around the meeting room to offer another option to the group.

- Harness a bloody huge dragon to the bridge!

I didn't know where I was going with this, and the stunned silence lasted long enough for me to worry that I'd blown the whole workshop. It was a few moments before a quiet voice from one of the young delegates offered an observation. *Now they are afraid of the bridge...*

This was sufficient to open the floodgates on the numerous means by which you can make someone fear a bridge.

- Loiter over the bridge with menace.
- Shoot the bridge with paint, just to prove you can do so whenever you want.
- Mine the bridge.
- Occupy the bridge with commandos, or ninjas, or pirates.
- Weaken the bridge by blowing it up, but just a *little* bit.
- Blow up every *other* bridge, to force a now highly suspicious opposition to use *this particular* bridge.

My little drama offered enough narrative, metaphor and impetus to get the solution process moving. A fantasy like this is often treated as a childish game, and can feel so to the player. A fantasy such as my bridge dwelling dragon can also offer a provocation that results in detailed, empirical, communicable knowledge [7]. A metaphor can lead to some small truth.

I am no stranger to the use of narrative and metaphor to drive the innovation process. Perhaps to the pre-scientific mind innovation was *all* narrative and metaphor? Despite my science and engineering roots Capra provided just enough structure to support my journey back to antiquity. After all, many of Humanity's finest innovators can be found there. If narrative and metaphor can offer an innovative framework, particularly for the pre-scientific innovator, then what are the oldest narratives that Humanity has to offer? This was the question that led me to the oldest stories of Humankind.

Steve Blank and Bob Dorf begin their work on start-up business practises with a reference to the hero's journey [4]. The text begins with Joseph Campbell's description of a ubiquitous hero often found in the narrative of art and literature.

A legendary hero is usually the founder of something – the founder of a new age, the founder of a new religion, the founder of a new city, the founder of a new way of life. In order to found something new one has to leave the old and go on a quest of the seed idea, a germinal idea that will have the potential of bringing forth that new thing [8].

The narrative offered by Campbell is familiar to most people as it offers a framework upon which heroic exploits have been hung for millennia. It forms the foundations of an endlessly repeated story that supports much of the movie industry. This character also offers appropriate motivation to begin a text for prospective entrepreneurs.

A hero ventures forth from the world of common day into a region of supernatural wonder: fabulous forces are there encountered and a decisive victory is won: the hero comes back from this mysterious adventure with the power to bestow boons on his fellow man [8]

This hero's story is far older than the modern narratives of movie screenplays. This heroic character selected by Blank and Dorf to begin their description of the entrepreneur's journey was a notable clue in my effort to find the very source of the innovation industry.

The archetypical hero identifies the anomaly that threatens home, faces the untamed forces of chaos with bravery, learns the adaptive principle that counteracts the new threat and returns home victorious with this new knowledge. The archetypical hero is both entrepreneurial and diagnostic. The hero is a problem solver, and the driving narrative behind this journey is a description of why and how these problems are solved. The hero's journey is a very old narrative that has been created by and has created Humankind. Ultimately, the source of this story now rests in human psychology itself. There is more to this fictional hero than meets the eye, for this hero is no fiction.

Pulling upon this thread of narrative and mythology led me to Jordan Peterson's *Maps of Meaning* [7]. This text ranges in scope from fairy-tale, mythology and religion, to studies into the ideologies that may lead to the nuclear destruction of Humankind. This work is accompanied by a lecture series that begins with interpretations of the movie *Pinocchio* and ends with an analysis of motivations that provoked entire populations to support the gulags of the Soviet Union and the atrocities of the Nazi regime. This text is tough going, but worth every step.

I cannot claim any expertise in the field of psychology, history, art or religion, and Peterson's strange, unsettling and frightening book seemed an unlikely text from which to draw some understanding of modern engineering. I struggled with this work, but my rudimentary understanding of its contents offered some insight into the roots of Human innovation. For a more expert interpretation I refer you to Peterson himself.

The scientific method has dominated how Humankind has observed, understood and described the Universe for only a short period of Human history. Over four centuries the scientific approach has allowed us to objectively describe the Universe and how each part interacts with every other. But the scientific method contains a hole that it cannot fill. This scientific perspective does not offer any framework to explain how to *behave* towards this Universe of interconnected nouns.

The scientific method can tell me the size and shape of a distant galaxy, but it doesn't tell me how I should behave as a result. It doesn't tell me how this galaxy will influence the decisions I must make. If innovation is the understanding of problems and making decisions about how the world should be transformed, then how does the scientific method help me? The scientific method can predict the destination of all the paths before me. How does it tell me which one I should choose? How do I get an *ought* from an *is*?

For much of Human history people have adopted a framework to describe the world that is quite different from my own. Human perception is not focussed upon a universe of nouns. Perception focusses upon *function*, and typically only the most immediate functions are of interest. Without looking up from the page can you describe in detail the environment around you? How much have you ignored in the pursuit of your current goals? The pre-scientific world was perceived as a world of *verbs* - a world of interconnected functions that may prevent one from starving to death, or being eaten by something fanged, clawed and horrific.

Peterson offers the example of the dragon to illustrate this classification by function. *Do dragons exist?* Answer that for yourself before proceeding, and contrast this with an alternative question. Do *birds* exist? It's a simple question which I guess you will answer positively. Birds exist. So, draw me a bird. What species of bird have you drawn? It's more likely that you drew a generic bird, much like that illustrated in Figure 1. You drew a representation of an object with bird-like features. Wings. Beak. Claws. Feathers.

Figure 1: Bird.

You have probably not drawn a bird, and nor have I. Figure 1 offers a representation of *all* birds. Figure 1 offers a symbol to represent a hierarchy of nouns we are likely to recognise as birds. A universe of feathered and flying nouns. What of dragons? Draw a dragon. What have you drawn? Perhaps you have drawn something like the illustration in Figure 2. Wings. Scales. Claws. Fangs. Fire.

Figure 2: Dragon.

A dragon is a creature that is simultaneously bird-like, snake-line, cat-like, and spits fire. What does this symbol represent? It may offer a symbolic representation of *all predators*. A chimera of features from creatures throughout Human history that would descend, pounce or strike at unfortunate Humans who are in the wrong place at the wrong time, to drag them off to some terrible end or simply incinerate them in some ghastly forest blaze. Our drawing of a dragon is not a representation of a noun describing a particular and singular creature that actually exists. Perhaps this creature represents a verb. A symbolic representation at the top of a hierarchy of horrors with a clear functional lesson accumulated from millennia of dreadful Human experience. *If you encounter something with any of these characteristics, then run as fast as you can!*

So, do dragons exist? Perhaps from a functional perspective, in a world of verbs, then they may represent the top of a hierarchy that describes all predators. The dragon could represent the apex of that malevolent side of nature that has scoured Humankind for all of our existence.

Peterson's work attempts to identify the fundamental narratives that have shaped the perceptions of the Human mind to offer each some advantage against a cruel and unforgiving universe. Consequently, a fundamental base narrative emerges that might be shared by many, and perhaps may even be sexually selected to ultimately shape our evolution. I will offer a simple summary of this narrative. Proof of this I leave to

Peterson.

Humans are social creatures, and so the elements of our stories are represented with Human actors. Consider a story with three characters. A Mother. A Father. A Hero. Each represents a different feature of the Human experience, and each exhibit both beneficial and harmful characteristics.

The strong association between birth and the creative powers of those natural processes observed by Humankind often results in a representation of the environment using a feminine character. The *Great Mother*. Mother Nature herself. This character is the source of all the natural bounty which has sustained Humanity for all of our history.

The physical environment is ambivalent to the survival of Humankind, and has inflicted all manner of flood, fire, plague, pestilence and famine upon us throughout the ages. The environment is not only a source of riches, but also the terror in the dark and the unpleasant end at the hands of a terrible beast or threatening stranger. The malevolent aspect of nature is represented by a predator – the *Dragon of Chaos* against which Humanity has battled throughout the ages. It seems that Dragons are often found resting upon a huge pile of gold. This repose reflects the contradictory aspects of the predatory environment by simultaneously offering both alluring bounty and utter peril.

Against this darkness Humanity is protected by the structures of our society and culture. Only a few square meals await between us no longer feeding ourselves, but instead feeding terrible dark creatures. These ancient stories typically represent the protective structures of society with a masculine character, the *Great Father*. The Great Father imposes rules and laws and order to structure society and puts every function in its proper place to keep the wolf from the door. Once more a character has two contradictory aspects. A rule of law too rigid and a society too inflexible to respond to change can become tyrannical. Under these circumstances the protective Great Father becomes the *Tyrannical King*. A King both heavy handed and arbitrary in his proclamations who is unable to cope with changes to the evolving situation.

Enter the *Hero*, who resides in a world encompassed by the Mother and the Father. The revolutionary hero of antiquity begins the journey protected by culture and by training. The Hero lives peacefully. Perhaps the story casts this hero as the offspring of a great warrior or King. This Hero lives a happy life in a world built upon the Father's own heroic exploits. Perhaps the hero is provided training at arms or diplomacy or politics, and will one day take the place of the Father to rule for many years over a happy, peaceful nation. The Hero draws knowledge and strength from the protective structures of the Great Father that nurtured the Hero's skills. As long as society is well adapted to the environment everyone is safe and the Hero is at rest. Introduce an anomaly and our story begins.

The Hero recognises a threatening anomaly which the Great Father is ill prepared to resolve. This new anomaly threatens all that the hero holds dear. The threat may be a terrible famine, or a flood, or a virulent disease. It may be a horrifying beast, or an overwhelming army of terrible foes. In this story the Father becomes afflicted in some way. Perhaps this threat renders the old King infirm, or blind to the threat, or kidnapped, lost, melancholic, mad or tyrannical. Take your pick, as you've seen this story a thousand times in some guise. This affliction transforms the Great Father into the Tyrannical King who becomes intent upon imposing order at all costs.

The Hero's quest is clear. The anomaly against which the Tyrannical King is unprepared could plunge everyone back into their base state. Thrown back into the tooth and claw of a raw, unsympathetic environment to starve, suffer or be torn asunder. The Hero rises to the challenge and descends into battle to face the Dragon of Chaos. The Hero is often the only one who can see the threat. Perhaps the hero must debate the presence of this threat with sceptical peers, or older siblings, or jealous rivals. The Hero's own internal fears and cowardice may create an obstacle, for even this character possesses a malevolent counterpart. Identifying this threat against all opposition to the contrary is the first step in this revolutionary, or innovative, journey.

The Hero does not simply build upon the Father's work, but returns to first principles by confronting the raw environment that threatens to consume Humanity. This descent to face battle is perhaps impeded by the Hero's own negative aspect – the *Adversary*. The jealous sibling. The ambitious and corrupt peers. The Cain to the Hero's Able. The dark, cowardly aspect of the Hero who begs to run from the terrible dragon and the horrors of a harsh world.

The Hero must leave the protective home to face nature in the raw, tooth and claw. The Hero is laid bare against the elements to determine the solution to this threat to home and hearth. The Hero must fight the unforgiving elements, the beast in the dark, the terrible foe.

The terrors of the unknown also contain great promise and advantage. After all, the Dragon sleeps upon a huge pile of gold. Successful combat with the Dragon of Chaos recovers new bounty from the Dragon's benevolent alter ego, the Great Mother. From Nature herself new knowledge, new materials or new adaptive strategies are discovered to defeat the anomaly that threatens the Hero's home.

The Hero returns from this trial replete with new riches from the Great Mother which the Hero does not withhold from others. This is the critical heroic act. The Hero shares these riches with his community. The Hero offers a solution to the threatening anomaly to save the Father from his tyrannical indisposition. This bounty may be a magic amulet, charm, sword or other assorted tools, but this is just a metaphor. After all, returning from battle against the Dragon of Chaos with a new method of crop rotation adapted for extended periods of drought is just not going to offer a sufficiently dramatic narrative. Cut to titles. Fade to black.

Is this a familiar story? I would expect so, as it seems to be the plot to just about every movie I've ever seen. But this is not a modern narrative. This story is old. This story is very old. For example, this narrative offers a framework for the oldest written story Humanity has to offer, the Babylonian epic of creation the *Enuma Elish*. Tiamat, the primordial goddess of the sea, dragon-like symbol of chaos and creation joins with her husband *Apsu* to create a lineage of gods. Tiamat is slain by her descendent *Marduk* for waging war upon the other gods for the murder of her husband. From Tiamat's remains Marduk creates the world.

The Hero's story commences when an anomaly is detected that presents a threat. This anomaly has never before been encountered and requires a return to first principles to resolve. The Hero is an innovator. Considering the age of these stories, perhaps the Hero of antiquity is the first innovator.

The Hero doesn't simply pick up the reins where the old King dropped them. This Hero deconstructs the assumptions upon which an earlier maladapted strategy rests to develop a new strategy to respond to the new threat. The Tyrannical King may very well recoil at this disassembly of his own gains, hard won from when he too played the Hero. However, the Hero does not sweep aside the old order to implement a new strategy. This Hero builds upon the skills provided by society and culture through long apprenticeship, building upon that foundation to respond to the new situation. Humankind has been doing this for centuries and the better we were at achieving this the more likely we were to pass these skills on to our offspring. Onto you and to me. Innovation is a trait selected for by evolution itself. Innovation is built into every one of us. Each of us start life with millennia of practise.

In this ancient story not only do we see why we are motivated to innovate, but also see how we should build upon the innovation of others. We learn how we should employ this innovation once it has been wrestled from the problem. In this ancient story we see why the old order may recoil at this effort, as the world that they built for us was itself once a hard-won adaptation to an earlier threat. This older solution has protected the community well up to this point, and people may be reluctant to concede their winning strategy to a new approach. The conflict between conservation and creation wrestles on throughout history. The story of the innovator is the oldest story of Humankind. Innovation is ancient.

*

The balance between chaos and order is older still. Consider the journey of life itself. Consider what is required to grow a complex biological structure. You need enough variation to allow the ebb and flow of information to present new and useful functions. You need enough rigidity to hold those structures together long enough to consolidate them into some greater whole. Life itself clings to a cliff face high above a boiling, crashing sea [9]. Off shore, information is fluid, unstructured, but plentiful. On shore, the land is fixed. Information is immobile, but is secure. For millions of years life has thrived on the interface between this chaos and order. Life harvests just enough information to adapt. Life retains just enough structure to grow. Life itself adapts. Life evolves.

Life is innovation itself.

4. FRAMEWORKS

The uses of not.
Thirty spokes
meet in the hub.
Where the wheel isn't
is where it's useful.

Hollowed out,
clay makes a pot.
Where the pot's not
is where it's useful.

Cut doors and windows
to make a room.
Where the room isn't,
there's room for you.

So the profit in what is
is in the use of what isn't.

Lau Tzu, Tao Te Ching [10]

Imagine yourself in a large open prairie on a fine sunny day. Green grass stretches under a deep blue sky. Tiny flowers of every type pepper this landscape, nodding together in a warm, gentle breeze. You lie back on the soft grass and gaze at bright clouds as they drift by far above you. How do you feel? Is this a suitable environment for some innovative thinking?

Alternately, you're in a small featureless room. The walls are painted a plain white and reflect harsh light from a fluorescent tube buzzing with menace along the ceiling. A dark line frames the edge of a door that hides flush within one wall. A small black keyhole in this door offers the only other feature on these blank walls. You can see the key to this door. The key lies at the bottom of a large, heavy fish tank that rests in the centre of the room and is full of water. A heavy glass bell jar protects the key from the water by trapping a pocket of air above it. This air pocket also protects spiders. Many killer spiders crawl all over the key.

It's likely that the open prairie and that sunny sky is forgotten, and you are already trying to work out how to get the key out from under the bowl without disturbing the killer spiders. You may even realise that if you lift the bell jar from the bottom of the tank the spiders may scuttle onto the jar to escape the water, leaving you free to retrieve the key from the bottom of the tank. We must assume, of course, that spiders cannot swim. I have no idea if this particular species of killer spider can indeed swim, but good luck with your plan.

Offer a clear objective that is thwarted by clear obstructions and the problem-solving skills possessed by every human seem to react immediately. This seems to be an instinct. It's a reflex.

There is a prevailing attitude that believes that people need space to be creative. This approach believes that people need to be relaxed and be supplied with sufficient time and bright colours and beanbags to unleash good ideas. Creativity is not provoked by a total freedom to act. It's not released if the mind is balanced and relaxed and happy. To be balanced is more or less to be at rest. Action is at the bottom. A swinging and flailing of arms to regain one's balance and keep afloat. Unbalancing keeps people active and striving [11].

For thousands of years Humankind has faced flood, famine and the beast in the dark so frequently that we have developed an efficient problem-solving toolset to save our skins quickly and efficiently. The desire to burst boundaries provokes creativity. Constrain a Human and they will break those constraints as soon as they can.

Boundaries do not only support problem solving by offering obstacles to overcome. These boundaries can also manifest as structure that can be used to describe a problem and develop a solution. To illustrate this, consider the format of popular movies.

Popular movies will often adopt a formal structure upon which the story is hung. Figure 3 illustrates the three acts that are employed in many movies to introduce the protagonists, unleash a compelling crisis and develop a satisfying resolution [12].

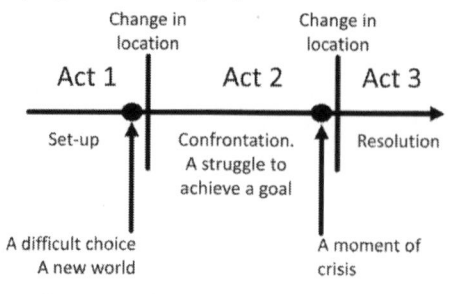

Figure 3: Movies often employ a firm and well understood structure.

Alternatively, return to the basic narrative of the hero described by Joseph Campbell [8]. The *Hero's Journey* described by Campbell forms a framework for many an epic journey. This journey can be illustrated as the wheel presented in Figure 4 and is likely to be a structure familiar to many movie goers.

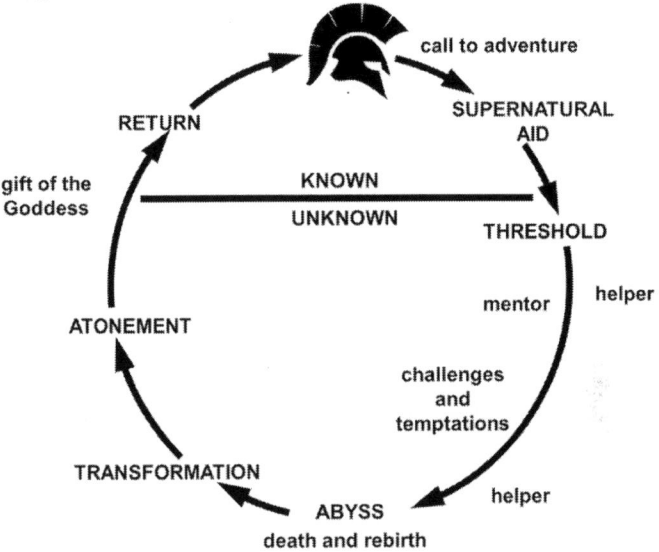

Figure 4: The Hero's Journey of Joseph Campbell

Stray from this formula and your movie may become lauded as an art house classic, or destroyed by the reviewer's wrath at your incoherent narrative and obscure characters. What purpose do these formal story telling structures serve?

The use of a formal framework to produce a well-structured story is a means to satisfy the expectations of the audience. A recognisable framework offers a shorthand that the audience can employ to understand who is who, where we are currently in the story, what is happening now, why people are doing what they are doing, what is likely to happen next, and why this might happen. If you execute these structures with skill then perhaps you have a blockbuster hit on your hands.

Perhaps you want to push things beyond the expectations of the audience. Perhaps you can invite the audience to leave the safe shores of this familiar structure to consider more challenging themes. A brave but impulsive young protagonist may receive a severe reprimand for his heroics from an atypical superior. The hero's enemy may understand the hero's position, face considerable danger to switch sides, only for the audience to find that he does so not out of bravery but only to save his own skin. A skilled and noble warrior well known to the audience from numerous daring exploits may turn his back on the whole franchise, to live as a hermit on a remote island wishing no further part in proceedings. One may even see multiple detours from a familiar structure occur in a single movie.

A formal and familiar structure offers the audience a known point from which to launch this exploration of unknown themes. The audience can be delivered back to this familiar structure when your experimental film making strays too far from expectations that the audience may have for a good night out, a satisfying date or boisterous children kept quiet for an hour or two.

In this case the boundaries placed upon the work by a formal structure are not employed to challenge the audience to break boundaries. This structure offers the audience a safe space from which boundaries may be exceeded and from which the unknown may be explored.

A formal structure can offer a chaos from which order must be constructed, or can offer familiar structures to be modified to derive something new from something old. Resting relaxed and happy on that sunny prairie offers you nothing. No problem to solve. No obstacles to overcome. No destinations to explore. No structures to build upon. No challenge to confront.

Developing a good framework to support your problem-solving efforts and to delineate that step into the unknown is essential to innovation, and has been so for as long as Humanity has been solving problems lethal to life, loves and liberty.

Note that in this ancient story the exploits of those heroes of antiquity are supported by the prior exercise and training nurtured during a peaceful youth. Revolutionary heroes do not make things up as they go along. They don't begin this journey with nothing. They often start their stories with tools provided by those who have also cast out on their own revolutionary journey during the prime of their youth. Perhaps the hero takes the Father's sword on this journey – a symbolic token of the culture and training that will be used to prevail. Perhaps the hero will gain further support from more ancient advocates of this cultural framework. Perhaps an ancient weapon that glows blue in the presence of danger is discovered. Perhaps invulnerable armour woven by smiths of old is recovered. Perhaps the hero purloins an ancient and magical ring that renders the wearer invisible.

The ancient hero does not often tear the old culture down to build something better from the undifferentiated ashes. The hero of antiquity builds upon what has gone before, to strengthen hearth and home against the new threat. After all, in this old story the hero often rescues the Father from his kidnappers, or finds this lost Father, or cures the Father of his ailment. The hero may recognise the good remaining in the heart of a tyrannical old King, and succeed in drawing this earlier hero back from the depths of a dark descent. Father rescued, problem solved, the revolutionary hero takes a place upon the throne to act as parent and monarch to a prince or princess who begins the cycle of anomaly, innovation and renewal all over again.

Note that the hero does not tear everything down just to rebuild everything anew. The hero builds upon the established framework, modifying it into something better suited to the new environment. The oldest innovators in Human history employ frameworks to structure their efforts. A good framework has been essential to solving the difficult problems faced by Humanity for thousands of years. Structure builds upon structure that builds upon structure over millennia, and a complex civilisation emerges.

Consider one of the simplest of frameworks upon which a problem-solving exercise may be hung. We'll call this framework *Time-Size-Cost*. We introduce a problem. Then we flex the time available to solve the problem. Then we flex the potential size of the solution. Finally, we flex the costs that we can endure in our efforts to resolve the issue.

To illustrate, apply this to an example problem. Imagine it's the year 2600BC. We're building Stonehenge in Salisbury, England. We will need to move huge blocks of stone weighing 25 tons each over 40 kilometres from a quarry North of Salisbury. How many solutions can you think of to achieve this feat of Bronze Age transportation?

To frame our thinking, we start by flexing the costs that we are permitted to employ on our solution. What kind of solution will emerge if we can spend as much resource as we like to solve the problem? Perhaps we could assemble an army of workers to drag each rock by hand for the entire journey? We'll need ropes, rolling logs, hundreds of slaves, hundreds of guards, food, provisions, the whole ancient engineering exercise.

Alternatively, perhaps our framework could impose a boundary upon the solutions available to us. What solutions emerge if we can only spend almost zero to solve the problem? We're going to have to drag the rocks ourselves. Perhaps we could encourage a few friends to help for free. But this is going to take time, which incurs costs of their own.

As we've raised the issue, let's flex the time available to solve the problem. What if we had all the time that we need to move these rocks? Together with our friends we could tug a rock a few centimetres per day. We will arrive in Salisbury eventually. Perhaps a single rock could offer a life's work. We could build a monument to our personal commitment. Alternatively, as we have time on our side, we could leave the rock right where it is and wait until someone else invents the means to move big rocks.

Conversely, what if we had almost no time to get our Stonehenge assembled? Perhaps solstice is just around the corner and the chief druid needs his henge as soon as possible. What is the fastest way to move a 25-ton rock? Perhaps travel by water will pick up the pace? We could construct a raft to float the rock on a convenient river.

Finally, how does the solution size alter the solutions available? What if the means to transport the rock could be as large as we like? The object we use to transport the rocks could be the size of the entire journey. Perhaps we could build a smooth road, or a canal down which we could float the rock on that huge raft?

Or perhaps we can place boundaries upon the problem and demand that the solution must be tiny. What solutions are now available? What the smallest way to transport the rock? Could we break the rock up into more manageable chunks so that a single person could transport a piece by hand to reassemble them all at the destination?

This simple framework offers six options to act as a starting point for our ideas and also bound our thinking, to force from us some innovative options,

- A high cost solution.
- A low cost solution.
- A solution that takes a very long time.
- A solution that must be available right now.
- A solution as huge as we like.
- A solution that must be tiny.

This framework also offers us eight combinations to consider.

- All the time we need to build a huge solution at high cost.
- All the time we need to build a huge solution at very low cost.
- A solution available right now that is huge and high cost.
- A solution available right now that is huge and low cost.
- All the time we need to build a tiny solution at high cost.
- All the time we need to build a tiny solution at very low cost.
- A solution available right now that is tiny and high cost.
- A solution available right now that is tiny and low cost.

This simple framework provokes many potential solutions.

- **Slow, huge, costly.** Thousands of workers dragging each rock with ropes and rolling logs.
- **Slow, huge, cheap.** Wait for tectonic plate movement to shift the rock.
- **Fast, huge, costly.** Dig a long canal and build a boat to carry each rock.
- **Fast, huge, cheap.** Build the Stonehenge next to a river and build a log raft to carry each rock.
- **Slow, small, costly.** Pay a few dedicated workers to spend decades dragging all the rocks by hand.
- **Slow, small, cheap.** Encourage some friends to help you drag a rock hundreds of miles for free.
- **Fast, small, costly.** Break the rocks up and carry all the parts by hand. Rebuild on site.
- **Fast, small, cheap.** Build Stonehenge next to the quarry.

Which of the characteristics result in ridiculous solutions? Solutions that are very large are perhaps feasible if we have a great deal of time to spend. Practical solutions emerge if we are willing to change the problem a little by building next to a river or by creating a giant Stonehenge shaped jigsaw puzzle. The most basic lesson this very simple framework can offer is why this problem is difficult to resolve. You can have your henge where you want it, but it's going to cost you. Alternatively, constrain your choice of site by building your henge nearer to practical transport links or the quarry itself and you have a more practical solution.

A firm framework that both supports and provokes can offer many more solutions than employing unstructured intuition. The most fundamental framework that you must have to solve a problem well is the problem statement itself. The problem statement provides a known starting point from which solutions can be explored, and also creates boundaries around your problem-solving exercise which you are at liberty to remain within, or stray beyond.

As the problem acts as a solution framework itself, any problem-solving exercise must be accompanied by a very well-crafted question. Without taking care to state the actual problem that must be solved the solution process will cast off towards shores unknown.

What does a well-crafted question look like? A good question is much like any good problem-solving framework. Delegates must be able to understand the problem and have the required background knowledge to answer it. A good question offers a known jumping off point from which each delegate's imagination can extend, but also allude to boundaries that they may wish to break.

Peterson explains that this is how young children might explore their new world around them. They cling to their parent's leg, hiding behind this familiar column for protection. After a few moments, if nothing startling occurs, everything can be treated as safe but hiding some unknown horror. The child takes a few exploratory steps out into the unknown. They learn something new about the world, and then scuttle back to parental protection when those explored unknowns that require new processing become overwhelming. A brief moment is taken to reflect before they take another bold foray out into the world, perhaps making a little more headway than the last adventure. This is how brand-new Humans explore the world, so there seems no reason to relinquish this habit.

A good question must offer firm footing back to which the problem solvers can return should the tangle of possibilities become too great to manage, process or negotiate. An effective problem-solving exercise will stray into unknown territory and may burrow into deep holes. A well-crafted question that offers the opportunity to return to the core problem and begin exploration anew can refresh an entrenched exploration.

A good question must also be motivating. Problem solving exercises can last hours, or days, or weeks, or even months. Perhaps your innovation may take years to discover. On what kind of question would you be willing to invest hours of your life? On what would you invest years? We have described a good problem as one that, in part, rests on dry land, as a good question offers a known starting point. But who wants to answer a question that many people have already answered many times before? Conversely, only the most brazen problem solver may wish to invest their time attempting to answer a question that many people have failed to answer.

If brazen is your approach then a good question offers a known starting point, and also presents delegates with an exciting boundary that has never before been breached. This assures the team that they may very well be the explorers that penetrate this final frontier. Penetration into unexplored territory will motivate a problem-solving team and may address a boundary that has never before been breached, but must offer the team some likely chance of success. If an often scrutinised but unsolved problem is to be faced, what advantages do the current team have that those failed teams did not possess? Has a new technology presented a new key to a yet unlocked door? Do we know something that earlier failures never knew? Does the team possess a particular set of skills that has never before been employed to address this particular problem?

A good question offers some metric of success. How will the team know that they have succeeded in solving the problem? How can the team measure their success? Consider the operators of a rail service who wish to improve their product. They assemble a team to solve the problem and ask the team to answer the following question.

- *'How could we improve our rail service?'*

This is likely to provoke the team to focus upon the word *improve*. This demand for improvement offers an ill-defined metric at the centre of this question and the team will spend a great deal of time trying to understand what the word *improve* means in the context of a rail service. This may be precisely what you want, for you too may have no idea what an improved service might look like. If this is the case, then be explicit and state that you do not know how an improvement may manifest itself.

If you don't want a meeting on the philosophical meaning of the word *improve* a more specific question would be more suitable. Perhaps you are trying to increase your market share. An alternative question may be,

- *'How can we double the passenger numbers?'*

Or perhaps you are trying to make your current customers much happier with the service they are receiving, so you could ask,

- 'How could we half the ticket price?'

Or perhaps your trains are overcrowded and uncomfortable, so your team might answer questions such as,

- 'How can we have 25% more rolling stock on the track?'

These questions will all result in very different problem-solving exercises. Think very carefully about how you craft your question. If you do, you may realise that you have no idea what question you wish to ask. In this case you should regress back to,

- 'What would improve our rail service?'

and hope that the team will discover the real question that you wish to address.

A good problem-solving framework is like a good martial art. This seems likely as a martial art is a problem-solving framework. Defending yourself from injury is the problem at hand, and this problem is solved by exercising a devious and effective repertoire. Each move is a response to a specific assault, and all the moves assemble into a unified and quickly referenced defensive framework.

A martial art that is complex may be hard to execute at speed and under stress. A martial art which employs techniques that are contrary to how you will flinch when under attack will demand years of dedicated training to transform your natural instincts into a honed killing machine. A martial art should fit the context in which it will be employed. A martial art that evolved to destroy armoured opponents on the medieval field of battle may be unsuitable to deescalate a minor misunderstanding in a modern public house. After all, erecting spear and shield walls against blokes who may have jostled your drink in the pub is often frowned upon by the local constabulary.

In many innovation workshops the majority of delegates are unlikely to be dedicated problem solving ninjas. Delegates are likely to be experts in their own field of interest and will have been drafted into the problem-solving exercise to offer their particular skills. Under these circumstances a suitable problem-solving framework is more like a basic self-defence class: easy to explain; quick to implement; brutally efficient. If your workshop is host to dedicated innovation experts then perhaps more esoteric and devious techniques can be employed. However, most of the time delegates will only need the basics to form them up into an efficient fighting force.

A related analogy can be found in the difference between swords and spears. A sword is a complex weapon that takes many years to both learn how to wield and learn how to craft. A great many manuscripts have been written all across the world throughout the centuries that describe the subtle art of swordplay. Men at arms have trained for entire lifetimes to wield these weapons, and if they failed to focus on their studies that lifetime could be very short. Smiths have bent their baking brows over the hot coals of a thousand forges to apprentice themselves in the ancient alchemy of steel to produce the finest weapons to arm those brave heroes.

Spears, on the other hand, can be hewn from a long pole and topped with technology that merely requires the combined attributes of both hard and pointy. It takes about fifteen minutes to school a peasant on how a long spear might be employed to be sure that a very few peasants working together can deliver a fine swordsman the worst, and last, news of his life. Get a large number of those peasants together and you have the start of your own army.

Few problem-solving exercises will be subtle duels between a pair of innovation experts. Usually you will want to fashion a gross of spears, offer some brief instruction to your assembled group and then distribute these weapons accompanied by a clear objective. With this analogy in mind, what characteristics do good problem-solving frameworks exhibit?

A good problem-solving framework is Human friendly. This can often translate into a simple, low tech tool that can be physically manipulated and aligns well with how Humans understand, discuss and solve problems. Good frameworks support collaboration and are often very visual. Good frameworks can be represented as diagrams, flows, charts or illustrations that can be reproduced on a large scale to allow a number of collaborators tgather around and discuss. A large, simple, low tech tool around which a group can gather will often manifest as a large poster onto which notes, icons or illustrations are appended and modified.

A good framework will also be predictable and accompanied by some proof that it can provoke valuable results. A good framework is likely to be widely and frequently used. There are few laurels available for employing an obscure approach just because it is obscure. The innovation should reside in your solution, not in the means you employ to reach it. Examples of a tool delivering the successful solution of previous problems should be available to assure the user that the tool functions as advertised. Good tools also offer examples of how the framework should be employed. If no prior examples are available, a good framework should allow you to pilot your problem-solving event to ensure that it will produce the results that you need.

If the framework might not produce the results that you require, a good framework should be flexible to allow its modification to match the specific problems you intend to address. If the framework cannot be easily modified to match your needs, then it may be a problem-solving framework developed for a particular field that is quite different from your own.

A good framework is likely to be consistent in its output. You can test a problem-solving exercise with a variety of different teams to determine if the framework will produce similar outcomes from the same inputs. A consistent framework will be predictable. The influence of any modifications that you make to the framework will also be predictable.

A good framework will have an effective means to deliver information into the problem-solving exercise. At the very least, a good framework will offer a clear and concise explanation of the problem itself. If the problem cannot be identified then a good framework will offer a mechanism to determine what the problem is. This may seem self-evident, but it's surprising just how often a problem-solving exercise will start in the middle with a ready-made solution that delegates are keen to implement and will enjoy discussing regardless of the actual problem at hand. Under these circumstances it is well worth checking that the group understand the problem. A good framework will allow you to determine this.

A good framework must deliver to the problem-solving team the question itself and any supporting information that the team can use to understand and answer this question. The simplest means to deliver information into a problem-solving exercise is by stating the question itself, as discussed above. Is this a sufficient quantity of information for the team to begin the process of discovery? Consider the problem of bridging a river. It is insufficient to provoke a problem-solving team with the straightforward question,

- *'How can we bridge a river?'*

Under these circumstances your team will spend most of their time debating everything they need to know to *start* answering your question: *What river? How wide is this river? How deep is the river? Where is the river? What is to be transported across the river? How often? Is there marine traffic on the river? Who in the group knows about building bridges? Who knows about rivers? How long do we have to complete this task? How complete does this task need to be? What does success look like?*

The information that a problem-solving team requires to answer a question could be endless. Perhaps the objective of your problem-solving exercise is to list these questions? Perhaps the exercise is to answer these questions? All are valid objectives, but it's important that your team understands the objectives and has all of the information they need before they start. Otherwise, valuable human resource will be wasted either recreating information that you already possess or creating new information at odds with your objectives.

A good framework will communicate all of the information required to the team in a clear and concise manner. Beware overwhelming the team with far more information than they can assimilate in the period before the problem-solving exercise begins. The information required to solve the problem must be easily referenced throughout the exercise. Always remember that not everyone in the group may be speaking in their first language. Often a simple, large, attractive and meaningful illustration can offer a team all the information that they need. Alternatively, a time line of events may suffice. Perhaps a shopping list of desires will help? A good problem-solving framework offers all the information the team needs to solve the problem and offers a mechanism to define the starting point of the exercise.

Similarly, a good problem-solving mechanism will also have a clear end point, and an effective delivery mechanism. How will the information created in the exercise be recorded? How will this information be translated from the workshop tool, stored in the long term and published to the customer of this exercise? How will those who endure the problem use the information that emerges from the problem-solving exercise? A list of ideas? An illustration of a concept? A designed, constructed and tested product?

A good problem-solving framework will allow the solution team to demonstrate to themselves and to the customer why their solutions solve the problem. Problem solving can be a complex exercise taking many blind alleys, may experiment with and discard ideas, may join many partial ideas together in a crude manner, or may take a maze of multiple routes to achieve the desired ends. Amongst this forest of ideas numerous blind faith assumptions and intuitive leaps may be made. Under these circumstances it may be very hard to link the problem statement to the solution offered. The customer of a problem-solving exercise is then expected to take the suitability of the solution to candidate problems on faith. It may irk your professional integrity for the customer to doubt that the solution you deliver solves the problem they offered. Alternatively, a customer may consider your solution elegant and your team ingenious if they can recognise a clear link from problem to solution, particularly if the problem at first appeared intractable. A good problem-solving framework will offer you the means to explain the link between the problem and your solution.

This text hopes to introduce you to problem-solving frameworks that exhibit the above characteristics. This isn't an exhaustive list of tools. There are many more to explore and to invent. Armed with the examples in this text perhaps further suitable examples can more easily be found by the reader. The problem-solving frameworks employed by this text as examples were developed by Steve Blank, Bob Dorf, Eric Reis, Alexander Osterwalder, Genrich Altshuller and Dan Roam.

The author employs the work of Blank, Dorf, Reis and Osterwalder in an effort to identify and understand the customer, their needs, and why their needs are not met. Blank, Dorf and Reis are responsible for the development and startling explosion of the *Lean Start-up* mechanism. Osterwalder builds upon this work, and introduces the canvas method of illustration. This workshop tool transformed the way I present, manipulate and solve difficult problems.

Genrich Altshuller was a Russian engineer who, during the latter part of the 20th Century, developed a powerful problem-solving framework теория решения изобретательских задач or *Teoriya Resheniya Izobretatelskikh Zadatch* (TRIZ) [13]. This Russian title translates into English as *theory of the resolution of invention-related tasks*. Albert Einstein was not the only patent clerk in history to dream impossible dreams whilst shuffling papers in the patent office. In his early career Altshuller also scrutinised many inventions for patent protection by the Soviet design bureau. Unlike Einstein's efforts to think the very newest of thoughts, Altshuller recognised just how often the very same thoughts passed across his desk. Many inventions employed similar strategies to achieve similar ends even if the problems to be solved were drawn from very different fields. This observation led Altshuller to formulate formal problem-solving strategies that reliably lead to creative solutions to difficult problems.

Dan Roam offers a toolkit that is peculiar in its operation. The mechanism offered by Roam is illustrated using Figure 5.

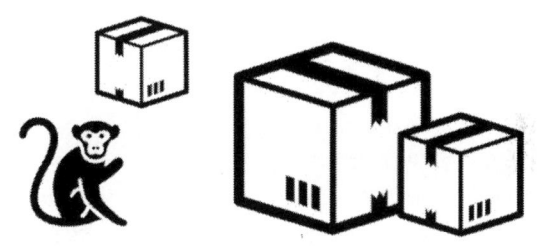

Figure 5: You've solved the problem the moment you see the problem.

The moment you see this illustration is it very likely that you have understood the problem and solved it with very little contribution from your conscious mind. Roam asserts that your conscious mind may very well have had little to do with this solution process. Your visual cortex can solve problems very quickly all by itself. If the problem presented is simple the visual cortex can solve it at lightning speed. This is a useful resource in both problem-solving, and in the presentation of your results to your customer.

The reader may already note a ready enthusiasm from the author to occasionally draw from the work of Jordan Peterson. Whilst not employing the psychological and mythological frameworks described by Peterson in any explicit manner, I find *Maps Of Meaning* offered by Peterson a useful framework to contextualise our problem-solving effort in a more historical and philosophical frame.

Humanity has been solving problems for many thousands of years and will continue to do so for many thousands more. Peterson's work places our efforts into its proper historical and philosophical frame, and teaches us that Humanity did not invent problem solving. We evolved effective mental processes and sophisticated cultural systems to support us in a multi millennia long workshop to survive, grow and prevail over an unforgiving universe. I find this perspective offers a certain much needed romance to the sometimes stale environment of office spaces, post-it notes and whiteboard pens.

A problem-solving framework suitable for employment by workshop delegates who may not be familiar with this material must be easy to understand, explain and employ. To this end, in this text I offer simplifications of the sophisticated and comprehensive techniques developed by these authors. To assemble a useful but simple toolkit I have selected those tools that I have found easy to present and teach and which deliver consistent and valuable results. In my effort to integrate these materials into a practical framework that you can employ amongst those less familiar with these authors, I have bent and stretched material to my own ends.

The reader can refer to these original texts to gain a thorough understanding of these sophisticated and comprehensive techniques. To avoid offending the purists, and perhaps the original authors, I will avoid referring to any of these frameworks by name, such as *Lean Startup*, *Value Proposition Design* or *TRIZ*, as this may result in dishonest misrepresentation. I will refer to the authors by name when referring to their material and indicate where a more comprehensive understanding can be derived.

This text will employ material from each author to illustrate the characteristics of an effective problem-solving exercise. These tools can be incorporated into the following basic problem-solving steps,

- Customer discovery
- Problem discovery
- Solution discovery
- Presentation to the customer

Note that the customer is present at either end of this basic schedule. This is an essential emphasis, as all too often a problem-solving exercise can focus upon the problem solver. After all, solving problems is an entertaining pastime. The process can become a means to entertain those solving the problem, rather than a concerted effort to serve the needs of a real customer with a real problem that must be solved. If your problem-solving team descend into an entertaining diversion, it is often a more efficient use of their time to draw them back to the problem at hand and to focus upon the customer and their needs.

To those with a creative streak, this need to impose a framework upon problem solving may sound a little restrictive. Those who want to roam freely around the problem may feel trapped by the idea of boundaries to constrain and pathways to be followed. This is entirely the point.

In this book I hope to argue for the presence of two distinct characters present in the effort to solve problems. The first is perhaps familiar, who I will call the *chaotic creative*. This individual will inject information into the effort to solve problems by asking endless questions, and by offering countless possibilities. The information may be unstructured, but will compensate for this chaos in sheer volume. To this chaotic creative, quantity is quality.

This character is unlikely to resolve the problem without a means to select, categorise, order and catalogue this information. This is achieved by a *conscientious curator*. Despite the name I have selected, this character is no less creative than its chaotic counterpart. The creativity of this character lies in the ability to construct a framework to illustrate the journey and offer a map to lead the team to those unexplored regions of the terrain. This structure is not a prison, but a guide. By structuring the problem-solving process and detecting the relationships between the information generated, the curator offers motivation for further action and establishes meaning to the mass of information offered by its chaotic companion.

These two characters exhibit different approaches to problem solving and are likely to quarrel. This is a desirable outcome, for it is in this clash that creativity is spawned. If they can be encouraged to appreciate one another's strengths and weaknesses then this can be a great benefit to their combined problem-solving efforts. These two characters may be two distinct and unique individuals, or may even reside in a single mind. In either case, if these qualities can be identified and can learn to work well together one will possess a powerful problem-solving tool.

In this text I want to illustrate not only the formal means by which innovation can be wrought, but also how it feels to be present within the interaction between these two characters. To be trapped between the desire for formal structure and the barnstorming of a creative process can be an infuriating experience. Just as the structured thinker manages to add the final component to a clear and well-constructed framework, the creative crashes into your structure with some new idea that knocks the foundations from under you. Just as the creative manages to scratch a hole in the problem with his bare hands to unearth some undiscovered possibility, the ordered thinker clears the site and erects a structure on top.

To illustrate this tension, I elect to occasionally change the voice of this text entirely. I aim to lurch from an ordered textbook in which the scientist or engineer may find a comfortable read, to a creative melting pot in which the topic of innovation is no less present but may be somewhat more obscure. If you find this shift in tone uncomfortable then I have succeeded in my efforts. Innovation can be both rewarding and infuriating in equal measure, and much of my everyday effort lies in carefully listening to the ideas of others and attempting to incorporate this into some shared whole. So, for the majority of this text the conscientious curator will dominate, at the risk of boring those with a creative streak. For the minority of this text the chaotic creative will take control, at the risk of infuriating or boring those who crave formality, structure and the satisfaction of expectations. If you can integrate these together, then I have prepared a taste of how a truly innovative experience feels.

This text offers a case study to reference the topics of each chapter and illustrate the utility of a widely shared and well understood framework. This employs a narrative structure likely to be very familiar to many readers, in which individuals encounter many simple problems that are resolved by formal means. If effective problem solving is a negotiation between a conscientious curator and a chaotic creative, then the former has held the floor throughout this chapter on structure and framework. We must make room for our chaotic character, or its efforts to make room for itself can be destructive to a carefully wrought process. To this end, we depart from the familiar framework of a textbook for a short time and offer the challenge of an altogether different structure to present this material.

For those that still prefer the comfort of a rational framework, then numerous footnotes are provided to offer some formal explanation of each problem and each resolution using techniques described throughout the wider text. Many footnotes may not be clear until later in the text. If these footnotes are intrusive, leave each to the end of the page. Alternatively, ignore them completely and read them later. If this material is not to your taste, you can ignore this fanciful diversion without losing much understanding of later chapters.

An abbreviation will indicate the source from which these footnotes are drawn. Authors will be indicated as Genrich Altshuller, (GA), Steve

Blank (SB), Eric Reis (ER), Alexander Osterwalder (AO). Those familiar with Jordan Peterson's work may recognise his influence throughout.

Are you sitting comfortably? Then I'll begin. *Once upon a time...*

DRAGON EGG

5. CASE STUDY: EMPLOYING A FAMILIAR FRAMEWORK.

Once upon a time there was a handsome Soldier who protected a peaceful kingdom. He was not of a high rank, despite being recognised as very skilled and very brave. All the other soldiers of the army agreed that he was just the sort of fellow that you'd want to stand at the very front of the rank and file between the kingdom and certain danger[2]. The Soldier's elderly Father was very proud of the young man, as he too had also served amongst the ranks of the army in the prime of his youth until age and deafness drew his long service to an end.

The Kingdom was ruled by a heroic King who had shared dark dangers and certain peril with the army in which the Soldier's Father had served. Many years ago, these old comrades had fought together to rid the land of fearsome dragons[3]. The King's great shield of dragon scales[4] hung above his throne in testament to this youthful camaraderie. The King and his army had driven dragons from the land, and with them had flapped and roared all of the magic in the world to who knew where? No one had ever known where dragons came from and no one knew to where they had fled.

Since the last dragon was banished from the world the Kingdom had enjoyed peace and plenty. Summers were long and warm. Winters were short and mild. The wind rarely blew more than a refreshing gust. Nature treated the people well. Harvests were plentiful and fishermen no longer feared the ocean's power. Life was easy, simple, quiet, and the years rolled on without distinction from one bountiful harvest to the next. Means to work the land were unchanging, traditions altered little and the unchallenged youngsters of the Kingdom even questioned whether their parent's adventures were simply stories. Had dragons had ever even really existed?[5]

---

[2] I've introduced a framework that is likely to be familiar to many. With this, perhaps we can construct a mnemonic for the content of this book.

[3] You're not the only one who has ever innovated. Others have had their adventures. If your room is warm and the lights stay on then you're building upon the innovation of others.

[4] A function drawn from the super system, the environment, to serve wider society.

[5] The innovation of others can be so taken for granted that it can be entirely invisible to those who benefit. They are all very obvious if you look with the right

DRAGON EGG

The aging King knew very well that dragons existed. During the final battle between the Kingdom and the very last dragon the King and his Queen had fought side by side. They fought together as they had for many years, on the very battlements that their daughter now took her morning walk. As she strolled along the battlements the Princess often recalled the tale her Father told of that final battle when she was only an infant.

The King had learned to use his prized dragon scale shield to great effect, using the great strength of his youth and the shield's fireproof layer to protect his Queen from the extreme heat and great pressure of a dragon's fiery breath[6]. From behind the shield, together they would press close enough to each beast for the Queen to strike at each dragon a mortal wound.

In their final battle the very last dragon had caught the King a near mortal blow to send him sprawling onto the stone underfoot. The shield flew from the King's hand which provoked the Queen to spring forward and stand her ground between the jaws and claws of the terrible foe and her beloved King[7]. Preparing for the charring blast that would extinguish her reign, the Queen made forwards to defeat the beast, only to be snatched away in one huge scaled talon. With a great roar and a flapping of leathery wings the dragon heaved itself into the air. The brave Queen and that final dragon had never been seen since.

The King survived his physical wounds but sank into a deep sorrow at the loss of his Queen that was only ever relieved over the years by the sight of his young daughter growing from an infant into a beautiful Princess[8].

The Soldier, when he was much younger and before he ever became a soldier, would on occasion visit his Father going about his military

---

kind of eyes. How many can you see simply from where you are currently reading this text?

[6]This is an example of one of Altshuller's standard solutions to problems, in which a harm is resolved. Numbered 1.2.1 and described in Chapter 21, we *block a harm by introducing a new substance.* Here we use the thermal properties of a dragon's scales to protect from heat.

[7] Another of Altshuller's standard solutions from Chapter 21 to block a harm, numbered 1.2.3. *Eliminate, block or reduce harms. Introduce a sacrificial substance to absorb the harm.* A Queen sacrifices herself for a King. Checkmate?

[8] Improve a measurement. Altshuller standard solution 4.1.2, Chapter 21. *Solutions for detection and measurement. Measure a copy or an image of a substance.* Remember a Queen when observing a Princess.

duties. The Soldier's Father shared great peril with the King over his years of service. He would therefore, on occasion, be honoured to guard that which the King's most prized, from the great grain store to feed the Kingdom during rare times of famine, to the great gold store to support the Kingdom during infrequent times of hardship, to King's greatest treasure of all, the Princess herself.

During these boyhood years the Soldier would sometimes see the Princess during the days she was protected by his Father[9] and had ever since his first sight found it so very hard to draw his eyes away from any but her. The Princess was bound to notice eventually, and occasionally treated the young boy to the briefest glance adorned with a sweet smile[10]. On a very rare occasion, when no-one was looking, she would offer a brief wave in his direction[11].

Under the circumstances there was very little that would stop the young man from entering into service with the King's army. The Soldier exercised, and practised with sword and shield, and learned to ride a horse as well as any prince and soon could enter the castle under his own authority as a protector of the realm.

The Soldier now saw his Princess often, and she saw he, and they continued to exchange glances and waves when the location permitted. Everything for the couple was as happy as one might expect for two born to such different stations[12].

The years rolled by and the Soldier's Father retired from the army leaving his son as the sole representative of their family amongst the

---

[9] A contradiction identified and formally resolved by Altshuller. A desire to meet, but for a commoner to meet a Princess would be inappropriate. They must meet but *not* meet. We separate this contradiction using formal principle 24 that describes an *Intermediary*. Use a Father's duties as a buffer and excuse to meet a Princess.

[10] Block a harm. GA. Standard solution 1.1.8.2 *Minimum field, enhanced where required*. Others may notice if attention is overt, but very little time and effort is required by the Princess to really make that boy's day.

[11] Block a harm. GA. Standard solution 1.1.8.1 *Maximum the field, but not everywhere.* A little more effort on occasion to provoke from the boy the widest and sweetest of blushing smiles.

[12] Resolve a contradiction. A desire to meet, but for a simple soldier to meet a Princess informally and with romantic intentions would be even more inappropriate. They must meet but *not* meet. GA. Separate this in space with principle 3, employ only a *Local Quality*. A formal relationship with rare informal interaction when hidden from view.

army that protected the Kingdom[13]. The Soldier would return home every day with a gladness in his heart to tell his old Father of his chance encounters with the Princess[14]. The Soldier's Father smiled and nodded at the tales, but could hear little of these stories. Frequent exposure to a dragon's roar can deafen. Now after long years of service the old man employed a large ear trumpet[15] he acquired during one of his adventures with the King. Despite this aid, the old man strained to hear. He didn't need to hear the Soldier's story for he could tell where the high points lay from the rise and fall of his son's face as he told of his day's duties and chance encounters[16].

These happy days could not last forever. The Princess and the Soldier grew towards adulthood and the sorrowful King added to his loss. It was time for the Princess to marry. The King would not rule forever and heirs must be born[17]. Of course, the strength of Kingdoms is derived from alliances[18] so the Princess must marry a suitable prince from neighbouring Kingdoms. Messengers were sent out in every direction to

---

[13] Resolve a contradiction. The Kingdom must endure forever, but its protectors are mere mortals. It must endure but *not* endure. GA Separation principle 27. *Cheap Short-Living Objects* collaborate over time.

[14] Resolve a contradiction. They want to be together, but cannot be together. They must meet but *not* meet. GA Separation in time with principle 19. *Periodic Action*. Meet one another on occasion, and be happy for it.

[15] Improve a measurement. Standard solution 4.3.3 *If a measurement system cannot be created from the resonant frequency of the entire system, measure the resonance of a joined object or the environment.* The ear trumpet resonates in response to the Soldier's voice. Measure that resonance rather than the voice directly.

[16] Improve a measurement. Altshuller standard solution 4.1.2, *Solutions for detection and measurement. Measure a copy or an image of a substance.* Follow a story by watching a face.

[17] The King represents established order and the security of a functioning culture. So, in the continuation of this long-established practise I doubt we'll see much innovation. You may wish to innovate by tearing the established culture down, but you are likely to be looking for supporters amongst the established order. If so, be sure that you can prove that the innovative alternative will work. Otherwise, you'll have a fight on your hands, and it's likely that a well-functioning established order is stronger than you.

[18] Resolve a contradiction. A single Kingdom must be sovereign but is also no match against multiple foes. The kingdom must be separate and *not* separate. GA SP5 *Merging*. Separate by system scale. The Kingdom remains predominantly sovereign but merges the top tier with an ally to resist assault by combined foes.

call for suitable suitors.

The Soldier knew this day would arrive and dutifully resigned to those royal duties to which a Princess must attend. He was saddened, but elected to keep this sadness from his face when the Princess might glance his way. Instead he confided his woes to his old Father[19] who in turn grieved at the loss of his son's happiness. The Princess hid nothing. The Soldier could see the sorrow at the impending loss of their remote but enduring adolescence tryst.

Princes would arrive at the castle to be met at the gates by an honour guard. The Soldier had long proved his worth to the army and was given the honour of leading the escort. Each prince was led to the throne room to be presented to the King and to the Princess. These princes would arrive laden with gifts for the Princess, but in the serious exercise of their official duties to both Kingdoms the one gift they never brought to the Princess was a simple smile[20].

Each prince would be escorted into the enormous throne room to stand before the King and before the Princess to be judged. Each arrival was treated as a memorable event of great importance, so a huge crowd of citizens would attend, crammed into the enormous chamber. The suitability of each prince would be announced by the booming voice of the court Chamberlain, who read aloud from a large almanac enthusiastically compiled by this Chamberlain ever since the Princess seemed even remotely of age to marry. Despite the press of bodies, a large empty space would surround the Chamberlain, as he was a large man with a large voice to match and no-one could endure to stand near him in full voice.[21] Each entry told a tale of great scholarship, or skill with arms, or expertise in diplomacy, or some other princely skill displayed by each suitor from the surrounding Kingdoms. Gifts would be presented to the Princess and then all the court waited with bated breath as she

---

[19] Block a harm. GA, SS1.1.7 *Protect the substance by putting the full required force elsewhere.* A soldier protects a princess from her sadness by expressing his feelings to his father.

[20] Blank, Reis, Osterwalder (SB, ER, AO). The suitors probably have a rough idea of what Princesses might like. Have any of these princes actually validated their hypotheses by enquired what *this particular* Princess would like? Seems not. A little customer discovery is demanded.

[21] Improve an insufficiency. GA SS1.1.6. *Be excessive*. A small quantity cannot be applied, so add a large quantity and absorb the excess. The Chamberlain's voice is loud and cannot be moderated, but throne rooms are large spaces that mercifully soak up this assault to the ears.

pronounced her decision on whether to marry this particular suitor. Each time the Princess pronounced in her clear and singing voice,

> *'I will not marry this prince'.*

The court's collective breath once more escaped in exasperation as another possible suitor was shunned. On each occasion everyone in the throne room once more missed the stress the Princess might place on her words[22]. Or nearly everyone, for one person knew precisely what the Princess was saying, as she was never gazing at each prince as she pronounced her rejection. The young man who had escorted each prince gazed right back, a Soldier and a Princess lost in their own shared and secret ritual. The entire court failed to answer a singular question. If the Princess would not marry a prince, then what kind of man *would* she marry? While the Princess carried out each act with a regal expression before the throne and before the entire court, the Soldier down amongst the crowd could not suppress a wide smile on each occasion[23].

This theatre was repeated many times, much to the frustration of the court and to the very great and growing frustration of the King whose sorrow transformed to anger.

One fine summer's day a very fine prince arrived alone on horseback at the castle gates. His horse was trembling and spent, for it had galloped at full speed for many miles and carried not one, but two. Accompanying this prince, a young peasant girl sat behind, clutching to herself a small bundle of rags. The urgency with which this prince hastened to the castle was evident by the additional unmounted horse tethered behind this prince's steed that was also spent and flecked with sweat and spittle [24]. With a determined glare fixed upon his face, this Prince bounded from his exhausted steed and swept the bundle from the peasant girl's hands.

---

[22] Listen carefully. What does the customer really want?

[23] Make a measurement. GA SS4.2.2 *We need to measure something, but cannot do it directly. Add something to make a measurement system. Measure a field that is connected to the substance measured.* Although the Princess is giving little away, if anyone was looking at the Soldier they'd have immediately worked out what she was really saying.

[24] Resolve a contradiction. Both fast and long-range transport is required but horses have limited endurance. A horse must have both endurance and speed. GA SP26, Separate in time with *Copying*. SP19, *Periodic Action*. SP20, *Continuity of Useful Action*. Use two horses. Change horses frequently. Ride at full speed all the way.

Wrapping the bundle in his fine cloak and with chin aloft, both girl and guard were abandoned. The Prince swept by the Soldier and made with haste for the throne room with as regal a strut as he could manage after such a long and jarring ride[25]. This prince seemed to possess no chests of gifts or boxes of trinkets for the Princess, but wrapped in his red cloak he carried a hot, dark, and now smouldering mass.

Whilst the honour guard collected at the gate the Soldier hurried alone after the Prince to ensure the propriety of offering at least some minimal escort[26]. After all, the Soldier took his duties very seriously and he was not going to let simple bad manners prevent their proper execution.

A mobilised court had yet to complete its assembly as the Prince strode with purpose towards the throne, pursued by the Soldier. The King received this prince with grace despite being roused from a pleasant afternoon slumber in the summer gardens. His crown sat askew on his head, which the Princess promptly fixed when she too arrived to hear from the hurried Chamberlin the many fine attributes exhibited by this next suitor.

The heat of a dark mass buried within the cloak burned the hands of the impatient Prince as he endured the flummery of the Chamberlain. The moment this formality was complete, the Prince raised an arresting finger before anyone had a chance to question him directly and reached into the folds of his once fine cloak that was now blackening with heat[27]. With a smoking flourish he produced the single gift he had brought for the Princess.

The King's eyes lit with both curiosity and avarice as he gazed at the huge blue gem the Prince held aloft upon a cushion of smoking cloak. The huge jewel glowed a blue of the bluest skies, and a blue of the deepest oceans. No one had ever seen its like, for it was the finest jewel ever to have been seen in the Kingdom.

---

[25] Resolve a contradiction. Prompt arrival is required, but also requires a formal manner. Arrival must be both prompt and formal. GA SP25. Separate by system with *Self-Service*. Leave the honour guard behind and try to make a regal entrance alone.

[26] Resolve a contradiction. No honour guard is available but a guard is required all the same. GA SP16, Separate by system with *Partial Action*. Offer those parts of an honour guard that are available.

[27] Resolve a contradiction. Whatever this thing is, it's hot. But we need to carry it, but not carry it. The object is hot but must also be cool. GA SP11 Separate by condition. *Cushion in Advance*. Wrap the hot thing in a thermal insulator.

The Prince had allegedly acquired the jewel on an adventure at the edge of the Southern sea. The jewel had been cut from the belly of a great leviathan beached by the Prince himself in a titanic struggle between man and beast. The court hung on the Prince's every word, for he must be a most heroic gentleman to have wrestled such a fine gem from such a beast. In truth the unfortunate marine leviathan was not so great as reported by the Prince and the poor fisherman who had landed the catch was paid only for the fish itself[28]. A good price for such a fish perhaps, but not the value of an entire Kingdom for which the Prince was attempting to negotiate with this gem.

The most unusual feature of the gem was not its size and not its bluest of blue, but that fact that only the fisherman's daughter who had accompanied the Prince on his journey could touch it without harm. It seemed that to the girl the gem may be cool to the touch, but to her Father and to the Prince and to any of his men at arms the gem was as hot as an ember from their camp fire. The Fisherman's daughter was a pretty girl, and so the Prince assumed to impress the Princess with a compliment wrought from the gem's peculiar properties[29].

A hush fell across the throne room as the court once more turned to the Princess for her verdict. The Princess once more caught the Soldier's adoring eye and stated once more in a regal tone,

'I will not marry this <u>prince</u>'.

There was little more emphasis that the Princess could place on her pronouncement without provoking a rather awkward public spectacle. The Soldier's heart was once more gladdened, but still the King was oblivious and he rankled at this rejection. The jewel held aloft by the Prince was magnificent. The King only had eyes for this wondrous jewel for it spoke of a heroic exploit. Remembering the adventures of his own youth the King saw something of himself in the tale, and with this his

---

[28] The only currency for innovators to trade is the value of ideas themselves. The battle to claim personal credit can fracture a team. Stick to the solidarity of a collective 'we' when presenting valuable ideas.

[29] Enhance a benefit. GA SS5.2.2 *Introduce a field under restricted conditions by using fields that are present in the environment.* If the princess has very particular tastes, and every other prince's man-made exploits do not catch the eye of this particular princess, then perhaps this oddity dragged from a lake might flatter her into agreement. SB, ER, AO. Still no-one is really listening to this princess.

patience wore so thin that he could see only one solution through it.

'You have rejected every fine prince from the Northern mountains to the Southern sea, and from the Eastern plains to the Western desert. There must be so few remaining of any quality that you may never be married. Young lady, you will indeed marry this Prince!', proclaimed the King[30].

With that statement the King strode towards the Prince and swept the wondrous jewel from his grasp. The King made to smile a Fatherly expression of thanks to the Prince, but soon realised that the wondrous gem now burned his hands as if he had grasped a coal from the throne room's great fire. In pain and without thinking he thrust it without ceremony into the hands of the Princess, only to balk at what he had done in such haste. The Princess now held in her soft and delicate hands a gem so hot that it must surely strip the skin from her sensitive palms.

A beat. A pause. The whole court froze as the realisation of a very rare and royal wedding was, at long last, imminent. The King cringed in preparation for his daughter's shriek of pain.

The dam broke and the court erupted into enthusiastic cheers. Trumpets sounded. Applause rang throughout the throne room. The King stared in wonder as the Princess clutched the gem in her hands as if merely holding a kitten. The Soldier forced his face to remain passive, neutral, and blank to the news.

Slowly at first, but at an increasing rate, the Princess's expression grew darker, and darker, and darker, as if a thunderous raincloud had swept across her mood...

*

I have introduced a well-known and well understood framework and characters into which we can introduce some creative chaos. More of this case study will be revealed later in the text. Meanwhile, in the next chapter I offer an explanation of what a problem actually *is*.

---

[30] Resolve a contradiction. You need to marry off a princess, but this princess won't marry anyone. GA SP21, *Rushing Through*, and hope your haste seals the match.

… DRAGON EGG

6. PROBLEMS

What's the problem? This is a common enough question that you may hear often. But what is *a* problem? If the raw materials of problem solving are problems, then we ought to know what a problem is before we attempt to solve one. What are they made from? Can we take them apart? How do they work? Why do we need a definition to describe what problems are? What happens if we don't define what we're attempting to understand?

If we don't identify what problems are and where they can be found we are likely to drive right by a problem altogether and lurch straight into formulating a solution. Unless you know your destination well, this impromptu journey is less productive than it sounds.

Consider a simple problem that you may encounter every day – tying your shoelaces. How should you tie your shoelaces? This has a question mark at the end, so it must be the problem to solve. Is that all you need to identify a problem? A question mark? Consider why you need to tie your shoe laces. To stop your shoes falling from your feet. So, tying shoe laces good and tight is a solution to the problem of your shoes falling off. Is stopping your shoes falling off the problem? Perhaps, but keeping your shoes on your feet serves a function. They keep your feet from the cold ground. Is keeping your feet from the cold ground the problem, with everything else in a chain of events only solutions to this end?

Yes. And no.

Problems and solutions are connected in a sequence of events that both lead you back in time to the very need for shoes themselves, and forwards to lead you through a chain of problems and solutions to eventually consider how long the shoelaces must be and what colour might be suitable to match your outfit. Problems and solutions are two sides of the very same coin, and to pick a point in this chain of events without some thought is to throw you randomly into the problem-solving fray. How do you know where to begin? We begin by understanding what we mean by a problem. There are many definitions to choose from.

CONTRADICTIONS DEFINE THE PROBLEM

Altshuller offers a formal definition to describe problems drawn from the demands of Soviet bureaucracy. The Soviet Design Bureau would not grant an Author's Certificate unless the inventor identified and resolved a clear contradiction. The discovery of a *contradiction* formed the basis for Altshuller's problem definition.

If a problem is to be defined as a contradiction, then what is contradicting what? There are only two options.

- You want something beneficial but cannot have it because something harmful prevents this. *I want a fast sports car, but they cost too much.*
- Alternatively, you want two benefits but cannot have them both at the same time. *I want a fast sports car, but also want my vehicle to carry a wardrobe around town.*

In a few brief words we arrive at a definition for problems that covers every case that you are likely to encounter. A desire for a benefit that is contradicted by a harm, or the desire for two benefits that contradict one another. Find your contradiction and you find your problem.

Your problem may be defined by far more than a single contradiction. In these circumstances it can be difficult to determine where the problem lies. Altshuller offers a means to identify the problem with some simple techniques. Let's illustrate this with an example. Consider the effort to offer a new kind of mail order store. A mail order store of the *future*. In this bold science fiction humans live in every corner of the Earth, and on flying platforms, and even reside in orbital habitats. However, those humans who inhabit this future still celebrate their birthdays. So, gifts from our mail order store must be delivered to the whole World, and up to giant floating airborne platforms, and up into orbit, and is illustrated in Figure 6.

Figure 6: Our delivery service must have a long reach.

The mail order firm wishes to design a new delivery vehicle that can transport packages from its single large factory. The further and higher this vehicle delivers packages the more successful it will be, so this service currently delivers using a rocket. This seems like a good solution, but what other options are available? If we can describe this problem in more detail, then perhaps we can find better solutions?

We should start by listing the benefits we desire from this *Mail Order Store of the Future*. We have already described two – range and altitude. To illustrate, let's add some more.

- The longest range,
- to the highest altitude,
- with the fastest delivery,
- of the largest payload.

All of these features working together should offer a suitable delivery vehicle with characteristics that are attractive to our customers. What specific solution will offer all of these benefits simultaneously? Can we devise a vehicle that offers long range, high altitude and high speed all whilst delivering hundreds of tons of payload? Does our desire to secure one of these benefits loosen our grasp upon any of the others?

If so, we could trade between these options to create the best vehicle we can. A rocket with just enough range, with just enough altitude, delivered at a speed that is just fast enough whilst carrying just enough payload. A rocket built from features drawn a little bit from column A and a little bit from column B. This is a typical approach to system engineering, and is an inevitable demand upon the development and construction of a practical solution. The project will eventually be passed onto a system engineer who will hopefully manage this trade with skill. However, at the early concept development stage perhaps we can do better than this? Can we help this system designer by removing some of those demands to trade between our desires?

Rather than try to solve this whole problem simultaneously with some grand trade between our desires, an alternative way to describe this problem is illustrated in Table 1. With this matrix we cross reference all of our desires against all of the others. With this tool we can deal with each contradiction separately. Each intersection describes a slightly different problem to be solved, which frees us from the multi-dimensional puzzle offered by even the short list of desires presented in this simple example.

Table 1: Deal with each contradiction separately to offer 6 separate and simpler problem statements

I want...	Without harming...			
	...the top speed	...the max range	...max altitude	...the payload size
...high speed		High speed and long range	High speed and high altitude	High speed and a large payload
...long range			Long range and high altitude	Long range and a large payload
...high altitude				High altitude and a large payload
...a large payload				

We consider how such a problem is solved in Chapter 10. Prior to an attempt at solving this problem we demonstrate at this earlier stage that a good description of a problem can deliver us halfway to the solution. Observation of the problem alone can provoke intuitive solutions that emerge without any formal problem-solving effort. Consider those solutions that immediately present themselves from inspection of the problem described in Table 1.

Table 2 offers a list of solutions strategies that may immediately and intuitively come to mind if each contradiction is considered in isolation. Only three contradictions may be resolved by our incumbent solution. High speed, high altitude and long range may be delivered by a rocket. The other intersections focus upon alternative solution strategies that prioritise our other desire - the desire to deliver a very large payload. By partitioning the contradictions within the problem space in this manner we may be provoked into considering solution strategies that we might ignore in an attempt to solve the entire problem all at once.

Table 2: Considering each contradiction in isolation can provoke new solution strategies.

I want...	Without harming...			
	...the top speed	...the max range	...max altitude	...the payload size
...high speed		Rocket	Rocket	Train
...long range			Rocket	Ship
...high altitude				Balloon
...a large payload				

In this example this decomposition of our problem description exposes a wider contradiction within our problem. A contradiction is evident between the flight performance that may deliver a high speed, high altitude service, and the solution characteristics that efficiently deliver a large payload to long range. This observation allows us to summarise these contradictions within the problem space into a simpler table which can be very useful when reflecting back to the customer why the problem they are expecting you to solve is so hard, illustrated in Table 3. A simplified description like this may provoke some sympathy and support from your customer when the problem is so plain to see.

Table 3: Summarising the contradictions can help you understand why the problem is hard to solve.

	But you can't because you want to...
You want to...	... carry a very large and heavy thing
...go very fast	✗
...go a long way	✗
...go very high	✗

The simplified matrix of contradictions summarised in Table 3 divides possible solution strategies into two broad groups. Consider the intuitive solutions suggested by Table 2. Large speed, altitude and range may be offered by high power, high speed solutions. A large payload seems to be offered by low speed, low altitude strategies that emphasise the use of the super system for support and motive power. For example, trains, ships and balloons are supported by the ground, the sea and the air. This perspective may provoke us into considering some hybrid of these competing strategies. What is like a rocket, but *also* like a balloon? What is like a balloon but also like a train? Alternatively, do we require two separate services to provide the two different solutions? Perhaps we can devise some hybrid solution?

You will know when you have described your problem well, as this description will begin to ask questions about the nature of the solution. These questions begin to encroach upon the method of solution, which we will address in Chapter 10.

In the meantime, this cross referencing of desires is not the only tool that can take you halfway to the solution by describing the problem well.

FUNCTIONS DEFINE THE PROBLEM.

If the word *problem* is defined by contradictions, then describing the interaction between those contradictory benefits you desire is only half of the definition. The contradiction that you face may also be found between a benefit desired and a harm that prevents you from achieving that benefit.

To illustrate with a simple example, consider a simple hammer. The benefit a hammer offers is the ability to drive nails into a material such as wood. Is this benefit achieved at no cost? What harms are introduced by a hammer? If we consider the interactions between elements of the problem, we can identify those that are harming our system. To achieve this Altshuller offers a convenient way to illustrate these interactions.

Consider how language describes the interaction between two objects. We have a *subject* acting upon an *object* through some *action*. Typically, a function is described using two nouns and a verb, and in English they are arranged as illustrated in Figure 7.

SUBJECT **VERB** ➤ **OBJECT**

Figure 7: A Subject does something to change an Object

A subject does something to an object. Basic grammar. We illustrate by returning to the hammer, in Figure 8. The nail is transformed by the hammer, as it is driven into a material.

HAMMER **DRIVES** ➤ **NAIL**

Figure 8: The nail's situation is changed by the hammer. It's now stuck into a piece of wood.

To describe the interactions of a system, we must be rigorous. To offer a useful description of a system the Subject must somehow *change* the object. Gadd [14] offers a useful example to illustrate how we might provoke an error by employing the tricky topic of romance. I could state, *I love you*, but how has that love changed *you*? In fact, my affection for you has changed *me*. A less romantic, but more accurate statement may be offered. *You have provoked feelings of love in me.* Less pithy, but at least we know who is doing what to whom.

Returning to the hammer, we are missing one more piece of useful information. *How* is the hammer driving the nail? What property of the hammer allows it to achieve this useful outcome? Here we encounter Altshuller's innovation. He separates the property, characteristic, or *field* exhibited by the subject from the subject itself. This offers a triangle of interaction illustrated in Figure 9 which is described as a *Substance-Field Interaction*.

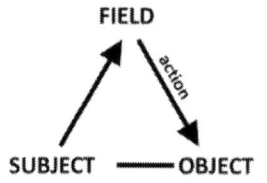

Figure 9: Separate the subject from its useful property

The Field is a property of the subject that interacts with the object to provoke a change. For a physical system this field will belong to one of eight basic types.

1. Gravitational
2. Mechanical
3. Acoustic
4. Thermal
5. Chemical
6. Magnetic
7. Electrical
8. Electromagnetic

Consider the useful work of a hammer, illustrated in Figure 10. The useful work offered by the mechanical field of momentum is illustrated by a black arrow. With a complete description of this simple system available we are now at liberty to modify the system to offer alternative solutions.

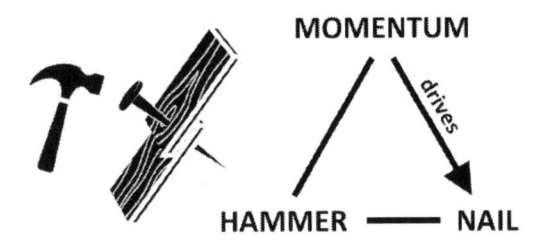

Figure 10: A useful property can be separated from the object that offers this property.

What if we did not wish to employ a hammer? We could remove it from the illustration without removing its useful work, illustrated in Figure 11.

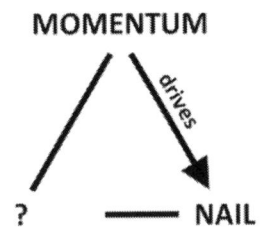

Figure 11: We remove the useful subject, but its work will remain.

This simple example shows that by separately illustrating the subject and its useful work we now detect an incomplete system. Our grammar is missing a subject. We must find an alternative tool that can offer enough momentum to drive the nail, illustrated in Figure 12. With a good description of the problem, solutions offer themselves with little effort.

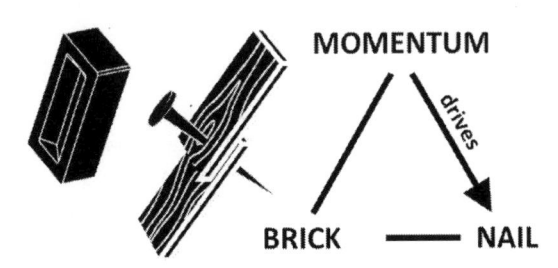

Figure 12: A simple house brick can offer the momentum required to drive in the nail.

This method of illustrating the system offers further detail. Perhaps the alternative solution is inadequate. No harms may be added to the system, but perhaps the brick does not offer enough momentum to drive in the nail. This inadequacy can be illustrated by a broken line, illustrated in Figure 13.

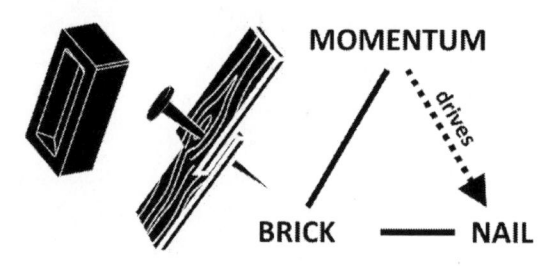

Figure 13: The brick is a poor solution.

The broken line indicates that the brick is a valid solution to the problem, but the momentum is insufficient to drive in the nail. The Substance-Field diagram highlights the specific problems within an inadequate system and provokes us to ask clear and unambiguous questions. If momentum drives in the nail, how might we increase the momentum of the brick? Without the focus upon the specific field that drives in the nail, one might be motivated to find a bigger brick. Momentum can be generated by more than this simple means. We could increase the speed of the brick by dropping it from a height, illustrated in Figure 14. Or we could secure the brick to the end of a long stick, which works us back to describing a rudimentary hammer.

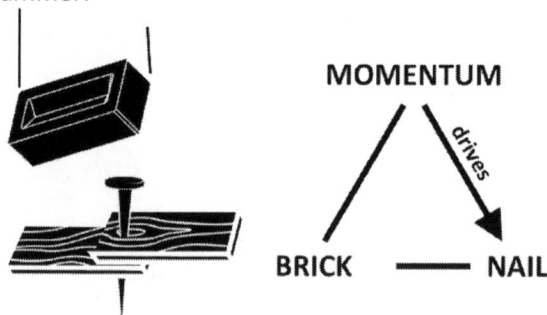

Figure 14: How many methods can you think of to create momentum?

The above figures illustrate with a straight black arrow the beneficial fields within a system. We can use a similar method to illustrate the properties of a subject that introduce harms. For example, poor accuracy from a large heavy hammer may result in a bent nail. We could illustrate this harm as a wavy arrow, shown in Figure 17.

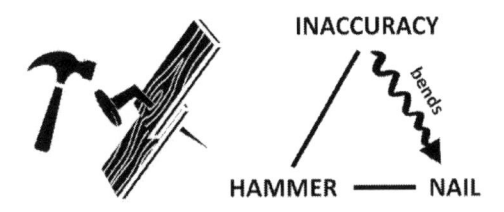

Figure 15: Inaccuracy arising from the hammer will harm the nail.

The poor accuracy of the hammer is a clear problem, but consider carefully how harmful fields are represented. For example, to illustrate this particular inaccuracy as a harm may not offer a practical tool to resolve this harm. What could you *improve* to resolve this harm? This harm is perhaps better described in terms of the accuracy of the strike, or in terms of the alignment of the hammer head with the nail. Focussing upon the accuracy of the hammer alignment offers a mechanism that we can improve to resolve this harm. To characterise this harmful bending of nails as an insufficient alignment of hammer and nail is illustrated in Figure 16.

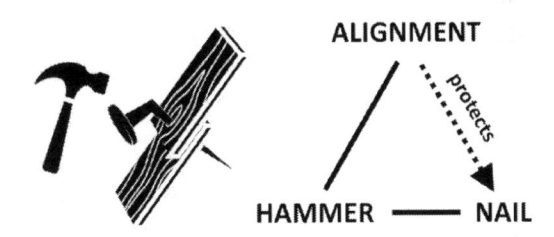

Figure 16: It is occasionally useful to cast a harm as an insufficient benefit.

To identify a harm, but subsequently recast it as an insufficient benefit can offer alternative options to resolve the harm. What modification may improve this alignment to resolve this insufficiency and reduce the interaction that we originally described as harmful? A nail gun may offer the alignment required, and may remove the harm altogether. Figure 17 illustrates how this improved control when striking the nail using the nail gun resolves this insufficiency, and resolves the underlying harm.

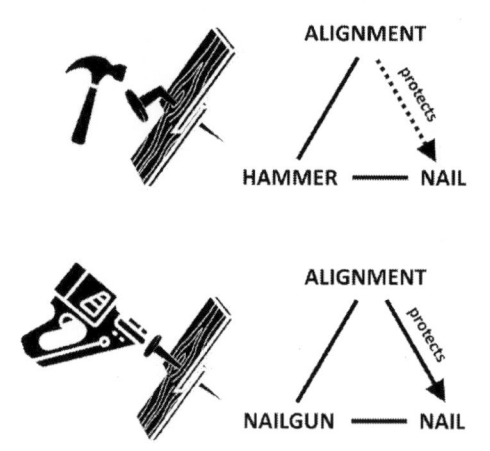

Figure 17: Harms can be illustrated as benefits and resolved.

Altshuller's Substance-Field diagram offers five basic grammatical connections with which we can describe a wide variety of complex systems. With only the five basic grammatical components described in the following figures a system can often be described in a clear and comprehensive manner.

SUBJECT ———— OBJECT

Figure 18: A black line without arrows indicates that a subject and object interact in some manner.

SUBJECT$_1$ ———— FIELD$_{1.1}$

Figure 19: A black line also indicates that a subject exhibits a characteristic represented by a Field. A suitable numbering system can be used to associate each field with the substance that created it.

FIELD $\xrightarrow{\text{action}}$ SUBJECT

Figure 20: A straight line with an arrow and a verb indicates that a field acts upon an object to transform that object in a beneficial manner.

FIELD ······▶ SUBJECT

with "action" above the arrow.

Figure 21: A straight dashed line with an arrow and a verb indicates that a field acts upon an object to transform that object in a beneficial but insufficient manner.

FIELD ∿∿∿▶ SUBJECT

with "action" above the arrow.

Figure 22: A wavy line with an arrow and a verb indicates that a field acts upon an object to transform that object in a harmful manner.

With these simple tools we can describe the benefits, insufficiencies, harms and dependencies within the system, illustrated in Figure 23

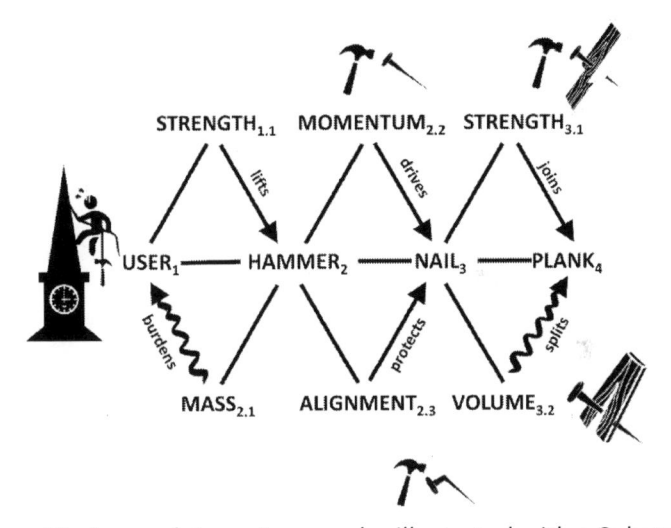

Figure 23: A complete system can be illustrated with a Substance-Field diagram.

Altshuller's deeper intentions in the development of this technique focus upon creating a 'molecular' view of problem descriptions and their solution. If a standardised means can be developed to describe problems, then a similar approach could be employed to describe standardised solutions. This tool would allow the user to identify the structure of their problem, relate this to similar problems and apply a standard solution 'molecule' that will solve the problem, much like the reagent of a chemical reaction might transform a physical substance into a useful material.

Note, that the effort to describe large systems with many interconnections can result in a complex illustration that can hinder the solution process as much as it helps. Under these circumstances the reader is advised to break their problem down into functional groups, and describe each in isolation using Altshuller's work, but noting the overlaps and interconnections between these groups.

The Substance-Field diagram can illustrate the problem by highlighting the benefits and harms within the system. Note that all of the harms within the system are present because they are associated with a desirable benefit. If they were not, then they would be easy to remove. The nail joins the wood, but the nail splits the wood. The hammer drives the nail, but the hammer burdens the user. A good illustration of the problem takes you half way to the solution, and the means by which harms can be removed from this system may present themselves with little difficulty. To illustrate more complex solution techniques that can be used to optimise this system, we will employ this illustration to solve these problems in Chapter 10.

THINKING IN SPACE AND TIME TO DEFINES THE PROBLEM

When you solve a problem, how far from the problem do you roam? Consider Figure 24, in which we want to transport livestock across rivers. If we exclude the construction of a bridge, for the sake of argument, we may immediately leap to a solution. We might consider a boat, or a raft some sort of floating mechanism to ferry the livestock across the river. How might we better describe this problem before we leap to a solution?

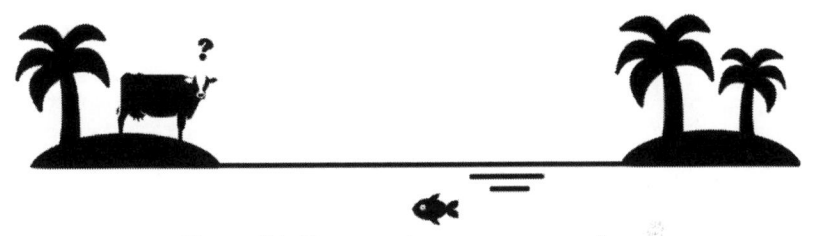

Figure 24: Transport cows across a river

Note that we're talking about a simple system. A floating transport of some kind. Is this as far as we are willing to describe the problem? What happens to the cow as it travels across the river? We can illustrate this in Figure 25.

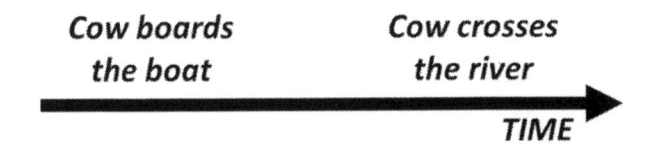

Figure 25: What happens to the cow over time?

The cow boards the boat. The cow travels across the river in the boat. This simple description of the functions we might desire as the solution to this problem unfolds doesn't seem useful, but it's common for a problem-solving exercise to remain at this simple level – to describe what we want at the level of the system. We want the cow to cross the river.

To continue this cow-sized analysis, what happens to the cow once it gets to the other side of the river? In Figure 26 we indicate that want to unload the cow from the boat. Perhaps by extending our timescale we also remember that we're going to want the boat to return to the previous bank.

```
                Cow leaves
Cow boards      Cow crosses    the boat
the boat        the river
                               The boat is
                               recovered
─────────────────────────────────────────────▶
                                          TIME
```

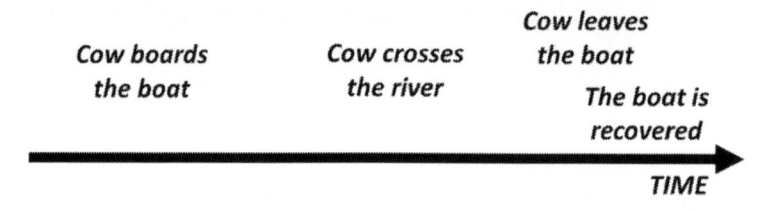

Figure 26: What happens once a cow has crossed the river?

Figure 26 illustrates that by stretching our time scale we may be provoked into describing the problem a little more fully. This is also true if we stretch our consideration over the size of things. So far, we have sketched out what we want from the system. What might we want from the sub components of that system? What do we want from the boat? How does the boat work? Figure 27 adds to our problem description what we might want from the subcomponents of the solution.

SYSTEM	Cow boards the boat	Cow crosses the river	Cow leaves the boat The boat is recovered
SUB SYSTEM	A mechanism to board cows Boat is big enough to hold a cow	The boat is powered The boat floats	A mechanism to disembark cows
	BEFORE CROSSING	WHILST CROSSING	AFTER CROSSING → TIME

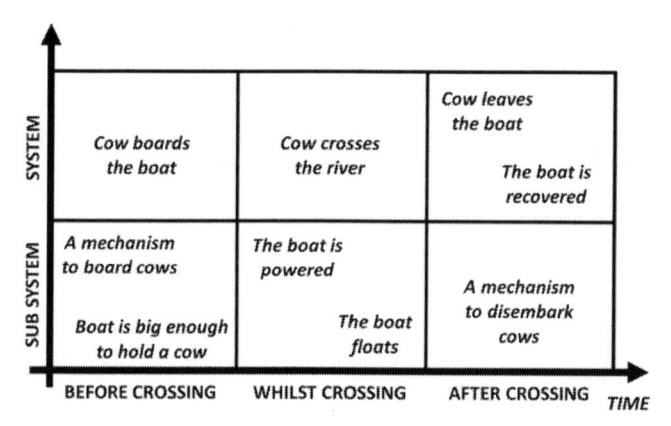

Figure 27: What do we want from the smaller scale objects in the problem?

Obviously, our boat must be big enough to hold a cow. But how many cows do we want to transport at once? The cow must also be able to board the boat with ease. During crossing the boat must float. But what propels the boat? A person with oars might be an obvious solution. Could anything else propel the boat? What about the cow? Also, once we reach the far side, we somehow want the boat propelled back to the original bank.

Note that we are still not solving the problem with this exercise. We are describing what we want. Now we have a description of what we want from the system and what we want from the sub components of that system. For example, we haven't stated that we will use a ramp to board the boat, but we have stated that this solution must allow a cow to board easily. A simple ramp is a good solution, but may not be the only solution.

We can continue this description of what we want by increasing the size of objects under consideration. We can think about the wider environment – the *super-system*. Figure 28 illustrates our consideration of the environment. We want each riverbank to be easily accessed, and a calm crossing would be desirable.

The problem space has been split into 9 boxes divided by space and by time. This means to describe our problem was developed by Altshuller and provokes us to consider what happens before, during and after a cow crosses the river, and also provokes us to state our desires for the solution subcomponents and how the wider environment may help or hinder our solution [15]. We are *Thinking in Time and Scale*.

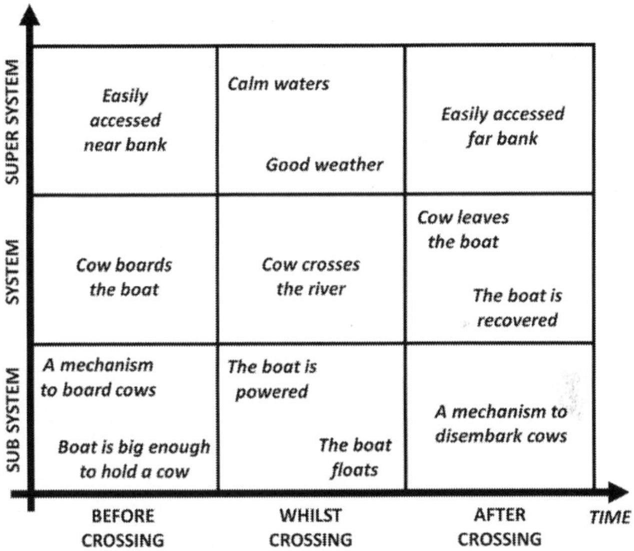

	BEFORE CROSSING	WHILST CROSSING	AFTER CROSSING
SUPER SYSTEM	Easily accessed near bank	Calm waters Good weather	Easily accessed far bank
SYSTEM	Cow boards the boat	Cow crosses the river	Cow leaves the boat The boat is recovered
SUB SYSTEM	A mechanism to board cows Boat is big enough to hold a cow	The boat is powered The boat floats	A mechanism to disembark cows

Figure 28: Considering the wider environment completes our description of the problem

We need not constrain ourselves to describing benefits. We can also subdivide the problem space and consider harms that may prevent us from achieving these goals. Figure 29 illustrates those harms that may hinder our efforts to transport our cows across a river. The environment may obstruct our objectives, or may sink our boat. The cows may not be as cooperative as we desire. Portions of the boat may fail.

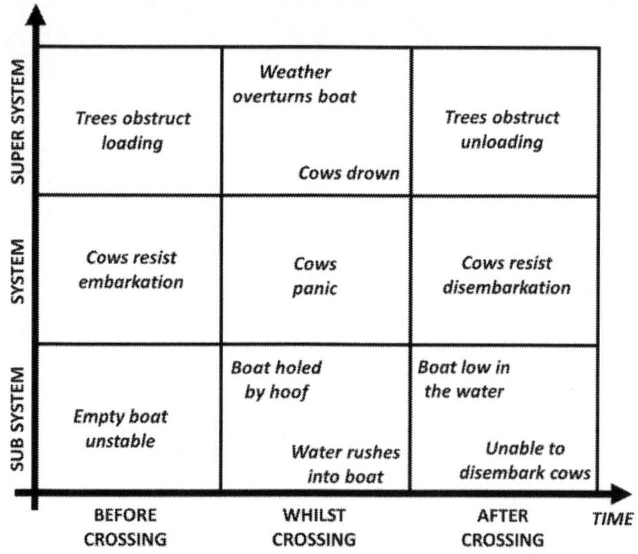

	BEFORE CROSSING	WHILST CROSSING	AFTER CROSSING
SUPER SYSTEM	Trees obstruct loading	Weather overturns boat Cows drown	Trees obstruct unloading
SYSTEM	Cows resist embarkation	Cows panic	Cows resist disembarkation
SUB SYSTEM	Empty boat unstable	Boat holed by hoof Water rushes into boat	Boat low in the water Unable to disembark cows

Figure 29: What may prevent us from achieving our goals?

One is well advised to consider the harms within the system in a separate exercise to describing benefits. You could attempt both simultaneously. After all, describing benefits may highlight those harms that will prevent the realisation of these benefits. Similarly, describing harms may reveal benefits that you desire. On your first pass through this technique it is easier to schedule two separate exercises.

Benefits and harms can be mistaken as opposites of one another. If you attempt to consider both simultaneously you may write a benefit, and then simply write its opposite. Benefit desired, *calm water*. Potential harm, *not calm water*. This approach is not a very useful exercise. Under these circumstances such a close association between benefits and harms will provoke your brain to vacillate between opposites. I've seen workshop delegate's brains lock up altogether as they overload with opposites.

It's more productive to subsequently describe the harms that prevent you from achieving a list of benefits. Benefit desired, *cows cross the river*. Potential harm, *the boat may overturn, the cows will drown*. Only after this consideration did I return to the benefits and add *calm water*. Split your consideration of benefits and harms into two sessions. The first session describes the benefits you desire. The second considers the harms that may *prevent you from achieving these benefits*. Once you have some material on the page, only then alternate back and forth between the two.

A good description of the problem could lead you halfway to solutions. We've stated that the system must be powered. We've stated that cows loiter on either store. We've identified that the trees might hinder our operation, but perhaps they can help? How could a cow and a tree be combined to solve the problem? Alternatively, we have stated our concerns about the weather. Might that too be turned to our advantage? A well described problem oozes with solutions. We will address the solution to these problems in Chapter 10.

Before we do, we provide some space for our chaotic creativity to once more take to the floor. No one was listening to the Princess, and she was growing unhappy. Problems soon arise...

DRAGON EGG

7. CASE STUDY: A PROBLEM ARISES.

The Princess's mood grew darker, and darker, and darker, as if a thunderous raincloud had swept across her face. On this bright sunny summer's day clouds had indeed massed over the Kingdom. They rolled down from the nearby mountains and rolled in from the shining sea. The mood in the throne room rose from shared delight to a high anxiety. All eyes turned to the focus of this sudden change. The Princess stood before the throne clutching the great blue jewel to her breast. An unexpected breeze whipped around her, picking up dust and blowing out candles[31].

The Princess's eyes grew ever blacker to grow as black as night, whilst the wind rose around her. Then the Princess uttered a low growl, at first, and then a scream, which ascended to a long high-pitched screech that forced the entire court to retreat back to the walls of the throne room in fear and confusion.

The King stared nonplussed at this transformation from his kind, gentle and beloved daughter to the howling monster that now hovered a few inches from above the floor. His daughter was not very pleased with his sudden choice for her husband. The Prince too was employing his long training in tactics and diplomacy to salvage his plans. He reached out a hand to grasp the King by a sleeve to yank him unceremoniously away from this new danger. His goal had been reached with far greater ease than he had anticipated. There was no way that the Prince was going to permit this turn of events to snatch this Kingdom from his grasp[32].

The Soldier stood his ground with such determination that soon he was standing alone in a wide circle proscribed by the court's dissolving bravery, accompanied only by the transformed Princess. The black eyes of the Princess caught those of the Soldier and softened for just a moment before blackening once more as the Princess raised a finger to point at the great stained-glass window that adorned the far end of the throne room. The Soldier turned to see a great bat-like shadow loom before the shining window.

In anticipation, the Soldier rushed to the Princess, grabbed her around

---

[31] Enhance a benefit. GA SS1.1.4 *Use the environment*. Whatever the princess is up to, the firmament is somehow definitely involved.

[32] Resolve a contradiction. You're trying to win the hand of a princess who now looks rather dangerous. Best take precautions. Separate this contradiction in time. GA SP34, *Discarding and Recovering*. Grab the King now, beat a hasty retreat and seal the deal. Recover the Princess's approval later.

her slim waist and together they dove beneath the great gilded throne just as the large stained-glass window exploded with a roar into a million colourful fragments. The Last Dragon burst into the chamber snarling and writhing, its huge wings kicking up the gale required to support this airborne monstrosity.

The court scattered with shrieks whilst the Prince hauled the King aside into to the safety of an alcove behind an ancient tapestry[33], despite the King's clear protests to again confront this beast as he once had in his prime. The great beast flapped lazily above the room, once more, twice more, and landed with a delicacy one might not expect from such a gigantic creature, its iron claws clattering onto the stone floor. The Dragon relaxed onto its haunches and surveyed the room with its large, piercing yellow eyes.

The Soldier shifted uncomfortably under the great throne where he and the Princess huddled for protection[34]. Despite the large size of the throne, there was very little room under this seat of power for two, and the Soldier realised that in this moment this was the closest that he had ever been to the Princess. In fact, he had never touched her at all in his whole life and this first time was to protect her from the most fearsome beast he had ever seen. He tore his eyes away from this terrible sight, to note that the Princess had returned to her more familiar state without the black eyes, the furious gale or the blue lightning, but clearly anxious. And soft. And warm. Together they waited for whatever fate would next befall them.

The Dragon continued its slow and deliberate investigation of the room until, in frustration, it roared a billowing gout of flame and smoke to torch the walls, the ceiling and the floor with its breath. The flags, carpets and tapestries all burned in a flash leaving the Prince and the King exposed to the Dragon's steely gaze. With a shriek of recognition, the Dragon recoiled and heaved itself once more into the air, dove through the shattered window and disappeared into the black storm clouds that boiled around the castle.

---

[33] Resolve a contradiction. We are trapped in a room with a dragon but do not wish to be seen. We must be in the room, but not in the room. GA SP30. Separate on condition by employing *Flexible Membranes or Thin Films* for cover.

[34] Block a harm. We are trapped in a room with a dragon who may cause us harm. GA SP1.2.1 *Block the harm by introducing a new substance. Introduce the third substance between the given two substances.* Hide under the throne.

A quiet descended upon the throne room, interrupted only by the faint crackle of a few still burning flags and a few blackened pews. With the Dragon departed, those of the court that remained in the throne room slowly emerged from under scorched tables and chairs, from behind sooted pillars and from under the charred remains of heavy tapestries that once adorned the walls of the throne room. The Soldier and the Princess struggled from under the great throne to survey the damage wrought by the Princess's Dragon.

The Prince took the King and the Princess's survival as a very good sign. As he had recently rescued the King from a terrible fate[35], and despite the surrounding devastation, felt that a rather indelicate question would pass scrutiny. The Prince cleared his throat, and after waiting a moment for the King's attention enquired after the King's health, the Princess's survival, the need for repairs upon the throne room prior to any grand events, how fine an event in high summer might be and … potential dates for a grand royal wedding?[36] The sorrowful King was driven further to shameful despair by his inability to face the departed monster and to protect his daughter, as he had failed to protect his Queen so many years before. In a quiet voice he agreed to terms, and with a wary eye to any further reaction from the Princess a date for the wedding was set. Despite this news the Soldier dutifully fell into line alongside the Princess. The Princess was crestfallen but continued to clutch the great blue jewel to her body. The gem remained red hot to the touch and no amount of encouragement could remove it from the Princess's grasp.

The King's troubles did not end there. Preparations were made for a royal wedding. Feasts were arranged. Fine clothes were gathered. Precession routes planned. Bunting was prepared. The King's trumpeters practised day and night. Guests were invited from all of the surrounding Kingdoms. All of this was presented to the Princess for her approval. Fire

---

[35] Resolve a contradiction. A topic that needs discussion, but may be received badly under the circumstances. We must discuss the topic but not discuss the topic. Separate on condition by adding a filter. GA SP11 *Cushion in Advance*

[36] Enhance a benefit. Being blunt would harm the objective. GA. SS5.1.2 *Indirect methods for introducing substances under restricted conditions. Indirectly achieve a function by segmentation. Divide the object into smaller units.* The Prince works in stages to the topical point in hand.

services were alerted[37].

Each time arrangements were presented to the Princess, great jewel in hand, it seemed not long after that the skies would darken and the wind would rise and a great Dragon would emerge from the darkness to torch yet another amenity. It may take only hours, or may even take days, but soon a whirl of wind would rise around the Princess, the jewel that would not leave her person would glow a malevolent blue, lightning would flash from walls to ceiling to floor and a Dragon would be summoned.

On one occasion the Dragon roasted a barn. On another it tore a grain silo apart with its claws. On another the army barracks were crushed under the weight of the Dragon and amongst the mad dash of troops that evacuated before disaster struck the young Soldier barely escaped with his life.

The King and the Prince recognised that the Princess was so very opposed to this match that she would even summon Dragons to avoid this fate. However, the King had given his word and the Prince ensured that he continued to do so. Together they hatched a plan and consigned the Princess to the deepest and darkest dungeon that the castle offered where the Dragons would not hear her shrieking call[38].

The King would not consign his beloved daughter to a dank, inhospitable cell. Prior to the Princess's sullen arrival, the deepest dungeon was redecorated in the finest manner to make incarceration as comfortable as possible. The only feature that remained to remind the Princess of her imprisonment was the stout wooden door of the cell, set with a small iron barred window. If we could just get through this wedding, reasoned the King and the Prince, then perhaps all this nonsense would end[39].

Despite the Princess's incarceration the King's troubles did not end. The Dragon continued to harass the Kingdom. A local inn was mashed and

---

[37] Block a harm. The Princess must be consulted, but the castle is inflammable. GA SS1.2.3 *Introduce a sacrificial substance to absorb the harm*. Just add water.

[38] Enhance a benefit. We cannot control the system directly. GA SS2.2.1 *Replace an uncontrolled or poorly controlled field with an easily controlled field*. Control the Princess and perhaps you control the Dragon.

[39] Resolve a contradiction. We want a Princess but do not want a Dragon. Princess and Dragon are linked. The Princess must be both present and not present.GA SP2 *Taking out*. Remove the Princess and we remove the Dragon. SP7. *Nested doll*. Keep the Princess but separate the Princess by nesting her deep within the castle.

the Dragon was not satisfied. An ironworks was crushed, and still the Dragon would not give up its search.

This last incident gave the Prince an idea. The Prince decided it was time to defeat this Dragon once and for all, and he should do so in the finest traditions of his martial tutelage. A huge iron bow[40] of his own design was fashioned. This giant bow was mounted on a huge wooden cart to permit some mobility. The arrow employed by this bow was twenty feet long and the whole contraption took twenty men to manoeuvre it into position and to correct its aim.

The giant bow was very heavy and very slow, so aiming this behemoth was a very tricky task indeed. Despite a long education in military tactics the Prince could never put the weapon in the right place at the right time. The bow was near the church, and the Dragon destroyed the school. The bow was near the remains of the school, and the church was demolished. The bow was hauled back to the church, and the town hall was crushed. The Prince never knew where the great bow should be dragged next, whilst the huffing, puffing team of red-faced men did their best to manoeuvre the great bow from place to place as fast as they could despite the futility of the whole effort[41].

Meanwhile, life was just as uncomfortable in the deepest, darkest dungeon in the land. Every time the Dragon arrived the Princess would scream and shriek in fits of rage, wind would whip around her feet and no one wanted to be near this maelstrom when it struck. Only one soldier was willing to guard that cell and attend to the Princess's needs. The Soldier who loved her more than anything in the whole Kingdom. The Soldier brought her food from the castle kitchens and books from the palace libraries. He could not predict her outbursts, so hoped that the comfort of fine cushions brought from the castle throne room might reduce their frequency[42].

The Princess would spend her days of protection and imprisonment reading aloud so that the Soldier who stood guard outside her door could listen to fantastic tales of knights and dragons from all over the world.

---

[40] Resolve a contradiction. Regular bows are effective but quite small. Dragons are quite large. A small bow must be large. GA SP16 *Partial or Excessive Action*. Build a huge bow to defeat a huge Dragon.

[41] Innovation is not just about solving current problems, but about predicting future problems.

[42] Resolve a contradiction. We must prevent a harm, but don't know when it will occur. GA SP11 Literally, a *Cushion in Advance*.

The soldiering of long ago sounded a most exciting vocation, which contrasted with the Soldier's own long days of training, guarding things that didn't ever seem to need guarding, and preparing for disasters and conflicts that never arose. On occasion, during his long days of guard duty, for there was no-one else who would volunteer for this task, the Soldier would pass the time wondering if such tall tales could offer him some clue to resolving the Princess's condition[43].

By day the Princess would read to him and by night the Soldier would listen to the sound of her soft breath as she slept. Despite the terrible events above ground during those days of the Dragon and the cruel imprisonment the sad King forced upon his daughter, the Soldier admitted to himself a guilty secret. In that dark, torch sputtered corridor, these days spent alone with his Princess were thus far the happiest of his young life[44].

Then, after a long campaign that had wrecked most of the town buildings at least once each, the Dragon finally attacked the castle itself. The Soldier knew that the Dragon would attack that day, for the Princess had launched into another maelstrom of wind and light and shrieking. The Soldier could hear the blaring of trumpets to alert the army and heard the brass refrain to call all of the reserves and all of the veterans to defend the castle walls. The Soldier's elderly Father would surely respond to that call, for he was and always will be a soldier and a protector of the Kingdom.

On one occasion, when only the echo of trumpets remained, the Soldier noted that the sound and fury from within the Princess's cell had unexpectedly ceased. The Soldier glanced through the bars of the Princess's cell to see the black eyes of the possessed Princess glaring right back. She stood stiff, bent, as if in pain, still clutching the great blue jewel to her stomach. Sweat beaded on her brow as if the Princess, through some great feat of determination, were stifling the storm with which she summed the Dragon[45]. Despite the blackness of her eyes the Prince could see the expression of concern for the King, for the Kingdom, and for the

---

[43] Don't be too enamoured by the genius of your own ideas. Take time to appreciate the ideas of others, as you are likely to find inspiration there. This is the essence of Altshuller's approach.

[44] Our hero suffers quite the contraction. GA SP22 *Blessing in Disguise*. If all that glitters is not gold, then perhaps the converse is occasionally true?

[45] Block a harm. GA 1.1.7 *Protect the substance by putting the full required force elsewhere*.

Soldier's own Father, for she too knew the loyalty of those who served the Kingdom.

With that glance the Soldier understood, left his station and dashed up the steps from the dungeons to join his comrades in defence of the castle. The journey from under the ground to the battlements themselves was a long and arduous climb, but this soldier was driven by a duty to the King and to his Father. Upon reaching the battlements the Soldier looked out over the town that surrounded the castle to see the great iron bow being dragged across a far field towards an old farmhouse. Despite its size the bow was a mere speck, but the Soldier could still make out his brothers in arms heaving the contraption. The Prince stood upon the bow, frantically flapping his arms and berating this Kingdom's protectors to redirect the contraption back to the castle. The bow began to turn back towards the castle so very, very slowly.

Once the bow had turned to begin its return journey the huge iron arrow nestled within the contraption now pointed directly at the Soldier. This arrow could never reach so far, but this weapon pointed to the heavens in a direction in which many other faces in that courtyard looked and pointed in concern[46]. The Soldier turned to look along the giant arrow's path. There, high in the sky above the castle was the huge, dark, flapping Dragon on its descent.

Soldiers rushed out onto the courtyard, clanking with steel helmets and shields and spears and swords. At the very vanguard was the King himself with his great dragon scale shield. At the King's side once more stood the Soldier's old Father dusting the years of idleness from his helmet and breastplate. His fervour to once more protect the Kingdom imbued the old soldier with fighting vigour. No longer did he clutch his old ear trumpet to his ear, but instead once more wielded a sword. The old man felt a full twenty years younger. The old earpiece was tucked into his sword belt, no longer betraying the old soldier's age and infirmity[47].

The Dragon swooped down at the assembled troops, knocking great stones from the castle walls with its mighty tail to send soldiers scattering as the rocks crashed to the ground. The King and his brave old companion stood their ground. The Dragon swooped by, turned, and landed with a

---

[46] Make a measurement. GA SS4.5.1 *Use more than one measurement system to get a more accurate result.* Everyone is looking over the Soldier's shoulder at something horrible.

[47] Make a measurement. GA SS4.1.1 *Change the systems so that there is no need for detection or measurement.*

mighty thump into the courtyard. The King and the old soldier glared at the Dragon. The huge Dragon glared back. They had all met many years before, and a moment to mark this recognition was demanded.

Well met, the great Dragon inhaled a huge breath as it prepared to roast the King and the old soldier. The King raised his shield with moments to spare as a red-hot stream of fire burst from the dragon's gaping maw at the old comrades. The dragon scale shield served its King well, as it had many times in the past, to protect both the King and the old soldier from certain death[48]. The blast rocked the old King, as the intervening years and hollowing sorrow had sapped his aging strength. Upon seeing the King stumble the old soldier drove into the shield in support of his King, and for a few moments longer together they withstood the dragon's fiery assault[49]. Under the heat and pressure, the pair sank to their knees behind the shield. Finally, this old bulwark crumbled onto their backs.

The young Soldier leapt to his Father's aid from the battlements overhead and landed with a thump onto the Dragon's wide head. The Dragon, interrupted in its effort to roast its old adversaries, swung its head this way and that to dislodge this new assault[50]. Meanwhile the young Soldier hacked and stabbed at the dragon's eyes and ears and nose with his sword, all the while clinging to the dragon's horns for purchase[51].

With the pressure released, the old soldier took his cue from his son. With a heave he tipped the large shield from the King and it fell with a dull clank to the courtyard stone. The Dragon had taken to smashing its own head against the massive stone walls of the castle keep to dislodge the young Soldier[52]. The Soldier dodged and dove behind the large horns for protection from the blows then leapt out from hiding to stab once

---

[48] Block a harm. GA SS1.2.1 *Block the harm by introducing a new substance. Introduce the third substance between the given two substances.* Dragon scales block the thermal harm of a dragon's breath.

[49] Enhance a benefit. GA SS3.1.1 *Improve systems by combining with another system or multiply/copy system elements.*

[50] Resolve a contradiction. A harm cannot be reached by conventional means. We must reach the harm, but cannot reach the harm. GA SP18 *Mechanical Vibration.* Shake the interloper loose.

[51] Enhance a benefit. GA SS5.2.2 *Introduce a field under restricted conditions by using fields that are present in the environment.* Avoid an attack using components from the attacker.

[52] Enhance a benefit. A harm cannot be reached by conventional means. GA SS1.1.4 *Use the environment* to interact with the harm.

more at the Dragon's eyes and ears and nose[53].

On seeing his son's predicament and before the King could gather his wits and his feet, the old soldier charged forward to the Dragon and to his son's aid. Standing under the rippling hawser of the monster's long neck that thrashed the young Soldier against the walls and the floor, the old soldier drove his sword upwards into the spot bald of scales between a dragon's broad shoulders and sinewed throat that he knew from long experience most pained such a beast[54].

With a shudder and a spasm and a roar the ferocious Dragon lashed its head one final time and tossed the young Soldier far across the courtyard. Beating wings swept dust into the old soldier's face and eyes as the Dragon thrashed itself into the air and out of the courtyard.

The old soldier turned from the Dragon's departure towards his son. The young Soldier had been dashed to near unconsciousness against the stone, and floundered in his efforts to regain his wits.

But the Dragon was not yet finished, for it rose high above the castle then swooped low, picking up speed as it dove amongst the towers and battlements. Flashes of its dark shape could be seen as it appeared from behind towers, over walls, and amongst the minarets. The old soldier tracked the monster for as long as he could until he lost sight of the dragon as it wove through the castle structure[55].

The old soldier turned his attention back to his son and made his way towards him across the large, now empty, courtyard. The young Soldier had regained some sense and climbed to his knees. Peering through blurred vision he recognised his old Father making his way towards him from across the large open space. As his eyes cleared, he could also make out the huge silhouette of the Dragon that loomed behind the castle wall and behind his old Father.

The young Soldier's legs were weak, but his breath remained strong

---

[53] Enhance a benefit. GA SS2.3.3 *When we have two incompatible actions, perform one action in the downtime of the other*. We cannot attack and defend simultaneously. We attack in the pause between assaults.

[54] Enhance a benefit. GA SS5.1.1.5 *Indirectly achieve a function by concentrating an additive at a specific location*. The sword is small compared to the beast, but its sharp blade and precision has an effect far larger than its relative size might suggest.

[55] Make a measurement. GA SS4.1.3 *Transform the problem into detection of consecutive successive changes*. We cannot track the Dragon smoothly, but perhaps we can discern its intentions by assembling intermittent successive exposures.

and he yelled to his Father a warning. Yet, the old soldier's ear trumpet remained tucked into his sword belt. He could not hear his son's warning. The Dragon swooped towards the courtyard with its claws outstretched. The young Soldier waved his weary arms in warning. The old soldier made his way across the courtyard, and he too made a cheery wave in return, gladdened that his son was no worse for wear from his ordeal. The young Soldier clambered to his feet, yelling and waving as a dark shadow loomed across the old soldier.

Seeing the skies darken all too late, the old soldier turned to see giant claws, great beating wings and a terrible snarling face fill his view. With an unbearable yank the Dragon plucked the old soldier from the ground, and such was the force of this departure that the old soldier left behind in his place his shoes, his sword and his old ear trumpet that clattered to the ground as the old man was lofted high into the air.

The young Soldier looked on astonished and grieved at his Father's sudden and violent departure. The pair were silhouetted against the summer sun as the Dragon stole the old soldier to whatever terrible fate would befall a man who had fought dragons for his whole life.

The young man cried out after his Father and, finding strength in anguish, rushed to where his Father had stood moments before. There on the ground lay his shoes, his sword, and his old ear trumpet. With that optimism that he had carried with him his whole life, he picked up the ear trumpet and tucked it into his own sword belt. He'll need that when he returns, thought the young man.

A moment later the Soldier remembered his sworn duty and helped the old King to his feet, who promptly berated him for leaving his daughter's side at such a precarious time. At that moment the courtyard gates burst open and a great iron bow thrust through the opening. The proud Prince inched ever forwards mounted upon his mighty bow, whilst his spent, red faced men heaved the weapon a final few inches. His triumph was complete, for the very sight of the mighty weapon had surely frightened the beast away[56].

Taking only a moment to lament the loss of his old comrade, the King surely and sadly agreed with the Prince.

*

So, we have a clear problem that terrorises the Kingdom. But what is the problem and who knows what is going on?

---

[56] Beware measurements of your success that stoke your vanity. Beware the *Innovation Theatre*.

8. CUSTOMER DISCOVERY DESCRIBES THE PROBLEM

The movie account of the 17th Century artist Johannes Vermeer in his efforts to paint *Girl with a Pearl Earring* offers a central scene in which an earring owned by Vermeer's wife is required to balance the composition of the painting. Griet, a young servant and the girl in the eponymous painting, is uncomfortable wearing the jewellery owned by the Mistress of the household, Catharina Bolnes. Griet offers an alternative approach.

"I've seen you paint with no one there.", Griet suggests.
Vermeer recoils at the suggestion.
"You want me to *imagine* how the earring would look?"
In this fictional narrative Vermeer believes that a painting of an imagined earring would be a poor representation of an earring in reality. Vermeer's objective is to reproduce an accurate image of the world. To represent an imagined earring would fail this objective altogether.

Similarly, should a potential innovator be satisfied with an imagined problem to be solved? Can an imagined problem offer an accurate enough representation of an objective to justify months or even years of solution development? An imagined customer with an imagined problem is no more accurate a sketch than the pearl earring of Vermeer's imagination. How can the problem to be solved be drawn with accuracy? By referring to reality. By observing the world directly.

*

The young graduate turned to me with an excited expression. It had been a few weeks since we hired him and a few months since graduation, and yet he had already had an idea. A great idea.

'*Mech suits!*', he began, with pride.
I suppress a groan as I prepare myself to once more entertain this idea. In my particular corner of the engineering world the weight of equipment is key, as someone has to carry it all by hand for many hours over many kilometres. By necessity our product can be weighty. To resolve this harm a mechanically actuated suit to help the user lift the equipment is the first solution that many leap to. In my world, when plunged into a sea of possibilities many new to innovation grasp for this idea first.

Graduates rotate throught our department frequently, and under these circumstances my job and my compulsion is not to discourage but to educate. In my experience if we carefully curate and encourage those first few faltering steps into innovation this can lead to some great ideas. Through this training we can mine great ideas from anyone.

Mechanical suits seem to be a *go to...* innovation. I've had this particular conversation many times before and settle into the routine. By far the most important question comes first. I repeat it frequently.

'What problem are you solving?', I ask.

The young graduate pauses for a moment as he reflects upon my unexpected question. The discussion is about to take a well-trodden path. The graduate's response is, as expected.

'It'd be *cool?*', he queries.

This is a frequent reply in the technical topics. If cool is indeed the value that your organisation offers to your customer, then I guess this is all the justification that you need to proceed. In my industry problems are practical, the budgets of customers are constrained, and the consequences of a solution prioritising style over substance could be lethal to the end user.

For the time being these considerations are beyond this graduate. The value he observes is based upon the characteristics of the technology employed to build a mechanical suit. At the time of writing actuators, computing processors and portable power are becoming widely available and small enough to place a mechanical suit within our grasp. Examples of sophisticated anthropomorphic robotic vehicles are widely publicised, with numerous examples performing spectacular feats of gymnastics. In these exciting times I am forced to pop this bubble of *technology push* with a common phrase that we repeat frequently in our department. You could call it our motto.

Cool has no value.

If this is the case, then why build a mechanical suit? From here our discussion of mechanical suits will then turn to the function of the mechanical suit, such as its ability to lift loads beyond that of a human or to protect the user from harm. But if a mechanical suit can stand, walk and operate by itself then why put a vulnerable human inside it and into harm's way at all? The vulnerability and reliability of a radio data link required to remotely operate a robot armature will be raised. The opportunity to reduce the vulnerability of the data link by locating this operator at close range but out of harm's way will be discussed. The specific need for legs rather than wheels or tracks will be discussed, and legs will often be rejected. For our particular corner of the engineering world, without understanding precisely *why* a mechanical suit is necessary the whole idea may collapse into a small autonomous or remotely operated off road wheeled or tracked vehicle. For us the ideal mechanical suit collapses into offering a fancy fork lift truck.

The young innovator looks crestfallen. I have no doubt that a mechanically actuated suit will eventually arrive, but it should do so for the right reason, at the right time, and to solve the right problem. I have a good idea of how this may eventually happen, and this genesis is likely to be motivated by more than merely its degree of coolness.

Very often a colleague will explain with excitement that if we attach one of *these* to one of *these*, and put *this there* and *that here* we are to believe that we have an innovation on our hands. A technology push innovation approach has its charm. It's a rewarding jigsaw puzzle. Some technical outcomes are indeed cool. The allure of cool ideas simply for the sake of cool ideas must be resisted. Ideas orphaned from any consideration of areal customer with a real problem I treat as *crutches.*

Consider a parsimonious man who discovers a single crutch discarded by its previous owner. What should the frugal fellow do with this lucky prize? Obviously, he should immediately find a means to break his own leg to offer him the opportunity to make good use of this new possession. An idea that does not solve a real problem for a real customer is a *crutch looking for a broken leg*, or more commonly described as a *solution looking for a problem.*

It's very tempting to believe that technology itself is the sole source of innovation. During my early career I was fortunate enough to work under a very experienced rocket scientist who seemed to have been involved in every advance in rocket technology throughout the latter half of the 20th Century before he retired from a long and successful career.

I did what I could to learn as much as I could from this mentor, and have had the great pleasure of watching this colleague command the centre of a circle of technical experts as they offer sub system suggestions from their various areas of expertise. Recent advances in high power rocket motors, sensor systems or high temperature materials were each drawn from experienced specialists to be extemporaneously assembled into an overall design by my colleague using only paper, pencil and mental arithmetic. Quit the sight and one I won't forget.

Considering his long experience, my senior colleague may have found my own enthusiastic speculation familiar and tiresome, and one day he explained why. Every idea that I might offer for his evaluation he had heard before, many times before, and many years previously. I had made the mistake of assuming that a concept was new because I could not find it instantiated in the world. The true explanation is so much simpler.

Throughout my colleague's career ideas have come and gone. I would offer a concept only to find that the very same idea had crossed my colleague's desk decades earlier. No doubt he had heard just about every idea in his time, but many of these ideas were dropped because the technology at the time was unable to offer the functions required at a practical size, weight and cost. Exciting ideas were not absent because no-one had deployed the insight and innovation that only I could muster. They were absent because up until now they had been impossible.

The difference that my senior colleague was looking for when I unearthed an old idea was whether or not technology had eventually caught up with the concept. If so, it might be time to take another look. If not, then don't waste any more time.

My technology push ideas were rarely new. Crack open the spine of any science fiction for evidence. I have often made the very same mistake as the junior colleague who opened this chapter. I have even on occasion suggested mechanical suits with enthusiasm. Under these circumstances the only skill I had deployed in my efforts to innovate was the fortune to exist at the very moment that technology had matured to realise the concept. Did I understand at all why the concept may be valuable beyond its current practical attainability?

Employment of innovation by technology push alone will unearth whether or not an idea can now be realised. The idea itself may be quite old. The very core of my senior colleague's consideration was whether or not an old idea allied with new technology now solved a real problem for a real customer at an acceptable cost.

Technology push innovation is perhaps an effort to employ the scientific method alone to innovate. Using a scientific framework of systematic observation, measurement, and experiment, and the formulation, testing, and modification of hypotheses, we can assemble all manner of technological wonders. The scientific method can offer us a description of how the world *is*. The scientific method can also predict how the world would be under proscribed circumstances or as a result of particular decisions. However, the scientific method has few tools to inform us which decisions to make, or how the world *should be*. Technology push innovation can show us all manner of possible technological futures, but cannot tell us which one is correct. We need some measure of value to make this choice.

Why is an accurate means to determine this value so important?

Consider the tale of Billy Beane, General Manager of the Oakland Athletics baseball team from 1997. His story is well known, as Beane is the central character of the book *Moneyball* [16] by Michael Lewis that was later adapted into a movie starring Brad Pitt as Beane.

Beane identified that his team did not compete on a level playing field. The rules of the game were fair and square on the field of play. However, the Oakland Athletics could not marshal as much money as wealthier teams in the effort to lure the best players to join their team.

This may seem an insurmountable disadvantage, but Beane noted an error in the established method of choosing good players. Baseball scouts had developed over decades of the professional sport heuristics by which good baseball players could be identified. A player many have *High ass,* suggesting a powerful player. *Red ass* describes a temperamental, argumentative player. *Country-boy build. Slight toilet-seat hitting approach. Feel for wood.*

Beane himself was described as having the *Good Face*, or maturity, confidence and charismatic star quality. Beane and his associates queried whether these features do indeed offer a prediction of baseball performance, and whether more rational and accurate means to determine the value of a player could be discovered.

Fortunately, the baseball world is strangely enthusiastic about statistics. Beane and his colleagues noted that the idiosyncratic assessment of players by the scouting fraternity was at odds with the performance of players measured through a statistical analysis.

Switching the selection of players to a focus upon statistical measures allowed Beane to purchase unrecognised talent at knock down prices. In 2002, with a cost-efficient team selected through statistical analysis, the Oakland Athletics became the first team in a Century to win more than twenty consecutive victories.

Billy Beane had noted that his team was unable to compete with better resourced teams. To resolve this contradiction, he found *new information* that was hidden from his opponents and provided a competitive advantage at a low cost.

Innovation can be high in risk and low in resources. You may find yourself competing with industrial titans who can throw mountains of money at the solution to problems. However, are they solving the correct problem? You may find yourself in a large and established organisation with an established product line. Under these circumstances you will be competing with the incumbent solution for resources. Is the established product well adapted to the future market?

Under powerful competition great ideas may not be enough to see off the competition, as your great idea may be solving the *wrong* problem. Like Beane and the Oakland Athletics, a strong focus upon discovering new information that is hidden from your competitors is the primary reason to *get out of the building* [4], and find that advantage. The customer is in possession of that information. Cool has no value. Consideration of the customer is key.

In previous chapters we are presented with an objective and attempt to dismantle and understand the problems that we might encounter in our attempt to achieve this objective. This disassembly can be achieved in a number of ways, and the examples offered so far focus upon identifying the fundamental contradictions within the problem statement, illustrating and identifying the harms present within the problem space, and expanding the focus in space and time to better understand how the problem is embedded into the wider world. A good description of the problem can take you halfway to the solution.

This disassembly does not describe the source of the problem. In these examples we are presented the problem to be solved. Where did these problems come from? *Why* do we wish to transport cows across a river? Or join wood with nails? Or deliver parcels to the Moon? Interesting and valuable problems are the raw material of innovation, and this is a raw material that your competition is also attempting to harvest. This wild crop can be found with the problem owner. If you can understand the problems faced by your customer better than the competition then you'll have the advantage.

Innovation is not only an application of both the scientific method and of system design that allows you to solve a difficult problem. Innovation is also the means by which we determine what the problem actually is. Innovation is a forum for action. A Universe of verbs. If you wait for someone else to discover those valuable problems that demand a solution then who is really innovating?

Understanding that interesting and valuable problems reside with the customer is one of the most valuable, and very obvious, lessons that I ever learned about innovation. It took me far longer to learn this lesson than it should have, lost as I was in the pleasures of a purely *technology push* approach. You are not going to innovate by imagining exciting futures from behind your desk or buried in your laboratory. This pearl earring must be observed directly.

Who is responsible for approaching the customer? Perhaps the sales and business development department will approach you with a new objective. Perhaps your role expects you to wait for a customer requirement to land on your desk before you take any action.

Often these customer facing entities may have a vested interest in keeping you, the innovator, away from the customer. These experts in customer relations may have a very good reason to do so. A disruptive approach has the potential to disrupt more than the competition. After all, if you do resolve the customer's problem with a novel but immature idea, this novelty may have as much power to disrupt your own organisation's current product line as it does the competition. If you do not coordinate well with your sales and business development function then your exposure to the customer could disrupt a carefully formulated sales strategy and attract the attention of hard-won customer away from an established product line. Under those circumstances the sales team would be well advised to keep you away from the customer.

If you work for a large, well established organization and hope to innovate, building a good relationship with the sales and business development team and understanding their sales strategy is a necessity. They can act as gatekeepers to the customer, and you will need access.

Reason being, it is very useful to determine for ourselves who the customer is and discover for ourselves their most pressing problems. If you are granted access, this task may also be obstructed by customers themselves. They may not understand their problem. They may not understand that a solution is possible. They may not even appreciate that they have a problem at all. They may not address a problem because they don't even know that the problem *can* be solved. A problem may have been identified, but solved badly. A rudimentary stop gap may be employed to resolve an identified problem. A comprehensive solution may have been attempted that employs established methods that are well known to the customer, but are methods inadequate to the task. The customer may be unwilling or unable to exercise solution methods that are found outside their own expertise.

Industry is littered with examples of businesses that failed to identify new threats and new opportunities. For example, established organisations may fail to identify new technologies that could supplant their incumbent solution. Technologies that replace an established solution can often emerge outside the field of this incumbent supplier. An external threat to the incumbent solution may not be observed until its impact is so large that it is well established, against which a response is too late.

The perfect storm is a customer that has identified a problem and has made a bad attempt to solve it. Customers may have cobbled together a rudimentary and inadequate solution from familiar components they have found in their immediate vicinity or which lie within their immediate field of expertise. Such customers are providing you with important information. They have a problem with a solution so valuable that they are willing to spend time and money creating a solution. If identifying the problem is half of the solution, under these circumstances the customer has done half the work for you and this is your cue to offer a more elegant option.

At the other extreme a customer may have no idea that they have a problem at all. Under these circumstances more complex probes will be required to detect the problem and dig it out.

All of these situations offer the innovator an opportunity to solve interesting and valuable problems. All of these situations also demand that the innovator pressure the customer to answer a great volume of difficult, irritating and impolitic questions. Pressing the customer with difficult questions could very well spoil the efforts your sales team may have made to get a valuable customer into the room in the first place.

You have to understand the customer, understand the objectives that they are trying to realise and identify the problems that prevent them from achieving these goals. You may have to consume valuable and scarce time with this customer to ask them difficult questions. The sales team may again be well advised to act as a buffer between your disruption and their carefully managed sales strategy.

If you need to query the customer you are well advised to collaborate and coordinate with the sales team. To achieve this, you may need a formal and repeatable interview framework that the sales team can review before they unleash you upon the customer. Effective customer discovery and problem discovery are valuable tools to the innovator and many frameworks exist to support this effort.

Eric Reis in *The Lean Startup* [5] and the follow up, *The Startup Way* [1], advocates an iterative experimental approach to discover pressing problems and assess the customer's reaction to potential solutions. This *build-measure-learn* cycle is an approach to aspire to. In this we make hypotheses about the customer problems and potential solutions. We then gather evidence on the veracity of our hypotheses through experiments upon the customer's reaction to an analogue to the final product that we are searching for. This analogue to the final product is typically called the *Minimum Viable Product*.

Reis observes that what a customer says and how a customer behaves may be at odds. A valid assessment of the customer's desires and future behaviour can be derived from observing their behaviour towards that functional analogue to the final hypothetical product. This minimal product could be a functional product that only offers a subset of desired functions, such as a functioning game with only one level. Alternatively, this analogue could be a functional mock-up of the proposed product. For example, the functions of a web site could be theatrically mocked up with paper and manually manipulated behind the scenes whilst a real customer attempts to select sketched buttons to manipulate an imaginary website. A hardware product such as a proposed smartphone could be manufactured in cardboard and the behaviour and reaction of the customer to this prototype assessed.

The Minimum Viable Product is a functioning solution with the least amount of functionality that will serve the customer's needs and inform the developers which functions are desirable, which are unnecessary and which are missing altogether. The customer will exercise this proto-solution and the developers will observe behaviour.

Note that this minimal product still an analogue of a *product*. Its purpose is to experiment upon the customer. This makes the Minimum Viable Product quite distinct from a *prototype* more traditionally encountered in engineering. A prototype provides an assessment of the technology employed to instantiate the solution. The Minimum Viable Product assesses the reaction of the customer to this solution.

The build-measure-learn cycle favours frequent and rich customer contact to validate the fit between customer problems and suitable solutions. In the uncertain world of start-up development, the trove of evidence drawn from an effective build-measure-learn cycle can inform a new business if it is on the right track, or warn it to switch strategies in good time. The build measure learn cycle is a fuel to drive product discovery campaigns towards success and the steering required to persevere with the current strategy or pivot to a new plan.

Alternatively, if you are embedded deep inside a large organisation that develops a complex, high performance product, you may encounter boundaries to the accumulation of hard evidence.

Product development timescales of complex technologies may be very long indeed. Years, or even decades, could span the time between the conception of an idea and the shipping of a product. Millions of dollars will flow under that bridge in the effort to construct complex, high-performance products. The gulf between conception and shipping within an organisation that may place a very strong emphasis upon product delivery can result in a concept development team with little true authority. Revolutionary, highly disruptive innovation may be relegated to a low priority. Under these circumstances the funds available to carry out a fully-fledged customer experimentation exercise upon a disruptive innovation may be very hard to secure.

Customers are important and busy people. Customers may be very senior and very busy decision makers. Customers may have far more important things to be doing than acting as experimental subjects for a speculative development.

Contact with these customers is likely to be a rare and valuable commodity that serves a long established and vital sales and business development campaign. If time can be found to interact with these customers, then this time is devoted to the essential task of developing close and fruitful business relationships.

For customers and an organisation with such time demands, being the experimental subject for a team of developers who are speculating about potential future products may be far down the list of priorities. Contact between such a development team and the customer may often be constrained to the presentation of innovations specifically in support of developing business relationships. Experimentation upon the customer's reaction to hypotheses may be restricted to the occasional snatched question within such a meeting. This too has its risks, as a searching and challenging query to a senior decision maker can be quite inappropriate and impolitic under these circumstances. Been there. Done that.

I aspire to the experimental programs recommended by Reis and direct the reader to his texts for a detailed understanding of this work. In its place I offer a simplified strategy to pursue if you do not possess the resources or authority to pursue a fully-fledged customer and problem discovery campaign.

It is true that a customer may say one thing, but then behave at odds with this rhetoric. If you labour in one of those unexpected places that Reis describes as a potential source of good ideas, you may not have the funding nor authority to exercise a fully-fledged customer experimentation programme to inform your problem-solving process. This funding usually *follows* the great idea, so you may need to get your preliminary information from the customer by other means. One ought to make one's best attempt to engage in proper experimentation to gauge behaviour, but when faced with many restrictions one may have to suffice with a truncated list of questions drawn from the works of Bank and Dorf, Reis and Osterwalder.

Reference to these sources can allow you to rehydrate the following interview questions into a fully-fledged customer engagement. Alternatively, this truncated list of queries can be used to snatch the occasional snippet of intelligence from a customer attending your presentation, meeting or brief encounter in an elevator. The more floors you are willing to travel, the more information you can glean, so be prepared. Ask your questions and listen very carefully indeed.

WHO HAS THE PROBLEM?

Before you attempt to find valuable and unsolved problems, do you know who is most likely to possess the information that you need? Could you describe an individual who has experienced the type of problems you are seeking? Could you write a hypothetical biography of a person who could offer you the greatest help? If you cannot, then how will you recognise them when you encounter them?

Before engaging in a customer interview or an extended workshop it is often useful to write a brief *persona hypothesis*. This brief is a hypothetical description of a hypothetical individual who has first-hand experience of the type of problem that you seek. Once you have this brief you then have the information that you need to find that individual to interview.

Consider a hypothetical example. You work for an automotive engineering firm. You're curious to know how one might improve the performance of those who drive for the emergency services. A fire fighter, perhaps?

You called a meeting of interested and relevant stakeholders within your organisation. The large oval table in the long meeting room is surrounded by suited individuals offering the corporate setting that one might find in a large automotive engineering firm. As host you introduce yourself and, as is the corporate custom, you ask each delegate to introduce themselves in turn. State your name and your organisation. You also introduce your persona hypothesis by asking each delegate to describe their most recent attempt to *drive a huge firefighting rig through a crowded city at breakneck speeds*.

As you might expect this will cause a brief stir, but considering the problem under scrutiny the result may be revealing. In a meeting room full of relevant and interested parties almost no-one may have any recent first-hand experience at all in the topic you intended to discuss. This is a revealing exercise, and it also gives the group the opportunity to be very clear about the status of their opinions they are about to offer to the discussion. In many cases the information offered may be second hand, out of date, an educated assumption or even a complete guess. One might want to include oneself in the latter group, as you too many never have *driven a huge firefighting rig through a crowded city at breakneck speeds.*

Introductions orbit the table, and soon you arrive at the final delegate. Name and organisation are offered and then you are treated to an emotive narrative. Despite working in the Human Resources department, this delegate is a volunteer fire fighter, and during the most recent experience *driving a huge firefighting rig through a crowded city at breakneck speeds* it was night. It was during a period of blackout, with the cold, cloying rain blotting out the remaining glimpses of moonlight. Vehicles had slowed to a crawl, and picking one's way through the darkened streets was an almost impossible task.

The destination was invisible in the dark, but illumination was soon to arrive. The windows on the rig shook as the chemical plant that was the destination of this dash through the streets erupted on the horizon in a huge, orange and yellow explosion that briefly illuminating the rain slick road ahead...

Under these circumstances it is very easy to determine who has first-hand experience of the problem and which opinion you may be paying the most attention to for the next two hours.

WHAT IS THE CUSTOMER'S JOB?

Customer jobs are the task they are trying to perform, the problems they are trying to solve and the needs they must satisfy [3]. A customer will have many jobs to perform. Some may be performed more frequently than others. Some jobs may have more impact than others.

Those who have some investment in your ability to solve problems will often be interested in the market size that your solution may serve. Clearly, the larger the market served the more valuable your solution may be. In the very early stages of a problem-solving exercise this evaluation may be impossible, particularly if you have little idea of what problems you may attempt to solve and the solutions that you may deploy.

Stakeholders may often insist on some measure of market size. Consider solving problems for this fire fighter. What market size might your problem-solving exercise serve? At this early stage do we simply sum the number of fire fighters in the country and call that the market we can access? Prior to any analysis of this potential customer's problem, how can we estimate the financial value of a solution that we have little idea about at this stage? How can we determine what customer to pursue and what job to support?

Alternatively, perhaps we can consider the problem space itself as our market place? Compared to all the jobs that the customer must perform, how much market share does each customer job possess? How much impact does each job have on the overall objectives that the customer must achieve? Imagine that we secure the opportunity to interview a fight fighter. Perhaps you have just enough opportunity to ask what jobs the firefighter must perform to protect the public. Perhaps we can encourage the fire fighter to arrange the hypothetical fire fighter jobs in the manner illustrated in Figure 30. Some jobs must be performed frequently. Some, hardly ever. Some tasks may have a large impact upon the overall outcome of the firefighter's role, some may have little impact at all. I have no more experience fighting fires than I do driving fire engines, so this illustration will serve as an example but is unlikely to be an accurate representation. Perhaps I too should get out of the building.

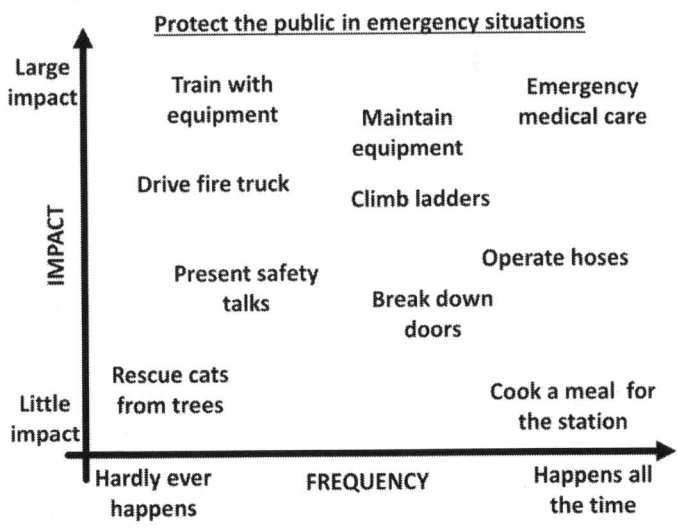

Figure 30: The relative frequency and impact of a hypothetical fire fighter's jobs

Assuming that this illustration is correct, if were intend to focus upon fire fighters, which jobs should we focus upon? One might assume it best to attack the most frequent jobs with the greatest impact. As fire fighters are first responders and may contact casualties first, providing emergency medical care may be a frequent activity and this life saving job may have a very large impact upon the outcomes of a fire fighter's duties. If there are valuable problems to be found, then perhaps emergency medical care owns a large market share of the fire fighter's problem space? Alternatively, perhaps a frequent and high impact job may already be well served with effective solutions.

Some jobs exhibit a high impact but are not frequently exercised. If these jobs are valuable then why are they infrequently exercised? One might assume that they are not exercised frequently because they are not required frequently. It is worth considering that these valuable tasks are not exercised frequently because the customer is *unable* to exercise them frequently? In the hypothetical example illustrated in Figure 30, if we could understand why training is not a frequent activity then perhaps we could offer a solution to increase the amount of training that a fire fighter could receive?

We could focus upon those jobs that occur very frequently but seem to have little impact upon outcomes. Why do these frequent tasks not offer more impact to firefighting outcomes? Do the fire fighters take turns to cook a meal for the rest of the team? Could this meal have more impact upon the fire fighters' duties? Might more nutritious food offer some valuable outcomes?

Figure 31 summarises the overall direction in which you might drive customer jobs to find valuable problems to solve. If you can assemble enough accurate information to build a simple illustration similar to Figure 30 this is likely to raise more questions than it answers. These will be concise and focussed questions with which you can return to your customer. If time for customer interaction is a rare commodity and you have little interaction with the customer, concise and focused questions are essential.

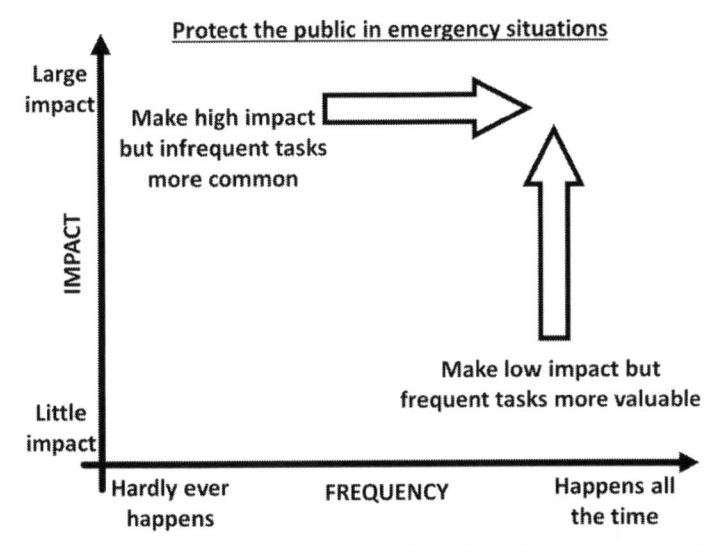

Figure 31: Valuable problems may be found by driving jobs to the top right corner of this illustration

WHAT BENEFIT IS THE CUSTOMER TRYING TO ACHIEVE?

From the perspective of Altshuller, a problem can be defined in one of two ways,

- An attempt to gain a benefit that is prevented by the presence of a harm.
- An attempt to gain two benefits that harm one another, so cannot be achieved simultaneously.

Under this definition, once the customer's jobs are understood then it is essential to understand what benefits they are attempting to achieve. Here a connection can be made between the works of Altshuller and Osterwalder. Under the TRIZ framework of Altshuller, the identification of the *benefits* desired is key [17]. Under the Value Proposition framework of Osterwalder [3] the customer interview hopes to identify the *gains* pursued by the customer.

Osterwalder's *gains* and Altshuller's *benefits* can be treated as synonymous. This creates a bridge between the customer discovery work of Osterwalder and the focus upon the practical instantiation of solutions in Altshuller's framework. We will return to this relationship in our discussion on workshop tools later in this text.

Much like our assessment of the market share experienced by each job within the complete market place of customer jobs, identifying the relative value of each benefit pursued is desirable. Ranking each benefit pursued relative to all of the other desirable benefits can tell us which benefit may be worth delivering with a suitable solution. For example, if we interview our hypothetical fire fighter and ask which benefits they hope to achieve during the *'train with equipment job'* illustrated in Figure 30, they may list and prioritise these benefits, as follows,

1. *Frequent training results in competent performance.*
2. *Realistic training tests our equipment for faults.*
3. *Accurate post training debriefings identify shortcomings.*
4. *Training displays help us to attract new recruits.*

The fundamental function of the job under scrutiny is likely to adopt the top priority. In this example, competent performance. The other benefits of training are subordinate to this primary benefit, but are desired. We want to develop competence through training, but we also want to identify problems, test our equipment and display our skills to attract new recruits. Do any of these desired benefits contradict? Can some of these benefits not coexist in the same training event? To determine if our benefits contradict, we can cross reference each, as illustrated in Table 4.

Table 4: Do we desire any benefits that cannot coexist?

I want...	Without harming...			
	...frequency	...testing	...scrutiny	...recruitment
...frequency		✓	✗	✓
...testing			✗	✗
...scrutiny				✗
...recruitment				

In this example, frequent training supports the desire to test our equipment. Frequent training events also support our desire to use training displays as a recruitment tool.

A detailed post training scrutiny may compete for time with frequent training exercises. The training debrief may consume time and effort that could be spent testing the operation of the equipment. The desire to test equipment in detail may contradict with the desire to host an exciting recruitment display for the public. A debriefing exercise to determine shortcomings may not be an interesting event for the spectating public.

A good description of the problems takes you half way to a solution. The benefits that arise from a customer job are the outcomes of functions that our solutions must offer. Which functions does Table 4 suggest may require attention? As we prioritised our benefits from top to bottom, the resolution of those contradictions on the top left of this matrix may be the most valuable to the customer. How might a training debrief be achieved quickly to permit more frequent training and testing? One could assume that this objective is more important than working out how a detailed training debrief could be made of interest to the spectating public. If a good description of the problem leads you half way to the solution, using this tool might inform you which contradictions should be tackled first.

WHAT IS STOPPING THE CUSTOMER FROM ACHIEVING THE BENEFITS THAT THEY SEEK?

Using Altshuller's terminology, the antithesis of a benefit is a *harm*. Under our definition of problem, a benefit may be blocked not by a mutually exclusive benefit, but by a harm provoked by the benefit itself or found elsewhere in the system. Under Osterwalder's framework the customer is attempting to achieve a gain. The antithesis of these gains is described as a *pain*. Once more, Osterwalder's pains can be treated as synonymous with Altshuller's harms, again providing a bridge between the customer discovery of Osterwalder and the solution generation of Altshuller.

Returning to our hypothetical fire fighter, what harms might prevent the realisation of the desired benefits described above? For example, harms experienced by our customer may manifest as follows,

1. Training does not represent real life accurately.
2. Training facilities are a rare commodity.
3. Training equipment is expensive.

We can incorporate these harms into our description of the problem illustrated in Table 4. The cross reference of desired benefits can be extended by inverting our list of harms into a list of desirable benefits. For example, our harms can be described, as follows,

1. Training should represent real life accurately.
2. Training facilities should be widely available.
3. Training equipment should be low cost.

By inverting our harms, our benefits and harms can be assessed and prioritised using the same scale – the more benefit we receive, the more desirable this outcome. This allows us to determine if contradictions are present between the benefits desired and the harms present. For our firefighter, this extended cross reference of benefits is illustrated in Table 5.

Table 5: Harms can be recast as desirable benefits.

I want...	...frequency	...testing	...scrutiny	...recruitment	...realism	...availability	...low cost
...frequency		✓	✗	✓	✗	✗	✗
...testing			✗	✗	✓	✗	✗
...scrutiny				✗	✓	✗	✗
...recruitment					✓	✓	✓
...realism						✗	✗
...availability							✗
...low cost							

The list of benefits described in the previous section are offered in order of priority. The inverted harms, now cast as benefits, could be prioritised and incorporated into this example wherever in this hierarchy the customer desires. In this example these inverted harms are placed at the bottom of our list of benefits for illustrative purposes.

The quadrant to the top left repeats the illustration of contradictory benefits in Table 4. The top right quadrant illustrates the potential contradictions between the desired benefits and our inverted harms. Frequent training opportunities may not be realistic, available nor cheap. Facilities to test hardware or scrutinise training performance may not be widely available nor low cost.

The bottom right quadrant illustrates the relationship between our harms. In this example resolving the harms within the problem space contradicts with every other harm mitigation. Realistic training may not be widely available nor low cost. Similarly, widely available training may also be costly.

An illustration of contradictions within the system can be a useful tool for negotiation with the customer. A customer who must negotiate between many jobs that hope to achieve many benefits and are obstructed by many harms may not have a full understanding of the problem space they inhabit. Objectives may be understood and the compromise between pressures may be arrived at with intuition drawn from long experience. If you lay out the conflict between these competing demands in a single, easy to comprehend matrix *does it feel right to the customer*? If it doesn't, we have an opportunity and a simple tool to rearrange until this description matches the customer's experience.

Furthermore, an illustration like this can be used to demonstrate why a solution to the problems that you are attempting to resolve is so very hard to derive. A simple illustration like this can generate some sympathy from the customer for the complexity of task they present you with, and can develop some willingness to collaborate further in finding a solution. If time to interact with the customer is at a premium, perhaps demonstrating your understanding of their problems may secure you further contact.

WHAT IS WRONG WITH THE CURRENT SOLUTION?

Before that great idea can strike you need to find a great problem. What makes a problem valuable? A problem that the customer is motivated to solve. The perfect storm is a customer who has a problem so vexing that they have already implemented a solution, and that solution is *bad*.

Customers who have gone to the garage or storehouse or basement and dragged all of their old junk out onto the front yard to cobble together some temporary, improvised, imperfect solution are clearly motivated to resolve their problem. The question to ask is, *what's wrong with this current solution?*

Obviously, an incumbent but inadequate solution tells us a great deal about the problem to be solved. The bad solution offers us the constraints that we need to focus our efforts and find a better solution. The bad solution acts as a problem-solving framework in itself. The benefits sought are clearly indicated. If multiple benefits are desired but contradict the bad solution is likely to tell us which have greater priority. Some benefits may have been rejected to resolve contradictions. The bad solution may offer only partial benefits in an effort to trade between equally desirable outcomes.

The bad solution will offer some measure of the relative priority of harms. Some harms may still be endured whilst the bad solution favours the complete elimination of other more painful harms. Multiple harms may be minimised but not resolved in an effort to trade away the dilemma of choosing between equally vexing pains.

The incumbent bad solution provides us with a complete but inadequate system that we can scrutinise in detail with a sketch using Substance-Field analysis. This sketch allows us to see which physical properties are used by the customer to create the desired functions. With this we can see which beneficial functions may be inadequate. We can see how the remaining harms interact with the overall system. We could offer a better solution by enhancing those fields with alternative components. We could offer the desired functions with alternative fields. We could remove the remaining harms.

A poor solution offers us a timeline of desired benefits and undesired harms, and also an understanding of the scale at which each act. This allows us to create an illustration of the bad solution in both time and scale. We could modify the system scale or time at which benefits and harms may act. We could separate contradictory benefits and harms in time, moving each to times when the other is not present. Similarly, we could separate contractions in scale. We could raise some benefits to the super system, allowing the environment to provide the desired function. Perhaps a benefit offered by the environment is better provided by a new specialised sub system. Perhaps some system sub components could offer more than one function?

The bad solution indicates the costs that a customer is willing to endure to resolve the problem. The bad solution tells us the type of solution the customer is expecting and some characteristics of their comfort zone. This allows us to remain within their comfort zone by offering an enhanced solution that exhibits similar characteristics to their bad solution. The poor performance of their improvised solution may make it easier to convince the customer that you can offer a suitable solution.

Building upon the characteristics that the customer is comfortable with can make convincing them to accept your solution a little easier. This is information also available to your competitors, so this conservative approach may result in a customer confronted by a number of similar solutions offered by a range of potential suppliers. Alternatively, the bad solution provides a starting point from which to encourage the customer outside their comfort zone and confound their expectation altogether with an elegant alternative.

IS THIS A CURRENT PROBLEM, OR A PREDICTION?

'Evacuate? In our moment of triumph? I think you overestimate their chances.'
- Star Wars, 1977. The late Grand Moff Tarkin, commander of the Death Star, just before he was killed in action by a small, agile competitor.

A common trigger employed to provoke innovative thinking to be found embedded within the TRIZ methodology is to reverse the problem, solution or the interaction between components. What if things were *the other way around?*[57]

Rather than considering an incumbent but bad solution to an existing problem, what if the customer's problem has yet to manifest itself? To identify a disruption to the customer's situation before the customer does is not as unlikely as you might think. It's possible that the customer is likely to know their business better than you. However, disruption to a customer's business can often arise outside their area of expertise. In fact, this may be likely, and there are many examples to choose from.

Consider the employment of ice to extend the shelf life of food. In the 19th Century this ice was provided by a well-developed industry that harvested ice from the East coast of the United States and from Norway. The innovation that began this trade was developed by Frederic Tudor in

---

[57] TRIZ Separation principle 13: *The other way around.*

1806, in which he delivered ice to wealthy residents of Martinique in the Caribbean. Tudor soon had many competitors as trade expanded to deliver ice all over the world. At its height, this industry employed nearly 100,000 people and was capitalised at over half a billion US dollars, in modern terms. The trade in the harvest and delivery of ice is no more. What happened to this industry?

During the heyday of this industry the nature of one's competition was easy to predict. To compete in this market, one had to scale behaviours and technologies that had been familiar and available for many years. A competitor would need skill in the harvesting of ice and the haulage and storage of thousands of tons of product from one part of the world to the other. Expertise in the reliable and efficient execution of these skills would see a contributor to this market flourish.

It seems likely that the innovation provoked by competition within this industry focussed upon the efficiency of harvesting ice, transporting this harvest and storing it at the destination in well insulated ice houses. If there was money to spend on problem solving and innovation to gain a competitive edge, then these problems would reside within a well-known toolset of this well-established industry.

Under these circumstances were any of these experts in the harvesting and haulage of ice likely to pay much attention to a small community of boffins in possession of a magic box made from science? If you pump the handle on the side a few times the box becomes a little cooler inside. So what? The temperature drop is very small, and the amount of fuel required to achieve this is very large. Hardly a threat to an established ice trade. And besides, all that ammonia probably makes the whole contraption decidedly unhealthily. I even hear that the whole thing might on occasion explode. A nasty business all somewhat removed from the pure lakes of Massachusetts and clean clear air of a fine ship at full sail on the open seas.

The ice transportation industry started in 1806 and survived for nearly a century, to reach a peak in 1880-1900. Immediately after this peak the industry collapsed in the early years of the 20th century, to be replaced by artificial ice production. In hindsight, this seems inevitable. Was it so hard to predict at the time?

If you had indeed noticed this disruptive technology, would the ice traders of the time have taken much notice of your observation? If you were invested in the ice industry, through employment or financially, how would you convince your employer or investment to take notice of this potential commercial disaster?

If you were an investor then perhaps you could withdraw your support until your investment could convince you that your money is safe. This text does not focus on business practises, so we focus on an alternative. How could we problem solve our way out of danger?

Imagine you are a middle manager of an ice trading company. You've worked hard to get where you are and possess a number of hard-won skills in the haulage business. You have a nice job, a nice house near nice schools and a nice pension from the ice haulage business that should see you nicely into retirement. For a few weeks you consider switching to the artificial ice manufacturing business with a few trusted colleagues. Considering how immature the ice making technology seems to be, a small start-up might present a considerable expense and risk to an otherwise comfortable life. Instead, you and your colleagues choose loyalty to a business that has treated you well over the years, over the rigours of casting out for yourselves into entrepreneurship. How are you going to warn the management of the danger that this new technology poses to their ice haulage business?

In this example your management are your customer, and this internal stakeholder is likely to be as busy and inaccessible as your external customer. How could you convince them of the danger as cheaply and quickly as you can?

Consider what you're asking the executive board to do. You're expecting the board of a successful company to begin the process of retooling and retraining to switch from a business model that has been successful for nearly a century to focus upon untried and untested technologies and customer reaction. In this tale this is an option that you and your colleagues have already rejected, whilst you demand that it must be implemented on a much, much larger scale. The sort of evidence or authority that you need to provoke this transformation is unlikely to be possessed by a comfortable middle manager like you.

You could return to work and keep your eyes open for opportunities to switch employment once someone else takes the risk to develop the ice manufacturing industry. Alternatively, why not present your observation to your board not in terms of transforming the business, but *protecting* it.

Rather than request the huge quantities of funding and risk required to transform the business, you could suggest that this ice haulage company invest a small quantity of funds in a *Red Team*[58]. The Red Team is not intended to be a profit-making entity. The small financial outlay should instead be treated as a form of *insurance*.

With these funds you and your colleagues could engage in some investigation into this new technology. Perhaps you could build a small working demonstrator to test its technical veracity? The product from this demonstrator could be used to gauge the reaction of potential customers to artificial ice. The Red Team creates a small technology start-up within the incumbent business, characterised as a small organisation designed to protect the business from disruption by detecting threats early.

The Red Team is an important concept when innovating in a corporate environment. To investigate immature ideas will demand funds, and the competition for funds will take place amongst every other demand for financing within the corporate ecosystem. Some of these funding requests will return an investment in the short term, and some will yield profit in the long term. In the competition for success and promotion in the corporate world, those projects that yield profit in the short term gain an advantage in the effort to catch the eye of internal fund holders. The exploration of new ideas and immature technologies with the intent to create a new product line will burn funds in the short term, only to potentially yield profit in the future. Innovation will always be disadvantaged in the competition for funds unless the project can offer some value in the short term. Preferably one needs to offer value in the current financial year. Innovation must therefore offer an *in-year benefit* to fund holders if it is to compete with established, profitable programmes.

This in-year benefit can be offered by the Red Team. An innovation may offer a potential product line at some point in the far future. An innovation that exposes a significant threat to the business model always yields value *now*. Sell to internal fund holders the imminent threat an innovation may pose to the established business. Add a hook with the potential product line that may emerge at some point in the future.

In this one can employ all of the business building techniques of Blank, Dorf, Reis, Osterwalder to build, measure and learn your way to evidence on whether this new technology is a threat. And, who knows? Perhaps

---

[58] In war games friendly troops are indicated in blue. The opposition is identified as red. Black and white hats from western movies are also sometimes employed to identify those in conflict.

this small insurance entity will indeed form the nucleus of a company transformation to ice manufacture once the inevitable disruption strikes.

So, if you are Moff Tarkin and you are in command of the Death Star, do take heed of a couple of enthusiastic pilots if they offer to spend a small amount of their free time dashing around the station defences in their craft looking for small vulnerabilities. This may be no self-indulgent aerobatic leisure activity. If they do find that small exhaust port, the future of the Empire could be quite different.

WHAT IS THE CUSTOMER'S *IDEAL OUTCOME*?

The opposite of the incumbent bad solution is the *Ideal Outcome*. This idea is drawn from Altshuller's TRIZ to highlight and mitigate the inefficiencies present in *Brainstorming*.

Brainstorming is one of the simplest problem-solving frameworks. Members of a group are encouraged to spontaneously and intuitively generate as large a list of ideas as possible in the time available. Contributors are encouraged to draw inspiration from the contributions of others, and the critique of ideas is prohibited to prevent the premature rejection of ideas before they have become fully developed. Brainstorming is a situation where a group of people meet to generate new ideas and solutions around a specific domain of interest by removing inhibitions. People are able to think more freely whilst they suggest as many spontaneous new ideas as possible. All the ideas are noted down and only after the exercise are ideas evaluated.

Altshuller describes the Brainstorming process as a wasteful and inefficient exercise [13]. Consider 50 contributors engaged in a Brainstorming exercise for a single day. 50 people working for a single day can generate many solutions, but this quantity offers the illusion of fast and efficient working. After all, a workshop of this size working for one day offers the equivalent labour of one person working for 50 days to derive suitable solutions. If the delegates of a Brainstorming exercise possess a wide range of skills and experience this session may offer breadth in the effort to mine for ideas. This must be contrasted with the depth that could be achieved by only a pair of delegates collaborating for nearly a full month on the problem.

Brainstorming is employed with little framework to constrain ideas beyond reference to the problem statement. Brainstorming is a trial and error process where ideas are generated at random and in quantity. Generating multiple ideas rapidly is a useful skill that can overcome inertia quickly, as it permits delegates to cast off in multiple directions as inspiration strikes. Each delegate starts from the problem statement and performs a random walk around the problem.

How do delegates know that they are searching in the correct direction? How does each delegate know where and when to stop a fruitless search and begin a new search in an alternate direction? How do delegates know that they have reached a valid solution? By lucky chance a search for solutions may proceed in the right direction. The structure of a Brainstorming session can inject inspiration from another delegate that can derail this positive progress. This can draw the conversation *away* from a valuable outcome.

The unstructured nature of Brainstorming can break a logical chain of reasoning that could have led to a valuable solution. Altshuller suggests that this deficiency can be resolved by the inclusion of an additional rule. Brainstorming prohibits the criticism and rejection of ideas as they are generated. To ensure that good ideas are developed to their logical conclusion the exercise could prohibit not just the criticism of ideas but the breaking of logical chains. New threads that are spontaneously generated could be noted and parked until the current logical chain of reasoning has run its course. This can result in better solutions, but is even more labour intensive than raw Brainstorming.

The Brainstorming technique is a random walk that orbits the problem statement. The result of this technique could be illustrated as shown in Figure 32. The vehicle of an intrepid explorer malfunctions in the middle of a long desert trek. The explorer elects to solve the problem by walking in a random direction from the stricken vehicle. After some time, if rescue is not discovered, the explorer chooses a new random direction. If the approximate direction of the optimal solution could be known before embarking upon this search, this would offer an improvement upon the trial and error approach.

Figure 32: Sometimes the problem may not point you to the solution.

Although a well described problem may take you half way to the solution, the problem-solving exercise may be unable to pinpoint that eventual solution before the exercise begins. However, the *direction* in which to search could be indicated by reference to the *Ideal Outcome*.

The Ideal Outcome is the *perfect* solution to the customer's problem. It is the delivery of every benefit desired without contradiction between those benefits and without any associated harms. The Ideal Outcome may not be a goal that can be reached through practical means. Gadd [17] describes the Ideal Outcome as the result of a magic wand waved to offer the customer what they really, *really* want[59].

To offer an example of how considering the Ideal Outcome can support an idea generation exercise, consider the problems that may beset the captain of a merchant ship, plying trade on the seven seas. In particular, this Captain is beset by pirates and Figure 33 might suggest a suitable solution. Blow them up.

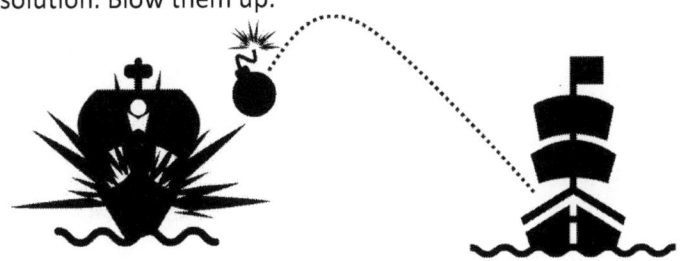

Figure 33: Is blowing up the pirates an ideal outcome?

---

[59] *'I'll tell you what I want, what I really, really want!'* The Spice Girls. 1996

Is blowing up the pirate ship the best solution to the Captain's problem? After all, if the merchant vessel can fire upon the pirates, then the pirates can fire upon the merchant vessel. So, this merchant sailor must be good at naval combat and have a brace of guns on board with a skilled and brave crew to operate them. Consider the chain of problems and solutions we presented in our effort to tie our shoe laces. Is blowing a hole in the pirate ship the problem to be solved, or the solution to a more general problem? What is the *ideal* outcome for the captain of our merchant vessel? All benefits. No harms.

Blowing a hole on the pirate ship is a solution to a more general problem - that the pirate ship floats. There are a number of means by which we could sink the pirate vessel beyond shooting cannon balls at it, such as fire ships, ramming the pirates or boarding the vessel with an axe or a hand drill. So, is sinking the pirate vessel the Ideal Outcome?

No, sinking the pirate vessel prevents it from getting its guns within range and taking the merchant ship by force. Perhaps preventing the pirate ship from *moving* is the ideal outcome?

Keeping the pirate ship away from the merchant vessel is a means to prevent them from firing their guns. Perhaps preventing the pirate ship cannons from *firing* is the ideal means by which we prevent the pirates from exhibiting their unsociable behaviour?

Preventing those pirate guns from firing prevents the pirates from acting in a piratical manner. Preventing the pirate canons from firing prevents the pirates from *being pirates*. So, perhaps the Ideal Outcome for the merchant captain is *no pirates*. A lack of pirates on the seven seas offers the merchant captain all of the benefits desired without any associated harms.

Under this Ideal Outcome the merchant captain does not incur the cost of bigger guns, nor the cost of additional weapons, nor requires the Captain to be a genius in naval combat, nor any of the other harms associate with further conflict with pirates. The Ideal Outcome is *no pirates*. Should we attempt to end piracy to solve our merchant sailor's problem?

How could our merchant captain achieve this outcome? Could this captain understand why pirates act as they do? Could an attempt be made to understand and resolve the economic hardships that might drive an individual to piracy? Perhaps an organisation could be funded to retrain and educate those likely to embark upon this life of crime. If this problem was owned by a much larger body, such as a government, then perhaps this sort of social and economic program might offer some resolution?

These solutions may be the Ideal Outcome for an entire nation, but are perhaps out of reach to the captain of our merchant vessel. Banishing all pirates from the sea may be an Ideal Outcome. From a practical point of view and considering the resources that may be available to our captain to solve this problem, this large-scale Ideal Outcome may not offer a useful tool to solve the merchant captain's immediate problems.

The chain of outcomes described above does offer an opportunity to choose an Ideal Outcome that is within the customer's control. If we summarise our chain of ideal outcomes, it looks like this,

1. Blow a hole in the pirate vessel.
2. Sink the pirate vessel.
3. Prevent the pirate vessel from moving.
4. Keep the guns of the pirate vessel out of range.
5. Prevent the pirate vessel from firing its guns.
6. Encourage the pirates to not act in a piratical way.
7. No pirates at all.

In this chain of solutions, which does our merchant captain have any control over? In the case of our merchant sailor, let's assume this ship captain only has control over the ship and its performance. The first four outcomes deal with this type of solution. The captain could better arm this merchant ship, which introduces a weight and volume harm to a ship that hopes to carry as much cargo as it can. The captain could keep the pirate ship out of range, perhaps by always retaining a speed advantage over the pirate vessel.

Considering the performance lost from carrying many heavy guns, perhaps the Ideal Outcome to the merchant captain is to carry *no guns*. After all, if no assailant can ever get within range of the merchant vessel, there will be no need for these guns at all. On the contrary, a pirate vessel would be advantaged by also striving for speed and manoeuvrability. However, the pirates must not only catch their prey, but must also subdue it with guns or by carrying a large enough crew to board and defeat the target crew. The pirates may also need to protect themselves from the authorities. As the merchant vessel has no need to perform either task, they will not experience these harms, have no need to make a compromising trade, and could perhaps always retain a speed advantage?

The Ideal Outcome for the merchant vessel is to possess the fastest and most manoeuvrable ship on the ocean. This offers all the benefits desired whilst removing many harms. Our Brainstorming exercise can now proceed in this direction, as it seems most likely to provide an optimal solution. Perhaps one very large and very fast ship is the solution? Perhaps a large fleet of much smaller, cheaper faster and manoeuvrable boats will move the captain closer to the Ideal Outcome? Under this Ideal Outcome if the customer seeks a fast and manoeuvrable ship, we now know what skills we need in the room to Brainstorm a solution.

The Ideal Outcome improves our efficiency in the pursuit of solutions by pointing us in the correct direction to search. A chain of increasingly ideal outcomes also offers a tool to choose the boundaries for our problem-solving exercise by indicating which kind of solutions we have control over, and which we currently do not.

9. CASE STUDY: A CRY FOR HELP IS EVENTUALLY HEARD.

The young Soldier sank into the deep dungeons, back to his duties and to despair with his old Father on his mind. Prior to retaking his post before the cell door, he took a moment to glance into the cell and check upon his charge. The Princess remained as she had before, straining against whatever force she employed to summon the Dragon to do her bidding should she be forced against her will to marry a Prince. However, the young man had just lost his beloved Father to her monster and could not hold her black eyes for even a moment. He turned his back to the door and to the Princess, despite her clear distress, and returned to his soldierly duties guarding the cell from without and from within[60].

In response to the young Soldier's rejection the Princess called out to him. The strain in her voice was clear, but the Soldier ignored her and thought of his duty and of his Father. An hour passed while the Soldier ignored the Princess and thought of his Father's fate. The Princess called out, growing weaker, and still the Soldier ignored her. Another hour passed. The Princess and her calls grew weaker. The cell soon grew silent.

The Soldier stood before the door for many hours and strained his ears to the silence. He listened for the soft breathing of the Princess to determine if she slept. He heard nothing. He listened for the trill of dry parchment as the Princess might flick through a book[61]. Nothing could be heard. He strained to hear the ring of a struck glass from which the Princess might drink[62]. Not a sound. The Princess must be at her wit's end, and surely must react to the slightest provocation. The Soldier reached into his pocket to find a small coin, which he dropped to the floor in the

---

[60] Don't be disruptive just for the sake of being disruptive. If in doubt, stick to what you know.
[61] Make a measurement. GA SS4.2.2 *We need to measure something, but cannot do it directly. Add something to make a measurement system. Measure a field that is connected to the substance measured.* If you can't hear the Princess, perhaps you can hear the book?
[62] Make a measurement. GA SS4.3.3 *If a measurement system cannot be created from the resonant frequency of the entire system, measure the resonance of a joined object or the environment.* If you can't hear the Princess, perhaps the wine glass might ring in response to her.

hope of startling the anxious Princess to react[63]. Not a single sound could be heard. It was as if the cell behind the Soldier was empty. Resisting no longer, the Soldier stole a glance into the cell to see the Princess curled upon the plush cushions he had provided. She said nothing. She did not move a muscle.

The Soldier began to take his meals at a rough wooden table, sitting on a small chair outside the cell door. While he ate, he thought of his Father, and he thought of the Princess, and he thought of the sad King, and he thought of dragons. When he delivered the Princess her meals she did not move from her nest and remained curled around the large blue jewel. Her black eyes stared blankly ahead. Days past and no news of the Soldier's Father arrived. Not a word passed the Princess's lips. No one came to visit that deep dark dungeon. In the silence and the foolish loneliness of his own making the Soldier became mired between his love for the Princess, his duty to the King and his desire to rescue the old soldier[64].

Over these few days the Princess barely ate the food he delivered. Full trays of food arrived. Full trays of food were recovered. Finally, when delivering yet another serving of fine food, and in concern, and being unable to stand the consequences of his one moment of cruelty any longer, the Soldier reached out a hand to the Princess curled on her mound of cushions.

And with a shriek the Princess lost her battle to resist the forces she had constrained for so many days, and lost all control. The wind rose and blew around her stronger than ever. Clouds and fog formed a whirlwind and blue lightning flashed between the Princess and the walls of her prison. The Soldier retreated from the cell, closed the stout wooded door against the distressed thrashing and terrible power of the Princess and turned his back once more to the cell door to wait for all this to blow over.

The wind howled and the clouds thrashed and the lighting flashed through the small barred window of the cell. The torrent rose and rose, bending the stout wooden door against its hinges, but still the Soldier did not turn. Finally, the thick wooden cell door gave way and blasted into the corridor in which the Soldier stood, propelling the young man, the

---

[63] Make a measurement. 5.4.2 *From a weak input field produce a strong output field.* Provoke a sound from the Princess by adding something to the system.

[64] The Soldier has adopted contradictory objectives between which he cannot trade. Can he separate and decouple all these contradictions? Can he resolve them all with a single action?

door, and all the howling winds against the far wall of the dungeon corridor[65].

For a second time the Soldier landed with a thump on the stone cobbles of the castle. Once more he climbed slowly to his feet, through the splintered remains of the shattered door. Light and noise and chaos streamed from the cell. Shielding his eyes from the bright blue light, the Soldier could just make out the silhouette of the Princess hovering just above the floor as she clutched the great blue gem to her breast.

The howling and the shrieking grew louder, and ever louder, forcing the Soldier to cover his ears in pain[66]. To his surprise, a few moments after his ears had adjusted to the muffled sounds, he could hear something else. Something new. With his ears covered by his hands, just under the sound of the shrieking and the wailing he could hear a faint cry[67]. As if very far away amongst all the noise he could hear the Princess crying out. A cry so pitiful and with such sadness that it melted his heart to a trembling tear.

Eyes welling with tears against the wind, the young man strained to hear the Princess's cry but he could not make out the words amongst the terrible shrieking and wailing. Crouched in the corridor. Buffeted by the winds. Kneeling amongst the remains of the cell door. Pinned by the glaring blue light of the Princess's rage. Covering his ears with his hands. Straining to hear this cry underneath the turmoil, the Soldier spied the old ear trumpet with which his Father had returned from a grand adventure so many years ago. The Soldier considered the old ear trumpet whilst he strained to hear these new sounds, and an idea began to form. Finally, he took the only course left to him under the circumstances.

Removing his hands from his ears the full force of the wailing and shrieking once more assailed him. He plucked the ear trumpet from his belt and tentatively placed it against one ear, fully expecting to be made utterly deaf from the combined efforts of the shrieking and the trumpet, but hoping that the trumpet might help him to hear the Princess's cry[68].

---

[65] Mechanical linkages are a common solution, but have you considered GA SP29 *Pneumatics and Hydraulics*?.
[66] Block a harm. GA SS1.2.2. *We cannot introduce a new substance. Block the harm by introducing a substance made from a modification of the other two systems.* Use your hands to cover your ears.
[67] Find signals hidden amongst the noise that your competitors cannot detect.
[68] At last, the Soldier's first actual innovation, but unstructured and simply drawn from a hunch based on a very simple and accidental observation allied with some

In this act, all went silent. Perhaps he had indeed become deafened. The powerful blue light remained. The strong winds continued to buffet. The lightning flashed and clouds loomed. All was silent to the Soldier. Some moments later, far off in the distance he could hear his Princess cry,

'*The Dragon returns!*'

The Soldier considered this for a moment. A threat perhaps? Was the Soldier, in his cruelty and rejection, himself now as much a target as all others?

'*I know where the Dragon strikes next!*', the Princess called.

The cry of the Princess was not a threat, but a *warning*[69]. The Princess no more controls the Dragon than the Soldier, but she knows something about it. Looking into the Princess's black eyes the Soldier finally understood. She knows when and where it will strike. She knows because the great blue jewel tells her.

With that realisation the winds died down and the lightning slipped away and the clouds cleared and the Soldier saw his Princess as he always had. She stood before him, still clutching the glowing jewel, with an expression that betrayed her strain and her relief that her trial had ended. Someone had listened.

There was no time to lose. The Princess picked her way through the wreckage of the cell door, grabbed the Soldier's hand, hauled him to his feet, and dragged him up the long journey back to light and air and freedom.

The pair passed through the throne room on their journey, where the Princess spied the King's dragon scale shield once more hanging above the throne. The Soldier would not dare to touch this artefact, but the determination of the Princess drove him onwards[70]. The Soldier climbed onto the throne, feeling somewhat guilty in the act, to struggle the shield down from its suspension. Despite its great size the Soldier was surprised

---

brave experimentation. This is the classic fictional inspiration leading to innovation, but is guessing and hoping for the best really an efficient and repeatable innovation strategy?

[69] Creativity provoked by the constraint of a framework. This Princess is no damsel in distress. She is actually the only person who can explain what's going on if only people would bloody listen to her. In the context of this manuscript the Princess is the Beneficiary, the Problem Owner, the *Customer*. SB, ER, AO: *Listen* to the Customer. If you don't, you are guessing.

[70] Enhance a benefit. GA SS5.1.1.4 *Indirectly achieve a function by using a small amount of a very active additive*. This Princess is no doubt a very active additive.

at its light weight. Up close, the shield was a simple but strong oak frame onto which dragon scales had been bound[71]. The Soldier hefted the shield in a single hand whilst the Princess grabbed the other, and out into the courtyard and into a commotion they both ran.

The courtyard was once more a hive of activity as trumpets blared in alarm and soldiers rushed to and fro. The menacing steel bow sat at the centre of the courtyard. Red faced, exhausted men loitered around the bow, two atop the contraption wound the giant bowstring back whilst four more slid the giant arrow into place. It was, of course, pointing in entirely the wrong direction.

The Princess ducked behind the fearsome machine and yanked the Soldier towards the highest of the castle towers. Up spiralling stairs the pair ran, round and round[72], the Princess in the lead, the Soldier following an arm's length behind, their hands clasped together. Their free hands clutched the King's shield and the large blue jewel that now glowed brighter than ever. Up the pair ran until they eventually reached the top of the highest tower and out into the open air.

The height was dizzying to the Soldier, who never had cause or permission to climb to the castle summit. He peered over the edge of the battlements to see in one grand view the roof of the keep surrounded by the courtyard protected by the strong castle walls encompassed by the outer moat[73]. Despite the grand vista all seemed so very small below. In the courtyard soldiers rallied around the King and the Prince and all looked Eastward in preparation for another attack along the arrow's future flight towards the town and into the farmland beyond.

Tugging once more at the Soldier's hand the Princess pointed towards the setting sun. Silhouetted against the bright horizon one could discern the shape of a huge, malevolent, flapping monster. The beast rolled into a lazy turn and made directly for the tower. The Dragon would, in fact, pass by the tower just below the dizzying perch adopted by the Princess

---

[71] Resolve a contradiction. A structure that must be both light and strong. GA SP40 *Composite Materials*.

[72] Resolve a contradiction. The staircase must be both long and fit inside a small building. A long staircase is coiled into a small footprint. GA SP17 *Another Dimension*. SP14 *Spheroidality. Curvature*. Wrap stairs into a cylinder.

[73] Resolve a contradiction. Defences must be simultaneously deep ditches, high obstructions and thick walls. GA SP7 *Nested Doll*. Embed each characteristic inside another.

and the Soldier[74]. The Soldier understood what he must do.

Steeling himself for action the Soldier released the hand of the Princess and stepped up onto the low wall that surrounded the top of the tower. The Dragon loomed closer, growing second by second. At first the Soldier could only make out its great flapping malevolent shape. Then he could discern its claws. Then its sharp teeth. Then its snarling countenance. The Soldier looked down. He had three outcomes before him. Leap onto this dragon. Fail, and plummet to the ground. Or retreat in ignominy back to the Princess and into the tower[75].

The Princess, responding to her Soldier's sense of peril, leapt up onto the tower wall beside him. The Soldier turned in surprise as she seized his face in both soft hands to plant a kiss squarely and firmly upon his lips. The Soldier grew concerned as the jewel crackled and the wind once more whipped around the Princess, who gathered up those storms from the North and the gales from the South, and the squalls from the East and tempests from the West to fill the Soldier with such a heady breath as he had never before experienced.

Lightheaded and filling with a euphoria the Soldier received this most wondrous kiss, whilst his lungs filled with winds from all across the Kingdom. The pair parted. The Soldier saw his Princess. The Princess saw her Prince. He was prepared. The young man turned back towards the setting sun and readied himself for the leap of faith required to find his Father.

The Dragon thundered by the tower in a snarling whirl of leathery wings and boiling fury, and the Soldier leapt into the wide space between the security of the castle and his home and his Princess...[76]

*

Our Hero has taken a dramatic step out of his comfort zone and will have to engage in some problem solving if he is to save his Father and return home. How do we solve problems? This question is the focus of the next chapter.

---

[74] Resolve a contradiction. We were very low, whist the objective is very high. GA SP12 *Equipotentiality*. Use the highest tower to equalise our altitude.
[75] To paraphrase Peterson, don't lose your fear. *Become more brave*.
[76] Steve Blank - *Get out of the building!* The information that you need to discover the customer and understand the problems that they face that will ultimately drive you to a valuable solution is not going to be found within the building where you work. Get out of the building, and employ footnote 75 if required.

10. SOLUTIONS

Problems and solutions are so closely related in a chain of cause and effect that one can often bleed into the other. This text is structured to separate techniques that describe problems and those that offer solutions, and yet it can be difficult to avoid referencing possible solutions when describing problems.

This is a good sign. I recommend that you describe your problems in as much detail as you can manage. I state often that a good description of the problem will take you half way to the solution. In fact, it may take you all the way there. As you describe the problem, solutions will seep into your process. Well described problems will become ripe with solutions. The further you dive into your problem statement the more it will ooze with solutions. A good problem discovery exercise will become ripe and succulent with potential resolutions.

You'll know that your problem description is complete when you cannot help but indulge in some problem solving. This does not, of course, insist that you cannot return to your problem discovery process. With some solutions on the table, an iteration back to problem discovery will improve your solution development. Problems and solutions are so closely related that one hand washes the other.

The examples presented so far burst with potential resolutions, so it's time to offer some solution generation tools. The form of these solution tools mirrors the close relationship between problems and solutions. In the interests of clarity and to help the reader parse this text these solution discovery tools will be presented in the same order that their related problem discovery tools were presented.

CLASSIFY AND TRANSFORM YOUR PROBLEM

In this text problems are defined in terms of the contradictions that they present. You are either faced with a benefit you desire but cannot have because a harm prevents this, or are faced with two desirable benefits that you cannot enjoy simultaneously.

These two types of contradiction suggest two solution strategies. If faced with a harm that blocks your ability to obtain a benefit then your strategy is clear. You must modify your system to find some means to remove this harm. When faced with two desirable benefits, removing one does not present a satisfactory solution. You want both.

The contradiction in which two desirable benefits compete can be classified further still. This is illustrated with an example. Imagine that we are about to embark upon a most exciting touring holiday. On this journey we will encounter winding roads through beautiful mountains, long fast autobahns, we will speed over beautiful lakes as smooth as glass, and hop between idyllic islands. It will be quite a trip that will demand at least two modes of transport. We will need to take with us a fast sports car and a powerful speedboat, illustrated in Figure 34.

Figure 34: This trip is going to be amazing.

The trouble is, these two modes of transport are incompatible. When we're speeding through those mountain passes, we can't do so with the boat. When we're bouncing along the wavetops with the wind in our hair, we can't do so with the car. We label this contradiction, a *Technical Contradiction*. We are faced with two independent desires that are incompatible. How can we resolve this problem?

The first solution may be to compromise. To trade between the performance of each. For example, during our journey through those winding mountain roads we could tow the boat, as illustrated in Figure 35. This compromise may not produce the driving experience desired.

Figure 35: This Car/Boat combination may be suboptimal.

Alternative hybrids may also not produce the experience desired. A car that can also float or a boat that can lumber onto the land may offer a poor boat and a terrible car. A compromise that trades between desires is inevitable during the design of any solution. However, at this early conceptual stage can we better resolve this Technical Contradiction to make these inevitable trades easier?

We could attempt to reach a better compromise by retaining all of the features desired from one of our options. For example, let's keep that sports car in its entirety. We will retain the speed, the handling and the looks of the car, and do something about that boat.

The boat alone now presents us with a contradiction. We want a boat that operates as a boat, but can also be transported by that sports car. We have collapsed our contradiction between two desirable benefits into a contradiction exhibited by one of these desires. The boat must not only be large to transport us across that lake, but must also be small to fit into the confined storage of a sports car. These are still two desirable benefits in conflict, but they reside within only one of our means of transport. We call this type of contradiction *a Physical Contradiction*. The boat must exhibit a contradictory physical characteristic. To be both large and small.

Under these constraints a solution may be obvious. The Physical Contradiction suffered by the boat can be resolved by making it inflatable, as illustrated in Figure 36.

Figure 36: A boat can be both large and small if it is inflatable.

This collapse of the Technical Contradiction into a Physical Contradiction can be achieved the other way around. Let's keep the style and performance of the speedboat, and modify that sportscar. Now the Technical Contradiction collapses into a Physical Contradiction suffered by the road vehicle. It must offer the desirable sporting performance on those winding mountain roads, but must also fit into our speedboat. Much like the boat, the road vehicle must also be large and small whilst retaining as many of its desirable characteristics as possible. This Physical Contradiction can be resolved in an alternate manner to the boat. A small but sporty road vehicle is offered by a motorcycle, as illustrated in Figure 37.

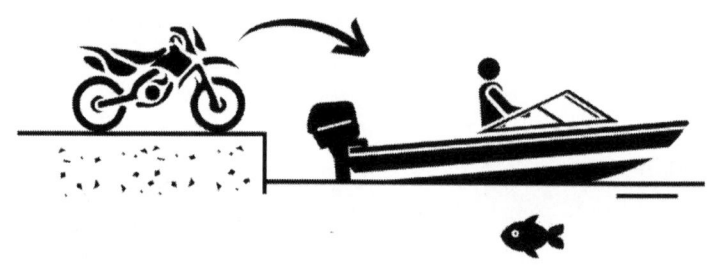

Figure 37: Can we fit our motorcycle into our boat?

Note that in each case we exercise a simple strategy. Identify a Technical Contradiction between two competing desires and collapse this into a Physical Contradiction that is suffered by only one of these choices. This strategy is useful because a Physical Contradiction is often much easier to solve than the difficult compromise demanded by a Technical Contradiction. This is the strategy to adopt whenever a Technical Contradiction is encountered.

SEPARATE YOUR CONTRADICTIONS

We return to our hypothetical *Mail Order Store Of The Future*, illustrated in Figure 38, and once again note that our means of transporting material exhibits a number of desirable but potentially contradictory benefits.

- Long range
- High altitude
- Fast delivery
- Large payload

Figure 38: Our *mail order store of the future* might not be serviced by rockets alone

A standard practice in Systems Engineering is to balance the extent to which each of these benefits is delivered. This trade, illustrated in Figure 39, will attempt to offer some portion of each benefit whilst degrading contradictory desires as little as practically possible. We design a solution by choosing a few features from column A, and a few from Column B.

Figure 39: An obvious solution to contradictory desires is to balance their relative influence.

This trade is a common and inevitable demand in engineering design, and is a valuable tool to be exercised with great care. An entire engineering discipline exists to ensure that our solution exhibits sufficient range at a high enough altitude, to deliver a reasonably large payload as quickly as possible. Good system design is detailed and painstaking work.

In the early solution process, before decisions are made and designs become fixed, we can take the opportunity to improve this trade. We can rearrange the solution to make a trade between competing desires much easier, or on occasion avoid the need to trade altogether.

During his early career Altshuller worked in the *Inventions Inspection* department of the Caspian Sea flotilla of the Soviet Navy. In his efforts to scrutinise and classify inventions he noted repeating resolutions to those contradictions within each problem. Despite handling problems drawn widely from disparate scientific and engineering fields, Altshuller noted repeating patterns within this very wide range of inventions.

Altshuller noted that when faced with a system trade between contradictory desires, innovative solutions tend to avoid trading between each desire. To offer the maximum of each desirable benefit, innovative solutions tend to separate the relationship between competing benefits, as illustrated in Figure 40.

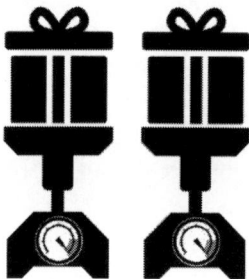

Figure 40: Can we separate the relationship between the desired benefits?

The scientific method offers sophisticated tools to describe how the world is, and can predict how the world might be under the influence of particular decisions. How are we do decide how the world *ought* to be?

The world ought to be *ideal*. All benefits. No harms. The complete separation of contradictory desires is how the world ought to be, for it allows us to have everything we want whilst enduring as few harms as possible. The separation of contractions is a central objective of Altshuller's TRIZ methodology.

Altshuller noted that the separation of contradictory desires to isolate them from one another can often be achieved. This separation provides the designer more freedom to offer the desired quantity of each benefit without an associated impact upon the other desirable benefits. The separation of contradictory benefits can be achieved in four distinct ways.

1. Contradictory benefits can be separated from one another in *time*. We could enjoy one benefit now, and enjoy the other later.
2. Contradictory benefits can be separated from one another in *space*. If we must enjoy both benefits simultaneously, we can isolate them from one another by placing each benefit in separate locations.
3. If we must enjoy both benefits at the same time and in the same location, we could place some filter between the contradictory desires to separate them on *condition* and prevent them from interacting.
4. If we must enjoy both benefits at the same time and in the same location, we could deliver each at very different *system scales*. One benefit could manifest its effect at the very small scale. The other benefit may only be felt at the very large scale.

Contradictions can be separated by time, space, condition and scale. Examples of each separation are offered for clarification.

Figure 41: Segment an antenna

The antenna of a radio, illustrated in Figure 41, must be both large and small. We separate this contradiction in *time* by making it segmented. It can be small *now*, during transport. It can be large *later*, when it must receive broadcasts.

Figure 42: Knives must be asymmetric

A knife, illustrated in Figure 42, must be both sharp and blunt at the same time. We separate this contradiction in *space* using asymmetry. At *one end* it is sharp, where it can cut. At the *other end* it is blunt, where we must hold it.

Figure 43: Meshes act as filters

I wish to catch a fish, illustrated in Figure 43, but I do not wish to catch the water it lives in. The fish and the water are present in the same place at the same time. We can separate this contradiction by filtering on *condition* using a net. The size of the fish contains it in the net. The properties of water allow it to pass through the net.

Figure 44: Chains differ in properties at different scales.

A chain, illustrated in Figure 44, must be both strong and flexible at the same time in the same place and we cannot place a filter between these properties. This contradiction is separated by *scale*. At the *small* scale subcomponents are manufactured from strong and rigid materials. At the *large scale* the small rigid links form a flexible cable.

    This separation of contradictory desires in time, space, condition and scale alone could form the basis of a useful problem-solving framework. Whilst scrutinising thousands of inventions during his time with the

Inventions Inspection Department Altshuller went further with his initial observation. Much, *much* further.

Altshuller noted patterns in solution methods far beyond time, space, condition and scale. During this analysis he noted repeating solution strategies which he documented and summarised. Some designers would segment system components to separate contractions. Other designers would do the opposite and merge functions together to resolve their contractions. Some might choose to mechanically vibrate a system to resolve their contradiction. Others might employ some intermediary to separate desires from one another. Altshuller was curious to know just how many ways there are to separate a contradiction and solve a problem. Despite scrutinising very different problems within very different engineering fields the total number of solution strategies Altshuller discovered was surprisingly small.

Forty. There are no more than forty methods to separate contradictions to solve problems. All engineering trades might be resolved by one of only forty different methods. This may be a hard result to believe. If you spend some time with these solutions you may be motivated to find more, but your additions are likely to be subsets or combinations of Altshuller's forty solutions. The forty methods Altshuller discovered within the patent database that can be employed to separate benefits in time, space, by condition or by system scale are described below.

1. **Segmentation.** Divide the object into separate parts. Fragment the object into powders, grains, droplets, etc. Split the object into independent functions.
2. **Taking out.** Extract and employ only the useful part, or separate the harmful part from the object.
3. **Local quality.** Optimise each part of an object to best perform its local function. Optimise the conditions around each part to best serve that part.
4. **Asymmetry.** Make an object asymmetrical, or more asymmetrical.
5. **Consolidation, Merging, Combining or Joining.** Bring together similar or related functions in space, or bring together functions that are closely connected in time.
6. **Universality.** Perform multiple functions with a single component and remove the redundant components.
7. **Nested Doll.** Place objects inside another object, or pass one object through another.

8. **Counterweight.** Compensate for the weight of an object by combining it with another object that has lifting power. Employ a lifting force from the environment.
9. **Prior Counteraction.** Counteract anticipated harms in advance.
10. **Prior Action.** Separate contradictions by performing a function in advance.
11. **Cushion in Advance.** Prepare in advance a function that will mitigate potential harms, should they arise.
12. **Equipotentiality.** Remove the need to change the height of an object, or use the environment to change its height.
13. **Do it in Reverse.** Reverse a function. Implement the opposite action. Place an object the other way around or upside down or inside out. Start at the end, and work towards the start.
14. **Spheroidality. Curvature.** Replace straight parts with curved parts. Replace motion in a straight line with rotation. Use rollers, or balls, or spirals, or domes. Use centrifugal force.
15. **Dynamics.** Make a stationary object move or interchangeable. Make parts of an object move relative to one another. Optimise the conditions around each part of an object at each stage of operation.
16. **Partial or Excessive Action.** If precision cannot be achieved, achieve too little or too much of the desired outcome. Remove excess or surplus.
17. **Another Dimension.** Increase the number of directions in which an object can move. Reorient an object. Use the reverse side. Use multiple layers.
18. **Mechanical Vibration.** Oscillate the object. Increase the frequency of an existing oscillation. Employ resonance frequencies. Use piezoelectric vibrations. Combine ultrasonic vibrations with electromagnetics.
19. **Periodic Action.** Replace a continuous action with an intermittent action. Change the frequency of a periodic action. Offer a benefit within the pauses of an intermittent action.
20. **Continuity of Useful Action.** Continuously work at full capacity without a break. Demand the full output from all parts of an object. Remove periods of idleness. Replace vibration with rotation.
21. **Rushing Through.** Perform actions as quickly as possible.
22. **Blessing in Disguise.** Transform a harm into a benefit. Use a harm to remove another harm. Increase a harm until it is no longer harmful.
23. **Feedback.** Feed information from the action back into the system. Change existing feedback. Increase automation.

24. **Mediator or Intermediate.** Use an intermediate object to transfer or exercise the action. Temporarily attach an object to an easily removed intermediate.
25. **Self-Service.** Allow an object to offer a benefit or remove a harm from itself. Employ waste energy or material.
26. **Copying.** Employ a simple or low-cost copy. Employ an image of an object as a copy. If an image is already used, employ a different frequency of light.
27. **Disposable, cheap short-lived objects.** Replace an expensive component with a disposable alternative.
28. **Replace Mechanical System.** Replace a mechanical system with an optical, acoustic, thermal, electrical, magnetic, electromagnetic or olfactory system. Replace fixed mechanical systems with dynamic or mobile systems.
29. **Pneumatics and Hydraulics.** Replace solid objects with gasses or liquids. Inflate components or create cushions. Use a vacuum.
30. **Flexible Membranes. Thin Films.** Replace components with flexible membranes or thin films. Use thin films as a barrier to isolate harms or benefits.
31. **Porous Materials.** Replace materials with porous substances. Fill porous materials with a beneficial substance. Use capillary action.
32. **Colour Change.** Change the colour or transparency of an object. Change the colour or transparency of the environment. Add a substance to make something easier to see.
33. **Homogeneity or Uniformity.** Manufacture subcomponents from the same material or from materials with the same properties.
34. **Rejecting and Regenerating. Discarding and Recovering.** Discard a useless component once it has completed its task. Restore components that have become consumed.
35. **Transform properties. Change a Parameter.** Change the concentration, density, flexibility, temperature, volume, pressure or other physical state of a component.
36. **Phase Transition.** Freeze, condense, melt or boil a material to change its state.
37. **Thermal Expansion.** Change the volume of an object with a temperature change. Exploit the different rates at which different materials change volume due to a temperature change.
38. **Accelerate Oxidation.** Transform an object by oxidising the material that it is made from.
39. **Inert Environment.** Surround components with an inert

environment. Introduce neutral substances into the system. Remove the environment altogether.
40. **Composite Materials.** Replace homogenous materials with composite materials.

Altshuller claims that if you can identify harmful contradictions within your problem one of the above solutions will separate your competing desires. Contradictory benefits or harms can be separated in time, space, condition or scale. Each of these Separation Principles will best serve a sub-set of these four dimensions. For example, the *Segmentation* of an object is perhaps best employed to separate a contradiction in time, space and by scale. *Segmentation* will allow one element of a contradiction to be enjoyed now, with the other enjoyed later. *Segmentation* will allow one element of a contradiction to be enjoyed at one location, with the other enjoyed at another. *Segmentation* will allow one element of a contradiction to be enjoyed at the large scale, whilst the other is enjoyed at the small scale. Alternately, if both elements of a contradiction must be enjoyed at the same time, location and scale, they can be filtered from one another using an alternative principle, such as *Porous Materials* or *Flexible Membranes*.

The use of these Separation Principles can be demonstrated if we return to our case study, *The Mail Order Store of the Future*. Table 1 cross references the benefits sought by delivering items all over the Earth and to high altitude and into orbit. This table documents the range of Technical Contradictions endured by this hypothetical transport. If we can transform each Technical Contradiction into a contradiction exhibited by a single physical property, then we can use the Separation Principles to build a list of solution strategies that together may solve our problem.

We first list the solutions that typically offer us each benefit in isolation. Without trying too hard we can state that,

- high speed solutions are likely to be offered by air vehicles,
- long range solutions are likely to be offered by solutions that require little fuel, can carry large fuel supplies, or can scavenge power from the environment,
- high altitudes are likely to be reached by air vehicles,
- and large payloads are typically carried by large scale transportation, such as container ships and cargo trains.

These isolated solutions are quite different from one another. If we engaged in a system trade, to solve our problem we must construct a very large air vehicle that can reach very high speeds at very high altitude by storing large quantities of power or scavenging power from the environment. Perhaps a solution is offered by a huge and efficient rocket? However, before we engage in the engineering trades that this particular solution will demand, *can we do better?*

We can attempt to reduce the number of compromises that must be made by scrutinising the relationship between each pair of benefits and looking for patterns. If we investigate each potential contradiction in isolation, we must consider the six relationships illustrated in Table 6.

This simple cross reference of benefits can be useful to offer an overview of where you are likely to encounter difficulties in designing a solution, and where your choice of benefits offers you advantage. For example, the desire for high altitude travel supports your desire to efficiently fly fast and fly far. Conversely, that desire to carry a very large payload a long way at high speed is clearly going to cause problems.

Here we reach the edge of the known World. Our *conscientious curator* has imposed a framework to describe the problem and to constrain our reflection upon what the solution may be. The six potential Technical Contractions to be addressed are illustrated in Table 6. Now it's time for our *chaotic creative* to do some work. We cling to the edge of the pool of potential solutions to become used to the water whilst practising our strokes with the firm support of dry land. Soon we must brave unexplored and unknown waters by employing our creativity to fettle solutions from this knotty problem. We have shrunk the pool of possibilities to as small a puddle as our constraints permit and also have flotation devices to aid us, in the form of the Separation Principles. Note that each principle does not offer us a definitive solution, but does provoke us to think in a particular direction and may also break us from treading familiar paths. The Separation Principles do not offer us singular, optimal solutions. This task is left to our creative skills. So, we grab some support from the forty principles and cast off into open waters.

Table 6: Which benefits contradict?

I want...	Without harming...			
	...the top speed	...the max range	...max altitude	...the payload size
...high speed		1	2	4
...long range			3	5
...high altitude				6
...a large payload				

With a solution framework in place to keep our creative skills on track we are free to bounce from one idea to the next without descending into unfruitful and irrelevant holes. Like a steel ball within a pin ball machine you are free to rocket around the obstacles with abandon. With a firm framework in place you are in no danger of exiting the confines of the machine. So, pull on that plunger and bounce with freedom from mushroom bumpers to kickout holes, under spinners and into jackpots. Keep that ball in play with the flippers, keep an eye on the back box, and watch that score climb.

1. *High speed and also long range?*

Consider our first potential contradiction in isolation. Our mail order service wants a vehicle to provide a high-speed delivery, but also wishes to deliver to a long range.

Both high speed and long range compete for fuel, so these two desires do present a contradiction. The more fuel we consume to gain a high speed, the less fuel we have to travel a long way.

High-speed delivery is typically offered by air vehicles. The fastest option is a rocket. If we retain this option how could we modify this high-speed solution so that it reaches a long range, but *does not* reach a long range? A Technical Contradiction is transformed into a Physical Contradiction. Long range, *but not* long range.

Perhaps not all of the rocket reaches the destination desired? We can separate these needs using the system scale. We could *Segment* the solution into a staged rocket, illustrated in Figure 45. The rocket discards unnecessary weight to reach the range desired by leaving parts of itself behind as it travels. Perhaps a staged rocket can offer greater range to this high-speed vehicle?

Figure 45: A stage rocket can offer high speed and high altitude.

Note that we could have reached this conclusion by considering an alternative Physical Contradiction. Consider a long-range option. Now the Physical Contradiction lies with the speed. The solution must be fast, but not fast. Perhaps not all of the solution is fast. Perhaps only the payload bay travels at the fastest speed reached by this solution. Once more a *Segmented* solution in which a staged rocket builds up speed, discarding mass as it goes might offer the performance that we need?

Can we do better? We fix the desire for very high speed and recover the fuel efficiency. A fuel-efficient vehicle is one which, once moving, keeps moving with little additional energy. However, energy will rapidly be drawn from a high speed vehicle by drag forces. How can the vehicle be high speed, but experience no drag? We can separate these features by condition.

We want a low drag vehicle, as low drag serves both speed and efficiency. The lowest drag is offered by an *Inert Environment*. If that rocket can reach orbit the lack of atmospheric drag can allow a body to travel at extremely high speeds using no further fuel. Achieving orbit offers high speed without further energy inputs, illustrated in Figure 46.

The Separation Principles don't offer you the solution. They simultaneously support and constrain your *chaotic creative*.

Figure 46: Reaching orbit could sustain very high speeds for a long period

2. *High speed <u>and also</u> high altitude.*

Consider the desire for high speed and also high altitude. In this case an increase in altitude provokes a decrease in drag, so these two desires actually support one another when a high altitude has been reached. The greater altitude we adopt, the higher speed we are likely to achieve.

This pair of desires ostensibly does not present us with a contradiction. The higher we climb, the faster we are likely to travel. However, this only describes the beneficial relationship between these desires at the end state, once at high altitude and at high speed. How did we achieve this virtuous relationship? After all, the more fuel we use to gain speed, the less fuel we have to gain altitude.

This relationship could be regarded as symmetric. If we can implement a mechanism that will reach a very high speed, we could use this speed to throw our payload to a high altitude. However, here we find our contradiction. If we attempt to throw our solution from the ground as high as possible by travelling as fast as possible, the higher we climb, the slower our vehicle becomes. We want both altitude *and* speed. Can we do better?

We retain the rocket to offer the high speed we desire and we transfer all of the responsibility for solving this contradiction onto the mechanism that offers altitude. Here we encounter the Physical Contradiction. We want a fast system that can reach high altitude, but *cannot* reach high altitude.

Perhaps some parts of our system don't reach high altitude? These desires could also be served by *Segmenting* the solution into a multi stage rocket that can offer both high speed and the endurance to reach high altitude, illustrated in Figure 45.

Alternatively, perhaps we could separate these desires in time? We could offer high altitude now and recover high speed later. Perhaps by employing *Equipotentiality* we could remove the need to change the height of an object, or use the environment to change its height?

This rocket could be carried to a high-altitude using an aircraft, and high speed could be offered by a small rocket that experiences low drag at this high altitude. This *Nesting* of solutions is illustrated in Figure 47.

Figure 47: Nesting a rocket in a high flying aircraft could offer both speed and altitude.

A high flying aircraft could store the goods we are likely to deliver, and when an order is received it is loaded into a rocket and propelled at high speed to the destination.

If we are to employ this *Prior Action* to separate contradictions by lifting the payload to the desired altitude in advance, can we do better? *Equipotentiality* could employ the environment to gain the desired altitude. Perhaps we could build our mail order store on the top of a high mountain or a high tower, or perhaps our mail order store should reside on one of those high altitude platforms or deliver packages from orbit, illustrated in Figure 48?

Figure 48: Use the environment to gain the altitude desired.

3. *Long range and also high altitude.*

An increase in altitude provokes a decrease in drag. Much like the relationship between speed and altitude, if we achieve a high altitude the low drag encountered at high altitude will create better conditions to achieve a long range. In this case the desire for high altitude travel supports the desire for long range.

Is this relationship symmetric? Does the desire for long range always support the desire to achieve a high altitude? Some mechanisms that enable a long range, such as a light weight or a low drag airframe, do indeed create characteristics that benefit high altitude flight.

However, some mechanisms to achieve long range do contradict with a desire for high altitude flight. For example, a very large and very heavy fuel payload will contradict with a desire to fly at very high altitudes. Can we use the Separation Principles to separate the contradiction between high altitude flight and the fuel load?

First, we fix the desire for high altitude flight by assuming that the solution is a high-flying aircraft. We then identify the contradiction forced upon the other physical property. We attempt to achieve long range flight with a vehicle that possesses large fuel resources but *has no* large fuel resources.

Perhaps we can restore fuel components that have become consumed through *Discarding and Recovering*? Perhaps we can separate in time the need for fuel but the desire for *no* fuel? Can we have no fuel now, and recover the fuel required later? Perhaps *Self-Service* could offer some mechanism to recover this fuel? Perhaps the high altitude desired is not a contradiction, but is a *Blessing in Disguise*?

Large fuel resources could be recovered at high altitude by refuelling from the sun, as no clouds will obscure this energy source at this altitude. The benefits of high altitude flight and long range could both be offered by a high altitude solar powered glider, illustrated in Figure 49.

Figure 49: Long range and high altitude could be offered by a high-flying solar glider

4. *High speed <u>and also</u> a large payload.*

Achieving a high speed and carrying a heavy payload compete for fuel, so this conflation of benefits results in a contradiction. The more fuel we expend gaining speed, the less fuel we have to propel a large payload. Put another way, for the same fuel load, the higher the speed we adopt the smaller the payload we can carry. How can we achieve both? Again, the order in which we consider our desires can have an influence upon the direction that our chaotic creativity takes us.

If we fix the desire for high speed with the most obvious solution, a rocket, how can we recover the additional desire for a large payload? The solution must carry a large payload, *but not* carry a large payload. *Segmentation* once more offers a solution by separating these desires in both space and time by creating *Copies* of our solution. A payload distributed amongst multiple small high-speed airframes could collaborate to deliver a single large payload. The high-speed delivery of a large payload could be offered by a multi-launch rocket system, illustrated in Figure 50.

Figure 50: Break up a large payload to deliver at high speed.

Alternatively, what if we first consider how a very large payload is typically transported? A very large and very heavy payload would not typically be delivered by air, but would be supported by the ground or by the sea. How can we recover the desire for very high speed from a surface vehicle? The vehicle must travel at high speed, *but not* travel at high speed.

Segmentation again could break a very large payload into smaller components that could travel at higher speed over land or sea. If joined to offer connected trucks and pulled by a single powerful engine we suggest a train. If each segment is individually pulled by multiple smaller engines, we describe a fleet of haulage trucks. How could these slower forms of transport, illustrated in Figure 51, offer a high-speed delivery? How could they move fast, *without* moving fast?

Figure 51: Break a large payload up to deliver with a high-speed rail network.

High speeds could be achieved by reducing drag. Perhaps we can separate this contradiction by system. Perhaps this vehicle could move slowly, but only relative to the system component that is slowing it down? If our train network ran through subterranean tunnels, we could pump the atmosphere through these tunnels to create a low drag environment. Perhaps this use of *Pneumatics and Hydraulics* could allow us to create an atmosphere that moves *with* the vehicle, illustrated in Figure 52. Perhaps this pneumatic mechanism could drive the train?

Perhaps an entirely *Inert Environment* could be employed by removing the air from these tunnels altogether, reducing atmospheric drag to zero?

Figure 52: High speed could be achieved with an evacuated, low drag tunnel.

5. Long range *and also* a large payload.

Long range and a heavy payload both compete for fuel, so here we find a contradiction. The more fuel we use to haul the payload, the less fuel we have to travel a great distance. Which of these contradictory benefits gets us closest to our overall goal?

Assume that employing a very large vehicle gets us closer to the ideal by enabling the carriage of very large payloads. This vehicle now experiences a physical contradiction. It must be able to reach a long range, without being able to reach a long range. How can we resolve this contradiction? How can a very large vehicle be moved efficiently?

Pneumatics and Hydraulics may describe the type of vehicle we must consider. We can ease the motion of a large payload by making it float. A large seaborne container ship could carry a very large payload for a very long distance, illustrated in Figure 53.

Figure 53: Container ships carry large payloads for great distances.

However, this does not resolve our contradiction. This resolution merely improves the trade between range and payload. The contradiction remains. For the same fuel load, the heavier payload this giant ship carries the less far it can travel. The further we deliver materials, the more fuel we will ultimately consume. Achieving long range whilst reducing fuel demands has the potential to contradict, so what options are available to us?

Can we offer fuel efficiency, *without* the need to be fuel efficient? We need not husband energy if we scavenge power from the environment. If we draw energy from the environment, we will have all the fuel we will ever need. Long range and fuel efficiency can be decoupled using *Flexible Membranes and Thin Films* which provoke us to scavenge power from the wind. A very long-range but fuel-efficient vehicle is offered by a sailing ship, illustrated in Figure 54.

Figure 54: A sailing ship could offer fuel efficient, long range transport.

Could we offer the same strategy to power land transportation? Can we increase the efficiency of a large train in a similar manner to a sailing ship? Large payloads could be efficiently hauled over land by scavenging power from the environment. Could a sail be attached to a train?

Here we encounter another contradiction, as the friction between a train and its support may be greater than that of a ship at sea. We could resolve this contradiction by *Replacing a Mechanical System* with an electromagnetic option. We could reduce the friction between this land vehicle and its support by lifting the train electromagnetically, illustrated in Figure 55.

Figure 55: A comprehensive problem-solving exercise can sometimes produce peculiar solutions.

A peculiar solution, such as illustrated in Figure 55, should not be rejected without scrutiny. An odd solution is sometimes merely a stepping stone to a better solution.

If we begin the separation exercise with fuel efficiency, we start by considering a vehicle that once moving requires only a small quantity of energy to keep moving. A large payload will be hauled by a large vehicle, but the larger the vehicle the greater the drag. We want a low drag vehicle that once moving does not stop. How could a vehicle that hauls a large payload exhibit extremely low drag?

Repeating an idea from our orbital option, an *Inert Environment* might offer a solution. Evacuate the atmosphere from a rail tunnel. Steal an idea from our sail powered train excursion, above, and *Replace a Mechanical System* with an electromagnetic option. We could reduce the friction between this land vehicle and its support by lifting the train electromagnetically. Ultimately, we return to the rail system travelling through a pneumatic or vacuum tube, but on this occasion it floats on electromagnetic support.

Figure 56: As this process unfolds, ideas are combined and refined

6. *High altitude and also a large payload.*

Achieving a high altitude and carrying a heavy payload both compete for fuel. For example, achieving orbit with an extremely heavy payload is wildly expensive as it requires huge, costly lift vehicles that must carry enormous quantities of fuel.

We retain the benefit that gets us closest to our ideal with an established solution. As with long range and large payload we choose a very large vehicle to carry a very large payload. How can a large vehicle that carries a very large payload, such as a ship, reach a very high altitude? The solution must reach a high altitude, whilst being unable to reach a high altitude.

This solution could remain at the altitude of the environment that supports it, just as a cargo ship might be supported by the sea. Perhaps *Equipotentiality* could allow the environment to change the height of the solution? However, this lifting environment cannot be at the surface of the Earth. We could again adopt the solution used to achieve long range but also a large payload, by making the vehicle float. In this case we employ *Another Dimension*, and float upwards. To achieve this, we could *Transform a Property* of the system by changing the concentration, density, flexibility, temperature, volume, pressure or other physical state of the material that supports the vessel. We could transform this lifting surface from a liquid into a gas.

We could lift very large payloads to a high-altitude using *Pneumatics and Hydraulics*. We could make our huge payload float, but this time on air. This *Counterweight* would compensate for the weight of the vehicle by combining it with another object that has lifting power. We employ a lifting force from the environment. To achieve both long range and high altitude a very large lighter than air vehicle could act as a dirigible cargo ship, illustrated in Figure 57.

Figure 57: Long range and high altitude could also be offered by a lighter than air vehicle.

We could further reduce the conflict between fuel demands by taking a lesson from our sailing ship to push our high-altitude vehicle along with the wind, illustrated in Figure 58.

Figure 58: Similar to the sailing ship, wind power could increase the fuel efficiency of a lighter than air vehicle.

7. *No vehicle at all.*

There is a seventh solution. This mail order company does explicitly demand the design of a vehicle that can deliver packages from a single large factory. This is merely a contrivance to focus our attention on the design of the vehicle, simply to illustrate the solution method.

However, this solution would not be complete without mentioning the obvious, and currently incumbent, solution. Perhaps the best high speed, high altitude, long range, high capacity vehicle, is *no vehicle at all*? Perhaps the wider system can solve the problem for us?

Perfect speed is being there. The solution to this problem may not be a special vehicle. If the package to be delivered to the destination was already present at the destination when ordered, then the travel time would be instantaneous.

We could *Segment* that single large factory. *Local quality* could optimise a distribution centre to best perform only its local function. *Copying* could distribute those local services all over the globe. By predicting what goods will be needed where, *Prior Counteraction* could remove the harm introduced by slow travel by performing the delivery function in advance, illustrated in Figure 59.

Figure 59: There's no need for high speed if you are already at the destination.

This solution is obviously a global chain of local shops that either delivers to the local community or which customers can visit should they wish.

Summarise and combine solution strategies.

The above discussion offers a framework that leads to some interesting ideas. Have we solved the problem? No, not yet. This exercise so far has not solved the problem in its entirety. We have assembled a number of solution *strategies* by considering each contradiction in isolation. These strategies range from high flying air vehicles to sailing ships of old. This collection of strategies continues to express the contradictions at the heart of our problem. To offer a concept that may ease the inevitable engineering trade that will be required to realise a practical solution will demand that we call upon our *chaotic creative* once more.

We may not have solved the problem, but we do now have a collection of formal solution strategies which can help to separate the dependencies between our contradictions. The strategies that we have been provoked to consider by the separation of contradictions are illustrated in Table 7. Can we combine these strategies in a creative manner to offer an alternative concept that combines the best features from our pool of strategies? Do we observe any repeating strategies that serve multiple contradictions?

Table 7: The solution strategies required to separate our problem contradictions.

I want...	Solution strategies
...high speed	• Segmentation, to break large payloads in to smaller, more manageable Copies or to discard unnecessary weight. • Inert environments to reduce drag. • Pneumatics and Hydraulics to drive motion
...long range	• Segmentation, to discard unnecessary weight and reserve fuel • Inert environments to reduce drag • Discarding and recovering, to receive fuel once tanks run dry • Self service, to scavenge energy from the environment. • Blessing in disguise, noting that at high altitude solar is unobscured • Membranes and Thin Films to draw energy from the wind • Replacing a Mechanical System to support large payloads on a low drag electromagnetic surface.
...high altitude	• Prior action, to lift a package to high altitude before delivery • Equipotentiality, to use the environment to lift packages to high altitude
...a large payload	• Pneumatics and Hydraulics to support heavy payloads with buoyancy. • Counterweight to support large payloads with the environment or a super system

Segmenting a payload into smaller pieces rather than haul a single monolithic package is frequently suggested as a method to move a large payload at high speeds and lift it to high altitudes. *Segmenting* the delivery vehicle into smaller components is also repeated to leave extraneous components behind when they no longer serve a purpose.

Alternatively, employing a *Counterweight* permits us to support a heavy payload in a fuel-efficient manner using *Hydraulics or Pneumatics*. This *Counterweight* is frequently offered by the environment. In some cases, the natural environment supports large payloads that float on the sea, or hang under lighter than air vehicles, or perhaps the dispatch site resides at the top of a high mountain. In other cases, the *Counterweight* is offered by another system component, such as electromagnetic rails, or wings.

Inert Environments are frequently employed to reduce the drag of a large payload, to increase fuel efficiency and speed. These vacuums are found naturally in orbit, or are created artificially by using *Pneumatics and Hydraulics* to pump tunnels free of atmospheric drag.

Self-service to *Discard* then *Recover* energy from the environment arises frequently, to fulfil the desire for long range or to avoid carrying a heavy fuel load to high altitudes.

We should also note that in both the desire to seek low drag environments and in the desire to recover energy from the environment, the higher our solution climbs the greater these benefits become.

Can we separate in time the desire for high speed and altitude from the efficient haulage of huge payloads? If we perform some *Prior Action* to lift potential deliveries to high altitude before a dispatch is necessary, our delivery can ultimately become very fast and very long range.

Despite this volume of strategies, we still retain a fundamental contradiction. The high speed, high altitude options are well served by air vehicles. Huge payloads are hauled efficiently by large surface vehicles, such as ships and trains. This perspective may provoke us into considering some hybrid of these competing strategies. What combination of solution strategies derived above will offer us characteristics like a staged rocket, but *also* like a balloon?

Nesting a rocket in a high flying aircraft could offer both speed and altitude, as illustrated in Figure 47. Range and high altitude could also be offered by a lighter than air vehicle, illustrated in Figure 57. Recovering motive power from the environment to move this lighter than air launch vehicle efficiently around the globe without an excessive fuel load is illustrated in both Figure 49 and Figure 58. Breaking massive payloads up into smaller packages will offer smaller, more manageable rocketry to nest into our air platform. We could simply add compatible solution strategies together to reach some suitable hybrid, by lifting the payload to altitude with a long range, high altitude balloon prior to the need for dispatch, illustrated in Figure 60.

Figure 60: Simply add compatible solution strategies together to offer the maximum number of benefits.

This summation of strategies may be sufficient to deliver the desired benefits to your satisfaction by separating contradictions sufficiently to offer both altitude and speed in the efficient delivery of hundreds of tons of cargo thousands of miles.

If we are not satisfied with this simple summation of strategies, perhaps we can push this framework further? The science fiction mail order dispatch office lazily drifting around the globe firing goods to their destination when required, illustrated in Figure 60, doesn't seem fast enough for me nor does it carry a sufficient mass of cargo. Can we deliver thousands of tons of material all over the world more quickly and more efficiently?

Segment the payload. Employ a *Counterweight*. Use *Equipotentiality* to allow the environment to change the height of the solution. Recognise that environmental power offers efficiency. Employ *Inert Environments* to gain speed.

Balloons are slow and offer insufficient payload. Don't act like a balloon. We want the payload of a large surface vehicle. Act more like a train. How could a train behave more like a rocket? Now we must get creative, and we can use the Separation Principles to do so.

We wish to behave like a train, but not behave like a train. We can modify our train to be more like a rocket by moving in *Another Dimension*. We can *Do it in Reverse*, by placing our train the other way around or upside down. We could move a train *vertically* rather than horizontally. This novelty is illustrated in Figure 61.

Figure 61: Could a train travel *up*, like a rocket?

A device that offers both the characteristics of a high speed, high altitude air vehicle and the heavy haulage of a train would satisfy many of our desires. A train that travels up is an elevator. This process of resolving contradictions to collect solution strategies that can be used to feed our creative inspiration perhaps may provoke us to reach the idea of the *Space Elevator*, first proposed by Konstantin Tsiolkovsky in 1895 [18] and illustrated in Figure 62.

Figure 62: Perhaps a high speed Space Elevator fulfils our desires?

Building a gigantic 35,786 kilometre high structure from the ground up is likely to be impossible as the structure would be unlikely to support its own weight. In 1959 Yuri N. Artsutanov suggested an alternative solution, by building *in Reverse* and hanging a cable from a *Counterweight* in geostationary orbit, such as an asteroid illustrated in Figure 63. Constant stresses were maintained in this huge cable by employing *Asymmetry*. The cable must be thick in orbit near to the counterweight, and taper to a thin cable near to the ground.

Figure 63: Could our factory sit at the base of a huge cable, suspected from a counterweight in orbit?

This enormous cable could act as the rail up which our rocket-like train will travel. *Nested Doll* could contain cargo within an elevator car as it climbs the elevator. Alternatively, *Do it in Reverse* and pass the elevator cable through the elevator car. The car could perform some *Self-Service* and provide the power to climb from internal resources or from power scavenged from solar or wind. Alternatively, as with our strategy to electromagnetically lift a train, we could *Replace this Mechanical* System. An electromagnetic means could be employed to lift this elevator car. Could some of the energy required to do so be *Discarded but then Recovered* from a similar car descending through this electromagnetic system that acts as a *Counterweight*? *Spheroidality and Curvature* help us in this task, as objects hauled up the elevator will gain horizontal velocity as they climb. Once they reached the top of the tower they will remain in geostationary orbit.

We could rapidly lift large payloads to orbit using this space elevator. Now a train acts more like a rocket. How do we offer the efficient and high-speed horizontal journey required to deliver products all over the world? Here we find the *Blessing in Disguise* we identified previously. Once hauled up to orbit the cargo is surrounded by an *Inert Environment*. In orbit we have no drag to slow our motion. We could *Segment* our cargo and boost each component with rocketry to continue its horizontal journey at very high speed.

Employing the *Equipotentiality* offered by the space elevator, this rocketry would have no need to contribute any energy to lifting the payload to altitude. This, combined with the *Inert Environment* could demand only a very small rocket system to offer the high speed desired. *Prior Action* could attach this rocketry to the payload before shooting it up the elevator and into orbit.

I admit, this proposal illustrated in Figure 64 is fanciful, but serves to illustrate the solution technique with some entertaining speculative science fiction. We list our desires. We separate the problem into multiple contradictions. We generate a library of solution strategies to separate each contradiction. We look for patterns in these strategies. We employ these strategies to develop a concept that solves the problem by separating the contradictions as much as we can.

It is important to note that this type of rhetorical concept development exercise does not solve the problem. This level of rhetoric cannot solve the problem alone. Alternatively, it is best to treat the outcome of this type of rhetorical exercise not as a list of answers, but as a list of *questions*.

After all, this exercise ultimately creates a long list of technical questions for the laboratory to assess. The concept description is a list of technical challenges. For example, is it possible to create a cable that must hang from orbit not only sufficiently strong, but also sufficiently long? How is this component to be constructed?

The solution strategies adopted to assemble the solution concept may demand materials that may not yet exist and require an enormous financial investment to develop. The answers to these technical questions may make or break the concept. This technological driver may be a show stopper, or may actually be the focus of a technology development programme that ultimately solves the problem.

Figure 64: Can small scale rocketry be delivered to orbit by a high speed space elevator?

TRIMMING THE FUNCTIONAL DESCRIPTION

The Substance-Field diagram developed to describe the utility of a hammer in Figure 23 is repeated below, in Figure 65. Straight arrows represent beneficial changes desired. Wavy arrows represent undesirable harmful changes. Dotted arrows represent beneficial changes that are desired but insufficient. In Figure 65 we note that the hammer head is so heavy that the user is having difficulty lifting it.

Note that substances and associated fields are assigned their own unique numbers, with a numbering system that associates each field to the substance that creates it. This allows us to keep track of properties, the values of which we could record in an associated table.

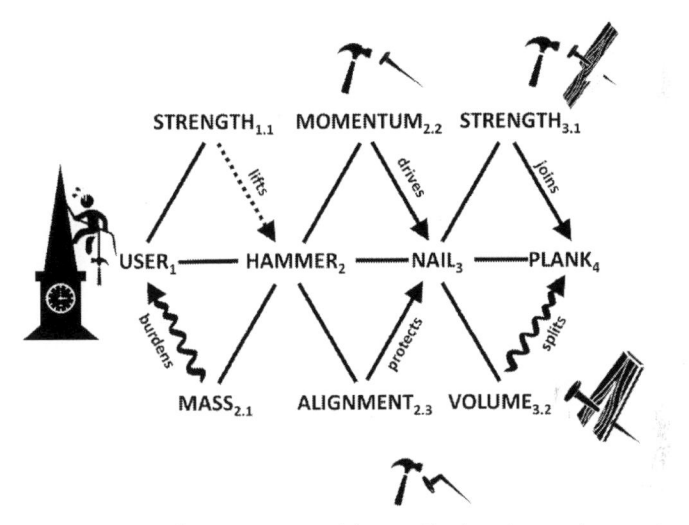

Figure 65: Our hammer can drive nails, but is too heavy to comfortably lift.

A scientific perspective offers sophisticated tools to describe how the world is. Similarly, the Substance-Field diagram offers a means to describe the world, and can be assembled from observing the world and describing the interactions that we observe. With this tool, can we decide how the world *ought* to be?

In Altshuller's view, the world ought to deliver the desired *ideal*. If we removed all of the harmful interactions from this system we should, by definition, possess an *Ideal Final Machine*. The Ideal Final Machine is the mechanism that offers the *Ideal Final Result*. Can we transform Figure 65 to represent this Ideal Final Result?

To hammer nails into wood the Ideal Final Machine is illustrated in Figure 66. Ultimately, this diagram illustrates how this small part of the world *ought* to be. How can we achieve this outcome?

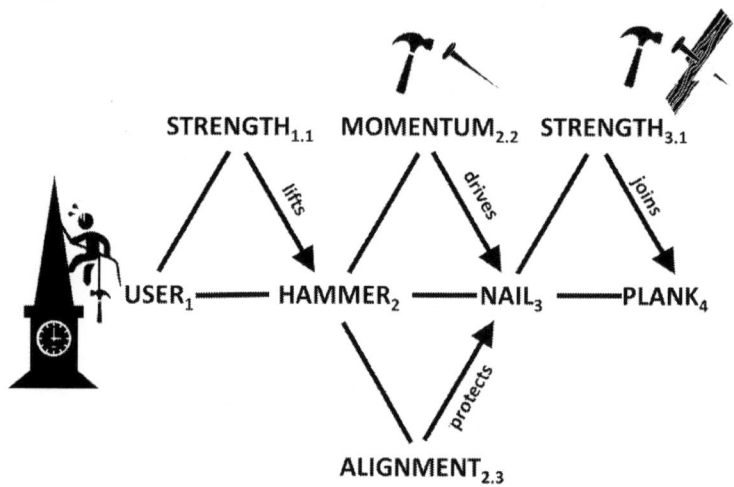

Figure 66: The Ideal Final Machine offers the Ideal Final Result. All benefits, no harms.

Our first step to solve a problem using a Substance-Field diagram is to decide how much detail should be included using this symbology. If we include every interaction these illustrations can become very complex. Under these circumstances we are not going to see the wood for the trees. A Substance-Field diagram must be as complex as it needs to be, and no more.

Each triangle illustrates the influence of one component upon another. Note that each triangle potentially hides a whole cascade of interactions within this relationship. Consider a firework rocket, illustrated in Figure 67. A burning taper may launch a firework into the air, but the chain of events that must take place from the heat of the taper, to the burning of the fuse, to the ignition of the engine, the constraint of the body material to permit an accumulation of pressure, to the conversion of pressure into a high velocity stream of gas using a nozzle, to the exchange of momentum between the rocket efflux and rocket body all contribute to the final motion of the rocket. Should one include all of this detail into one Substance-Field diagram? If we accept this, should we go further? Should we include a detailed description of the chemical interactions within the taper, or the rocket fuel? Should we describe in detail the pneumatic interactions within the pressure vessel or the nozzle?

If you do, there is no end to the chain of events you will unravel. You may have little hope of constructing a comprehensive and complex illustration that helps you to identify and solve problems that the illustration may expose. A diagram that illustrates the interaction between components is constructed to serve a particular purpose, not to describe the entire Universe in detail.

A system that exhibits only benefits and no harms is an ideal system. Such a system needs no modification to offer you all that you want. An illustration that highlights no harms nor insufficiencies can serve little purpose. If your illustration contains no harms or insufficiencies, illustrated in Figure 67, you are either in fortunate possession of an Ideal Final Machine, or the harms within your system lie a little deeper inside the interactions described.

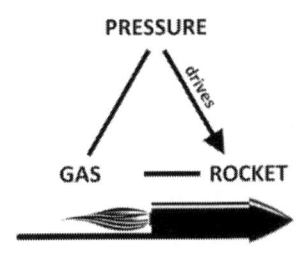

Figure 67: No harms. No insufficiencies. Perfect?

We must try to align the detail of a Substance-Field illustration with its purpose, and in particular we want to highlight influential harms and insufficiencies in the system. If burrowing down into an interaction will reveal little more of value then keep the illustration simple and search elsewhere for opportunities to improve the system. Keep to broader summaries of interactions unless you need to drill down and expose further detail.

For example, our Substance-Field description of a hammer, illustrated in Figure 65, includes two fields generated by the hammer. We have indicated the mass of the hammer acting as a burden upon the operator, and the momentum of the hammer driving in nails. We note that momentum is a product of the mass combined with the velocity of that mass. We could illustrate this relationship as a velocity field acting upon the mass field to produce momentum, as illustrated in Figure 68.

In this illustration we delve deeper into the functions of a hammer by separating the subsystems that create the desirable mass from those that generate the required velocity. The hammer head offers mass, whilst the hammer handle accelerates that mass to the desired speed.

To add this more complex description to our original illustration may result in a complex structure that is difficult to assemble and manipulate. Under these circumstances it is often more practical to manage these two illustrations separately, and cross reference the relationship between them.

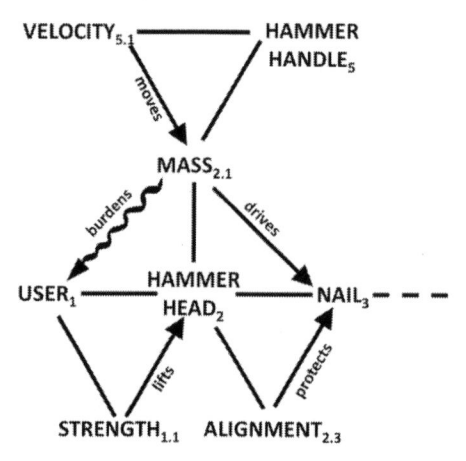

Figure 68: Momentum is a product of both mass and velocity

Altshuller's analysis of the patent database not only revealed standard methods with which to separate contradictions. This study also worked towards identifying common methods to remove harms from a system or to increase benefits that are insufficiently strong. Altshuller's standardised Substance-Field symbology not only offers a means to describe a problem. This symbology also offers a standard means to describe solutions.

To demonstrate how this Substance-Field symbology can offer a standardised solution framework we can impose a single problem-solving rule to this symbology and apply some basic intuition. Our simple, illustrative rule is to ask a single question, *what new solution can we derive if we delete a harm?*

To illustrate, we start on the far left of Figure 65 and reduce the burden upon the operator. To achieve this, we must reduce the mass of the hammer until it no longer provokes a harm upon the operator, illustrated in Figure 69. Our alternative analysis of the fields that combine to produce momentum, illustrated in Figure 68, tells us that if we diminish the mass of the hammer head, we not only unburden the operator but also reduce the momentum of the hammer. This may result in a hammer that is insufficient to drive a nail into a piece of wood, illustrated as a dotted line in Figure 69.

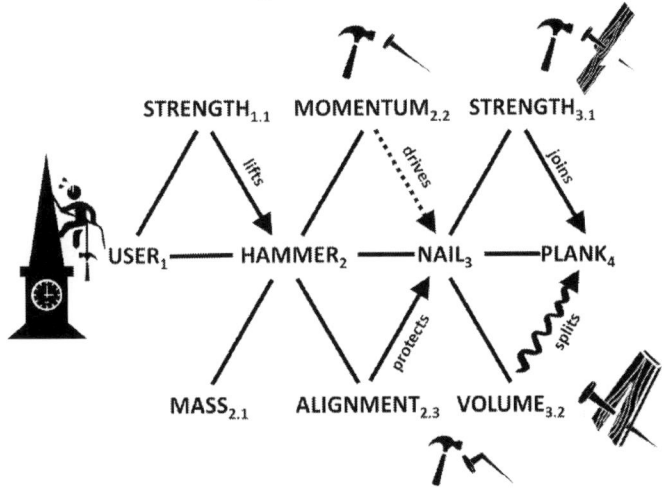

Figure 69: Remove the mass of the hammer to unburden the operator, and the nail is no longer driven through the plank.

Note that this modified diagram becomes a new description of a new problem, and a well described problem takes you halfway to a solution. Intuitively, how could we resolve this new problem?

Momentum is a product of mass and velocity, and our illustration of the hammer subcomponents, in Figure 68, tells us that velocity is generated by the hammer handle. We could increase the speed of the hammer by increasing the length of the handle. If this is likely to decrease the accuracy of the hammer then the benefit introduced by the hammer alignment required to protect the nail is likely to result in more bent nails. Perhaps increasing the handle length will simply remove a protection that our nails already enjoy in our Substance-Field diagram. If the ideal is our objective, an increase in handle length will not lead us there.

If more bent nails are undesirable, the Substance-Field might provoke us to ask how we can drive nails through wood without increasing the momentum required? We could make our nails sharper, which requires less momentum to drive them through wood, but may be more likely to split our wood. Half an idea can still lead you to the solution. Following on from this idea, to prevent splitting we could drill a small hole through the wood to ease the passage of the nail through the wood. Through the simple formal process of removing a harm, a number of intuitive ideas appear.

Ultimately, we want to remove the mechanism that bends nails altogether. We could dispense with the need for good alignment to ensure that the nails do not bend by removing the hammer, illustrated in Figure 70.

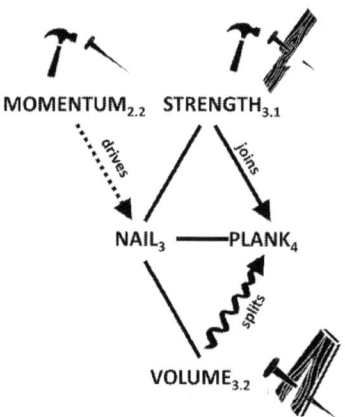

Figure 70: Removing the hammer results in an incomplete system.

We have removed the harmful bending of nails by removing the mechanism that bends nails, but the dangling field of momentum now exposes an incomplete system. From where could we gain the momentum required to drive the nail through the wood?

Note that the function we desire is to drive the nail through the wood. We need not use momentum, and could employ some alternative field to achieve this. We've already proposed a sharper nail, or drilling a hole through the wood to ease the passage of the nail. What if the nail drilled its *own* hole through the wood, illustrated in Figure 71.

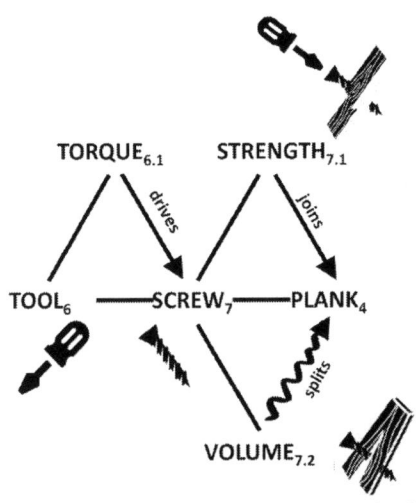

Figure 71: Could the nail drill its own hole through the wood?

By removing the harms in our system, we create new problems that propose new solutions. Through this mechanism we have invented a means to drive a nail through wood whilst decreasing the weight of the tool required and increasing the accuracy with which it is applied. With the single question, *'what happens if we remove a harm?'* we have invented the screwdriver.

We can go further. Perhaps the screw still has the potential to split the wood. We apply the same, singular solution process of removing harms once more and remove the volume of the screw, which removes the screw altogether. Without a screw we don't split the wood. Without a screw we need no screwdriver. Figure 72 illustrates that we once more have an incomplete system. This simple process offers an iterative means not to generate the right solutions, but to create the right questions. We now need some means to strongly join our planks that possesses little volume, or does not pass through the planks.

STRENGTH

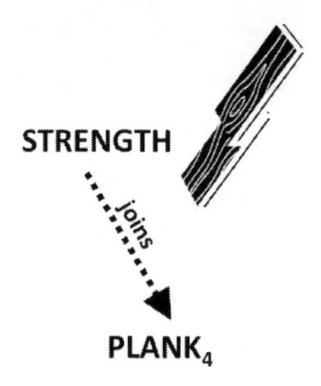

..joins..

PLANK$_4$

Figure 72: We need a strong join but without volume.

Glue could offer a means to join two planks of wood whilst exhibiting little volume and without passing through each plank, as illustrated in Figure 73.

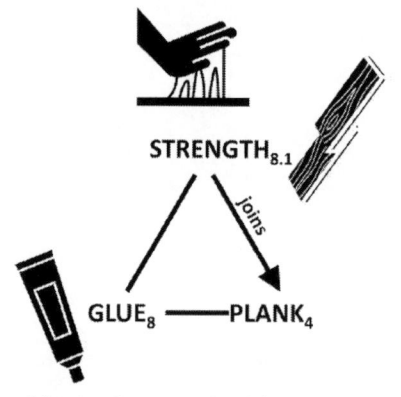

STRENGTH$_{8.1}$

joins

GLUE$_8$ ——— PLANK$_4$

Figure 73: Glue could join the wood without passing through each plank.

This very simple solution strategy could take us further. Consider the harms that an adhesive might exhibit. Perhaps the glue fumes are harmful. Glue that is sufficiently strong may not exist. Can we complete this system without adding into the system a means to join the planks? Can the planks join themselves? Of course they can, as an effective joint between the planks could be fashioned to join the planks together without any intermediate means, illustrated in Figure 74

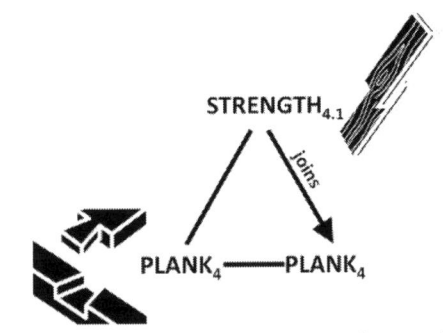

Figure 74: Could the planks join themselves?

We have illustrated how a single, simple solution strategy of *trimming* could be applied to our Substance-Field diagram to describe new problems that provoke intuitive, creative solutions. With this simple example we could trim *everything* from this system. Figure 75 illustrates that we could solve our need to join two planks together by *using a longer plank*. All benefits. No harms. Ideal?

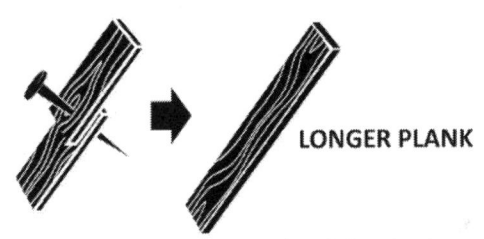

Figure 75: Why do we need to join planks at all?

The basic strategy of removing harms from the system and resolving the new problem that emerges serves to illustrate how a standard strategy might be applied to the Substance-Field diagram to reach an ideal. By now you are likely to assume that Altshuller would be unsatisfied with a single basic strategy. Altshuller's understanding of the patent database offers a comprehensive toolbox of strategies to solve problems described in this manner.

This method of describing problems offers a concise means to describe possible standardised solutions. To illustrate, consider the problem that might arise if an interaction was beneficial but insufficient. In Figure 76 we illustrate the desire to transform a substance S_1 in a beneficial manner using a field $F_{2.1}$ generated by a substance that we label S_2. The broken line in this illustration tells us that this benefit is insufficient. We want this benefit, but to a greater degree.

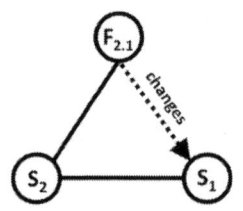

Figure 76: Substance 2 provokes a beneficial but insufficient change in Substance 1

Note that we have departed from describing what each substance is and the specific nature of the field. We need only present a generic description of a problem to illustrate how the Substance-Field operates.

If we wish to employ a third substance, S_3, to behave as some *intermediate* means to enhance the benefits provoked by field $F_{2.1}$, how many different ways are there to interpret this solution strategy?

This support from an intermediate may take the form illustrated in Figure 77. The new intermediate substance, S_3, is indicated with a box. This third substance might act upon the second substance in some beneficial manner to strengthen the effect upon the first.

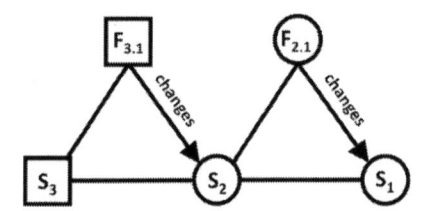

Figure 77: A third substance changes the second to enhance its effect on the first.

This is not the only manner in which an intermediate substance can manifest its support. Perhaps the third substance might reside between the other two, to act upon the first as a result of action by the second, as illustrated in Figure 78.

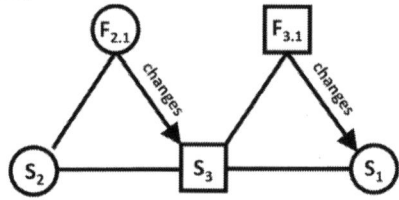

Figure 78: The third substance resides between the other two.

The action of an intermediary can manifest as a further alternative strategy. Perhaps the third substance could make the first substance more sensitive to the second? In this arrangement the third substance might act directly upon the first, as illustrated in Figure 79.

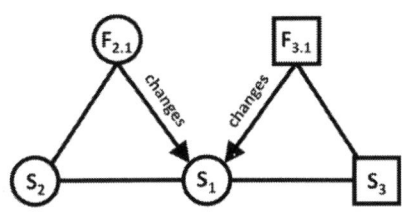

Figure 79: The intermediate substance may make the first more sensitive to the second.

Perhaps the action of an intermediate substance might not directly act upon another substance, but upon the field that it produces. This action upon a field by an intermediate substance is illustrated in Figure 80.

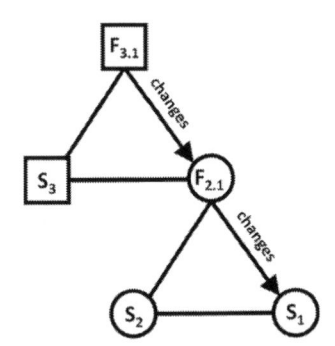

Figure 80: Perhaps the intermediate only acts upon a field.

Finally, perhaps the field of the second substance can only act upon the first substance via the modification of the field generated by this intermediate, as illustrated in Figure 81.

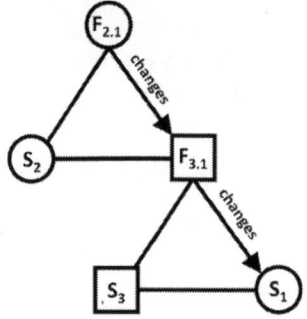

Figure 81: The second substance can only act upon the first by modifying the field of the intermediate.

What if the change Substance 2 makes to Substance 1 is harmful, and we wished to remove this harm? This situation is illustrated in Figure 82.

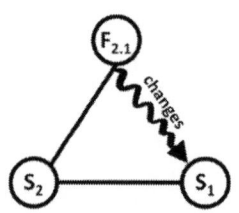

Figure 82: How might an intermediate mitigate a harm?

The intermediate substance might act upon the second substance to prevent the harmful field from arising. This would mean that the first and second substances do not interact at all, as illustrated in Figure 83.

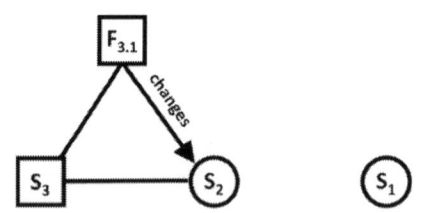

Figure 83: Through the action of our intermediate, the field from the second substance does not arise.

Alternatively, perhaps the intermediate substance acts as a buffer between the others, to absorb the harm generated by the second, as illustrated in Figure 84.

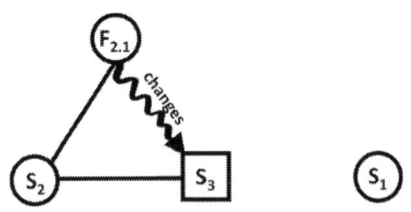

Figure 84: The intermediate substance could absorb the harm.

The intermediate could act upon the field generated by the harmful substance, to prevent this field from harming the first substance, illustrated in Figure 85.

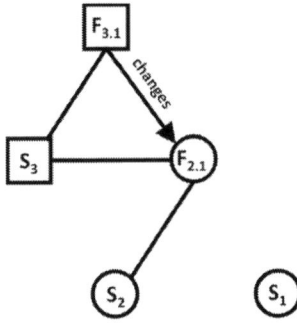

Figure 85: The intermediate modifies the harmful field so that it is no longer harmful

Finally, the field of the intermediate substance could absorb the harmful effect to act as a buffer between the harmful effect and the protected substance, illustrated in Figure 86.

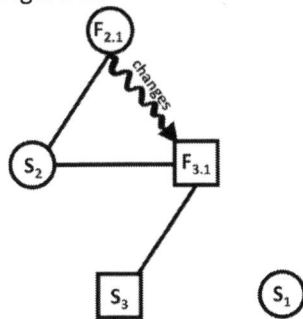

Figure 86: The field of the intermediate substance absorbs the harmful effect.

The solution strategy of a *mediator*, Separation Strategy 24, can be interpreted in ten different ways. The Substance-Field analysis developed by Altshuller allows us to describe each solution in a unique and explicit manner.

Altshuller developed his Standard Solutions to problems described by Substance-Fields through much the same means as the Separation Principles. In his scrutiny of many thousands of successful solutions, Altshuller assembled a catalogue of all the strategies that could be employed to improve a Substance-Field diagram to better deliver benefits. This work revealed a total of 76 solutions that will block or trim the harms within a system, will improve the influence of desired but insufficient interactions, or measure the properties of a system.

Note that in the fanciful case study that threads through this text, our heroic Soldier carries with him both a shield and an ear trumpet. The shield blocks harms. The ear trumpet increases insufficient benefits or enhances measurement. Each offer the same standard function regardless of the context, but each is employed in many different ways to achieved specific ends depending upon the problem that our hero must resolve.

You can treat these standard solutions as a catalogue of design patterns from which you can cut your own specific solutions, much like a tailor would employ patterns to create and copy a standard style of clothing. These standard patterns cover five primary classes.

Figure 87: Standard patterns are drawn from prior solutions.

Class 1. The construction or destruction of those fields that allow one component to influence another.

Substance-Field systems may be incomplete or offer insufficient benefits. Complete the system to offer sufficient benefits. An incomplete system is illustrated by a Substance-Field in Figure 88. A sufficient pressure field could be offered by water?

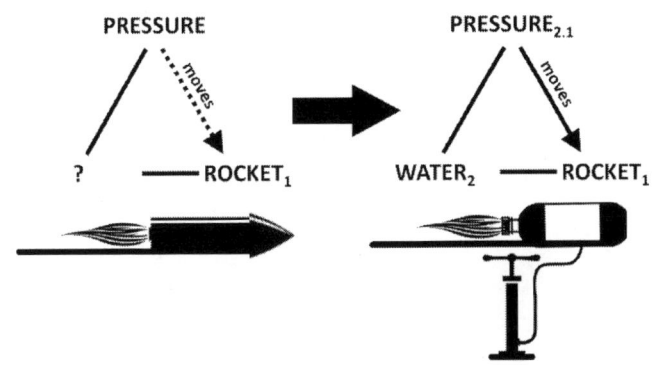

Figure 88: Our rocket has no means to create pressure? To complete the system, just add water.

Alternatively, we could counteract a field by introducing a sacrificial substance to absorb a harm, as illustrated in Figure 89.

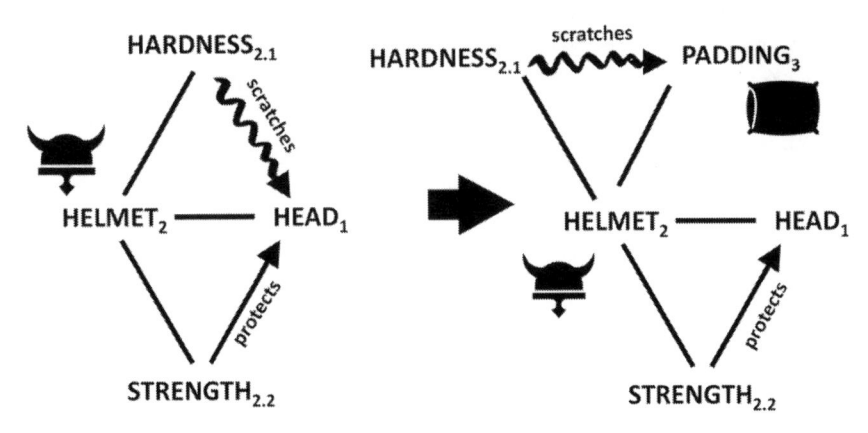

Figure 89: The hard material of a helmet hurts my head. Add padding.

Class 2. The development of Substance-Field models into more complex systems.

If a Substance-Field is insufficient, we could make it more complex to improve benefits. For example, if we wished to move a substance, we could introduce magnetic additives into this substance, as illustrated in Figure 90.

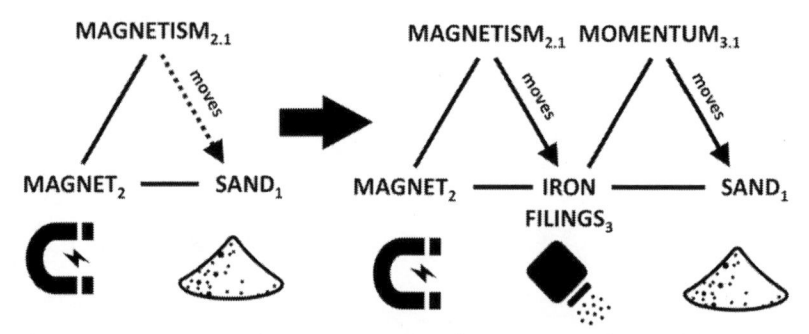

Figure 90: We can only move sand with a magnet if we add iron particles.

Class 3. Transition of functions to the super system or sub system

The system could be improved by creating copies of system components, and using their combined efforts to create the desired benefits. For example, an aircraft wing creates lift which we can use to support the fuselage along the centreline of the aircraft. If only a single wing is attached to the side of the fuselage, as illustrated in Figure 91, we achieve the lift we need but introduce harms into the system. A complete Substance-Field is created if we employ two copies of this wing on either side of the fuselage, the combined lift of which supports the aircraft.

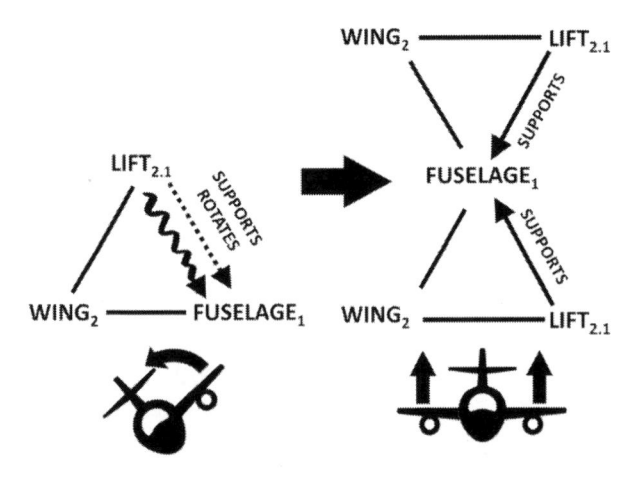

Figure 91: Two copies of the same wing are required to lift our aircraft.

Alternatively, multiple components that offer related functions could be consolidated into fewer components, whilst retaining all of the functions desired. For example, consider the simplification of a system. Achieve all the functions desired whilst reducing the number of components. Integrate several components into one but still deliver all the functions. Take a radio and a telephone, and offer all functions with a single component, as illustrated in Figure 92.

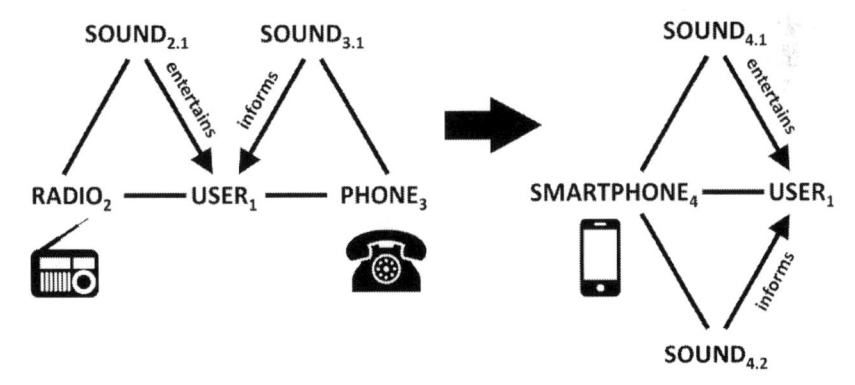

Figure 92: Deliver the function of phone and entertainment with a single object

Class 4. Solutions for detection and measurement

Altshuller's analysis of problems and their solutions as described by the patent database revealed a great many mechanisms designed specifically for the measurement of conditions within and without the system. These measurement solutions can be described using the Substance-Field mechanism, and Altshuller offers numerous standard means to measure system properties.

For example, consider the need to measure something, but this measurement cannot be made directly. Add something to make a measurement system. Measure a substance that is connected to the substance measured. Consider the need to measure the volume of fuel in a tank, illustrated in Figure 93.

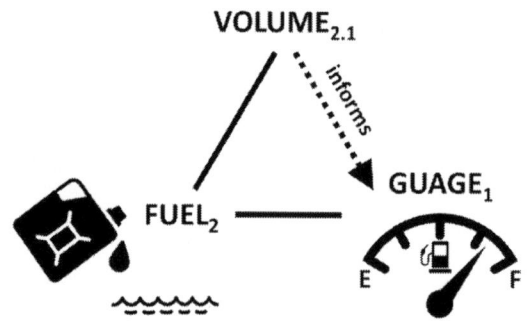

Figure 93: How does the fuel inform the gauge about its volume?

If there is no way in which the gauge can be directly informed of the fuel volume in the tank, perhaps we could measure the quantity of fuel in a tank by measuring the height of a float and inferring the volume of fuel from this height, as illustrated in Figure 94.

BOUYANCY$_{2.2}$ HEIGHT$_{3.1}$

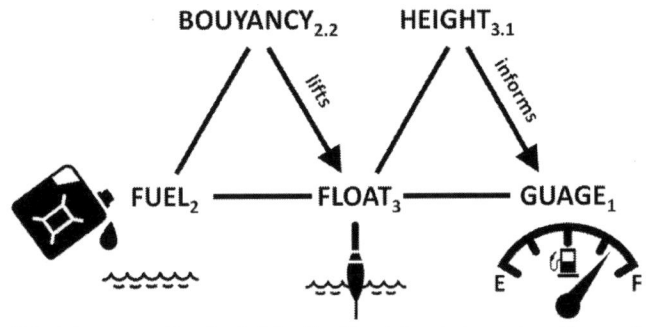

FUEL$_2$ ——— FLOAT$_3$ ——— GUAGE$_1$

Figure 94: Measure the height of a float to determine the volume of fuel.

Class 5. Additional patterns that support the above objectives.

Altshuller offers the ideal as the final objective of any system design. The ideal will offer only benefits, and exhibit no associated harms. A minority of problems will permit you to wring the ideal from the Universe. Despite our best efforts to separate contradictions or eliminate harms, under most circumstances we attempt to approach this ideal as closely as we can, but must ultimately trade between our desires to reach a final, practical outcome. Consequently, although the ideal may not be reached, ever more ideal is an aspiration that we can pursue. The more ideal the system, the more benefits we recover and the fewer harms we must endure.

The ideal is an aspiration, but the closer we can get to the ideal, the better. Altshuller incorporated into his 76 Standard Solutions a collection of strategies that will help the designer to apply the four classes of solution described above in such a way that the ideal will be more closely approached.

For example, consider our effort to move sand using a magnetic field, illustrated in Figure 90. The addition of iron filings into the sand offers a suitable solution. However, once the sand has been moved, a harm remains. The sand is now mixed with iron filings, which may be undesirable. We could therefore achieve a more ideal outcome by introducing this additive only temporarily. We could extend the example offered in Figure 90 by removing the magnetic material once it has done its useful work, illustrated in Figure 95.

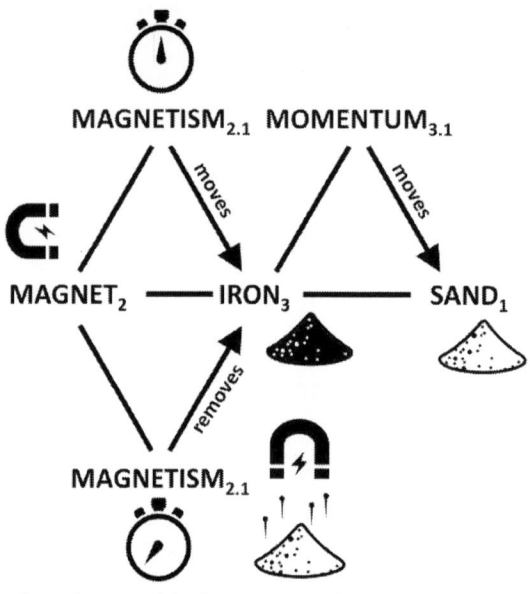

Figure 95: If we have added iron particles to move sand, use the magnet to remove them once the action is complete.

All 76 Standard Solutions that can transform your Substance-Field diagram to block or trim the harms manifest within your system, improve the influence of desired but insufficient interactions, or measure the condition within a system are described in Chapter 21.

To illustrate the use of these solutions, we can employ this catalogue to improve our hammer described above. Once more we have constrained our problem description as far as we can. We have drawn a precise diagram of the system, with all the relevant benefits and harms indicated, illustrated in Figure 65. We wish to modify this system to block or remove the harms, and we wish to enhance those benefits that are inadequate to perform our task. We have a list of 76 generic strategies to provoke our creative engine. Armed with these tools our chaotic creative must now once more push off into the unknown and do some work.

The simplest modification we could make is to build beneficial fields, or destroy fields that harm our system. Techniques to achieve this are offered by Class 1 strategies. We don't want the user encumbered by the hammer, so we need to block or remove the harm introduced by the weight of the hammer. The following strategies drawn from the 76 Standard Solutions described in Chapter 21 provoke questions that may offer some means to reduce the weight of the hammer.

The mass of the hammer is a benefit, as it offers momentum to drive a nail. However, this benefit imposes a harm upon the user. Standard Solution 1.2.3 suggests that we could draw this harm away from the user by introducing a sacrificial substance to absorb the harm. A formal Substance-Field illustration of this Standard Solution is illustrated in Figure 96. Such a solution might provoke us to ask the obvious question, *where else could we impose the weight of the hammer other than the user?*

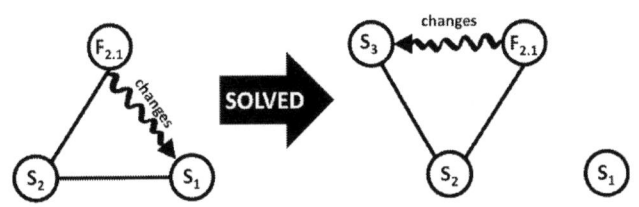

Figure 96: Standard Solution 1.2.3. A new substance, S_3, draws the harm delivered by S_2 away from S_1

This question may seem very obvious, and it seems likely that many will not require a complex solution framework to be driven to such a question. However, for Altshuller's framework to be comprehensive, it must include the obvious solution strategies by definition, which we use here to illustrate the process.

Some alternate means could bear the weight of the hammer whilst our operator is engaged with other tasks. In our Substance-Field diagram we could replace the burden that the hammer inflicts upon the user with a burden placed upon something more capable of lifting the hammer, such as the crane illustrated in Figure 97.

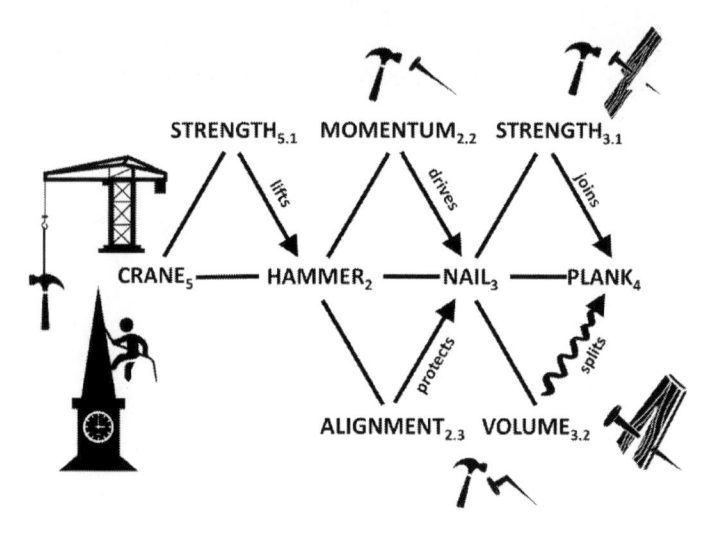

Figure 97: Add a new substance to absorb the weight of the hammer.

Here we note a very strong relationship between Altshuller's 76 Standard Solutions and his previous innovation on the separation of contradictions. These tools are designed to constrain and provoke our creativity, and we could have reached the same conclusion by considering the physical contradiction that the hammer presents to us. The hammer must be both heavy, and not heavy. We may be provoked to resolve this contradiction by considering the following Separation Principles. 8, *Counterweight*. Compensate for the weight of an object by combining it with another object, such as a crane. 24, *Mediator*. Use an intermediate object to transfer or exercise the action. Temporarily attach an object to an easily removed intermediate, such as a crane.

All of these roads may lead us to consider a crane to lift the hammer to its place of operation. It's doesn't matter how you get there, as long as you get there.

Can we do better than this? After all, the addition of a crane into our system will carry a long list of new harms into our problem. We turn back to our Class 1 list of Standard Solutions for new inspiration.

Consider solution 1.1.4 described in Chapter 21. Use the environment. Introduce an additive from the environment to enhance an insufficient benefit. An obvious option in the environment to lift the hammer up a structure is the structure itself. A block and tackle at the summit would transform the structure into a crane. When a function is lifted up into the super system, or the environment, there are often many options to choose from. The sky is the limit, and sometimes literally. Figure 98 illustrates a novel alternative means by which the environment could lift the hammer. The buoyancy of a balloon could support the weight of the hammer as the operator is engaged in other tasks.

Note that once again we could have reached this solution by separating our contradictions with one of Altshuller's 40 Separation Principles. The hammer must be both light and heavy. Separate these desires using principle 8, *Counterweight*, and employ a lifting force from the environment in combination with 29, *Pneumatics and Hydraulics*. These strategies also lead us to buoyant balloons that could lift the burdensome hammer for the operator.

Once more this introduces new harms into the system, as the balloon may blow away. The addition of new components is likely to introduce new harms so we must once more analyse our modified system and resolve these new harms. Perhaps we could tie the balloon to the user with a short piece of string?

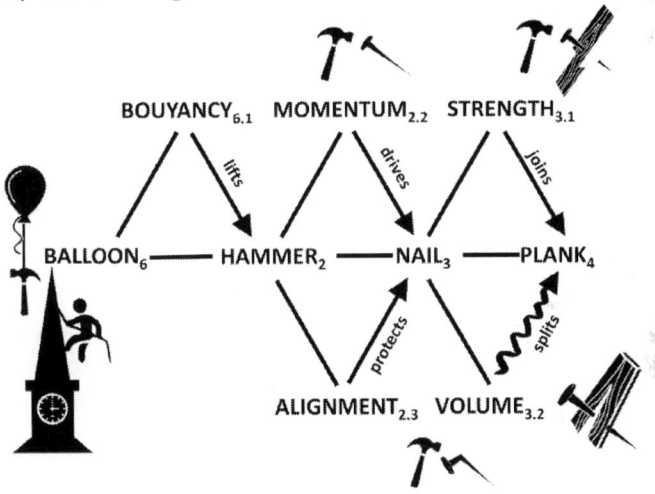

Figure 98: The environment could lift our hammer.

Can we transition to a more complex model and evolve our current solution to offer the benefits we want whilst removing the harms present in the system, or removing the new harms that we may have introduced in our effort to improve the system?

We note from the Substance-Field diagram that illustrates the operation of our hammer that it is momentum that drives in the nail, not weight. The momentum of a hammer's head can be increased by increasing its mass or its speed. We first try to improve this system by attempting to increase the mass of the hammer without encumbering the operator. The hammer presents us with a physical contradiction. The hammer must be both heavy, but not heavy. We can separate this contradiction in time. Heavy when in use, but not heavy when in transport. We can separate this contradiction in space. Heavy in the location that it must drive in nails. Light when stored in our toolbox.

In either case we can choose one of these states and solve the system to offer the alternative property. For example, when the hammer is light, during transport or stored in our toolbox, it exhibits too little mass to drive in nails if we should need to make use of it. The mass of the hammer is insufficient. What strategies might be available to temporarily increase the mass of the hammer? A brief return to Class 1 gives us our first clue, illustrated in Figure 99. Note the use of the suffix associated with substance 3, to indicate the environmental origin of the new substance.

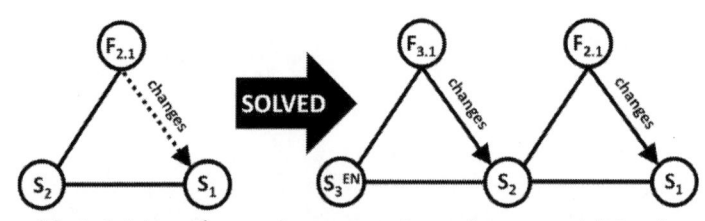

Figure 99: 1.1.4 Use the environment. Introduce an additive from the environment to enhance an insufficient benefit.

This strategy may provoke us to ask, *what could we add to the hammer from the environment to make it heavier?* Here we might review our list of resources available in the environment, and consider adding bricks, earth, rocks or rainwater to our hammer at the time or location that it must become much heavier.

We might determine which of these environmental resources may offer a suitable addition by considering the mechanism employed to add this substance to our hammer. This mechanism will require Class 2 strategies, as we are likely to make our hammer more complex if we must include an environmental additive.

Consider solution 2.2.3, illustrated in Figure 100. Note that the insufficient benefit illustrated has become sufficient because the substance that it acts upon now exhibits cavities, indicated with the suffix 'cp'.

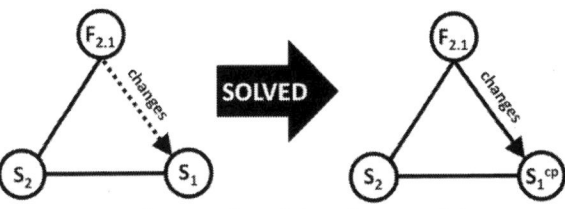

Figure 100: 2.2.3 Change the object from solid to a porous or capillary material that will allow gas or liquid to pass through.

This improvement in the system, provoked by adding voids into the substance acted upon, might provoke us to ask, *can we make our hammer hollow? Could a hollow hammer hold liquid?*

Figure 101 combines these strategies to offer a potential solution. If a hammer need only be heavy when it is in use, the hammer could be filled with water from the environment when mass is required. Of course, this demands that water be available, which may not be assured on the roof of a tall structure on a building site.

Rather than lofted to the top of a structure, a hammer that must be carried a long distance may also offer this physical contradiction – to be both light and heavy. Perhaps this water filled hammer is employed to nail tent pegs into the ground? This standard solution strategy suggests a camping mallet that can be filled from a nearby stream when mass is required. Perhaps this hollow structure stores those tent pegs? If the additional mass of the hammer is bearable, this hollow structure also doubles as a water bottle.

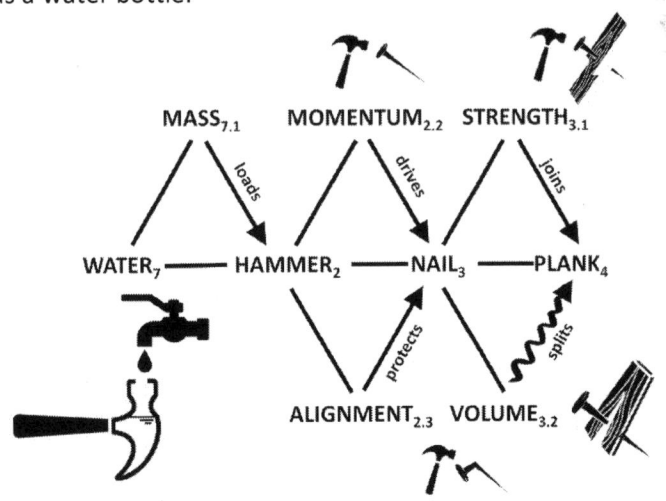

Figure 101: Could water from the environment load the hammer?

We began this process by considering the physical contradiction presented by the hammer's mass. With the contradiction understood, we treated the lack of mass as an insufficiency that must be resolved with a temporary additional mass. Note once more that this solution could have been reached by considering the Separation Principles that resolve contradictions.

The hammer must be both light and heavy. We can separate these benefits in time. It must be lightweight now, and sufficiently heavy to hammer in nails later. We could separate this contradiction using principle 2, *Taking out,* by extracting and employing only the useful part or removing the harmful part. We remove the mass when we don't need it.

Principle 15, *Dynamics*, could have driven us to a solution. *Dynamics* optimises the characteristics or environment of an object at each stage of operation. Make the object light when it needs to be light, and heavy when it needs to be heavy.

Principle 19, *Periodic Action*, may have offered help. Principle 19 offers a benefit within the pauses of an intermittent action. The hammer becomes heavy between periods of transport.

Principle 29, *Pneumatics and Hydraulics*, could have offered inspiration. This principle replaces solid objects with gasses or liquids.

Principle 31, *Porous Materials*, could have driven us to consider a hollow hammer, by replacing materials with porous substances and filling porous materials with a beneficial substance.

Principle 34, *Rejecting and Regenerating*, discards a useless component once it has completed its task.

Altshuller presents a great many possible chances to discover the *Water Filled Camping Mallet*. An advantage of a formal solution structure is that one can be more confident that every possible solution strategy has been considered and scrutinised. Let's take this process further, to ensure that we have thought of everything. The momentum of a hammer's head can be increased by increasing its mass or its speed. We previously discarded the idea of increasing the speed by making the handle longer. Perhaps a very long hammer handle could indeed be attached to a very light hammer head to offer a lightweight but effective hammer? We can illustrate this by modifying our Substance-Field diagram, illustrated in Figure 102.

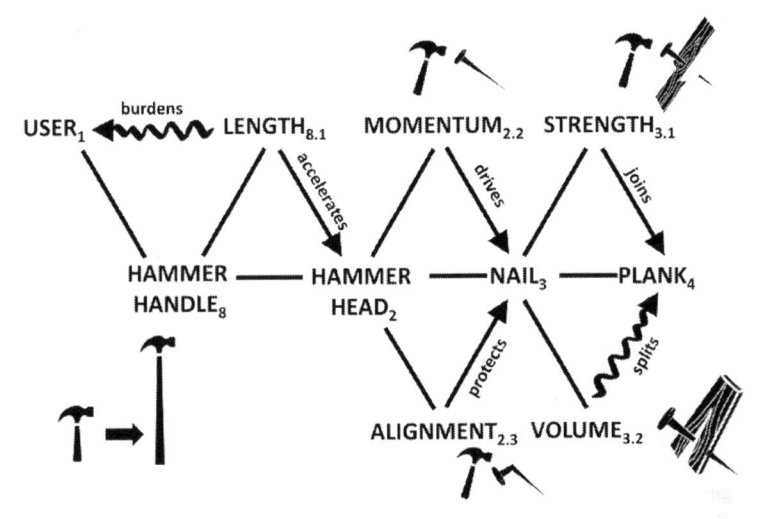

Figure 102: We can modify our Substance Field diagram to include the influence of handle length.

Once more, attempts to resolve a problem are likely to introduce new harms. A hammer with a long handle may very well encumber the user as the mass does, but through a different mechanism. We turn to the Standard Solutions to determine how this new encumbrance could be resolved.

This long handled hammer again presents us with a physical contradiction. The hammer handle must be both long and short. This can be separated in time, where the handle is long when in use, and short when momentum is not required. How might this be achieved?

We accept one of these conditions, and solve for the other. Consider the outcome if we retain the short handle on the hammer. How might this short handled hammer be modified to temporarily act as a long handled hammer? We could transition the system to multiply or copy system elements, illustrated in Figure 103.

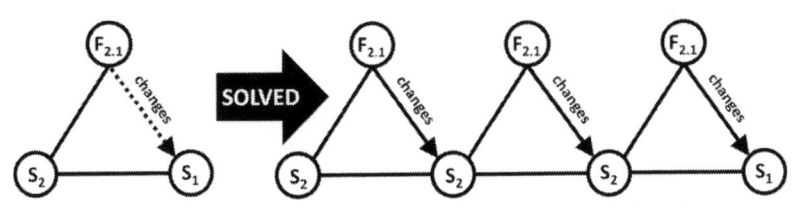

Figure 103: 3.1.1 Use multiple copies of components already present in the system.

A single short handle does not offer the speed required. Might multiple copies of this short handle all acting upon one another offer the speed required? This solution strategy might provoke us to ask *how might segmenting our hammer reduce the burden on the operator?*

A hammer handle constructed from multiple copies of a short handle that changes length over time describes a segmented or retractable handle. This *Segmentation* could allow us to fold the long handle when not in use, but extend the handle when we need more power, as illustrated in Figure 104.

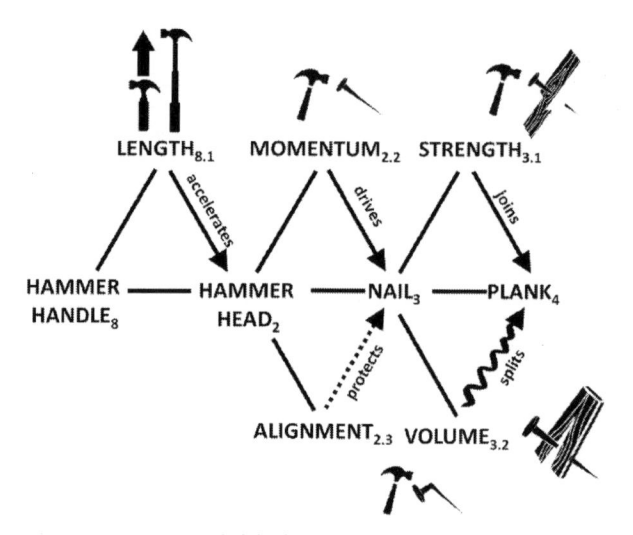

Figure 104: An extendable hammer could be both light and convenient.

Scrutiny of the Substance-Field has provoked solutions that resolve the burden imposed by the hammer, but have diminished other benefits in the system. To focus on deficiencies in only one part of a system may have consequences that harm connected functions. The Substance-Field not only offers a system wide view of the solution, but can also alert us to these new *Benefit Induced Harms*.

For example, a longer hammer handle may offer a less controllable hammer. The harm introduced by inaccuracy in the hammer strike seems likely to increase with a long handle. The hammer alignment required to protect the nails has become insufficient. This inaccuracy may result in more frequently bent nails. Can we resolve this new problem introduced by our new solution?

If nails are more likely to be bent if the handle length increases, the control we currently enjoy represents an insufficiency that introduces the inaccuracy exhibited by the head of the hammer.

These control forces arise from the handle, this addition to the Substance-Field diagram provokes us to ask the question, *how could we better control our hammer?* We need to influence the position, and in particular the alignment, of the hammer head. We can describe this relationship between the hammer handle and head with a further modification of the Substance-Field, illustrated in Figure 105.

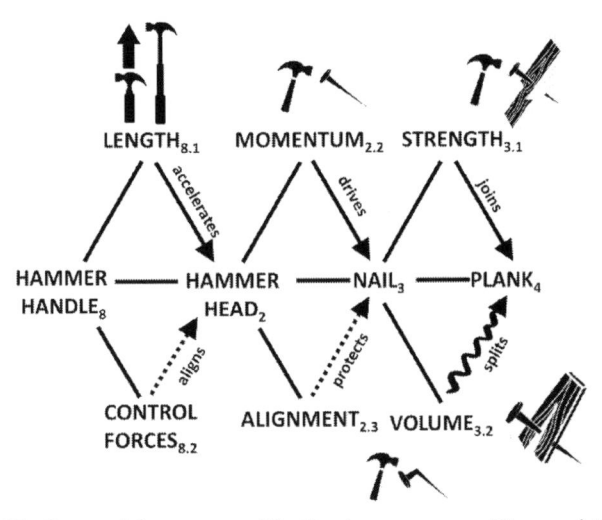

Figure 105: Control forces modify the hammer position, which seeks to improve alignment and protect the nails from bending.

To resolve the Benefit Induced Harm that has arisen from an increase in handle length we must enhance the control forces that direct the hammer. Can we offer an additional field that will enhance these control forces, the Standard Solution for which is illustrated in Figure 106. What field could we add to enhance the forces that draw the hammer squarely onto the nail?

The Substance-Field allows us to search the established solution for an existing resource that could help to raise this field. The nail is precisely in the location to which we wish to draw the hammer head. Could the nail itself offer a contribution to the creation of this additional control field? What could we add to the nail to raise this control field?

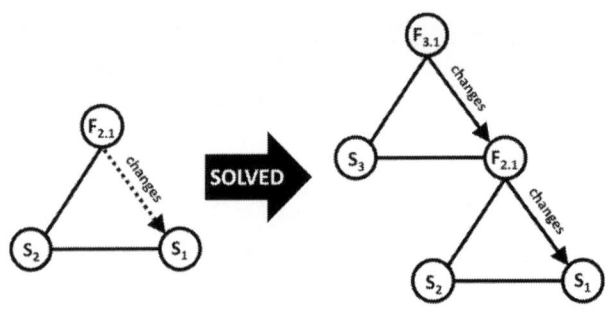

Figure 106: 2.1.2 Create a double field. Use the field of one substance to enhance the field of an insufficient benefit.

Figure 107 illustrates a subsection of our Substance-Field diagram that describes this control mechanism. We add a spring to the system that is held in place by the nail, and this spring raises a field that supplies elastic forces that draws the hammer onto the nail. A peculiar solution, and perhaps an impractical solution, but perfectly valid in the context of a Substance-Field.

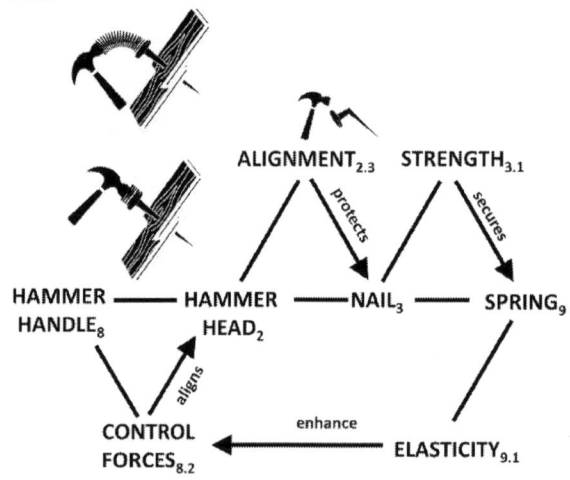

Figure 107: Can the nail draw the hammer onto itself using a spring?

This solution offers an example of how the Substance-Field allows you to experiment with possible solutions that may not necessarily produce a practical outcome but may offer inspiration towards a more ideal solution

Perhaps by attaching a spring between the hammer and the nail one could indeed draw the hammer onto the nail, but it does seem a little impractical. One shouldn't stifle the creative process by discarding such an idea immediately. A novel idea that is half stupid is still half an idea. Half ideas are very valuable. The integration of two half ideas can lead you to a whole idea, so don't discard these odd diversions because you feel foolish. For example, I had no idea that *Impact Spring Hammers* existed until I wrote this paragraph and then searched the Internet for arrangements of hammers and springs that may reflect Figure 107.

It is through the constraint of a formal framework upon a creative process that novelty can arise, and in this example we now encounter a cognitive leap. It is this leap that you are waiting for. It is in these irrational leaps that interesting solutions can be discovered.

We now start to investigate arrangements of hammers and springs to improve our solution. An Impact Spring Hammer is used to test the durability of materials by delivering a precisely controlled force from a precisely directed head. Within an Impact Spring Hammer a compressed spring accelerates a striking element to hit the target. The spring is released by pressing the striking end of the impact hammer against the target, which permits great precision. Not quite the spring drawing the head onto the target illustrated in Figure 107, but an employment of a spring to accurately direct the hammer allows us to make a leap and consider using the spring as the driving force not the control mechanism, illustrated in Figure 108. Now we have the precision we desire, potentially in a small, lightweight package. However, can we generate the power we need to drive a nail through a plank of wood using only a hand operated spring?

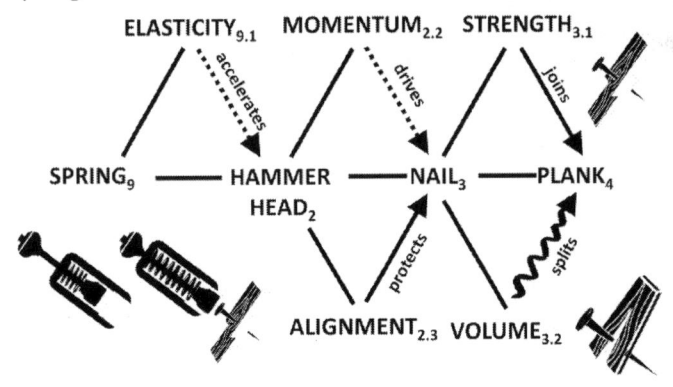

Figure 108: Use the spring to drive the hammer, not aim it. Does the spring offer sufficient power?

Altshuller's Standard Solutions allow us to take this system further by improving the control of both power and accuracy. The 76 Standard Solutions offer strategies for improving control, illustrated in Figure 109.

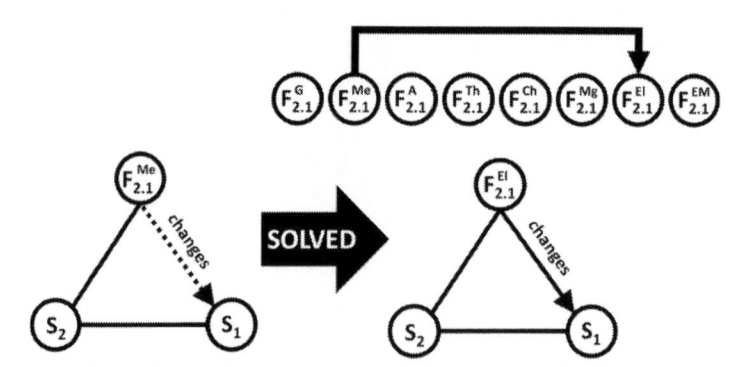

Figure 109. 2.2.1 Replace an uncontrolled or poorly controlled field with an easily controlled field. Escalate the type of field from gravitational, to mechanical, to acoustic, to thermal, to chemical, to magnetic, to electrical, and finally to the most controllable field, the electromagnetic.

The standard solution described by 2.2.1 offers a particularly interesting strategy. Altshuller notes that some fields are more controllable than others. We have little control over the gravitational field, and as a consequence a system controlled by gravity offers the least control. A control mechanism that uses mechanical linkages can offer greater control than a gravity controlled system. If more control than that offered by a mechanical mechanism is required then acoustic or perhaps thermal fields offer a better control mechanism. If control must be greater still, our escalation of field type transitions to a chemical field and then to a magnetic field. Finally, the greatest control can be offered by electrical and electromagnetic fields. This escalation of control mechanism might offer strategies to mitigate the lack of control introduced by the long handle of our hammer. *How could we better control our hammer by escalating the driving field?*

This escalation is echoed by a particular focus upon magnetic fields to improve insufficient fields with solution class 2.4. In particular, we could improve the control and power of our hammer by escalating the driving field using Standard Solutions 2.4.1 and 2.4.11 illustrated in Figures

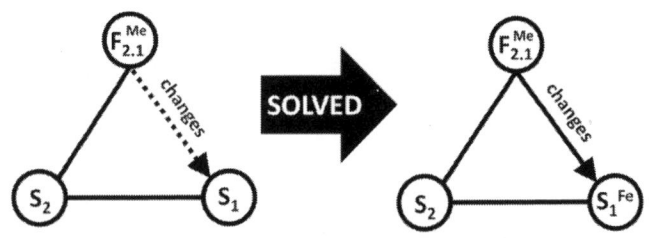

Figure 110: 2.4.1 Use ferromagnetic materials and/or magnetic fields to add functions. Note that the subject acted upon has transformed to exhibit ferrous properties.

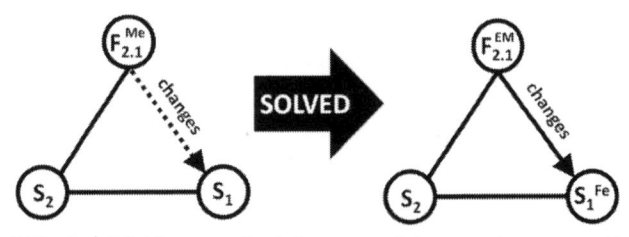

Figure 111: 2.4.11 Use an electric current to create magnetic fields.

If we transform our system driven by a mechanical spring using these standard solutions, we may improve the power and precision of our solution, illustrated in Figure 112. We have invented the convenience of a rapid-fire nail dispensing tool.

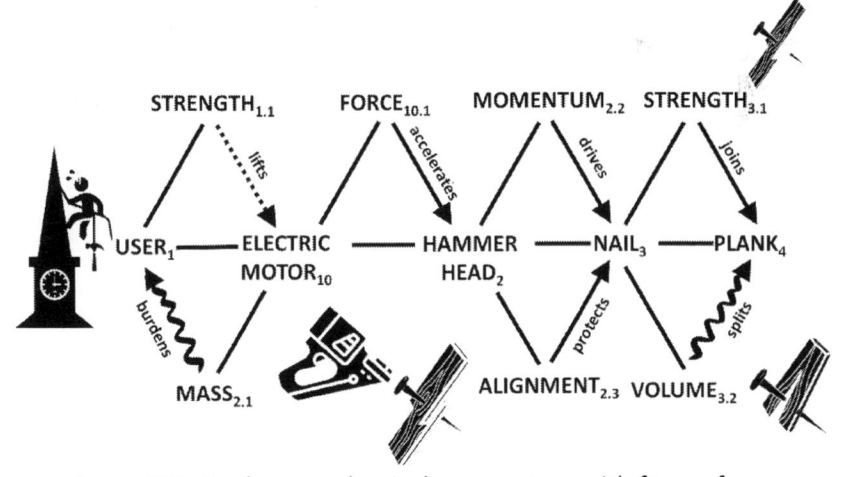

Figure 112: Replace mechanical momentum with forces from magnetic fields

Is this electric nail gun a better solution than the simpler impact spring hammer? Our hammer is certainly more accurate and more powerful, but these new benefits are achieved by reintroducing a harm we had previously removed – the burden upon the operator.

Let's have one last try to create a powerful, lightweight precision hammer to drive nails. Consider Figure 108. If we can use a small spring to create a more controllable hammer, can we retain this form factor whilst employing an alternative motive force to make a more powerful hammer?

We have a suitable system, but we wish to drive this system closer to the Ideal Final Machine. This may provoke us to peruse the Class 5 Standard Solutions, designed specifically to pursue a more ideal outcome. We need a small volume of substance to create a large effect, illustrated in Figure 113.

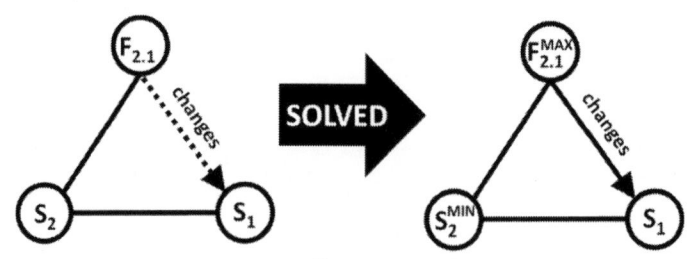

Figure 113: 5.1.1.4 Use a small amount of a very concentrated or active additive.

We have previously escalated our driving field from a mechanical system to an electromagnetically driven mechanism. This escalation results in a bulky, heavy system. If we moderate this escalation, we are led to consider a system controlled with a chemically driven element. Helper functions from Class 5 suggest that a more ideal system could be achieved if this chemically driven system accompanies a change of phase. Consider Standard Solution 5.3.3. Use a phenomenon which accompanies a phase change. *Can our chemical driver transform from a low volume solid that into a high volume gas?* We could further reduce the mass and volume if we discard this element once it has done its useful work, as described by the helper function 5.1.3. Indirectly achieve a function by introducing a substance that disappears after carrying out its work. *A propellant that disappears?*

A very active chemical compound that changes phase from a solid to a gas might offer us the force we need. This solution hints at a solution that already exists. Standard Solution 5.4.2 suggests that from a weak input field we could produce a strong output field. A substance could be pushed to the very edge of transition, then pushed over this boundary using a small input field. These helper functions are driving us towards a *rifle cartridge* that contains a highly active chemical compound to produces a very powerful field by striking a sensitive primer.

The assembly of the above Standard Solutions leads us to the integration of a nail with a rifle cartridge, illustrated in Figure 114.

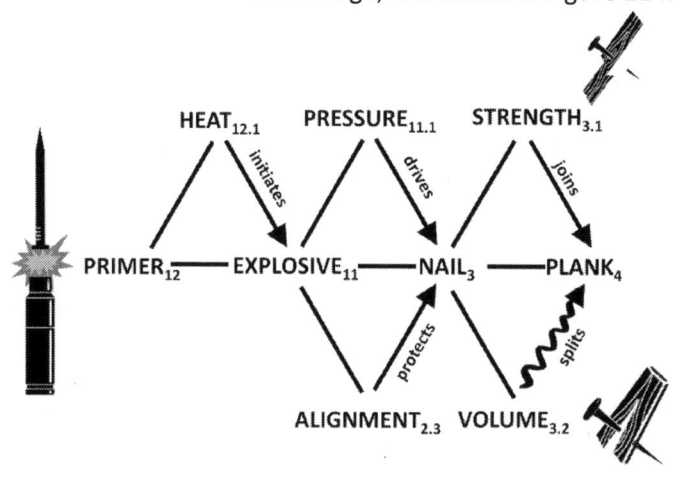

Figure 114: A rifle cartridge could powerfully drive a nail using a small lightweight package.

We have a final harm in our system to resolve before we can rest, satisfied that we have driven the humble hammer as far as we can. Blasting the nail through the plank with an explosive force may still split the wood which we wish to join together. We have previously proposed that a small guide hole could ease the passage of the nail and prevent splitting.

Under these circumstances we have now added another tool to our toolkit. We would require a drill. Standard Solution 3.1.4 suggests that we might improve our system by consolidating our fields into fewer substances. We can simplify our system and remove elements if some components offer more functions. Could the nail drill the hole itself?

DRAGON EGG

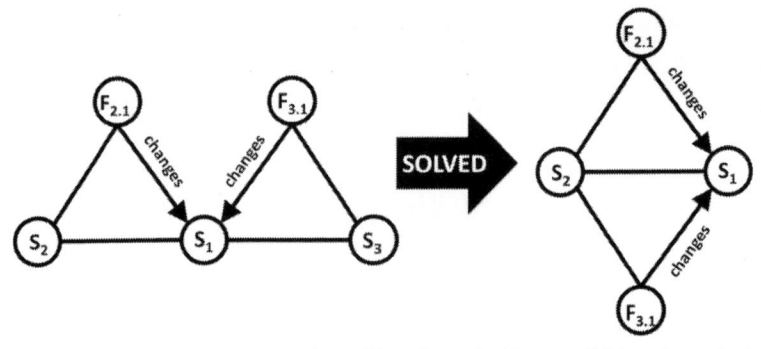

Figure 115: 3.1.4 System simplification. Achieve all functions but reduce/trim components. Integrate several components into one but still deliver all the functions desired. The field offered by Substance 3 is now supplied by Substance 2.

If we incorporate a drill bit into the head of the nail, perhaps there is sufficient power available in the cartridge to also torque this combination of nail and drill, much like rifling spins a bullet. This could drive a narrow guide hole through the wood and prevent splitting. This simple nail now possesses an integrated drill that drives itself into the plank whilst drilling a path for its entry, illustrated in Figure 116. We have invented the self-drilling screw.

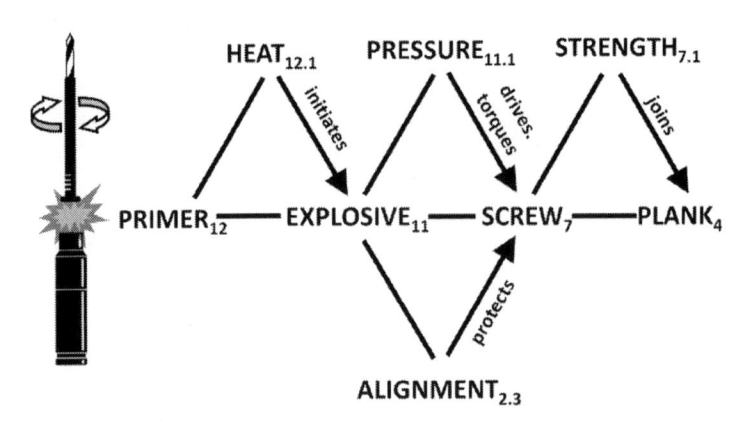

Figure 116: A rifle cartridge could drill a hole and drive a nail through a plank.

Note how many solutions we can create for one simple objective that incorporates only a small number of harms if we use a formal framework to drive our investigation. This ability to create a large catalogue of potential solutions is a feature of Altshuller's work that prevents us from clinging to a single clever idea that we have wrenched from the problem space and must husband into existence. With such a glut of solutions we have no need to be precious about any single idea.

Altshuller's work helps us to solve problems by drawing upon the mountain of prior art created by our engineering forebears. On occasion it is fun and informative to solve a solved problem using Altshuller's frameworks without direct reference to extant solutions. Think of this as practise, with ready answers to refer to. Reinvention of the wheel is not a wasted effort if it offers some experience in employing these problem-solving tools and demonstrates that these tools work.

I was convinced that I was onto something by combining a gun cartridge with a nail to create a small, lightweight and powerful nail driver. I found this *Drill-Nail-Pistol* a far more satisfying idea than the *Water Filled Camping Mallet*. For a minute or two I thought I'd invented a clever and unique solution to a simple problem. However, hold the patent presses. Fortune does not await around the corner. *Powder-Actuated Tools*[77] have been around for some time.

Easy come. Easy go.

---

[77] A type of nail gun used in construction and manufacturing to join materials to hard substrates such as steel and concrete. This technology relies on a controlled explosion created by a small chemical propellant charge, similar to the process that discharges a firearm.

SOLVING THE PROBLEM IN SPACE AND TIME

Thinking widely in space and time to provoke creative solutions to difficult problems is perhaps the most frequently employed tool from Altshuller's repertoire, but is also the simplest. Without careful employment, this next technique can become little more than glorified brainstorming. However, if used correctly, this tool will force one to think expansively about a problem, and can unstick a persistent psychological inertia. Recall our desire to transport cows across a river, illustrated again in Figure 117.

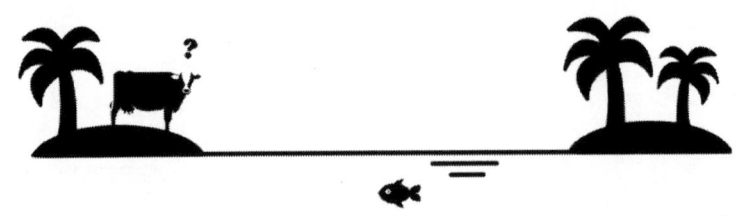

Figure 117: What is the best method to transport cows across a river?

The benefits desired and the harms that may prevent us from reaching these goals are integrated together into Figure 118.

	BEFORE CROSSING	WHILST CROSSING	AFTER CROSSING
SUPER SYSTEM	Easily accessed near bank Trees obstruct loading	Calm waters Good weather Weather overturns boat Cows drown	Easily accessed far hank Trees obstruct unloading
SYSTEM	Cow boards the boat Cows resist embarkation	Cow crosses the river Cows panic	Cow leaves the boat Cows resist disembarkation The boat is recovered
SUB SYSTEM	A mechanism to board cows Boat is big enough to hold a cow Empty boat unstable	The boat is powered The boat floats Boat holed by hoof Water rushes into boat	A mechanism to disembark cows Boat low in the water Unable to disembark cows

Figure 118: The benefits desired and the harms that prevent them.

Before we attempt to derive solutions that may either offer these benefits or block the potential harms, we should consider those resources that may be available in the surrounding environment to help us to resolve the problem. Solutions that make use of elements that already exist in the environment are often elegant. We can once more use the segmentation of the problem in space and time to identify these helpful resources.

Most of the problem and solution discovery techniques presented in this text constrain the demands we make of those solving the problem. We reduce the cognitive demands upon delegates to give them the freedom to focus upon a specific part of the problem space. During problem discovery we reduce this load by separating the assessment of benefits and the identification of harms, and iterate only after we have assembled a useful volume of material.

Similarly, our consideration of potentially useful resources in the problem space should at first be attempted separately from our attempts to generate solutions. For example, Figure 119 illustrates the resources that may be available to support our effort to transport cows from one side of a river to the other.

The most obvious resources in this problem are found in the surrounding environment. Trees on either bank of the river. The sun and the wind. Gravity itself. At the level of system, we obviously have cows and cow hands, plus their particular behaviours and properties. Cows herd and float. Until I assembled Figure 119, it had never occurred to me to ask if cows can swim?

The purpose of reviewing the resources in the problem space is to discover new and elegant solutions. If you only seek resources that support specific potential solutions you will constrain your search to only those resources that support solutions that you have already discovered. This is the reverse of the outcome we desire.

Of course cows can swim. Apparently, they swim well. I had just never had a reason to ask if cows can swim, so I had to look it up. If you feel dumb asking a question, then ask it quietly, write down the answer and offer this to others with authority. Certainly, don't mention your ignorance of cow capabilities when authoring a book.

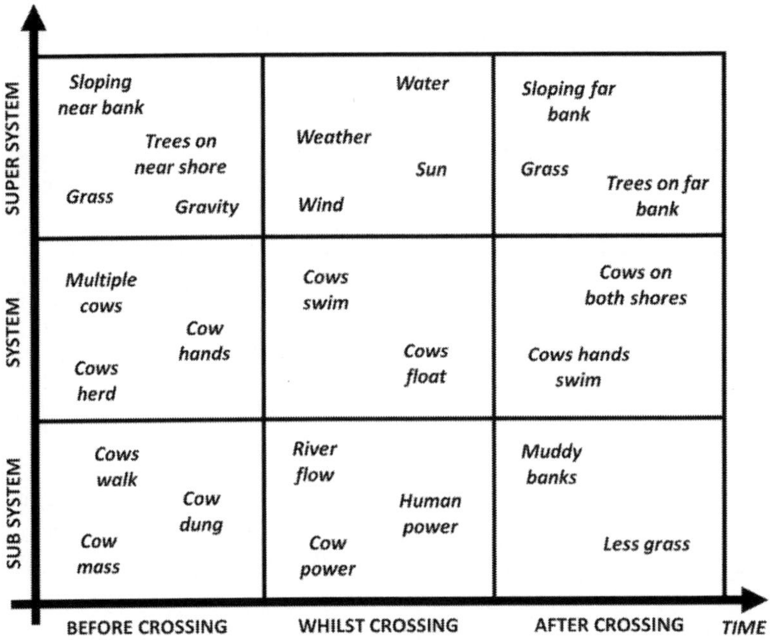

	BEFORE CROSSING	WHILST CROSSING	AFTER CROSSING
SUPER SYSTEM	Sloping near bank; Trees on near shore; Grass; Gravity	Water; Weather; Sun; Wind	Sloping far bank; Grass; Trees on far bank
SYSTEM	Multiple cows; Cow hands; Cows herd	Cows swim; Cows float	Cows on both shores; Cows hands swim
SUB SYSTEM	Cows walk; Cow dung; Cow mass	River flow; Human power; Cow power	Muddy banks; Less grass

Figure 119: Discovering useful resources in the problem space may lead to novel solutions.

It is easy to discover useful resources in the environment and in the system. In fact, consideration of the wider environment can consume all of our attention. Dividing the problem in scale isolates the opportunity to also focus upon resources that can be found in the behaviour and characteristics of those sub systems of each component.

First consider only the cows. Obviously, cows can move themselves around, which will come in handy. They also weigh approximately a ton. This mass may constitute a harm to whatever mechanism we devise to transport cows across the river. Could this mass offer a benefit? Cows also can become less heavy over time, as they produce dung. We have searched for energy sources in the environment, such as wind and solar power. Might the cows themselves offer some source of energy to drive our mechanism?

We roll forwards in time and descend into the subsystems encountered as the river is crossed. Cows or humans could power this mechanism. Until all of the component subsystems were considered it had not occurred to me that the flow of the river itself could be harnessed to drive our mechanism. This source of power could have been encountered when considering the wider environment, but I found it when considering the sub components of the river itself. It does not matter how you discover advantage, just as long as you discover it. This consideration of time and scale offers multiple opportunities to stumble over a useful resource.

Finally, we have cows and cow hands on both banks of the river, and those river banks are likely to become quite churned with mud during this operation. I doubt that this mud will offer a beneficial resource. However, consideration of resources can also drive one to discover potential harms that emerge as the scenario unfolds. Leave this mud on the list of resources, or transfer it to your assessment of harms. Or both. You choose.

We have now used this segmentation in time and scale to describe what we want, to predict what may prevent us from achieving our goals and to list the resources that may help us in our effort to provide a solution. We are now ready to employ this framework for a fourth time, to brainstorm solutions.

Of course, we are not employing pure, unconstrained brainstorming, as we now have many constraints upon our thinking to focus our creativity. The nine segments in this framework force us to focus upon only part of the time and scale of the solution space. The problem is well described as we can refer to a clear list of benefits that we wish to achieve. The obstacles we must overcome are clearly indicated. The resources at our disposal are listed. With so much material at our disposal, offering multiple solutions can become easy. Some possibilities are illustrated in Figure 120.

	BEFORE CROSSING	WHILST CROSSING	AFTER CROSSING
SUPER SYSTEM	Trees provide building materials A loading ramp Grass keeps cows occupied	Sail pushes raft across river Water wheel pulls raft	Attach pulley to far shore tree
SYSTEM	Cows attract cows onto raft	Rope pulls raft across river	Cows attract cows off raft
SUB SYSTEM	Loading ramp prevents mud	Human pulls raft Cows pulls raft Water plus dung. Steam engine	Rope recovers raft

Figure 120: Many solutions exist to transport those cows across this river.

Figure 120 describes a raft constructed from the trees found growing near the river. The raft could be pulled across the river by ropes attached to the remaining trees along the riverbank. We want a loading ramp to mitigate any difference in height between this raft and the riverbank. This loading ramp could offer multiple functions, as the ramp could protect the shoreline from becoming muddied. Perhaps the herding nature of cows could attract them onto and off this raft? A number of energy sources are available to draw upon this rope. The cow hands could pull upon this rope themselves. Alternatively, we have plenty of power available in the cows themselves to pull the raft across the river, illustrated in Figure 121.

Figure 121: Cows could perform *self-service* to cross the river.

If this power source is elevated to the environment, we could blow the raft across the river using the wind, or use a power drawn from the flow of the rover itself, illustrated in Figure 122.

Figure 122: The environment could offer motive power.

Finally, perhaps an unexpected solution derived from this consideration of time and scale is the possibility that the cows themselves could fuel a steam engine, as illustrated in Figure 123. Is there enough energy in cow dung to transform into power that can draw a cow across a river? I leave this calculation as an exercise for the reader.

Figure 123: Could the cows provide power to run a steam engine?

THE IDEAL MACHINE.

'Sometimes nothin' can be a real cool hand.'
- *Cool Hand Luke, 1967*

The temptation to launch immediately into solution generation can be strong. If we don't have a clear understanding of the problem and know little of the direction in which to look for a solution, we are likely to foray out into a jungle of possibilities. The objective of this text is to demonstrate the importance of carefully planning a problem-solving campaign, and to demonstrate how quickly and easily a comprehensive plan can be assembled. The objective of this text is to demonstrate that one should embark upon a journey of solution discovery only once the problem description is pregnant with many possible solutions.

If there is a singular overarching philosophy to the discovery of elegant solutions it can be found in the definition of the *Ideal Outcome*. If the Ideal Outcome is, by definition, that outcome that delivers every benefit desired without exhibiting any harms whatsoever, then the *Ideal Machine* is that device or mechanism that can deliver all of the benefits desired without provoking any associated harms.

From a practical perspective one might expect the Ideal Machine to be an impossible aspiration. Any machine, no matter how elegant in its artifice, must introduce some harm to the customer. Even if the machine imposes a cost for ownership, or consumes some undesirable mass or volume, a cost will be imposed upon the customer.

The Ideal Machine need not be a hypothetical and an unattainable theoretical goal. Note in our efforts to separate the contradictions within the problem how often we turn to the environment to provide solutions. In one example we attempt to deliver a large payload at speed to high altitude and long range in a fuel-efficient manner. To achieve this, we turn to high flying solar gliders, we consider lighter than air vehicles that support large payloads using the buoyancy of the atmosphere, or employ dynamic forces using wings to loft large payloads at high speeds. Similarly, we support very large payloads with the ground or the sea. We turn to wind power to blow air, land and marine vehicles around the globe. Alternatively, we artificially modify the environment around our vehicle to blow our payload through evacuated tunnels. We fling vehicles into a high orbit to exploit centrifugal forces and a lack of atmospheric drag to enable very long range and high-speed transport. In every case we turn to the environment, or modify the super system in which our vehicle operates, to offer some useful function.

Consider our efforts to build a better hammer. In this exercise we trim away extraneous objects whilst retaining all of the benefits we desire with multi-functional components. Note that to retain this functionality with fewer components we again appeal to the environment or to the super system to provide the functions that we desire. A crane lifts a hammer. The building under repair becomes part of a crane. The wider environment itself lifts the hammer by exploiting the buoyancy of a balloon. Functions of the hammer itself are drawn from the environment. A hammer is filled with water from a nearby river to provide sufficient mass to drive in a tent peg.

In our efforts to transport cows across a river frequent appeals are made to the environment for support. We could have smuggled a petroleum powered outboard motor into the problem space to provide motive power to our raft. Alternatively, we considered wind or river power to drive our mechanism, or scavenged energy from material expelled by the cows themselves.

This elevation of functions up to higher spatial scales and potentially all the way up to the environment is a frequent strategy in the drive towards the Ideal Machine. The more functions that can be elevated up to the environment, the fewer are delivered by our mechanism. The fewer functions that our solution mechanism must fulfil, the fewer harms are likely to accompany our solution.

It may be possible to elevate *all* of our desired functions up to the surrounding super system or to the wider environment. Once we have recruited the environment to serve all of our functions, our solution mechanism should no longer exist. If the Ideal Machine delivers all of the functions that we desire whilst provoking no harms, then elevating all of our desires up to the super system or the environment should provide the Ideal Machine. The Ideal Machine is no hypothetical, impractical, unattainable fantasy. The Ideal Machine is delivered by the environment.

If you can solve the problem without building anything, then you have constructed the Idea Machine.

The Ideal Machine is *no machine, at all.*

SOLVE THE PROBLEM BY PREDICTING THE FUTURE

We can avoid the complex task of solving a difficult problem if we merely travel into the future and observe the mechanism that eventually solved the problem. A time machine would certainly make the task of problem solving far more convenient. If we could invent a time machine, then all subsequent acts of invention become trivial acts of tourism. How could this technological marvel be achieved?

Altshuller's analysis of the patent database scrutinised a vast number of problems and their associated solutions. This exercise detected similarities in the solutions contained in the database and collated the most common and most successful strategies available to the problem solver. There is more than one way to slice this cake.

Alternatively, one can compare successive attempts to solve the *same* problem. Old attempts to solve problems could be contrasted with the solutions that superseded these earlier attempts. The mechanism that improved solutions to the same problem could be identified to determine how these solutions evolve over time. As solution mechanisms evolve, repeating patterns can be observed. This method of analysis allowed Altshuller to summarise the essential features one is likely to observe in the evolution of a solution, which in turn may permit predictions on how a solution may evolve into the future.

This evolution of solutions allowed Altshuller to make nine predictions about the transformation of technologies as they evolve. Two of these predictions we have already encountered in this text. The others should be familiar to the reader, as they typically match one's expectations, as a good solution framework should. We will review each technological evolution identified by Altshuller in turn, and describe how this evolution might manifest in the development of our new and improved hammer described throughout this text. To address this case study, the fundamental question we ask is *how might our hammer evolve to improve its performance?*

1. Systems become more complete

Altshuller recognised that solutions tend to become more complete as they evolve. At first, a solution may offer only the primary function demanded of it. The environment within which this early iteration operates will supply the auxiliary inputs required to make the solution function as desired.

Consider our hammer. In its first evolution, once supplied with energy the hammer only offers the momentum required to drive nails into wood. The energy required to drive nails is supplied by a component outside the hammer. The first evolution of our hammer relies upon the operator to supply the energy required to drive a nail through wood. This energy is delivered to the hammer via the handle gripped by the operator. Similarly, the control required to guide the hammer onto the nail is also supplied by an external agent. Again, the operator guides the hammer head using the hammer handle as it flies through the air to eventually strike the nail. The detection of the nail by eye is also offered by the operator, to allow these control forces to be determined and delivered via the handle.

Altshuller's observation suggests that systems become increasingly complete as they evolve. The operating part of the system that delivers the required function will ultimately be joined by a self-contained store of energy required to achieve this function. Energy in this context not only refers the motive power, but also to the information required to carry out the function. Consequently, a function will evolve to adopt its own internal energy and information stores, a means to distribute this energy and information amongst its own components, and a means to control that energy and therefore its own operation.

The evolved hammer in our case study ultimately no longer has to rely upon the operator to supply it with energy. The final version stores its own motive power as a chemical explosive that can drive a nail through wood. Consequently, as the hammer evolves it becomes more complete.

We could save ourselves the complex task of solving a difficult problem if we merely travel into the future and observe the mechanism that will eventually solve the problem. We can predict a future evolution of our hammer by answering the following questions. *How could the system possess its own energy or information store? How could the system distribute this energy or information amongst its own components? How could the system control its own operation?*

2. Systems get better at conducting energy.

The second technical evolution that is typically observed as solutions improve is related to the first, and involves the flow of energy or information through the system,

As solutions evolve, they not only lose their reliance upon the wider environment and incorporate new energy or information flows into the system. Solutions also evolve to become more conductive to that energy or information flow. As a solution evolves, it becomes better at distributing the flow of energy or information to each functioning part of the system.

Consider the need to control the hammer head as it moves to strike the nail. The first incarnation of our hammer requires the operator to manually detect the nail and guide the hammer head onto the target by hand. Once better evolved, this control becomes unnecessary, as the hammer's own starting position informs the hammer head precisely where to strike. Information flows from the target against which the body of the chemical powered hammer is placed, to the hammer head through the body of the powder actuated tool. Motive power from the chemistry is well connected to the hammer head as the pressure drives the head back towards the nail.

We could determine a better solution to a problem by using this transformation to predict future evolutions. We could achieve this by answering the following question. *How could energy or information flow more easily through each functioning part of the system?*

3. Coordination between functions improves.

A system may get better at transmitting energy or information as it evolves, but that transmission of energy or information must be coordinated to achieve a specific end. An effective solution may incorporate a number of sub systems that must work together to achieve a desirable goal. In the early incarnation of a solution, the system components may act in a poorly coordinated manner. Outputs from one component may not be delivered in good time to those other parts of the system that they feed. Alternatively, coordination may be made in good time, but in undesirable quantities.

Our first iteration of our hammer exhibits precisely this problem, which was originally described as a harm but subsequently recast as an insufficient control over the accuracy of the hammer blow. Poor coordination between the motive force that drives the hammer handle and the control forces from the handle to the hammer head leads to poor coordination between the hammer head and the nail itself, which bends the nail. Evolution of the hammer design specifically sought to improve this coordination between components. The evolution improved the coordination and integration of subsystems. The operator must no longer direct the hammer as it descends upon the nail. The body of the hammer is coordinated with the nail, and the body guides the hammer head onto the nail as it is propelled towards the target. The hammer itself controls the head as it strikes the nail.

We could predict a better evolved version of an incumbent solution by answering the following question. *How could the components of a system be better coordinated so that they work together more effectively?*

4. A system will become more ideal.

The fourth method by which systems may typically evolve we have already encountered in this text. As a solution evolves and improves its operation, by definition the system becomes more ideal. The benefits that a system offers will increase in performance or increase in number, whilst costs and harms will reduce. The ultimate outcome of this evolution towards the ideal is a system that exhibits only benefits, with all costs and harms trimmed from the solution. Consequently, this evolution may end when all functions have been elevated to the super system, or to the environment itself.

Our new and improved hammer transforms from a heavy, unwieldy tool with a potential to bend nails, into a powerful lightweight package sufficiently accurate to never bend nails. Benefits have increased whilst harms have diminished. The hammer becomes more ideal.

To evolve our system into a more ideal state, and to therefore predict the future, we should answer the following questions. *How can we increase the benefits delivered by this system? How can we decrease the harms and the costs?*

5. Uneven development of system components

Altshuller's fifth system evolution is of particular interest, as it is not only a subtle observation, but this observation offers considerable scope for identifying opportunities to evolve a solution in fruitful and surprising ways.

Altshuller noted that the subsystems of a solution do not necessarily all evolve at the same rate. Some parts of a solution may enjoy considerable scrutiny and development, whilst others remain undeveloped. This non-uniform evolution may be borne by a system for some time. However, eventually subsystems may evolve so far apart that contradictions arise between system components.

Consider the development process of our hammer designed to pound nails into wood. Which components of the system evolved the slowest, and did that lack of development introduce contradictions into the system?

A great deal of scrutiny is placed upon the driving force and the control mechanism of the hammer head, which ultimately trims the long handle from the system altogether, which results in a more ideal system. The *last* component to receive any attention is the nail itself.

Although the hammer transforms into a powerful, lightweight and accurate means to drive a nail into wood, the nail does not transform at all until the end of the process. The nail remains a straight shank of iron with a flat head and a sharp point, perhaps little different from those employed hundreds of years previously. As a consequence, the potential for the nail to split the wood remains, despite the evolution of the hammer.

No matter how small and how powerful we evolve the hammer, this potential harm will remain. The nail may split the wood as it is driven home. Perhaps the more powerful our evolved hammer, the more likely this nail may split the wood. This results in a technical contradiction. The hammer must become more powerful, but must not split the wood. This contradiction that arises from this uneven evolution of system components is resolved by eventually evolving the nail into a device that could drill its own small guide hole and prevent splitting.

We could offer a more evolved version of a system with the following questions. *Are all of the components of this system of the same maturity? Do some components outperform others? Which parts of the system must improve in performance to permit an overall increase in performance?*

6. Become a super system or transition to the super system.

The next technical evolution that Altshuller observed can be described in two stages. The first describes the interaction of system components, the second describes how you might regard these interacting components.

As a system evolves those subsystems within the solution that compete for resources, such as the overall mass, volume or power budget, will integrate together to better share these resources. Those subsystems that offer opposite functions may merge together to share resources. Functions that are complementary will merge into a single component. This third evolution is repeated by Standard Solution 3.1.4, illustrated in Figure 124

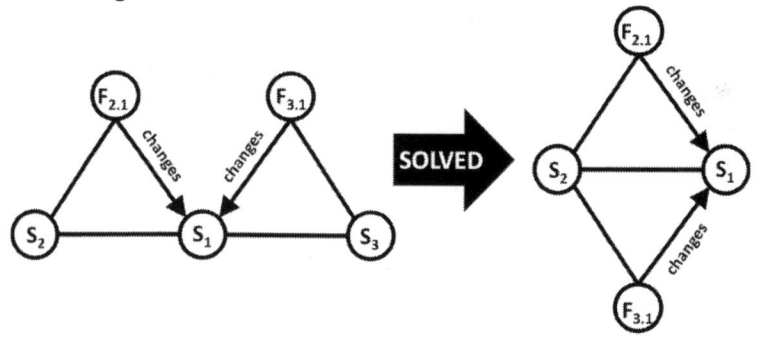

Figure 124: 3.1.4 System simplification. Achieve all functions but reduce or trim components. Integrate several components into one but still deliver all the functions desired. The field offered by Substance 3 is now supplied by Substance 2.

Functions that complement one another may at first be offered by their own specialist sub systems, but ultimately evolve to be delivered by the same component. The transformation of telephone and entertainment illustrated in Figure 92 offer an example of this evolution. At first separate electronic components may offer the functions of a telephone, a radio and a media player. Ultimately the system evolves to offer all functions using the same multipurpose processor.

This evolution describes a solution that begins life offering a single function, described as a mono-system. This solution may evolve to offer two functions, to become a bi-system. This evolution continues until the solution offers multiple functions, to become a poly-system. This evolution leads to the second manner in which this evolution may be treated.

Once subsystems have become sufficiently integrated the poly-system is then able to support multiple functions. As a consequence, the system becomes a supersystem to which additional functions can be elevated. The transition from mono-systems to bi-systems to poly-systems either elevates the required functions to the supersystem, or becomes a supersystem in its own right.

Consider opposite or complementary functions offered by a hammer. The hammer must drive nails into wood. However, we may also wish to draw nails from the wood, to remove the component fixing planks together. If each function is offered by a specialist tool, these tools compete for space in our tool box.

Consider the claw on the head of many hammers that offers the reverse function to hammering in nails. This claw offers the reverse function to the hammer head whilst sharing the hammer handle with its opposite counterpart, illustrated in Figure 125.

Figure 125: Hammer and 'Reverse-hammer' share the same handle.

This clawed hammer therefore transforms from two separate tools into a bi-tool. This evolution could continue, to transform the hammer into a multi-tool, to ultimately transform into a super system into which additional functions may be incorporated, illustrated in Figure 126.

Figure 126: Hammer-axe-spanner- crowbar-torch-saw. Poly-systems become super systems into which new functions can be incorporated. What new function could we add to this multi-tool?

We could predict a better evolved version of our solution by answering the following questions. *Can competing components integrate? Can complementary functions share components? Can opposite functions combine? Are functional improvements limited by the system? Does this integration create a supersystem? Can new functions be added to this super system? Can functions elevate to the environment?*

6a. Dynamization

The next technical evolution is a later addition, described as a subset of the sixth. Altshuller recognised that as solutions evolve into improved systems an increased ability to change parameters in time is observed. Functions become dynamic.

For example, a single, solid, monolithic system may improve its operation by incorporating a flexible joint. If a single joint offers an improvement then perhaps multiple joints offer further improvement? These joints multiply until the solution is offered by a fully flexible system. This increase in dynamic properties can be offered by an escalation in the sophistication of the field. The ultimate expression of this increase in joints may be the delivery of functions using thermal or chemical effect, to ultimately end with functions delivered by electrical or electrometric fields.

Consider the evolution of our new and improved hammer. The system begins its development as a monolithic device where functions are fixed firmly together. The handle of the hammer is fixed firmly to the hammer head. As the hammer evolves, functions begin to move relative to one another. The handle transforms into a tube that contains the chemical explosion and guides the hammer head as it travels towards the nail.

The nail begins its evolution as a monolithic object that is forced through the wood in a single motion. As the nail evolves it exhibits more than one motion. The nail not only moves forwards, but also rotates to drive the new drill bit integrated into the point of the nail.

We can improve our solution by predicting how it may evolve. We could achieve this by answering the following questions. *Would allowing component parts to move relative to one another improve the system? Would more degrees of freedom result in greater benefits? Would allowing fixed parameters to vary in time improve benefits or remove harms?*

7. Transition to the micro level

The seventh technical evolution identified by Altshuller involves the shrinking of system components and the segmentation of the system into smaller, separate parts.

One might be motivated to treat this segmentation as the reverse of the integration described in the sixth evolution. However, one should consider a subtle difference. The sixth evolution integrates complementary or opposite functions to deliver these disparate functions with the same components. The segmentation described by this seventh evolution breaks the system into multiple copies of the same function. This evolution continues until the function is delivered by copies that exhibit micro scales, such as granules and powders. The ultimate expression of a function offered by small scale components might employ an electrical or electromagnetic field.

The evolution of our new and improved hammer hopes to improve benefits by reducing the burden upon the operator. Consequently, by definition, subsystems will shrink in size and may require delivery by alternative mechanisms.

The long handle of the first iteration of our hammer shrinks so much that it is trimmed from the system altogether. The head of the hammer shrinks in size as the momentum required to drive this head is supplied not by the mass but by explosive powders and pneumatic expansion that increase the velocity of the hammer's head.

To predict how our current solution may evolve, we could answer the following questions. *Would segmenting components offer greater benefits or diminish harms? Could system components shrink in size? Could components shrink to the micro level?*

8. Increase the sophistication of the Substance Field

In this text we have previously encountered the evolution of solutions through the escalation of the Substance-Field to offer more complex fields. This solution is offered by Standard Solution 2.2.1, illustrated in Figure 127.

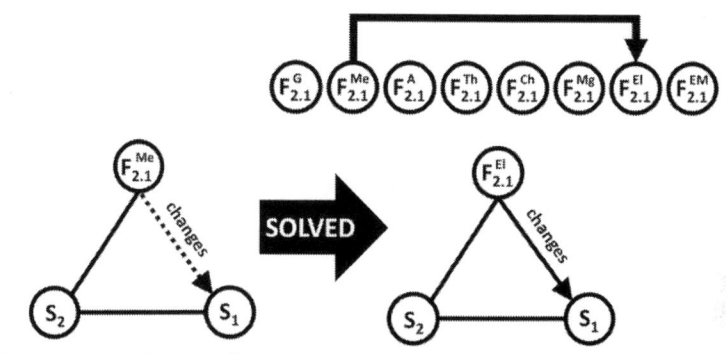

Figure 127. 2.2.1 Replace an uncontrolled or poorly controlled field with an easily controlled field. Escalate the type of field from gravitational, to mechanical, to acoustic, to thermal, to chemical, to magnetic, to electrical, and finally to the most controllable field, the electromagnetic.

The field that offers the desired functions will evolve in subsequent iterations into a more complex form. Gravitational fields are subsequently served by mechanical fields. Mechanical fields are supplanted by acoustic fields, which may then be replaced by thermal fields. Thermal fields give way to chemical fields which are ultimately replaced by electrical or electromagnetic effects.

Consider the development of our hammer. The momentum that drives the nail into the wood is offered by a simple mechanical action that amplifies the power offered by the operator through the length of the handle, and delivers this power into the mass of the hammer's head. This simple mechanism is replaced by an alternative mechanical force offered by a spring. The spring was unlikely to offer the power we require, so these mechanical options are replaced by a chemical field that can offer explosive power.

The technical trend offered by Altshuller suggests that a function offered by a chemical field might escalate to an electromagnetic force. However, when we employ these technical evolutions we must remember that contemporary technologies may not yet offer the evolved function desired. In this case study, as mass and volume are primary drivers to our design, the practical instantiation of the chemical power source is currently lighter and smaller compared to an electromagnetic motor one may find in a contemporary nail gun.

This observation directs us to the fundamental power behind the evolutionary trends that Altshuller identified. The current solution is dependent upon the current state of our technology. The technical evolutions identified by Altshuller allows us to travel into the future and observe the future form of the functions desired. We can use this observation to not only skip over intermediate steps but also to propose hypothetical future technologies and direct our laboratory towards a novel research effort.

The best contemporary solution to drive a nail into wood using the smallest and most powerful mechanism that we can may currently be offered by a chemical explosive. This chemical explosive may introduce harms of its own, from toxic gasses, the carriage of dangerous substances, or even a loud report. The evolution of this solution is likely to transition to a system that drives the nail with electromagnetic forces. A nail driven by an electric motor already exhibits this property. Can we do better?

What research is required to offer an electromagnetic driving force at a mass and scale offered by the chemically explosive option? One might propose a further shrinking of the hammer head to zero, with the ferrous nail itself driven through the wood by electromagnetic forces alone. What technical development must we embark upon to evolve our hammer into a powerful, lightweight electric coil gun, illustrated in Figure 128.

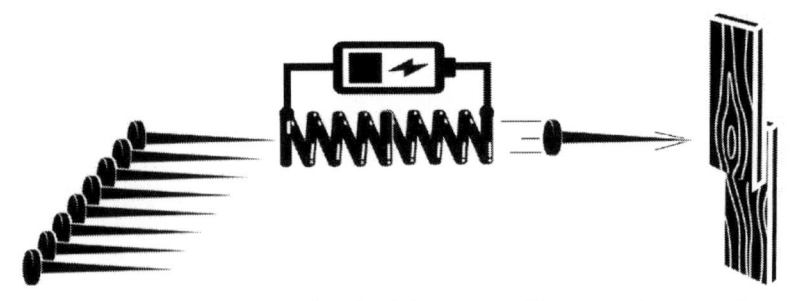

Figure 128: A question for the laboratory. How much power is required to electromagnetically drive a nail through wood?

A WARNING

With solution methods described and demonstrated, we now turn to a warning. This is a warning so significant that it deserves its own section as it can transform one's entire approach to the innovative design of new concepts and the solution to difficult problems. This is important.

Chapter 6 offers strategies that will allow the question under scrutiny to be well formed. Chapter 10 offers strategies that may allow us to formulate a solution. Once we have exercised the techniques described, have we solved the problem? Unfortunately, no. Not at all.

The solutions described above, be they modified hammers, the means to transport a cow across a river or even an enormous space elevator are used to illustrate the techniques that form the focus of this book. However, these solutions can only ever be treated as strategies with which the problem might be solved should the physical limits of a practical instantiation permit. Before we can suggest that these strategies constitute a valid solution to the problem, we must face reality itself.

At the genesis of a new idea, it may only be supported by a rhetorical device, perhaps derived from the techniques described in this book. In these early days, such solution strategies may not be supported by any evidence derived from the physical reality of practically creating this solution.

Consider Figure 56. In this example the rhetorical device of our solution framework suggests that an evacuated tube might permit a rail car to travel at high speed. Can we treat this strategy as a solution to the problem? Consider for a moment how much energy it might require to evacuate several hundred kilometres of tube. Calculate the thickness of tube required to resist this pressure. Count the number of pressure seals that may be present along a track that spans hundreds of kilometres, and how frequently these seals may fail. Imagine the consequences of a tube rupture, in which a wall of supersonic air will blast down the tube to encounter a rail car in a terminal confrontation of shattered steel, glass and plastic. The solution strategy illustrated in Figure 56 does not solve the problem, it asks a question. Can we safely build and operate an evacuated tube down which a rail car might move at high speed?

Consider Figure 64, in which we rotate our rail line to point to the sky, and propose a space elevator. Have we solved the problem? Or have we asked a question? The ribbon up which the cars must ascend must be

35,786 kilometres long. What material would offer sufficient strength to adopt this function? Is this even physically possible? Consider the rock from which this enormous ribbon must be suspended. How much must this rock weigh? From where will this rock be sourced? What will it cost in time, energy and money to gather this rock from the solar system and place it in the desired orbit?

The proper measure of an idea's value is not its ability to attract investors, marketing campaigns and awards. These baubles represent nothing if a little scientific rigor can demonstrate that the idea is utter nonsense. If one aspires to innovate and engage in the very genesis of design ideas, one must learn and apply a most important lesson. Once you are flushed with success, and believe that you have indeed solved a problem, the very next thought to pass through your mind should form along the following lines.

These ideas are not solutions.
These ideas are <u>questions</u>.

Treat this as a mantra. Stick it to the wall, to remind yourself every day that a rhetorical argument that proposes a possible solution strategy is not a solution. It's never a solution. It's a question. When engaged in the discovery of new problems and new solutions, a good design idea is a list of good questions. If you have not yet spent much money, a good idea can only be a list of questions. A valid solution will demand proof, and proof demands numbers. The rigor of numbers costs money because laboratories, scientists and experiments cost money.

This means that if you aspire to innovate, you must deliver your ideas to the laboratory or to the library for scrutiny. The laboratory is the very place in which your reputation may be saved. If a room full of technical experts suggest that you go no further with the idea, they may very well prevent you from making an utter fool of yourself.

This is the pact between the innovator and those laboratories full of scientists, technical experts or specialists in the field that you are investigating. Those who aspire to innovate must be willing to make fools of themselves. They must be willing to ask the stupid questions. To step outside the box. To look in from outside the box and query those long-established truths that may form the foundation of a psychological inertia that separates a problem from a solution. To dive from that cliff of certainties and plunge into a crashing ocean of unknowns and possibilities.

In return for the self-sacrifice of one's credibility, the specialists are there to rescue you. Once you begin to drown, they'll wade into the surf and drag you out. If you do return from your fishing trip with some small treasure dragged from the depths, then you've all won.

The far more likely outcome is that you will be dragged from that ocean empty handed, embarrassed but still alive. If you are thinking far outside the box a little scientific rigour will often demonstrate that your idea is bogus. If so, you should be thankful to those specialists, for they have probably saved you a vast sum of money, your reputation and a decade of your life trying to make something work that a simple experiment might demonstrate had no hope of ever succeeding.

If you are innovating well you are generating ideas and posing questions that for most of your career will act as target practise for a laboratory or a library full of specialists. Design is an iterative process. Entrepreneurship should contain a build-measure-learn cycle in which business ideas are constructed, experimented upon, and modified. However, before you start burning money building anything, the genesis of a new idea must also traverse this iteration. Start this cycle small. Find a sceptical specialist, some paper, and a pencil. If you get past this first scrutiny, do a small experiment, then from this seed grow the physical evidence that will support your rhetorical argument.

The value of an idea is not drawn from passion for a project or a belief in the team or fancy graphics or the quantity of money that it can attract, or even the strength of a rhetorical argument. Value is drawn from evidence. Cold, hard evidence. This is why the concept design techniques that are described in this text are simple, fast, and produce a volume of ideas that are mostly disposable. A good innovation process will create hundreds of questions, and if you don't have the technical expertise to answer them all, you must cast your ideas into the laboratory and hopefully others can offer an argument to convince you that an idea is indeed viable.

Usually, it is not. This is the sad truth of innovation. The generation and test of ideas in volume will result in an extremely low success rate. If only one in ten of your ideas are getting a positive response, then you're doing well. However, this iteration is not simply a high-volume trial and error process. After all, each question imposes a financial liability, as each question will cost money to answer. The job of innovation is to ask the *right* questions. To employ that laboratory as efficiently as possible. Despite one's best efforts to offer the most succinct and most focussed questions, a 10% success rate is to be expected and appreciated.

If you're achieving a much higher success rate then perhaps you should step a little further outside that box. The specialists are the safety net. They are there so that you can have the crazy ideas, and to keep having the crazy ideas without the ignominy of burning other people's money. Unless you are a billionaire, it's likely that you'll only get to do that once.

Do this enough, and one day you might ask the right question. If the specialists return with a positive result, you might be in business. So, if you have an enthusiasm for innovative exploration and you feel that you may have solved the problem, always remember the following simple truth.

Your ideas are not solutions.
Your ideas are questions.

11. CASE STUDY: SOLVING THE PROBLEM.

The Soldier landed with a thump on the wide shoulders of the dragon as it sped by the tower, and tumbled head over heels down the creature as he attempted to gain some purchase from the huge scales that tiled the long coil of creature[78]. Jamming the edge of the shield into a crevice between two scales arrested his fall, and the Soldier came to a stop clinging to the creature's knotted and rippling back[79].

The thick, iron-like scales of a Dragon's back are its greatest protection, but now they served to protect the Soldier from discovery as their considerable thickness deadened any clue to the Dragon that it had picked up a passenger[80]. Wind whipped by the Soldier as he clung to the Dragon's back, but he couldn't cling to this precarious position forever. The Soldier began to climb, using the light but sturdy shield in one hand as a pick to jam between scales. With this commotion the Soldier would no doubt be discovered in moments. He laid himself as flat as he could against the dragon's back, jammed hands and feet between great scales and threw the King's shield over his body. The Dragon flexed its thick rope of neck to turn its head and investigate the bothersome tick that it may have gathered. All it spied was row upon row of fine, broad scales that lined its magnificent back[81].

A circling of the castle thrice more exhausted the Dragon's current search of the Kingdom, and the Dragon turned away from civilisation to head out over the landscape and towards its home. Unobserved and with more care the Soldier continued his slow climb up the creature's back until he found a better purchase at the neck of this enormous steed. Despite his leap into the unknown the Soldier was beginning to gain some confidence, and with a smile swung his leg over the dragon's broad neck

---

[78] Resolve a contradiction. The dragon must be both flexible, but possess a hard and armoured exterior. Separate on scale. GA SP1 *Segmentation*. Many small stiff plates work together to create a flexible large-scale structure.
[79] Enhance a benefit. The Soldier needs to be attached more firmly to the Dragon. GA SS2.1.1 Chain substances together. Add an intermediate substance to amplify the influence of an insufficient field.
[80] Resolve a contradiction. We must land on the Dragon, and not land on the Dragon. GA SP22. *Blessing in Disguise*. The thicknesses of a Dragon's scales serve to deaden a presence.
[81] Resolve a contradiction. We need to be present but not present. GA SP32 *Colour Change*. Camouflage.

to sit astride the creature for the duration of their journey together. In doing so the Soldier drove the heel of his boot into the deep injury his old Father had inflicted upon the Dragon some days previously[82].

The Dragon roared with a pain that shuddered and convulsed its whole body. The beast whipped its jagged head around once again to winkle out the tick it now knew for sure it carried. Without time to camouflage himself with the shield the Soldier was now eye to eye with the Dragon, balanced upon its back, travelling at speeds he could never have imagined, many thousands of feet in the air. The Soldier's new-found confidence evaporated in the wind that whipped by[83].

The fanged maw of the Dragon stretched open as it lunged at the stowaway, intent on biting him in half. The jaws clanged shut mere inches from the Soldier's face, for the nape of the neck is that one place on a dragon that it cannot reach[84]. Claws snatched and grasped at the Soldier. Wings beat frantically as the Dragon performed all manner of aerial gymnastics in an effort to shake the parasite loose[85].

The Soldier hung on with great determination as he was swung to and fro, up and down, right way up, upside down so when he looked up the Soldier was staring at the ground. From this vantage the Soldier saw the coastline of the Southern sea swell into view. Righting itself once more, the Dragon drove on out to sea and lunged for the salty waters.

Faster and faster the Dragon dove. Wind tore past the Soldier like a hurricane, but still he hung on. The Southern sea grew large, then grew huge, then grew to encompass his whole view. The Dragon meant to dive into this great water to drown the Soldier from its back[86]. As the wind whistled by the Soldier accepted that he would soon be deluged and drew a great breath, and in drawing his deepest breath found that he could draw more, and more, and more. From the Princess's kiss the Soldier was

---

[82] If others are attempting to solve the same problem as you, there's a strong chance you'll be working at odds, or even competing. Either coordinate with other teams or keep out of each other's way, or you'll see conflict before you know it.

[83] It's easy to lose confidence in a very new idea. Find evidence that you are astride the correct dragon. Find evidence, not faith.

[84] Who knew?

[85] Resolve a contradiction. GA SP18. *Mechanical Vibration*. We must reach the pain but cannot reach it directly. We can reach that to which it is attached. Shake it off.

[86] SS5.2.2 *Introduce a field under restricted conditions by using fields that are present in the environment.* Use the sea to remove the Soldier.

filled with all the winds from the North and from the South and from the East and from the West. Within this maelstrom the Soldier found that he could draw an endless breath as he and the Dragon sped like a meteor towards the surface of the sea. The Soldier jammed the shield into the scales of the Dragon's neck and braced himself for the inevitable impact[87].

The water slammed into the shield as if the castle walls themselves had been thrown at the Soldier, but the shield held fast in its crevice and the Soldier held fast behind the shield. Once immersed the Dragon slowed rapidly and soon was thrashing not the air with its wings, but the deep waters of the Southern sea.

The Soldier hung on, sure that his breath would hold out for only a moment. After a time, as the Dragon insinuated itself through the thick kelp forests of the deep, the Soldier realised that his breath held. With the Princess's kiss his breath may even hold forever[88].

After some leagues of swimming through the deep the Dragon was sure that his irritation would have long ago drowned, but turned its head to survey its back, just to be certain. Sure enough, all the Dragon saw were the fine scales of its magnificent back[89]. Pleased, the Dragon swam on.

After a few more leagues of lazy, sinuous swimming the Soldier could see the dark entrance of a submarine cave through the gloom. The Dragon made straight for the cave and the wide entrance swallowed the Dragon and the Soldier whole. After some brief minutes negotiating this undersea cavern the Dragon angled its swimming upwards. Above, the Soldier could see the underside of a bright pool that hung like a shining full moon.

With a splash the Dragon broached the surface of a wide pool within a dark cave. Light spilled from the pond into the cave, casting a shimmering gloom around the cavern. Salt water washed down the flanks of the Dragon as the beast slid out of the water. As it did so the Soldier decided that he had pushed his luck far enough. As he broke the surface

---

[87] Resolve a contradiction. The presence of a passenger and the sea are about to contradict. GASP11 *Cushion in Advance*. Prepare in advance a function that will mitigate potential harms, should they arise.

[88] Resolve a contradiction. We must breathe but must enter an environment in which we cannot breathe. GA SP9 *Prior Counteraction*. Counteract anticipated harms in advance. SP29 *Pneumatics and Hydraulics*. Take a very deep breath.

[89] Clever ideas don't have to be new. If a trick works, keep doing it.

of the pond he gently floated from the scaled back as the Dragon heaved itself from the waters[90]. The Dragon splashed its way onto land whilst the Soldier drifted to the far edge of the silvery pond, slipped silently out of the water and crouched for cover behind a large, cold rock, still able to hold his breath for fear of alerting the Dragon to his presence.

The Dragon flopped and splashed its way from the lake and down a dark tunnel and out of sight. Only then did the Soldier permit himself a breath, and with a heave he expelled all the winds from all the Kingdom to replace this rush with a much-needed breath of his own.

The Soldier took some moments to assess his new situation. The cave was cold, dark and dimly lit by the moon pool. The walls and floor were not rock, but damp brown earth through which oozed musty, stale moisture. This constant trickle ran down the walls and pooled on the floor to transform the footing to a greenish slippery mud. The dank cave was punctured by large entrances to a cavern system that stretched out in every direction. The Soldier considered what to do next. It seems likely that the Dragon had carried the Soldier to the same location to which it stole his Father. The Soldier could still faintly hear the Dragon slapping its way down a cavern and could see the imprint its claws scrabbled out of the earth as it walked[91]. Following the Dragon seemed the sensible choice, so the Soldier forged onward in his effort to find his Father and return to the Kingdom.

The Soldier tracked the Dragon, stumbling, slipping and dragging his boots through the thick mud of the cavern floor. The Dragon soon outpaced the young man, its sounds fading into the thick gloom. The damp cavern floor was churned with years of clawing, slithering and sliding through the earth, and soon the Dragon's trail was much too obscured to follow. Pathways branched and joined in every direction, the tunnels shrank, the roof dropped and eventually the Soldier was completely lost with no idea of which direction to take, or even what

---

[90] Resolve a contradiction. At full height on land the back of the Dragon will be many metres from the ground. We need to be on the ground. GA SP12 *Equipotentiality*. Remove the need to change the height of an object, or use the environment to change its height. GA SP8 *Anti-Weight*. Use our buoyancy to descend from the Dragon with little disturbance.

[91] Make a measurement. GA SS4.4.1 *Create a measurement system by using a suitable detectable substance*. We can navigate the cavern if we can detect the Dragon. GA SS4.1.2 *Measure a copy or an image of a substance*. Follow the Dragon's footprints.

destination he sought[92].

The Soldier lay the shield upon the sodden sludge and sat upon it to think through his next plan[93]. Sitting cross legged upon the shield, chin supported by a hand propped against a knee, only a few moment's thought revealed a startling contradiction to the Soldier. He was deep underground and some good distance from the light of the moon pool, and yet he could still see the walls and floor of the earthy tunnel. Vision was hardly the best, perhaps as bright as a clear night with a full moon. Yet, since his departure from the moon pool this lunar light had now transformed into a shimmering, phosphorescent green.

Scanning around this tunnel the Soldier soon noticed the source of this eerie light. Along the roof of this earthen cave ran a leathery tree root as thick as a man's thigh. The dim green glow that lit the cave pulsed from this thick root[94].

The Soldier regarded this for some time, until he noted that the thickness of a tree root is unlikely to be uniform[95]. The Soldier peered into the gloom as far as he could see down each end of the tunnel but the faint glow was insufficient to discern any detail. The Soldier stood, reached up and ran his hands along either side of this trunking. With his hands he could easily feel this change in thickness, and in this manner the root was noticeably wider at one end of this tunnel than the other.

This is the root of a tree, the Soldier mused. Trees can be climbed. If I have no idea in which direction to go, then perhaps pursuing the trunk of this tree might offer some means to escape this labyrinth and see where I have been brought? His mind was set. Travel to the centre and see where it takes him.

The Soldier slung the shield onto his back and reached up with both

---

[92] He could *Brainstorm* his way out, but this would send him on a random walk. This Soldier needs a framework to follow.

[93] Resolve a contradiction. I need to sit down, but I cannot sit down because the ground is wet. GA. Separate on condition. SP11 *Cushion in Advance*. Prior to sitting down protect our britches from the wet mud with the shield. Similarly, block a harm. GA SS1.2.1 *Block the harm by introducing a new substance*. Introduce the third substance between the given two substances. This third substance will remain unchanged. Block the damp with the shield.

[94] Enhance a benefit. Improve the lighting GA SS1.1.4 *Use the environment. Introduce an additive from the environment to enhance an insufficient benefit.*

[95] Resolve a contradiction. We must navigate using the environment, but the cavern offers no navigation cues. GA SP4. *Asymmetry*. Perhaps the asymmetry of a feature could offer some value?

hands. Sliding his hands down either side of the root he made for the direction that grew the root in his hands. If an intersection was reached, the direction towards the thickening root was chosen[96].

The Soldier felt a relief, for as the tree root grew, so did the tunnel[97]. Soon the tunnel grew to such a height that he could no longer reach the root to feel its width. This was of little concern, as the wider the root became the brighter it lit the tunnel, and the Soldier could soon see in which direction the large root grew[98].

The Soldier arrived at the focus of this forest of roots. He paused at the mouth of a tunnel that emerged into this convergence and hid himself against one wall. In the roof of the earthen cavern before him the great wooden limbs converged at the base of a gigantic tree.

Under this nexus, nearly hidden by the gloom, the Soldier could see row upon row of iron grey egg-like objects arranged in a cluster. The Soldier had arrived at a nest that could only belong to the Dragon itself.

Edging forwards and peering through the green gloom the Soldier could also make out another shape. The shape of a man lay curled up in the mud next to this iron nest. The man was still, muddied and as grey as the eggs next to which he lay. The Soldier recognised this figure immediately and rushed to his aid. With a hand he rolled the prone man onto his back to reveal his dishevelled and haggard Father. The old man seemed in great pain, and clutched his curled hands to his chest. The Soldier in concern unfurled the bony and wrinkled hands of his Father to reveal terrible burns that creased his Father's palms, who reflexively clawed his hands back to his chest in pain.

Kneeling, the Soldier rested his Father's head on his lap and attempted to reach through the pain with soft words of encouragement. The old man slowly opened his eyes and his pained face transformed, to crease into a broad smile. There they both sat in the gloom, Son comforting Father, until the old man had gathered enough strength to tell his Son

---

[96] Make a measurement. We must navigate using the environment, but the cavern offers no navigation cues SS4.3.1 *Create a measurement system using natural phenomena*. Use the flora and fauna to navigate.

[97] Make a measurement. GA SS4.1.2 Measure a copy or an image of a substance. We do not have a map of the cavern, but we do have a conceptual map of a tree's roots. It gets thicker towards the centre. Measure the root not the cavern.

[98] Resolve a contradiction. The increase in root width provides me direction, but the increase in cavern width pulls the root out of reach. GA SP22. *Blessing in Disguise*. The illumination becomes brighter as the tree root thickens.

what he knew of this place and how they might escape.

The old man had already discovered a stone stairway under the huge tree trunk. Together, Son supporting Father, they made the short ascent through an archway into daylight and onto the shores of a tiny island in the middle of a wide ocean. The island was so small it was barely large enough to graze a single cow. This cow would still grow hungry, for only bare earth rose a few feet from the surrounding sea.

From the centre of the island rose the gigantic tree, plunging far into the sky, and so huge that its wide canopy could be seen to spread far beyond the confines of the island and out over the sea. The altitude of this canopy attracted lightning that flashed amongst the branches, gathered to the centre and plunged down, winding electric blue around the glowing trunk to discharge into the iron brown earth.

The Soldier helped his Father to the nearby shore, and together they gently washed the old man's burned hands in the ocean. The salt stung the old man terribly at first, but the combination of numbing brine and cool waters soon offered the old man some small relief from his injuries.

The pair sat at the water's edge intent to rest from their journeys, but a great roar and leathery flapping cut this respite short. The old man grasped his son's sleeve in his burned hands with a wince and dragged him back to the cavern entrance.

Crouched on the stone steps and hiding within the entrance to the cavern the two men watched as the Dragon swooped down from the branches of the great tree. The Soldier's sharp eyes could see a figure clutched within the cruel talons of the Dragon.

Swooping down at great speed, and with little care to slow much, the Dragon released its catch to dash the figure against the bare earth of the island not far from the cavern entrance[99]. Face down the figure ploughed a short furrow into the earth of the small island and quickly came to a stuttering stop.

The figure lay still for a moment, indignant, then levered herself from the impression made in the earth. The Soldier was shocked to recognise this face, for it was not a face he was ever likely to forget and yet he had never met its bearer. This likeness was of his greatest love.

The lost Queen clambered slowly to her feet, her face exposed a dark rage. Despite her long absence at the hands of the Last Dragon, the

---

[99] Resolve a contradiction. We wish to quickly deposit a payload on the ground but landing will take time. GA SP 21 *Rushing Through*. Skip the landing to perform the desired action as quickly as possible.

indignity she currently suffered seemed new to her. She brushed the mud from her clothing with irritation and made towards the cavern entrance. The old man once more grasped his son's sleeve and in pain dragged his son further back into the cavern and down the stairs to avoid discovery by the Queen.

Finding refuge in a tunnel entrance deep inside the cavern the pair watched the Queen as she strode to the nest of steely grey eggs. Dropping to her knees, the Queen scraped handfuls of the iron earth into a rough facsimile of the eggs already present in the collection[100]. Her task complete the Queen settled into the brown earth beneath the nexus of giant tree roots and began to sing.

The Queen's strong, clear voice filled the dull earth chamber and the smooth iron eggs began to shine. The rough egg-shaped mound of brown earth joined this transformation, becoming smooth with a bronze iridescence and transforming on to a grey steel sheen. As the Queen's song continued the soft glow began to brighten to an electric radiance. A breeze began to rise inside the enclosed space, and sparks began the crackle between the shining eggs. The Queen raised her voice still further, and the eggs began to move. Every elongated egg slowly tipped until each rested on a narrow end, aligned with one another, pointing towards the roof of the cavern.

Song complete, the Queen reached into the nest and selected that egg with the brightest chrome shine. Clutching the egg to her breast she retreated back up the stone stairs.

The two soldiers followed, and emerged back into the daylight in just enough time to see the Queen retire to an alcove cut into the side of the great glowing tree. The central axis of this great tree formed a hollow chimney to the skies.

The old soldier turned to his son with a mischievous expression, for the boy was about to witness a truly miraculous sight. Clutching the egg to her body the Queen began to rise off her feet. As she ascended she was soon no longer visible, as if drawn by some magical source up through the centre of the trunk to vanish aloft[101].

---

[100] Resolve a contradiction. We need more eggs but do not have the means to create them. GA SP26 *Copying*. Employ a simple or low-cost copy.

[101] Employ a magnetic benefit. GA SS2.4.11 *Use an electric current to create magnetic fields*. SS2.4.1 *Use ferromagnetic materials and/or magnetic fields to add functions*

12. INNOVATION

Innovation is an extremely overused word with little explicit definition. You hear it everywhere, from the internal mantras of corporate mission building, to the catchphrases of marketing teams, and endlessly in the pitching of new ideas to potential investors. What does such an overused word mean? Every text that covers this subject seems to make an attempt at a definition, and this one will be no different.

The first problem one may encounter with this word is the standard definition itself. The Oxford English dictionary describes innovation as *a new method, idea, product, etc.* The Cambridge dictionary agrees with *the use of a new idea or method.* Merriam-Webster offers *the introduction of something new, a new idea, method, or device.* This requires an idea or an object to exhibit only novelty to be regarded as innovative. Mere novelty cannot be the sole characteristic that all those corporate missives and product pitches proudly pursue. What characteristic pushes an idea from unfamiliar to innovative?

An alternative definition involves the intersection between need and resolution. Figure 129 illustrates these two domains. On the left we encompass everything that we want. Perhaps we want to carry a hammer up a tall building, or deliver packages into space, or transport some cows across a river. On the right are illustrated all the technological means to achieve these ends. Cranes, rockets, sails, etc.

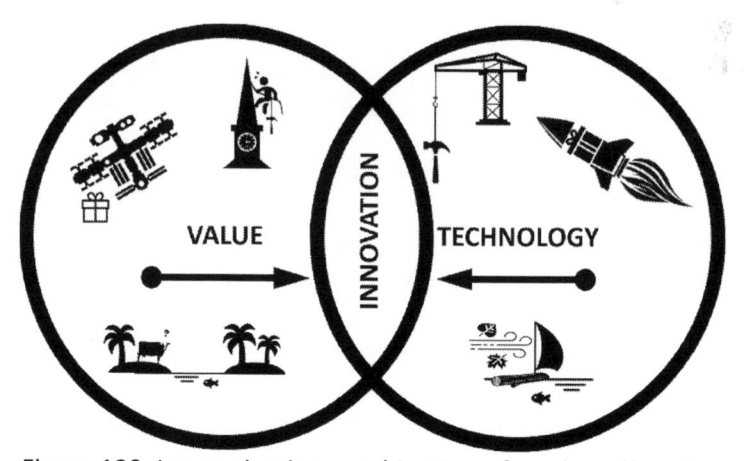

Figure 129: Innovation is a combination of a value offered by technology.

Our task as innovator is to pull our technology towards the customer need and to find those customer needs that we can resolve with available technology. In the intersection between these two domains lies our innovation.

This is a reasonable and functional definition of innovation. A clever technology that does not serve a recognised and valuable need is not an innovation. To identify a valuable problem and to derive a solution without a practical means to realise this solution is also not an innovation. Conjuring up crazy ideas without reference to problems, solutions or practical means to achieve an end is not innovation, even if your enthusiasm for the idea might make you feel in your bones that your idea is the most innovative thought you've thought all day.

This definition has one flaw. This definition of innovation encompasses *all* of problem solving. If we identify a need and resolve that need, perhaps using the techniques described in this book, then using this simple definition we have innovated. If innovation is merely problem solving then this definition of innovation makes the word rather redundant. We already have a means to describe problem solving in the phrase *problem solving*.

Considering how the word innovation is used, innovation must mean more than novelty and more than problem solving. Not all problems demand an innovative solution and not all solutions are innovations.

For many years I have observed many groups attempt to solve difficult problems. Through this observation I have developed a definition of innovation that seems to identify those solutions with true potential to hold the mantle of innovation. This definition is straightforward and easy to spot when you see it.

Innovation is funny.

Not *funny strange*. Funny *ha ha*. Amusing. I'm sorry that this revelation is not a little more sophisticated, but it's true. Whenever a group discovers a clever idea that was hidden from view and difficult to unearth, everyone will laugh. When the group laughs, I have learned to sit up and pay attention.

You may have experienced this yourself. Have you ever struggled with a problem only to discover the solution in an unlikely place, or staring you in the face but obscured? Have you ever suddenly seen the wood, despite the trees? Under these circumstances you may have laughed. Not necessarily a loud laugh. The laugh following an innovative leap is not the belly laugh of bawdy humour or high comedy. The innovative laugh is the self-satisfied chuckle. An audible smirk. Amongst groups it is the brief congratulation for a well-wrought gag. If you witness this, don't discard the source as mere entertainment. Listen carefully, tease the comedy aside and scrutinise the contents of this humour. As they say, it's funny, because it's *true*.

This leads us to a hypothesis that I have developed that is supported by no actual evidence or hard science that I am aware of whatsoever. The observation is functional, so treat it as one of our metaphorical truths until disabused. I'll call it *Dr Hart's Evolutionary Theory of Humour*. I doubt you'll ever see it referenced in a scientific journal, as I made it up with no more supporting evidence than a guess.

Long observation of problem-solving groups led me to wonder why clever ideas are often amusing. After all, problem solving has been a serious business for Humankind for many thousands of years. From the difference between life and death for many Humans, to the difference between promotion and obscurity in the modern corporate workplace, problem solving has been key.

I've noticed a positive disadvantage in pursuing the humour in a corporate problem-solving exercise. In my opinion if the group is laughing, then the group is innovating. To an outside observer, if the group is laughing then the group is wasting time and money on their own amusement rather than concentrating on the job in hand. Engineering is a Serious Business, after all. So why are innovative ideas funny?

We act before we understand why we act. Under these circumstances, if I am willing to harm my professional credibility by encouraging a little wit in a problem-solving exercise, then there must be some value in this that I am willing to take a risk to secure.

Haines-Gadd offers a piece to this puzzle in her text on Altshuller's work [14]. Difficult problems can be accompanied by *phycological inertia*. Einstein explains that the definition of insanity is doing the same thing over and over again, but expecting different results. Yet many attempts to solve problems do precisely this. Have you ever attempted to solve a problem, but ploughed down the same rut over and over in search for a solution? You have laid out all of the pieces of a problem before you, attempted every solution you can think of, and yet all of your solutions seem to only offer many variations on a single theme? Haines-Gadd describes this impasse as *phycological inertia* and offers examples to illustrate.

- *I said to the gym teacher, 'Can you teach me how to do the splits?'. The teacher replied, 'How flexible are you?'* and I said, *'I can't make Tuesdays'*. Tommy Cooper.
- *'I want to die like my Father, peacefully in his sleep, not screaming and terrified like his passengers'*. Bob Monkhouse.

As painful as this choice of jokes is intended to be, they are also funny. Each presents a situation about which we have clear expectations. The joke then confounds these expectations and we laugh. Why?

Furthermore, it's not just the comedy that attracts people's attention. It's the comic. People are willing to sit for hours and listen closely to the observations of a good comic. A good comedian will not recite a list of unrelated jokes. Comics assemble a narrative using observations about the world and often resolve these observations in a comic way. They set up a situation, then break your phycological inertia. *It's funny, because it's true.*

The clinical psychologist Peterson engages rapt audiences with long presentations ranging across complex fields from psychology, religion, mythology, moral philosophy and political thought. Peterson has long praised the delivery methods and objectives of stand-up comedians, and you can see in his presentations an attempt to draw from the observational comedians some of their presentational power. Peterson does not seem to prepare a presentation word for word, but notes a number of themes to cover and solves problems with the audience during the event. The effect is very like stand-up comedy, despite the observations on occasion being as far from comedy as one might get.

I observe a group trying to solve a problem. The group bring to the exercise expectations about the problem. A solution is hard to find and psychological inertia builds. Tension builds. Then someone makes a humorous observation about the problem. Everyone laughs. A pregnant pause. Then often someone will say, *wait a minute, you might have something there…*

Humankind has been beset by tooth, claw, disease, death and disaster for many thousands of years. Humans have so far overcome all that the Universe has thrown at us. Despite the terrible end that many have met at the hands of fate, the standard of living and life expectancy of many has risen throughout this journey. There is still a long way to go, but our problem-solving skills have so far taken us a long way from our cave dwelling beginnings. Our problem-solving skills are our greatest asset, and we seem to have evolved mechanisms to ensure that the best problem-solvers hand their skills onto the next generation.

A creature who has learned to be attracted by psychological inertia and also gains great pleasure from its resolution must advantage itself when running the great Human race. Humans who can indicate to others their ability to overcome psychological inertia and resolve difficult problems must attract the attention of other Humans. If I laugh when I overcome problems, then perhaps I can advertise this skill if I can make you laugh too. Humans love solving problems. For Humans to still be around, Humans must also love other Humans who can solve difficult problems. Everyone must have endured a friend who, although perhaps not the most physically attractive member of the Human race, has an unerring ability to amuse the object of their desires. Have you ever had to suffer the success of a friend who can easily laugh a potential mate into bed? I have, and it is both an insufferable and fascinating skill. Funny is sexy, and sexy always has an evolutionary advantage.

So, *Dr Hart's Evolutionary Theory of Humour* has no scientific foundation whatsoever other than frequent observation and idle musing during long hours of collective problem solving. The breaking of psychological inertia required to solve difficult problems is amusing. Innovation is funny because Humans who gain and advertise pleasure from problem solving are likely to be those Humans with whom other Humans will vigorously collaborate to pass those problem-solving traits onto their children. Laughter is perhaps a creative endeavour in more ways than we realise.

*

Alternatively, perhaps innovation can only be identified in retrospect? Consider some of the greatest innovations of the 20th Century. Consider, for example, the digital camera. This is a technology that many now carry with them embedded within their mobile devices. When the digital camera was first invented, did the inventors hail this creation as an innovation?

The charged couple device lies at the heart of the digital camera. In 1975 Steven Sasson, an engineer at Kodak, invented and built the first hand-held, self-contained electronic camera that used a charge-coupled device image sensor. This first camera weighed 3.6 kilograms and produced a black and white image only 100 by 100 pixels in size. Each image took over 20 seconds to record onto a cassette tape. The effort that Sasson must have put into this solution suggests that he well understood the value of this work.

If you were presented with a very slow, 100x100 pixel, black and white camera the size of a small typewriter, would you have hailed this mechanism as an innovation that would eventually cover the Earth? The Kodak executives to whom Sasson must have presented his work most certainly did, as Kodak briefly became the largest manufacturer of digital cameras in the world. Whilst they focussed upon offering high quality cameras, what they did not seem to predict was the incorporation of digital camera technologies into every smartphone, holiday trip and selfie on Earth. This eventually drove their company out of existence.

A more general description of this specific example is offered by Clayton Christensen, author of the *Innovator's Dilemma* [19]. Christensen advises that new entrants into a marketplace avoid competing with the incumbent supplier at the high-quality end of this market. Alternatively, a new entrant with a new solution to an old problem should enter the market where the incumbent competition places the least value. Christensen offers the manufacture of steel as an example.

Consider the development of new technology that solves an old problem – the manufacture of steel. New technology allowed small steel mills to manufacture a low cost, low quality steel from scrap by employing electric furnaces. The low-quality steel manufactured by these early electric furnaces could not compete with high quality material manufactured by the large, incumbent steel mills.

Those who recognised the electric furnace as a potential innovation could have ploughed money into the development of this technology until it could compete at the high-quality end of the market and return a larger profit. Alternatively, these smaller firms employed electric furnaces to create low quality material to compete with the large established mills in the manufacture of concrete reinforcing bar, or *rebar*.

This electrically produced rebar was manufactured at low cost. When these smaller companies began to compete for the rebar market did the established mills recognise this electric means of manufacturing steel as an innovation? No, they regarded this new entry into the marketplace as a convenience. The established mills were offered a reason to retreat from the low-quality marketplace and concentrate upon more lucrative manufacturing. Little did they recognise that this new steel manufacturing technology was an innovation that would improve over the years to chase the established steel firms right up their product line and out of business, starting with rebar and ending with the manufacture of high-quality steel.

A clever solution is likely to be hailed as an innovation only *after* it has proved its value and driven its competitors from the market place. To describe oneself as *intending* to innovate is a bold claim. How do you know before the fact that valuable problems will be identified, contradictions can be separated, harms can be blocked, clever solutions exist, and in this you will overcome your physiological inertia? To innovate is perhaps a verb that is best employed in the past tense, after the fact.

Many books have been written to explain why you should innovate. You *must* innovate! Innovate or *die!* This text has presented examples of organisations who were disrupted or destroyed when they did not innovate or did not recognise innovations in time to save themselves. Plenty of other examples litter commercial history.

The definitions of innovation I present above relegate innovation to either a label with which we market our problem-solving skills or an award we offer to clever ideas after they have proven their value. Under the circumstances it would seem hypocritical to proceed much further hailing the benefits of innovation.

Perhaps less has been published on when to *avoid* innovation. After all, ideas labelled as innovative often share a common feature. Innovation is *disruptive*. Disruption is often redefined as beneficial innovation only *after* the disruption has proven its value, so consider the definition of the word. Disruption is a disturbance or problem which interrupts an event, activity, or process. Is this a behaviour that your employer will reward you for?

If you labour within a large and well established organisation, consider the source of your employer's success. If you're intent upon provoking disruptive innovation within your existing organisation, it is a good idea to recognise that your company is already making money. It wouldn't exist if it did not. The company has identified a real customer with a valuable problem, has solved that problem, and has developed the means to realise and sell that solution to a satisfied customer, illustrated in Figure 130.

Figure 130: Your company is making money for a good reason.

Your company already offers a desirable product to a known customer. Your company has knocked down the technical barriers required to deliver this product. Your company has managed its supply chain and operating costs so that it can reliably make a profit from producing and selling this product. How does your company manage the risk of embarking upon all this effort?

Your company knows who their current customer is, the problems this customer suffers, and what products will solve those problems. Your company manages the risk of being in business by firmly fixing the scope of requirements and carefully managing the cost and time required to deliver this product, illustrated in Figure 131. Your company will make a plan and will execute this plan well.

Figure 131: Manage risk by fixing what we make very firmly, and negotiating on the time and cost required to deliver this solution.

If you have internalised that the company must innovate or die, then you want to disrupt all of this with new business practices that you have not yet developed, with new customers who you have not yet approached, with new problems that you have not yet discovered, and hope to offer new products that you have not yet developed. If this is your intent, I have a question for you.

Why would you do this to yourself?

You hope to creep into the lair of a large happy dragon who slumbers upon a huge pile of gold that it has hoarded over many years. You want to confront that dragon with a disruption to its carefully carved business case. You want to consume the company profits to pursue products that may displace a product line that has taken years to establish.

In the early stages of your drive to innovate your disruption will consume the company's resources. The journey from customer discovery to the shipping of your first product will cost the company money, time, and resources illustrated in Figure 132. Blood and treasure will be expended upon your ideas, and by the time a new product is ready to deliver to a new customer you may not even be a member of the team who delivers those profits to the company.

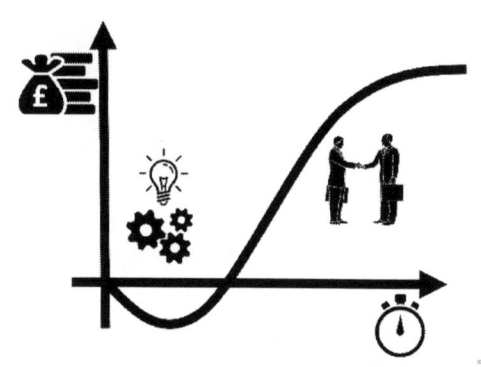

Figure 132: A new idea will consume resources in its early stages. Only later will it show a profit.

Even if you do succeed, you may fail spectacularly. After all, if you catch the eye of the customer with a competing product you may spoil a long established and carefully constructed business strategy, illustrated in Figure 133.

Figure 133: An exciting new product could spoil an established and hard-won sales strategy.

If you threaten the company's established product line, customer relationships and business strategies then you are going to provoke an immune response. If you become labelled as a biohazard, you'll find that an established company may have a very effective immune response indeed. And for good reason, for this protects the company from threats, and that threat may now be *you*.

For example, a large established company must constantly manage risk and be on guard to detect potential threats to the business. To manage that risk, they will promote a *safe pair of hands*. If you are disrupting an established company with innovative products, technologies and customer relationships you will not be regarded as that safe pair of hands. You will be the *loose cannon*. The immune response is unlikely to promote a loose cannon unless you are spectacularly successful, and successful innovation will often only emerge from a long chain of small successes. You may be considered a loose cannon, and may now be the most obvious and easily detected threat for a newly promoted safe pair of hands to gain his first scalp. Good luck.

So, how does a team of disruptive innovators avoid becoming labelled as a team of risky renegades? We hope that if we are successful our disruptive innovations will one day become an established product line, customer or business practise.

Your experiments in disruptive innovation may have some very senior support, with its roots in a visionary Chief Executive who understands that the company must innovate or die. This creates two companies in competition, illustrated in Figure 134.

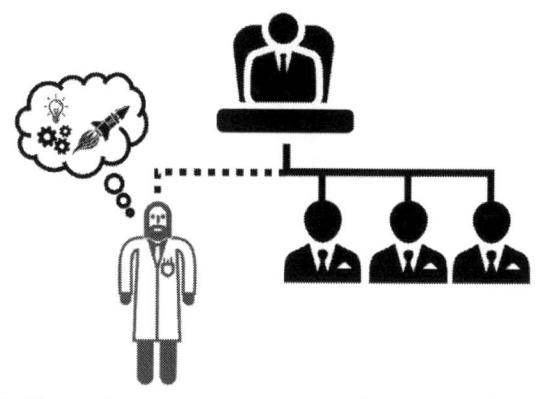

Figure 134: Disruption can start as a special case, isolated from the main organisation.

You and your team cannot rely upon the Chief Executive's benevolence forever, nor can you remain isolated from the parent company if you aspire to innovate your way to a new product line. Unless you can convince your organisation to support an isolated innovation cell, to survive in the long term your disruptive, innovative approach cannot act as a pet project for the CEO. You must benefit and become an established component of the wider organisation, illustrated in Figure 135. Don't forget that these intermediate levels of management may have one thing on their minds. This is your population promoted because they are all regarded as a safe pair of hands. A primary function of this population is risk management, and you're asking them to take a risk.

Figure 135: You can't be the Chief Executive's pet project forever. You must to appeal to the risk managers.

Your funds must eventually come from established sources within the organisation. To achieve this, those sources must understand the benefits of your approach and become your internal customer. And when you succeed, it's not your innovative new exercise that will break, nor will the established working practises suffer. It's the *interfaces* between these contrasting processes that will creak and groan under the weight of mismatched objectives and timescales.

In my own efforts to exercise disruptive innovation within a well-established framework I have often worked under the impression that I was attempting to harness a high-speed sports car to a large, secure and very heavy safe, illustrated in Figure 136.

Figure 136: If you put the pedal to the metal, what's going to happen?

Obviously, the safe represents the secure, established framework of our parent company. Filled with resources and protected by thick, heavy defences, this safe is designed to resist shocks and be difficult to move. In our efforts to make progress quickly and efficiently using all the references presented in this text we construct a light, fast sport car to take us on our journey. To remain part of our corporate structure we must harness one to the other at some point. Under these circumstances you might have to press that accelerator very gently at first, otherwise a suboptimal outcome may result.

You are unlikely to hurt the safe, as your parent company will have as a matter of policy reduced its exposure to your adverse outcomes to a minimum. You will be risking a small quantity of cash, your access to the customer will be restricted and controlled, and your outcomes should come under great scrutiny before they are associated with the wider corporation.

Your vehicle may tear in half, of course. This is an outcome that you should prepare for. A tight, trusting team with a shared objective and responsibility may just manage to keep the vehicle in one piece. Repairs and modifications are likely, and repeated shocks may force you to transform your sleek sports car into something less powerful and more practical. You may need some hybrid that retains some disruptive intentions but better fits the wider organisation. A practical Prius, perhaps?

That chain will snap, and when it does you want to avoid its flailing report. For example, the difference in timescale between the corporate payment process and the needs of small external suppliers may be mismatched, leaving the supplier in serious deficit and working at risk until the corporate gears have turned their slow turn. The corporate structure may demand that the small players in the new, agile supply chain be assessed and certified for quality, or security, or for their ability to keep supplying what you need into a future far beyond your immediate experiments. This assessment may be longer than your entire experiment. You may be sourcing new and untried technology from academia, who may have no mechanism or enthusiasm whatsoever to understand and cater to the needs of industry. Some link in the interfaces between your effort to innovate and business as usual will snap, and until it does snap that weak link may be hard to identify. The illustration in Figure 136 remains stuck to my office wall, as a reminder.

Under these circumstances it is well worth considering one of the roles that middle management play in a large organisation. The call to innovate is often made by the upper management, and the organisational structure busies itself to respond to this call. If you are tasked to discover new customers, problems and solutions and are embedded into the organisational structure as illustrated in Figure 135 then you may have several layers of management between you and that internal customer who made that call to arms.

Reis describes in detail that the objective of those management bodies is to follow the plan, and follow it well. The plan will fix the scope of the project to offer repeatable and scalable processes and will monitor performance indicators to execute and measure the performance of the project. Once a programme is under way it is unlikely to accept changes to the scope, with innovation and improvements focussed upon processes, procedures and costs that are incurred. Reis explains that those responsible for executing the plan are rewarded for following this plan to the letter, *even if it's the wrong plan*. The purpose of making a plan is to squeeze uncertainty and risk out of the project. Careful planning and precise execution are essential, as this drives risks from the organisation, produces profits and keeps the wolf from the door.

Those engaged in the search for new customers, problems and solutions work in an environment that exhibits great uncertainty and many unknowns. Under these circumstances you will have to find some means to work within the established risk management regime. You need to indicate to the reporting chain how you are managing the risks of innovation and how you are delivering value. To avoid attracting the attention of those risk management antibodies within your organisation you must explain what you are doing, why, how long it will take and how much it will cost or you will often be in conflict. This is at odds with the chaotic creative cliché of the lone genius innovator.

How can we convince the wider organisation that we are not a risky proposition? We show them that we are *also* managing risk, but in a different manner. We don't know who the customer is, or what their problems are, or what product might solve these problems. So, we fix the timescales and budgets to reduce our exposure to only those losses that we can endure, as illustrated in Figure 137. Under these constraints we experiment with the customer, the problem and the potential solutions to find that business winning product. We *are* managing risk, but unlike the wider business who fix the scope and negotiate the time and resources, we are flexing the scope under a fixed time and budget to find that valuable new product line. *Fail fast, fail cheap* is the cliché, but it's a cliché for a reason.

Figure 137: We can manage risk, but with the opposite mechanism to an established company.

In your efforts to discover a new customer, or a new problem, or a new solution you might fail. This search for disruptive innovation is an experiment, as you have little idea what the outcome may be. After all, an experiment that cannot fail is not an experiment at all.

An experiment that teaches you a valuable lesson, no matter how harsh, is always a success. If you do intend to engage in disruptive innovation, do not sell the idea of a new product line to the wider organisation. An established and successful company is a creature that is focussed upon delivery. In your effort to release funds to finance a campaign of disruptive innovation, if you sell to this kind of organisation a potential new product line then they *will* expect you to deliver it. In science a negative result is still a valuable result. In business, not so much.

Don't sell that potential product to the wider organisation. *Sell the experiment*. Sell your organisation an experiment to discover new ways to make more money, not the product that may emerge. To re-task a cliché and summarise Reis in only a few words, *learn fast, learn cheap*.

Do pick your battles carefully. Don't innovate with the core products and core customer unless you can link yourself into a mainstream sales and business strategy to win new customers or delight established patrons. Similarly, don't step outside the company business boundaries, unless your shareholders are keen to see their profits retained to expand the company scope. Your best chance to gain wider support from the established business may lie somewhere in between these two extremes. Pitch your stall just outside the city gates. Not competing with established and powerful merchants within the city, but not too far into the wilderness. Within sight of resources, advice and protection.

If you do succeed in finding an innovative, disruptive and desirable product for a new or an established customer, one may be well advised to collaborate with the existing business strategy to get that innovation into the hands of customers. Despite the desire you may have to be creative, innovative and disruptive, you do *want* your innovation to become part of the established product line.

Figure 138: Your company will be making money from your innovations for a good reason.

DRAGON EGG

13. CASE STUDY: A NECESSARY INNOVATION.

The young Soldier looked on, astonished at the Queen's ascent skywards up through the hollow trunk of the great tree. His bewilderment did not last, for it was quicky forgotten. The island upon which they were trapped was tiny and to escape back through the moon pool would demand both he and his elderly Father swim to the bottom of the great Southern sea and across its face, assuming that they could even find the pool at all in the labyrinth of roots below. The Soldier wistfully reminisced over the help that would once more be required from his Princess to achieve such a feat of submarine navigation. Up to the Heavens and into the unknown seemed the only promise of progress[102].

The trunk of the tree was extraordinarily wide and rough with ancient bark. The Soldier had climbed many trees in his boyhood, but a few nostalgic experiments soon demonstrated that climbing this vast trunk would become a gruelling ascent.

The Soldier investigated the chamber inside the trunk. The archway through which the Queen accessed the tree led to a chimney driven up through the very centre of the trunk. The Soldier noted that this funnel was sufficiently narrow to span the space with his body to brace his back and knees against the walls. Looking up from the centre of the chamber the Soldier observed the dizzying channel as the smooth walls converged high above to a tiny dot. There was no way he could brace himself within this space and slowly shuffle to such a great height, and to his old Father this challenge counted double. The whole climb seemed an impossible physical feat.

A strong wind must blow across the summit of this tree, mused the Soldier. A steady draught was pulled in through the archway and up this vertical shaft. The Soldier considered for a moment whether this draught could have propelled the Queen, and could similarly propel these adventurers. With a sail stretched across the chamber perhaps some support could be generated[103]. However, no sail was available to the

---

[102] Resolve a contradiction. We can neither travel down, nor horizontally to reach home. GA SP 17 *Another Dimension*. Perhaps travelling upwards can take us home?

[103] Resolve a contradiction. We need to rise up through this channel, but our weight prevents us. We could lose that weight with some means to generate GA SP8 *Anti-Weight*. This could be achieved by SP29 *Pneumatics and Hydraulics*. We

Soldier, and although no sailor he doubted whether this draught was sufficient to support their combined weight.

The Soldier peered upwards once more into the towering chimney. The lightning attracted by the broad branches of the tree penetrated the trunk to present the Soldier with blue swirling energies coiling around this channel from the top of the tree, down past the Soldier and into the roots.

Only the Queen's magical union with the iron grey eggs offered the single remaining option. Both son and father had been trained as soldiers, and knew little of the magic in this world[104]. This was going to require some experimentation[105]. The Soldier and his old Father returned to the dank cave beneath the tree to investigate the nest of iron grey eggs that the Queen had wrought[106].

These eggs clearly had some affinity with the tree that the Soldier could not understand. A brief experiment was in order. To carry an example up to the chamber within the tree, the Soldier reached out to the nearest egg.

The old man lunged at the younger, slapping his hands aside as he reached for the egg. It was no stretch of the imagination to associate egg with tree, and the old man had already paid a price for his own experiments, in the terrible burns upon his hands. It seemed that only the Queen could touch these eggs without dreadful injury.

Perhaps the shield of dragon scales could act as a container to carry

---

could employ air pressure, generated by GA SP30 *Flexible Membranes/Thin Films,* via a sail or parachute.

[104] The *axis mundi,* or world tree, is a suitable metaphor for innovation in this fairy-tale framework that is grounded immovably in the world of chaos, with branches reaching to the heavens. This structure unites three distinct domains: the chaotic, subterranean, oceanic, hellish, reptilian land of the unknown; the mundane, conscious domain of humankind, trapped uncomfortably between the titanic and the heavenly; and the heavens, the ideal, the utopian state, a fantasy that follows its own rules, governed by its own denizens. Here the world tree can serve a ritual purpose as a bridge between the profane individual domain and the realm of the gods. One must climb the tree to face the unknown and gain wisdom, for this is the tree of knowledge in which lurks a serpent. [6]

[105] Or alternatively, *'I'm going to have to science the shit out of this.'* Mark Watney (Matt Damon), in *The Martian,* Riley Scott, 2015, based on the book of the same name by Andy Weir.

[106] At some point the questions that arise from your problem-solving framework must eventually be addressed to the laboratory.

an egg to the chamber[107]. The Soldier swung the shield from his back and handed it to his Father, who clutched it in his pained hands.

The Soldier would need to leaver the egg onto the shield with some tool, so drew his sword[108]. Sword drawn, the moment the weapon saw the Dragon's eggs it lunged of its own will at the nearest. The Soldier struggled to control the weapon as it attacked of its own violation these impending dragons, as if possessed by a searing hatred for the creatures. Despite the Soldier's efforts to control the disobedient weapon the steel sword struck the nearest malevolent egg with a dull iron clunk.

The sword was stuck fast to the egg[109]. Placing a foot upon the egg the Soldier made to draw the weapon from its target, only to notice an uncomfortable rise in temperature in the handle of his sword. The magic that attacked his Father now attacked the Soldier through his own sword. Try as he might the Soldier could not separate sword from egg, whilst the temperature of this weapon rose ever higher. Soon the blade began to glow a faint red hue, and the Soldier struggled to retain a firm grip upon the heating handle, as one might struggle to maintain a grip on a poker left too long in a roaring fire.

At the moment of crisis, with the blade glowing an angry red, the sword released its grip sending the Soldier tumbling back into the red earth[110]. The sword hissed as it met the moist ground, and its angry red

---

[107] Resolve a contradiction. We need to touch the egg, but not touch the egg. Touching the egg provokes a terrible harm. GA SP11 *Cushion in Advance*. Block a harm. GA SS1.2.1 *Block the harm by introducing a new substance. Introduce the third substance between the given two substances.* Use the shield to block the harm.

[108] Resolve a contradiction. I need to touch the egg, but not touch the egg, GA SP24 *Intermediary*. Move the egg with your sword.

[109] 13 of Altshuller's 76 Standard Solutions employ magnetism to either block harms or improve an insufficient benefit. Altshuller seems to have an affinity for employing magnetic fields, introducing ferromagnetic substances, suspending ferromagnetic particles to create magnetic fluids, or employing electromagnetic fields. Altshuller's emphasis upon the usefulness of magnetic properties should not be forgotten in the resolution of your own problems.

[110] Make a measurement. Whilst the problem in question does not specifically involve measurement systems, it's worth referencing GA SS4.4.5 *Create a measurement system using the Curie point, Hopkins and Barkhausen, etc*. The Curie temperature, or Curie point, is the temperature above which certain materials lose their permanent magnetic properties. This temperature change allows us to switch permanent magnetic fields on and off.

hue retreated back into the depths of the blade.

The Soldier climbed to his feet, marvelling at the temporary vitality of the sword in his hand. The burning sword seemed to have returned to its usual passive behaviour, but as it cooled seemed to recover its new found and independent vigour. Once more the weapon embarked upon the offensive with a will of its own.

This time its target was the Soldier's own Father, who cowered behind the iron scales of the shield he held. The sword met this shield with a thunderous blow that knocked the old man from his feet and into the mud. The sword was now stuck fast to the shield. However, on this occasion the sword did not betray its aggressive ardour with heat or colour, as the handle remained cool.

The Soldier regarded the sword stuck fast to the iron scales of a long dead dragon with curiosity. There was nothing special about his sword. Up to now it had happily coexisted with this shield and had even ridden upon a dragon's back with no sign of independent action. The sword was like many others, and had been issued to him by the quartermaster of the King's army who had made no mention of any particular animosity that this particular sword had towards dragons, nor of a fickle nature in this regard. In fact, the Soldier had never even heard of a sword exhibiting a life of its own in this manner.

Contact with the eggs of dragons had perhaps transferred some properties of these eggs to his sword? Perhaps the sword could now act as the eggs do within the tree?[111] Together the Soldier and his Father returned to the surface to test this hypothesis[112].

Above ground the Soldier immediately noted an affinity towards the tree from his newly animated sword. Even approaching the trunk to within a few paces drove the sword to hysterical and near uncontrollable jerking and shuddering as it attempted to haul the Soldier towards the trunk and twist the sword out of his hands. Even the shield of dragon scales now seemed infected by whatever animation had been contracted from the Dragon's eggs. The Soldier and his Father backed off and considered their options.

Assuming that they now held the right tools, boldness was their only option. Steeling themselves with their soldier's spirit, together they prepared to rush for the chamber at the centre of the great tree and

---

[111] A new technology pressed to a valuable goal. Now we're *innovating*.
[112] ER. A rapid build-measure-learn cycle will allow you to test numerous possible solutions and discover the correct course. [4]

resign themselves to whatever fate the sword and the shield intended for them. This risk gave the Soldier pause for thought[113].

First, perhaps a test was in order. Only iron and steel seemed susceptible to the contagion contracted from contact with the eggs of dragons. The Soldier removed a boot and prized one of the iron hob nails from the sole with his thumb. Sure enough, the moment the nail came in contact with the sword it stuck fast. Prizing the nail from its new companion the Soldier drove his weapon into the earth for temporary security and approached the tree. He could feel the affinity from the nail for the tree as he grew close. He released the nail and, as expected, it flew to the tree and stuck fast. If they had rushed the tree with sword and shield, they would now surely be stuck fast to the trunk[114].

The Soldier attempted to pluck the nail from the surface of the tree, but this new-found affinity was too strong. Try as he might, he could not pull the nail free. However, with a twist he could remove the nail's grasp, and in this act, now he felt a heavenly tug skywards[115]. They were going to have to orient their tools to gain the magical support they desired.

The pair approached the tree carefully, twisting and turning the sword and shield as they approached, seeking just the right orientation to sense that Heavenwards tug. Once prepared, and losing control of their contraption, they once more adopted the soldier's approach and boldly charged for the tree[116].

As they rushed for the tree a great silent wind pummelled their weapons, which they struggled to control. On they drove through the archway and into the chamber at the centre of the tree, to be swept up by this mysterious and ethereal wind that only caught at the sword and at the shield. The pair were yanked into the tall duct and up towards their fate.

Clutching the sword and shield the Soldier and his Father were propelled upwards at an alarming rate. The chamber below shrank to a tiny speck, air howled past their ears, and the summit of this channel grew from a tiny spot to a brightly lit aperture that announced an end to

---

[113] If gripped by an innovative fervour, do remember that risk management is a *good thing*.
[114] ER. Fail Fast. Fail *Cheap*. [4] Don't risk everything on a single experiment. After all, experiments should be allowed to fail, or they are not experiments at all.
[115] Resolve a contradiction. If something doesn't work one way around, try the alternative. *GA SP 13 The Other Way Around*.
[116] Eventually, those risk managers simply need to let you try.

their vertiginous ascent.

The pair were propelled out into the light and air of the great tree's canopy. Their ascent slowed. Without support from the trunk's power they were sure to descend. For just a moment, at the apogee of their ascent, the Soldier saw the wide canopy spread out below. A tangle of branches and boughs stretched out under him like an open hand, ready to catch their fall.

Crashing through forks, limbs, spurs and twigs the pair came to rest on a large platform of tree limbs twisted and entangled into a wide cathedral sheltered by an arching dome of interwoven branches. White knuckles continued to clutch the sword and the shield as the Soldier and his Father took a moment to recover from their ordeal as they lay amongst the dry brown leaves that carpeted this natural basilica. The gentle rain of leaves and twigs that had followed them as they punctured the canopy soon abated, and it was time to take stock of their new surroundings.

14. WORKSHOPS

Throughout this text it's worth noting the persistent contradictions to be found in the effort to solve problems. Problems are also solutions, and both are associated together in an endless chain of cause and effect. Structure is required to contain a creative chaos. We consider all of our contradictory desires but we never compromise. Considering the nature of innovation, what kind of personality can navigate these conflicting objectives?

As problem solving requires a creative approach, an effective problem solver is advantaged by intellectual curiosity, creativity, and is drawn to novelty and variety. Effective problem solvers are imaginative and independent and prefer variety over routine. A flexible and spontaneous approach is useful but can also result in a lack of focus. These personalities seem easily bored.

Problem solving also requires a firm framework to fix the fruits of creativity long enough to build an effective solution. Effective problem solvers must be organized and dependable, show self-discipline, and prefer planned rather than spontaneous behaviour. A conscientious attention to detail is essential in problem solving. This ability to focus upon the task at hand is very useful, but may provoke a stubborn fixation to the known.

What kind of personality can exhibit both positions? More than one personality working together. The idea of the lone genius boffin working in isolation is a cliché that may very well, on occasion, be true. In the majority of cases I have found that great ideas do not emerge from a single Human mind, but appear within the space between the creative efforts of an effective team.

Great ideas are less likely to appear in the space between people who are very much alike. Similar problem solvers tend to reinforce the position that each takes and reinforces their own position in turn. The problem-solving frameworks presented in this text demonstrate that great ideas emerge from resolving contractions. The power of contradiction is no less true when we consider the contradictions amongst those solving the problem. If disparate personalities can reach a conclusion without accepting some insipid compromise to resolve that contradiction, they are likely to solve the problem well.

An unstructured engagement between delegates who hold very different positions may result in a confrontation or a rapid dissolution of the discussion. To manage and maintain an effective interaction takes careful planning, practise and moderation. This typically takes place in a *workshop*, and the design and management of an effective workshop can be a tricky skill to master.

In the context of this text, workshops are extended meetings with the objective to either define or resolve a problem. For example, the output of a workshop may be to interview the customer and assemble a list of desirable benefits, or to scrutinise these benefits and discover the problem to be solved, or to employ a problem-solving framework to resolve the contradictions within the problem. It all depends upon your objectives, and this demands that you be very clear about your objectives before the workshop event.

The raw material into which you must mine for ideas is the Human mind. There's no other resource for you to turn to if you are to achieve your objective, so you must treat this resource well. Working hours are a valuable commodity, and pulling a number of busy and expensive delegates into a room for an afternoon may be an expensive proposition. You may find it difficult to assemble a workshop in the future if your current exercise is not productive, and not *seen* to be productive by the delegates themselves. This latter point is important. Delegates regard hours spent in a workshop as working hours. They should leave a long workshop with the feeling that those hours were well spent. A well-structured, well-prepared and well-executed framework which exercises the intellect of each delegate helps to provoke a good impression upon such a valuable commodity, and helps to ensure the opportunity for a repeat performance.

A well-executed workshop in which you mine deeply for information should tire your delegates. If your delegates leave the meeting either relieved that the boredom is over or refreshed and alert, then it's likely that your workshop has not drawn all that it could have from these delegates. Delegates should leave the workshop feeling stimulated, satisfied, but a little spent. A workshop has gone well if delegates take a moment to rest and reflect upon the experience, and you can often tell from their facial expression if you have hit your mark.

This can be achieved with a few hours work. A whole day can be exhausting if frequent breaks are not scheduled. Alternatively, a single hour is the bare minimum required for a group of delegates to understand the objectives, become competent with your workshop framework and tools, and exercise this framework to come to some worthwhile conclusion.

A mistake often made by those designing a workshop is to assume that the more people who attend, the more minds will be applied to the problem and the better the result. I've seen huge meeting room tables surrounded by thirty delegates attempting to solve a single problem. Within a large group, many will opt out and hide amongst the throng. Others will dominate the discussion to ensure that their voice is heard. This results in a workshop between two or three of the most senior or outspoken delegates in the room, and twenty spectators. Every minute that passes you are paying for these spectators to sit silently and watch.

Alternatively, if a large group do all contribute, they will often talk over one another. Skilful moderation is required to manage a large discussion. Discussion amongst such a large group is likely to exhibit undesirable behaviour that can grow out of control very rapidly. The moderation of a workshop discussion and exercising the problem-solving framework is the role of a workshop *facilitator*. Facilitating a workshop does not require authority over the workshop delegates, but it is a true skill that takes practise to do well.

The primary function of a facilitator in a problem-solving workshop is to *ask questions*. A facilitator must arrive at a problem-solving workshop armed with sufficient questions to keep the delegates happy for the duration of the exercise. As a consequence, the facilitator must also ensure that everyone has the opportunity to offer answers to these questions.

In a discussion amongst a large group with no delegates playing spectator it can take some time for the facilitator to get around everyone and draw a contribution from each. In fact, it can be quite hard to spot the desire to contribute. Even if you do, in a large group the waiting list can grow very quickly, particularly if the discussion moves on and those who have already contributed want to secure another opportunity to contribute.

Under these circumstances, those with a burning point to make will make their point regardless. If you have engaged your delegates well, they will not be able to resist. Without a prompt opportunity to contribute to the wider group they will soon find an alternative avenue and turn to their neighbour to make their point. Their neighbour and those around them will reply, if only out of politeness, and your workshop is now split.

This outcome is inevitable in a large group, and is a disaster. You now have two workshops to moderate simultaneously, and this is almost impossible if you are improvising. You can choose to either stick with one discussion and let the breakaway group continue unmanaged, or silence the breakaway group. Both outcomes are undesirable. It is better to prevent this split from occurring altogether.

This outcome can be avoided by managing the size of the group. The smaller the group, the less likely it will be to split. You can't eradicate this behaviour, but infrequent splitting seems to occur at about six or seven delegates. With six delegates everyone is prominent in the discussion and talking over others in an attempt to split the group is obvious enough to be avoided by good manners. With six delegates you can spot splitting easily, you can hear and table the point that a potential splitter is making and return to it once the current discussion thread has reached a suitable break. Put simply, if your group splits, put it back together again as quickly as you can. This is easy with approximately six delegates.

This does not mean that an effective problem-solving workshop is actually much smaller than people usually expect. This limit means that you need one discussion and one facilitator for every six delegates. Large workshops should be split into multiple smaller groups, but it is a mistake to host multiple groups in a single room, unless the room is very large and the acoustics are excellent. A number of groups competing for the audio bandwidth of a room can once more provoke the splitting of groups. If it's hard to hear what delegates are saying, due the number of people in the room or the room is a large echoing chamber, delegates will once again turn to their nearest neighbour to discuss the exercise with someone they can hear, and once more the group is split. The harder it is to hear, the closer knit the groups will become and the worse the splitting problem. Noisy rooms or poor acoustics will force delegates into small huddles. If you are offered a choice, distributing small teams throughout multiple small rooms is preferable to hosting everyone in one large chamber.

As each contributor imposes a cost upon the exercise, I've often seen organisers skimp on the number of facilitators whilst being lavish with the number of delegates. This is a mistake and your workshop will suffer for this imbalance. Don't be sparing with discussion facilitators. Facilitators are desperately important to structure and manage the discussion and are also your primary means to record the outcomes of the meeting. Too many is better than too few.

This means that your discussion facilitators will require training. Moderating a discussion, particularly amongst people more senior to oneself, is a difficult task that requires practise. They say that you can't learn how to swim in theory, and the same goes for managing a discussion. This takes practise, as you must impose a structure to the discussion and must also be listening carefully to the points made by delegates, expanding upon these points by taking the discussion down new paths, watching for those who may have a point of their own to make and also noting those who have not contributed for some time.

Those with loud voices and bullish temperaments will drive the discussion. Senior delegates with strong opinions are senior for a reason, so they should be listened to as their contributions to the discussion are likely to be valuable. However, their opinions can drown out those with less seniority or confidence to contribute. The trick is not to silence the more vocal members of the workshop, but to somehow wind the quieter opinions into the discussion. You only have to delay the stronger opinions for a moment. Despite the cliché, in most cases a dominant contribution does not necessarily suggest poor manners. In my experience, most people are more than happy to stop for a moment and let others speak if they are directed to by the facilitator. Curtesy is the rule adopted by most delegates.

I'm not denying the existence of rude, arrogant and overbearing contributors. They occur on occasion and can require some considerable skill to manage. I'm simply observing that they are more rare than you might think. In many cases the appearance of rudeness can arise because it can be quite hard for delegates to spot if someone else wishes to contribute, particularly if they are in full flow. Detecting that someone has a contribution to make to the discussion is the facilitator's job, and can be quite tricky. In this setting there are many reasons for delegates to sit in silence, and there are many opportunities to do so. As a discussion facilitator it is your role to detect those more retiring contributors and draw them into the discussion.

Even half an idea is valuable. Occasionally two partial ideas combined together can often result in a single spectacular idea. However, many delegates will avoid making a contribution to the discussion until they have a complete and coherent contribution to make. By the time they have assembled their thoughts, the discussion may very well have moved on. I've seen engineers avoid contributing to a discussion until they have *solved* the problem in hand. I've seen groups of engineers assembled to solve problem retreat to opposite corners of the room to solve the problem in silent isolation before regrouping to discuss their respective efforts.

If you're looking closely you can sometimes see half a thought flitting through a delegate's mind. They'll write something down. Or eyebrows will raise at another comment. Often a delegate will adopt a quizzical look as half a thought is distilled into something more coherent. The cues are varied and fleeting, but if you're watching carefully you can often tell if someone has something to contribute. Alternatively, cues can be more explicit. Half a sentence cut off by another delegate is an obvious sign. A raised finger to attract your attention. An attempt to split the group by turning to a neighbour to provoke a separate discussion.

Watch for those cues that will provoke you to politely pause the more outspoken delegates and ask a leading question to the rest of the group. Someone with a contribution to make will take the opportunity. If you are very sure that someone wants to speak you can address them directly. Do try to be *very* sure when directing the attention of the group to an individual. If you are wrong and they have nothing to add, you are going to make them look foolish to a now silent group all paying careful attention. This may spell the end of your victim's contributions altogether. Expose the misunderstanding, take the blame, and move on. Alternately, whilst more vocal contributors are engaged in discussion you can often check the commitment to speak with non-verbal cues. Point a finger, raise eyebrows, mouth a question. *Do you have something to add?* You may get a nod.

It can be difficult for delegates to identify a more reluctant or less pushy contributor, so delegates may talk over less forthcoming attendees. This can be misinterpreted as poor manners, but this may only indicate inattention. It's your job as facilitator to look out for the less confident contributors whilst the others debate. It's your job as facilitator to draw the more reserved delegates into the group. If these contributors do not secure a voice in the discussion then the facilitator is to blame, not the other more vocal delegates. Facilitators facilitate. It's all in the name.

If you do have a rude, arrogant, pushy, poorly mannered delegate dominating the discussion remember that you can split your workshop into numerous smaller groups. There's nothing stopping you from drawing a less vocal contributor into a group better suited to their manner, or excising a troublesome delegate from the discussion, perhaps by pointing out that this group over here would be fascinated by the issues they have raised. If you can corral all of your overbearing delegates into one group, then all the better.

TOOLS

Much like basic brainstorming, a workshop that drives off in *any* direction towards *any* objective is unlikely to produce valuable results. A successful workshop needs a clear structure to describe the objectives and to drive the exercise towards defined ends. This is achieved by asking questions. I seem to spend my life asking questions, and often they are the sorts of questions delegates would either never have thought to ask, or don't want to answer.

From where do we find all these questions? You can prepare a large pool of questions in advance. This will suffice at the start of your workshop. However, as your workshop proceeds and delegates offer answers that will shape how the conversation will unfold you may find that your prepared pool of questions become less relevant as the workshop proceeds. What we need is a method to generate questions as the workshop unfolds. We need a method to track the unfolding discussion and generate relevant questions as the shape of the workshop emerges. Crudely put, we need to make questions up as we go along. This is achieved with a workshop framework.

This framework will be manufactured from a selected group of workshop tools. One might be more familiar with these tools described as games, exercises or tasks. I prefer to call these resources *tools* as this is their role. A device or implement used to carry out a particular function. A workshop tool helps us to achieve our ends as surely as a hammer helps us to drive nails. A workshop tool allows us to ask questions and record answers, which will provoke new and relevant questions.

A workshop tool will offer a framework into which the contributions of delegates will be incorporated. The simplest tool that many will be familiar with is the tool that accompanies brainstorming, illustrated in Figure 139. A carefully designed question is formulated, and the workshop delegates are then confronted by a large, empty, blank space. Typically, this space will be a wall onto which self-adhesive notes can be fixed.

Figure 139: A blank wall offers an open space in which to collaborate.

The advantage of a large empty surface such as a wall is that it allows a group of workshop delegates to gather around it and collaborate. Delegates can offer ideas to the group through notes fixed to this space. Others can read, digest, cluster or rearrange these notes to form a collective view of the workshop progress.

Osterwalder likens such a workshop tool to a painter's canvas and applies these tools to the generation of business models [20]. Osterwalder's canvases allow us paint pictures of business models. These canvases act as practical workshop tools when printed upon large surfaces to allow groups to sketch and discuss elements of each business model together.

I often treat Osterwalder's canvasses much like a detective might employ a pin board onto which evidence is assembled, connected and assimilated, illustrated in Figure 140. With such a tool our plucky movie detective will arrange evidence in such a manner that hitherto undetected information will be identified not long before the denouement and final shoot-out. This dramatic prop is also a useful visual tool with which a discussion between a team can be framed and visualised, or with which our detective will explain her reasoning to a supporting character, and ultimately to the audience. With every new piece of evidence pinned to the board, new questions arise and the case evolves.

The work of Dan Roam describes a problem-solving mechanism that employs the fast, subconscious pre-processing of visual information before it is delivered to the slower heavyweight processes of the human mind [21]. By arranging information on a canvas, the pattern matching mechanism of the visual cortex can be used to detect relationships between elements, discover gaps in one's knowledge or provoke new lines of enquiry. Much like the movie prop, if the physical size of a canvas is large this tool can be employed by a group and also used to explain findings to a wider audience.

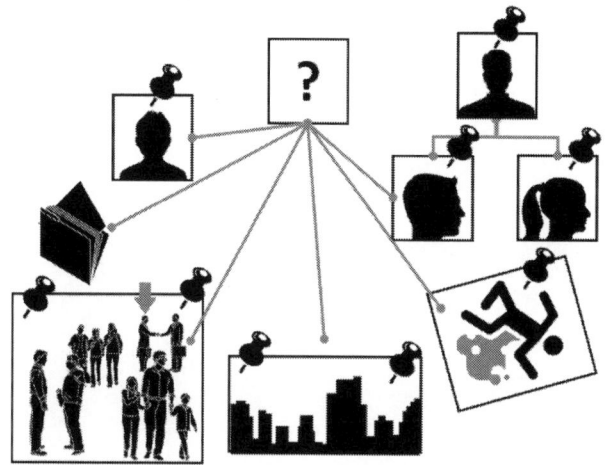

Figure 140: A visual representation of the connection between evidence can be a useful visual tool

Osterwalder's canvasses transformed the manner in which I host workshops. A suitable canvas can be wrought from most frameworks, and the best canvases exhibit a number of essential features. A good canvas will,

- ask specific, focussed questions,
- segment the problem space to focus the attention of delegates,
- co-locate and link related parts of the problem space,
- employ text sparingly,
- be seen and read from several metres away,
- act as a record of the workshop outputs,
- lead us to new specific, focussed questions.

Osterwalder's work offers some inspired canvasses that seldom fail to work with a wide variety of settings and delegates. Many of Osterwalder's canvases focus upon the discovery of customers, the development of products and services and the evolution of a suitable business model to deliver these products. For example, Osterwalder's

Value Proposition Canvas, illustrated in Figure 141, segments the problem space that considers the customer discovery process and the development of products or services that might serve that customer, and is invaluable in many of the workshops that I facilitate.

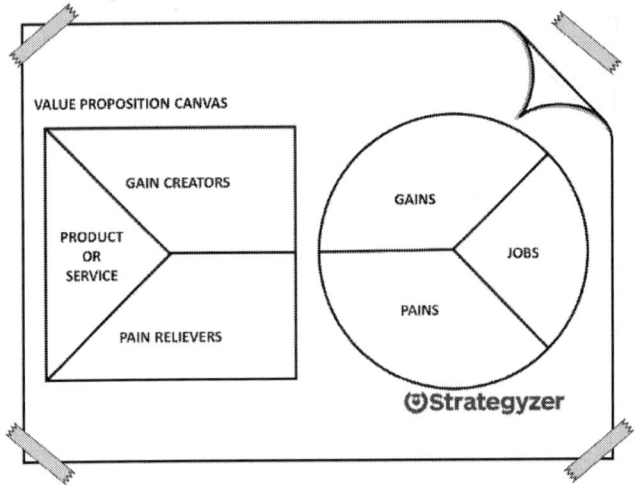

Figure 141: The Value Proposition Canvas offered by Strategyzer is an invaluable customer and product discovery tool.

(*The Value Proposition Canvas is copyright Strategyzer AG, strategyzer.com*).

This text will widen Osterwalder's concept of a workshop canvas to encompass the problem-solving frameworks that are the focus of this book. I shall refer to a canvas as any tool that allows group collaboration to develop a shared picture of the workshop progress. Most of the problem-solving frameworks described in this text can be employed as workshop canvases. They are unlikely to function well without careful selection, design and rehearsal.

What does our basic, blank brainstorming canvas say about a brainstorming exercise? What instruction does it offer? This workshop tool illustrated in Figure 139 represents our large open prairie on that fine sunny day. Go anywhere. Do anything. Cast off in whatever direction takes your fancy. Change direction whenever you please. This blank slate offers little help in the pursuit of the workshop objectives beyond offering the time and space to think, a repository to deposit your answers to the question raised and some space to cluster or arrange this material. In particular, this blank canvas does little to provoke new questions.

A better tool would focus the workshop delegates on different parts of the problem space, and would direct the delegates towards specific workshop objectives. We could improve upon this tool by dividing the problem in space and time to offer a more structured tool with which a group might collaborate. Figure 142 illustrates a canvas that employs Altshuller's thinking in space and time to segment the problem space.

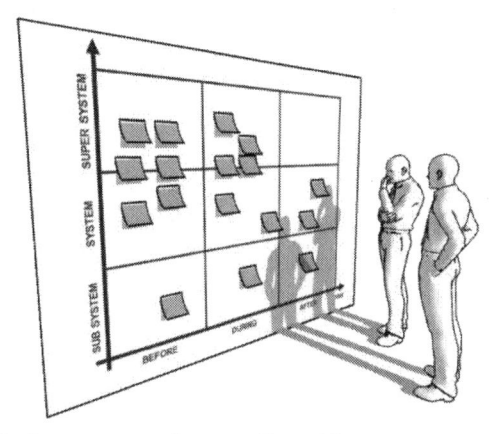

Figure 142: Some group focus offered by segmentation of the problem space would improve performance.

These nine boxes could be used by the group to question the benefits desired by the customer, the harms that may prevent these benefits from becoming realised, the resources that are available in the problem space, or functions that would serve to deliver these benefits whilst resolving the harms.

When solving problems, delegates often focus upon their comfort zones. For example, delegates may offer material drawn from their particular area of expertise, or focus upon topics in which they are particularly interested, or obsess about one particular solution to the exclusion of all else. Any canvas that segments the problem space presents the facilitator with an extremely useful property. The tool illustrates those parts of the problem upon which the group has focussed, and *also* indicates those parts of the problem that the group has ignored. This clear and unambiguous indicator is invaluable to a facilitator. The neglected regions of a canvas offer gaps in the discussion that the facilitator can fill with many new questions.

It's clear in Figure 142 that the group has made an attempt to consider the system and sub system, and have offered some ideas to reflect this. The super system of the wider environment has also been considered, but it's very clear that no one has yet offered any ideas about what happens in the wider environment after the problem has been solved. A canvas that segments the problem space in this manner makes it very easy for the facilitator to note that the box on the top right is empty. This allows the facilitator to direct the delegates away from their comfort zone and into this portion of the problem space. A facilitator may simply ask, *what is happening in the wider environment after the problem has been solved?* This may on occasion make your facilitation seem insightful, but is simply the result of directly reading the blank spaces on the workshop tool.

For example, imagine a group of rocket scientists developing new air vehicles. I can guarantee that these delegates will keenly consider the launch mechanism and the means by which the vehicle will propel itself. The group will enthusiastically drill down to consider the sub systems that practically promote this behaviour. They will even consider the wider environment that supports the rocket prior to launch. This results in a canvas similar to the example offered in Figure 143.

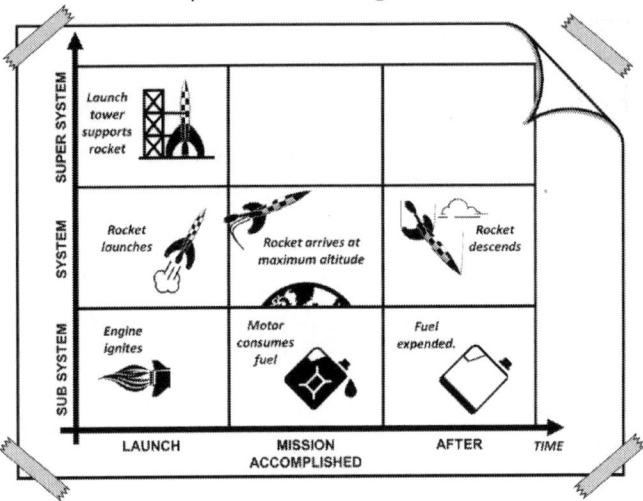

Figure 143: Rocket Scientists are interested in both the whizz and the bang.

This canvas offers a very obvious question for the facilitator to ask. *What's happening in the environment when the rocket is descending? What is on the ground, under the rocket? What is going to happen when the rocket meets the ground? How might you mitigate any harmful contact between the rocket and the ground?*

At this point the group may suggest a parachute. Such a solution offers a simple launch point for further questions. *Can you think of an alternative solution? What is like a parachute, but not a parachute? Under what circumstances is a parachute not the best solution? What is the Ideal Outcome?* From here the Ideal Final Machine could be stated, contradictions can be stated clearly, Separation Principles could be considered, Standard Solutions attempted, or perhaps a Substance-Field diagram sketched.

In this example a possible Ideal Outcome may be that the rocket completely vanishes once its mission is complete. We could create a means to destroy the vehicle once its mission is over. This offers the opportunity for further questions. *Perhaps this function could be elevated to the super system, allowing the environment to destroy the vehicle? Can we tear the vehicle apart with the airflow? Could the vehicle burn up on re-entry?*

Perhaps the Ideal Outcome demands that the vehicle is recovered intact. We could slow its descent with a parachute. Perhaps retro rockets land the vehicle softly? We could cushion the rocket's landing with pneumatics and hydraulics using an inflatable bladder. With a few more solution strategies suggested, we can even ask the same questions again and gather new answers. *Can we elevate this cushioning to the super system and allow the environment to protect the vehicle?* Perhaps the delegates then suggest that we could we splash down in the sea.

The quantity of questions that unfold when you focus the group upon a small part of the problem space is often counterintuitive. One might imagine the converse to be true, as a small part of the problem space should only provoke a small portion of inspiration. When released from the need to consider the entire problem space simultaneously, inspiration often seems much easier to find when only a small part of the problem must be considered. Segmentation of the problem space is a vital tool for a facilitator. A tool that segments the problem space always offers prior warning of where the workshop must investigate next, will always keep you one step ahead of the delegates, can allow you to generate leading questions and can structure the workshop *ad infinitum*. This can make you seem quite competent but is perhaps only a form of *cold reading*.

Cold reading is a set of techniques used by mentalists, psychics, fortune-tellers, mediums, illusionists, and scam artists to imply that the reader knows much more about the person than the reader actually does. Without prior knowledge, a practiced cold-reader can obtain a great deal of information by analysing the person's body language, age, clothing or fashion, hairstyle, gender, sexual orientation, religion, race or ethnicity, level of education, manner of speech, place of origin, etc. Cold readings employ high-probability guesses, quickly picking up on signals on whether their guesses are in the right direction or not, then emphasizing and reinforcing chance connections and discarding errors.

As a facilitator you need not guess which direction the workshop should take. The delegates have indicated very clearly on the workshop tool where focus is required, and the tools described in this book offer you material from which to draw searching questions. From here the appearance of competence is a mere packaging exercise, rehearsal and a clear delivery.

Consider another potential canvas, this time drawn from the consideration of system contradictions. Perhaps a previous workshop employed thinking in time and scale to determine the benefits that the customer desires, or the harms that they experience. These harms and benefits are transformed into a list of desirable outcomes, and these in turn are cross referenced with one another to create a canvas for consideration by a group illustrated in Figure 144.

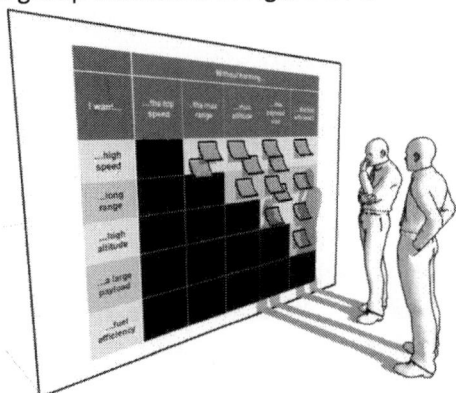

Figure 144: The consideration of contractions could offer a simple but powerful workshop canvas.

This cross referencing of benefits offers the facilitator a set of simple questions that can be asked over and over again. *Does this benefit contradict with this other benefit? Why does this benefit contradict with this benefit? Do these benefits support one another? What outcome is improved by the support?* The question may seem repetitive, but the constantly shifting context offers the workshop delegates a different question every time. With these simple questions drawn from a matrix of contradictions you can keep delegates working and contributing for hours.

In this example we constrain the options to an even greater degree. For a few minutes the group could debate whether the need for long range and high speed contradict. The group can ignore the entire problem and focus on that one question. Perhaps the group could even avoid any attempt to solve this contradiction. Discussion could focus only upon explaining if these two features do or do not contradict, and why. Under these restrictions, even when not explicitly attempting to solve the problem, the group will spontaneously generate solutions no matter how hard you focus on this singular question.

What are the delegates physically doing when exercising a canvas? Is this only a cognitive exercise? In my experience I have found workshops to be most effective if your delegates are quite active, and in particular if they take ownership of the workshop tools. As a facilitator it's tempting to stand in front of a canvas and exercise it yourself. The workshop delegates will happily permit you to take the time and trouble to append their material to the canvas. You should encourage them to do this themselves.

When delegates are *standing* the facilitator can more easily encourage delegates take the opportunity to physically interact with the canvas. Once interacting with the canvas, delegates can be encouraged to take some ownership and modify the canvas themselves by offering them some stationery. This gives them something to do with their hands, but more importantly gives them a means to note their ideas down if they don't currently have the attention of the group. As facilitator, keep a keen eye out for this. If you do not encourage delegates to add their ideas to the canvas then they will take notes, but clutch their little collection of these notes in their hand for the rest of the meeting. Giving delegates a means to record their ideas. Encouraging them to add them to the canvas as they are written will prevent delegates from turning to their neighbour and will once more help to prevent the group from splitting.

Every other delegate must be able to comfortably read each note, which brings us to some practical considerations with some stable outcomes. Consider the physical location of each delegate. They stand before a large canvas onto which each delegate is encouraged to append notes.

Delegates will be used to writing with a standard pencil or ball point pen, and are likely to have taken some writing materials to the meeting for just such a reason. This creates two problems. First, the notes that delegates take may be extensive. It is surprising just how much a motivated engineer can scribble onto a small self-adhesive note when they are possessed by the creative spirit. Second, handwriting cannot be easily read from a conversational distance. Under these circumstances, delegates are now expected to quickly consume screeds of tiny handwriting from a conversational distance.

We need to encourage delegates to write less and write larger. The solution is obvious and illustrated in Figure 145. Some people loath the workshop cliché of adhesive notes and thick pens. These essential tools provoke some valuable behaviours.

Figure 145: Innovation demands fat pens and small notes.

A short two or three word note on a small self-adhesive note provokes a very particular, clear and quite standard font size no matter who writes the note. Thick marker pens also offer a wide variety of vibrant colours, which can be useful to identify the author of each note if you encourage them to keep hold of their pen. The workshopping exercise is a negotiation, so delegates will change their minds about the contents and location of an idea. It is undesirable for them to write directly upon the workshop canvas. A self-adhesive and movable note is ideal. If standing, the delegates will adopt a location approximately one metre from a canvas. Too near and it's hard to focus upon the whole canvas and delegates must also stand uncomfortably close together. Too far and delegates tend to lose contact with this workshop tool. Fortunately, the font size forced by thick pens and small notes can be easily read from a metre or two away.

Here we encounter a significant and consistent feature of a workshop group standing before a canvas tool. Delegates will stand about one metre away from a canvas annotated by thick pens. If a group of delegates all stand around the canvas without obscuring one another, how many delegates can physically fit around the canvas? Figure 146 illustrates this scenario.

Figure 146: Approximately six people can crowd around a canvas.

Approximately *six* delegates can surround a workshop canvas without getting in one another's way. This matches the optimal size of a workshop group that maximises the number of collaborators without frequent splitting, described earlier. If more than six delegates attempt to interact with the canvas you will begin to see two rows forming. When the rear row loses contact with the canvas, they will form their own group, as illustrated in Figure 146. Once the group splits, then it will be much harder for the facilitator to structure and manage both discussions.

You might think that this is no big deal. As facilitator you could remain in contact with the tool and let the breakaway group manage themselves. I can guarantee that the group who remains in contact with the canvas will host a discussion amongst those of a confident, forceful and opinionated disposition. The second row that is ejected from the contact with the canvas, and distant from the facilitator, will contain those delegates who *need* the facilitator to draw their contributions into the discussion.

THE FACILITATION TEAM

A workshop is often successful not due to your carefully crafted framework, but success may result from the diligent efforts of your team of facilitators. This is particularly the case if unexpected difficulties arise during the workshop that demand that your facilitators take control, make a new plan and keep the whole workshop driving towards the planned objectives.

A facilitation is not like a presentation. With a presentation you have a topic which you can plan and rehearse. You may have an unstructured period at the end of a presentation during which the audience may offer questions. At worst, one can pass if you don't have a ready answer.

As you must create questions that respond to material the delegates offer in the workshop, a facilitation is like presenting a talk that you have not yet written. You have an overall structure to pursue, but that framework is an empty vessel that must be filled. You must exercise the workshop structure, listen carefully to the delegates and assemble presentation material as you proceed that arises from the interplay of your questions and their answers.

A good team of dedicated facilitators is a valuable resource. A workshop is perhaps the most public evidence of your problem-solving expertise. A workshop will be well remembered if it is either very successful, or if it is a waste of everybody's time. Your team of facilitators are the cast in your performance, and should be appreciated for this. Delegates can experience a significant sense of satisfaction from a good workshop, and the successful delivery of the workshop by your team of facilitators will, in turn, make you look great.

Facilitating a workshop is a little like a performance before a small audience. If the workshop starts to go wrong, then the facilitator is expected to handle these problems and modify or rewrite the performance in front of this audience, *ad hoc*, whilst continuing to host the workshop. This public exposure in a fluid, uncertain environment can be a stressful experience, particularly if the facilitator is inexperienced or the delegates are in a position of authority or scrutiny over the facilitator. No-one wants to appear in disarray in front of their boss or their customer.

The worst facilitation I have experienced was provoked by a very vocal delegate with little interest in the group objectives who insisted upon imposing his views and objectives upon the workshop in opposition to the desires of the assembled delegates. Furthermore, these delegates were rare and influential customers who were very difficult to gather in one place at one time. The disruptive influence had no self-consciousness whatsoever, but could not be ejected as they were an industry partner. Consequently, to mitigate this disruption I had to concede to the disruptor's demands, re-plan the workshop in front of the rest of the group, and exercise my now improvised workshop structure *in reverse, for five hours.*

An often-neglected activity that precedes a workshop that can have a significant impact upon the success of a workshop is *rehearsal*. We have characterised a workshop as a tool employed to exercise the collective minds invited to the event. Each workshop may demand a custom tool to achieve its particular objective, and the careful design of this tool is key.

The custom nature of each workshop tool demands that this tool functions as you anticipate. You can predict how it might function, but the most accurate means to assess your tool is to try it out on a suitable audience.

I often discover that workshop tools and structures that I have designed don't work as expected. The questions asked may seem ambiguous to the audience. The tool may be too complex for the group to understand and employ quickly. Activities may take longer than you expect. Carefully planned objectives may easily be derailed by a determined dissenter. You may even require a backup structure should the workshop not follow the planned path.

Facilitation can be a skilled but stressful activity. Offer some experience with the workshop tools to your team prior to their public performance. A rehearsal tests whether the proposed tool functions, and also offers to your facilitation team the practise that they need to become familiar with the material and acclimatise to the inevitable stresses. Finally, in your efforts to accustom your facilitators to the material, make your own attempts to derail the workshop. This will offer the facilitators experience of this disruption and can allow you to detect those opportunities available to disruptive delegates for which you can prepare in advance. To summarise, if you rehearse your workshop your event will be better. I guarantee it.

Your facilitators offer more to your workshop than managing the event. Your workshop tools should be designed to explain the problem, raise questions, provoke delegates to solve the problem, and provide a record of the workshop outputs. The facilitator will be listening very carefully to delegates and directing the discussion for many hours. Under these circumstances, a facilitator can gather a very detailed impression of the group's approach.

Once the workshop is complete it is well worth asking your facilitators to record their personal impression of the workshop. This impression is extremely volatile, but your facilitators will be fatigued after a long workshop. Give your facilitators time to reflect, but do encourage them to record their impressions soon after the event. No later than a couple of days. It's likely that your facilitator's impressions of the group will match the material gathered by the workshop tool, but may offer some narrative that joins the group's ideas in an accessible manner.

The outputs of a workshop will be fragmented summaries of the delegate's solutions. Even with their ideas recorded on the workshop tool, this output can also be as volatile as the delegates' impressions. You must process these outputs as soon after the workshop as you can. Pens and paper are an effective, tactile, engaging tool for delegates to employ during the workshop. At the very least you should translate this physical material into a digital format. If appropriate, you could distribute this raw material to the delegates as evidence of their hard work, and as a reminder of their ideas should you need to follow up with some queries of your own. If you don't immediately translate this material into a digital format, your office will fill with mounds of paper remarkably quickly.

You have a great deal of work to do after a workshop. Be sure that you schedule time after the meeting to process these results. You may need to refer back to the delegates to clarify their thoughts summarised on their numerous notes. Be very aware that memories will fade fast, particularly with very novel ideas. I have delayed processing the outputs of workshops, and I have regretted it every single time.

CHAIN TOOLS TOGETHER

Workshop tools help to generate questions in response to the delegates' contributions. It should be obvious that workshop tools can be combined. Some tools can be chained together, with the outputs of one exercise feeding the inputs of the next. Other tools represent details within another, to embed one tool within a portion of another. Examples of how tools can be used to raise questions, and how these tools might interact will be offered with an example of a workshop campaign.

Imagine it's the mid-1940s and technology is making the world ever smaller. You are a respected science fiction author and you recognise the value of long range, worldwide communication to the global population. How might you begin to consider this issue?

A well described problem takes you half way to the solution. In a workshop setting, a well described problem also offers you a pool of relevant questions. So, our best place to start is to better describe the problem. In this example, we need to think about that global population and to understand what they might want.

Osterwalder's *Value Proposition Canvas*, illustrated in Figure 147, asks us to consider the connection between the desires of the customer, represented by a circle, and the product or service that will fulfil that desire, represented by a square.

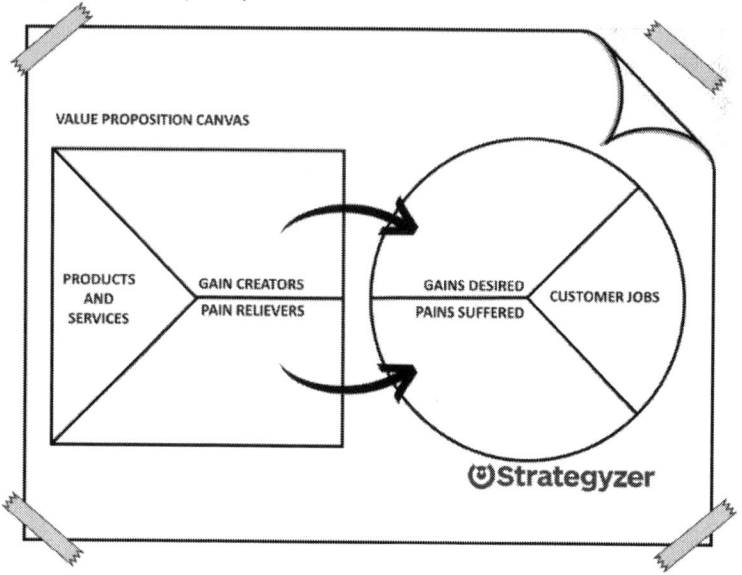

Figure 147: The Value Proposition Canvas
(*The Value Proposition Canvas is copyright Strategyzer AG, strategyzer.com*).

This canvas segments the question that queries the fit between the customer's needs and the proposed solution. This is a segmentation of the problem space that functions much like the nine boxes of Altshuller's thinking in time and scale. On the far right we consider what jobs the customer must fulfil.

For the sake of a simple argument let's assume that our customer must only *communicate with others at a long range*. This communication will confer a number of benefits to the customer. Osterwalder describes these as *Gains* that the customer seeks. In the case of our simple long-range communication problem, this job allows our customer to *coordinate actions with others who are far away*.

Of course, communicating and coordinating with others at long range is not going to be easy. A number of harms will accompany this long-range communication. Osterwalder calls these harms *Pains* that the customer must endure. In our simple example the desire to communicate at long range may demand a radio with *a very tall, very large, vulnerable and static antenna*. The jobs to do, gains desired and pains endured will populate the Value Proposition Canvas as illustrated in Figure 148.

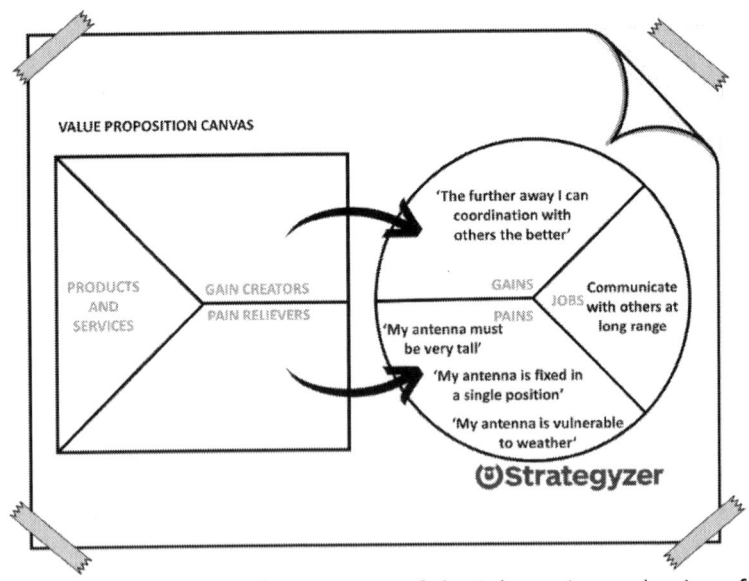

Figure 148: A very simple summary of the jobs, gains and pains of a customer communicating at long range.
(*The Value Proposition Canvas is copyright Strategyzer AG, strategyzer.com*).

Figure 148 suggests that the effort to communicate and coordinate with others far away is constrained by the need for a tall, static and vulnerable antenna. When Arthur C. Clarke considered this problem, he was first credited with proposing geostationary communications satellites, along with Vahid K. Sanadi building upon work by Konstantin Tsiolkovsky. In October 1945 Clarke published an article titled *'Extraterrestrial Relays'* in the British magazine *Wireless World*. Clarke's proposal could be summarised on Osterwalder's Value Proposition Canvas as illustrated in Figure 149.

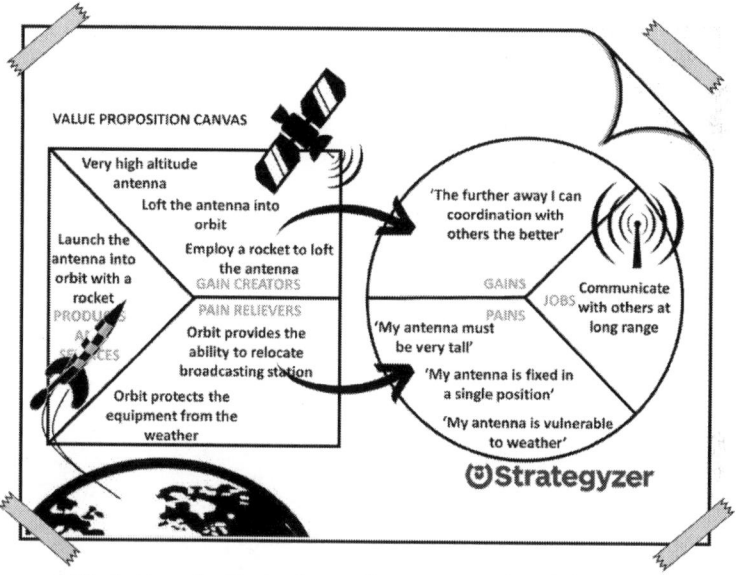

Figure 149: Arthur C. Clarke leapt from one side of the canvas to the other to propose satellites launched by rockets.
(*The Value Proposition Canvas is copyright Strategyzer AG, strategyzer.com*).

A very tall antenna allows our customer to communicate at long range. Clarke proposed that a very tall antenna could be offered if a repeater station was lofted into orbit with a rocket. These *Gain Creators* offer the Gains desired by our customer. This fit between the Gain desired and the Gain Creators and the fit between the Pain endured and the *Pain Relievers* creates a Value Proposition which can be embedded into a wider business model [20].

The reach of this orbital antenna means that our terrestrial broadcasting station need only reach the satellite in orbit. This station is no longer fixed to the site of a very large world spanning antenna. Furthermore, this orbital antenna is protected from the rigours of wind and rain.

On the far left of Figure 149 Clarke proposes to launch our world spanning antenna into orbit with a rocket. Clarke's proposal presents us with a puzzle. *How* did Clarke make that leap from the customer need to his proposed solution? With a little inspiration one might leap from your description of the customer to a product or service that fulfils their needs, and being an accomplished science fiction author probably helps. Can one make a more formal bridge between the customer description and a desirable product? To offer a formal framework to make this journey might require an additional tool that resides between the customer description on the right of the Value Proposition Canvas, and the description of our product on the left, illustrated in Figure 150.

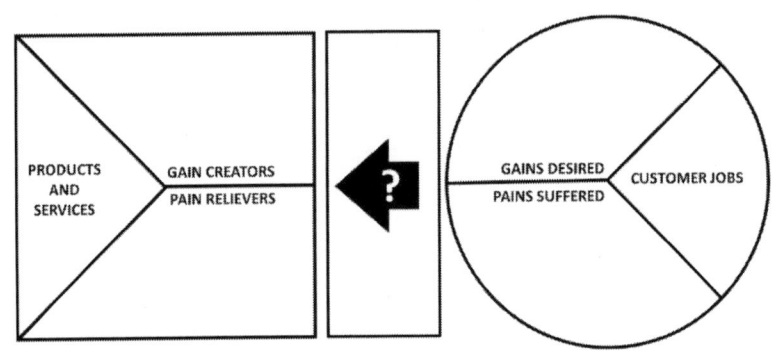

Figure 150: An additional tool may allow us to create a bridge from problem to solution.
(The Value Proposition Canvas is copyright Strategyzer AG, strategyzer.com).

What questions might such an intermediate bridge ask? A clue is offered by noting the similarity between Osterwalder's Gains and Pains and the Benefits and Harms employed by Altshuller. In most cases Gains and Benefits are synonymous, as are Pains and Harms. This allows us to embed our understanding of Altshuller's work *within* the Value Proposition tool offered by Osterwalder.

Our workshop can employ the Gains and Pains appended to the customer discovery illustrated in Figure 148 as inputs to a tool that employs Altshuller's problem solving framework to determine the product or service that will fulfil these desires. From the customer canvas in Figure 148 the customer states the following desirable benefits.

- Communication between remote actors.
- Tall antennas for long range.
- Mobile antennas.
- Windproof antennas.

A more extensive problem-solving exercise may discover far more customer objectives, but for the sake of a simple illustration we suffice with four. Do beware that beyond ten and the exercise can become unwieldy.

To follow Altshuller's framework we should attempt to define our problem in terms of those contradictions found amongst the customer desires. This cross-referencing exercise can be structured with a simple tool, illustrated in Figure 151. This contradiction matrix can furnish our workshop with a great many questions that derive from simply investigating the contradiction of one benefit with another.

On this canvas we cross reference each of the customer desires, and indicate contradictions with a strike through Desires that support one another, or at least do not harm one another, are indicted with a white background.

We want... \ Without harming...	Communication between remote actors	Tall antennas for long range	Mobile antennas	Windproof antennas
Communication between remote actors		Tall antennas offer long range	Remote actors may be on the move, or inaccessible	Remote actors may reside in poor conditions
Tall antennas for long range			~~Tall antennas will be large and hard to move~~	~~Tall antennas will be vulnerable to weather~~
Mobile antennas				Mobile antennas can withdraw from conditions
Windproof antennas				

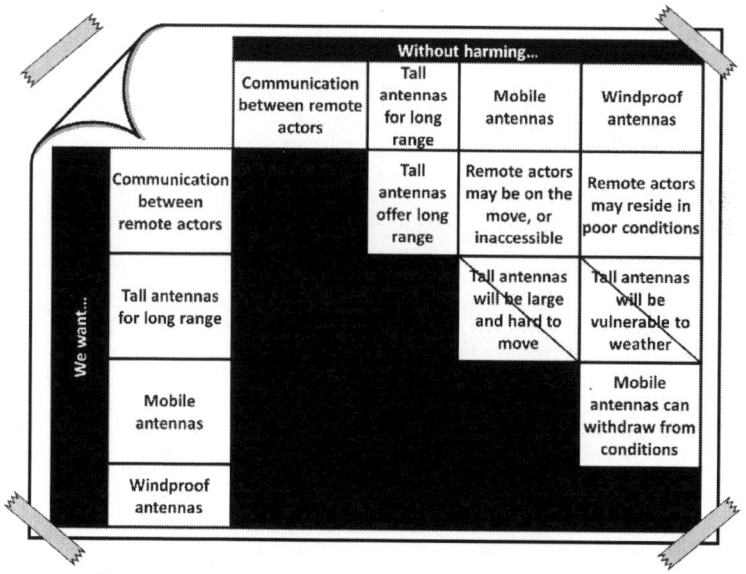

Figure 151: Do the customer desires contradict?

Communication between remote actors is enabled by tall, mobile antennas that can be deployed in all weathers. Similarly, the desire to weather proof an antenna is enabled by making it mobile, as it can be moved away from poor weather or moved under cover. By embedding this tool inside the Value Proposition canvas our workshop delegates will determine that the major contradiction amongst the customer's desires is provoked by the large antenna size required for long range, and the small size desired for mobility and protection from the wind. This clear identification of the central contradictions offers our workshop the focus it needs to solve the correct problem in easy, structured stages.

To avoid these contradictions, our antenna can be tall but not mobile or windproof. Alternatively, our antenna can be mobile and windproof, but not tall. These are technical contradictions that we must collapse into a physical contradiction.

From here a great number of questions unfold. We proceed by offering one of these contradictory desires in an established manner, and recovering the other by provoking our workshop delegates to invent some novel means. The questions are clear.

- *How could we retain the large size of or our antenna, but recover its mobility or wind resistance?*
- Alternatively, *how could we make the antenna mobile using an established, well understood mechanism but recover its large size?*

We start by considering how these characteristics that might be realised in *isolation* in an established manner. We start with the solution we would choose if no contradiction was present.

- Delegates may suggest a very tall antenna offered by a large metal pylon supported by its own mechanical strength or perhaps supported by long cables that stretch from the top to the ground, much like the supporting ropes of a tent.
- Delegates may suggest a mobile antenna that is small enough to be mounted on a truck, or a boat, or a train, or so small that it can be carried in a backpack or held in the hand.
- Delegates may suggest a windproof antenna that is short, squat and aerodynamic to present as little surface area to the oncoming wind as possible.

In this worked example this desire to retain a characteristic of the solution with established means whilst separating and recovering the contradictory elements with some cunning device raises four possible questions that our workshop delegates must consider.

- *How can tall, robust antennas become mobile?*
- *How can tall antennas become windproof?*
- *How can mobile antennas become tall?*
- *How can windproof antennas become tall?*

Note that the facilitator is not answering these questions. It's tempting for the facilitator to contribute to the solution process. However, whilst the solution process is taking place, the facilitator must always focus on the next step. The facilitator's role is to create and ask these questions.

For example, Altshuller offers four primary means to achieve these four strategies, which once more raises questions.

- *What resources are available to us? Can the environment resolve our problem?*
- *Does any prior art suggest that these problems have already been solved?*
- *Can we separate our contradictions using the 40 separation principles?*
- *Can we employ the 76 Standard Solutions to block harms or strengthen insufficient benefits?*

We start by investigating the resources available in the environment that may help us to solve these problems. To focus our workshop delegates upon the environment we could segment the problem space using Altshuller's nine boxes that help us think in time and scale, illustrated in Figure 152.

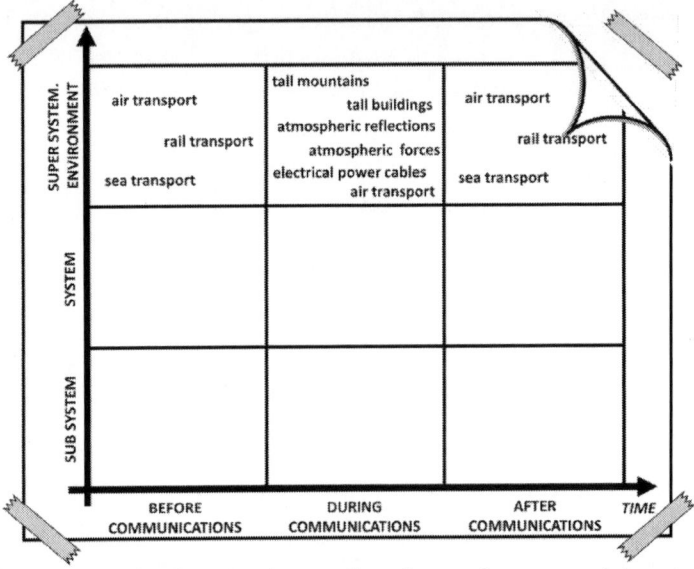

Figure 152: Thinking in time and scale can focus our delegates.

By simply applying resources as time progresses, the nine boxes provoke a great many questions for consideration by our delegates.

- Which resources might help us to move the equipment around <u>before</u> the antenna is used to communicate?
- Which resources might offer support <u>during</u> the operation of the communication device?
- Which resources will be useful once we have <u>finished</u> our communication?

In your facilitation of the workshop you could make direct reference to our four contradictions.

- Which resources could make tall antennas more mobile?
- How can the natural environment make tall antennas more windproof?
- Which human-made structures could allow mobile antennas to become tall?
- How might the wider world make windproof antennas taller?

Large-scale transportation, such as rail, sea or air travel could be used to move a large antenna around. During transmission a number of environmental resources could help us to lift the antenna to a high altitude. Multi-functional solutions are always desirable, as air transport serves to move the large antenna around and also to lift it to a high altitude. For clarity, we transpose these ideas from the canvas to indicate how these resources solve our four objectives. Despite only considering the available resources, your delegates might quickly discover a number of possible solutions.

- *If a tall antenna must become mobile, can we move large antennas with sea transport or move large antennas with rail links?*
- *If a tall antenna must become weatherproof, can we stabilise it with aerodynamic forces from the wind or embed it into tall buildings?*
- *If a mobile antenna must become tall, can we place it on a high mountain, or lift a repeater station with aircraft, or place it on tall buildings or bounce the signal around the world with atmospheric reflection?*
- *If a windproof antenna must become tall can we place it on a high mountain, or embed it into a tall building or lift it with aerodynamic forces from the wind?*

Note that in your workshop you are not the only one who can contribute questions to proceedings. Problems and solutions reside on either side of the same coin. What may be considered a solution, is actually a problem for another to solve. Consequently, ideas offered by your delegates can easily be transformed from statements that suggest solutions, into questions in their own right. In this manner, a workshop can become self-sustaining.

Next, we can again employ Altshuller's partition of the problem space into nine boxes to focus our workshop delegates on prior art. We direct our delegates to append those obvious, existing systems that already solve the problem for us, or we could encourage delegates to browse through patent applications or technology databases to derive the type of solutions that are appended to the canvas in Figure 153.

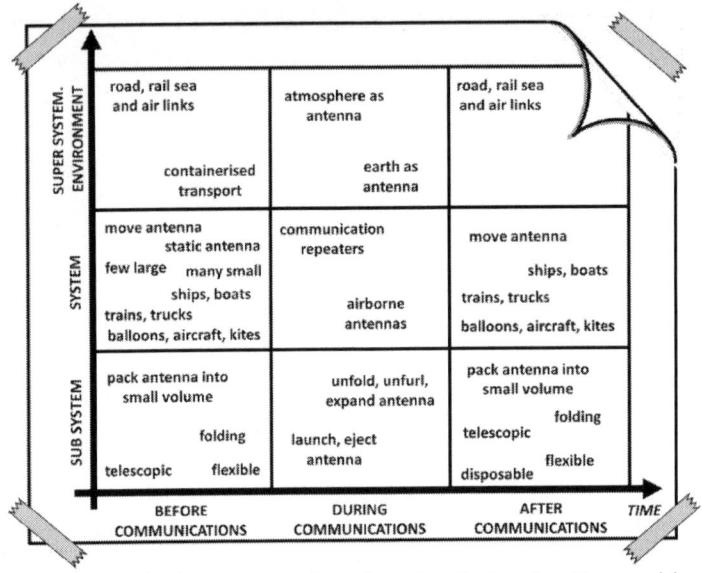

	BEFORE COMMUNICATIONS	DURING COMMUNICATIONS	AFTER COMMUNICATIONS
SUPER SYSTEM. ENVIRONMENT	road, rail sea and air links; containerised transport	atmosphere as antenna; earth as antenna	road, rail sea and air links
SYSTEM	move antenna, static antenna, few large, many small ships, boats, trains, trucks, balloons, aircraft, kites	communication repeaters; airborne antennas	move antenna; ships, boats, trains, trucks, balloons, aircraft, kites
SUB SYSTEM	pack antenna into small volume; folding; telescopic; flexible	unfold, unfurl, expand antenna; launch, eject antenna	pack antenna into small volume; folding; telescopic; flexible; disposable

Figure 153: Which systems already exist that solve the problem?

Once again, we can draw these ideas from our workshop tool and describe how this prior art solves our four contradictions. Delegates might suggest dismantling or retracting an antenna for transport or during poor weather. Perhaps delegates might wish to lift the antenna with some buoyant mechanism Perhaps delegates offer a series of small repeater stations. Whatever the suggestion, be sure to transform these ideas into further questions.

- *If a tall antenna must become mobile, then what mechanism do we know of that could pack the antenna into a small volume during transport?*
- *If a tall antenna must become windproof, could the same mechanism pack the antenna into a small volume during poor weather?*
- *Describe the mechanism that could lift a long antenna with a balloon or kite? Must we stop moving to operate this mechanism?*
- *If a windproof antenna must become tall, then how could we transport a windproof antenna onto the top of a mountain?*
- *How can we employ a series of small, weatherproof antennas to act as repeating stations? How many will we need?*

By only considering resources in the environment and considering solutions that the workshop group are already aware of or can find easily, the delegates can generate a large number of possible, but obvious, solutions quite quickly. These solutions can be transformed into questions and presented back to the delegates for further consideration.

To dive deeply into the resolution of our contradictions requires us to expose our workshop to Altshuller's more sophisticated observations. Next, we employ the 40 Separation Principles that can separate contradictions and the 76 Standard Solutions that can enhance insufficient benefits, block harms or enhance measurements. With these tools, yet more questions arise.

40 STRATEGIES CREATE A BRIDGE FROM PROBLEM TO SOLUTION

A motivated group of workshop delegates might be encouraged to familiarise themselves with the 40 Separation Principles and the 76 Standard Solutions prior to the workshop. As delegates are unlikely to do this, this material must be presented to them during the workshop.

Consider the 40 Separation Principles. Unless you and your delegates have a great deal of time to spend it is unlikely that you can work through every single one to consider how each might resolve the contradictions you unearth.

To introduce Altshuller's solution tools to those unfamiliar with their operation, we can employ the selection and distribution of Altshuller's principles in games for our workshop delegates. Principles can be printed onto postcards and shuffled like a deck of playing cards. You could offer solution strategies at random for consideration by the group. You could group solution strategies into separations in time, space, condition and scale, and encourage the group to consider one type of separation at a time. *How might an antenna be tall at one time and small at another time, only using Segmentation?* Perhaps the group might suggest a telescopic antenna? *How might an antenna be tall at one place, and small in another place, only using Segmentation?* Now the group might propose that the antenna be dismantled and loaded onto a train carriage for transport?

The pack of 40 principles could even be employed to provoke a little competition that could drive group to inspiration. Groups could be offered different principles to solve the same contradiction and challenged to conjure up ideas that may outperform the efforts of the other group. *Could tall antennas be made windproof using Periodic Action? Might a Mechanical Vibration do better?* Inject a little innovation sourced humour into proceedings and you could have the groups riffing back and forth with ideas. With a little careful motivation your workshop group can begin to fill a canvas with ideas very quickly and in great volume. A brief example is illustrated in Figure 154. I have hosted workshops that papered their canvases several layers deep with sticky notes.

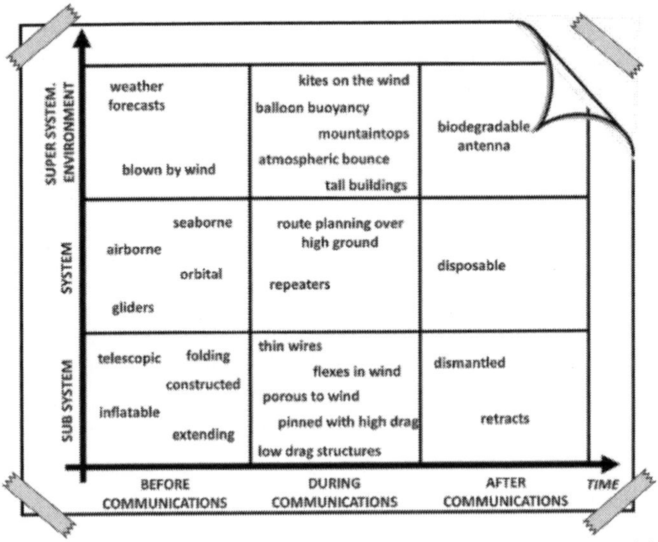

Figure 154: A well facilitated group can fill a canvas quickly.

Do not be concerned if successive visits to the solution process generate repeating solutions. The objective in pursuing this variety of solution strategies sourced from the 40 Separation Principles is to squeeze as many ideas out of your delegates as possible. Once you feel you have squeezed out as much as you can, Altshuller will offer you yet another approach to squeeze just a little more. You want your delegates to feel energised but wrung out by the end of the session.

Each of the 40 Separation Principles constitutes a question that you can ask your delegates. If a comprehensive list of solutions is desired one could explicitly reference every single Separation Principle against every contradiction within your problem. Although comprehensive, this is a method that may generate mountains of potential solutions. This comprehensive list of questions may provoke something like the following.

How might tall antennas become mobile using the following Separation Principles?

- *Segmentation?* Antennas that are telescopic, folding or dismantled in transport.
- *Nested Doll?* A telescopic antenna that retracts in transport.
- *Prior Counteraction?* An antenna that folds in transport.
- *Cushion in Advance?* An antenna retracts prior to transport.
- *Do it in Reverse?* Avoid moving the antenna at all. This suggests many static repeaters.
- *Spheroidality and Curvature?* Consider orbit to offer high mobility and great height.
- *Dynamics?* A tall antenna dismantled for transport.
- *Partial or Excessive Action?* An antenna that is so tall that orbit is achieved.
- *Periodic Action?* Only transmit from a large antenna when stationary and deployed.
- *Blessing in Disguise?* Might weather enhance mobility? Could the antenna be blown by the wind?
- *Copying?* Multiple low-cost repeaters that offer an antenna at every location.
- *Short Lived Objects?* A supply of tall but disposable antennas that we don't transport once we have finished using them.
- *Pneumatics and Hydraulics?* Lifting the antenna with a balloon.
- *Flexible Membranes and Thin Films?* Lift and transport a lightweight antenna with a kite.
- *Porous Materials?* Porous and therefore lightweight antenna that is easily moved.
- *Thermal Expansion?* Expand upon the balloon idea, suggesting that a hot air balloon lifts and transports an antenna.
- *An Inert Environment?* Inject a repeater into orbit

How might tall antennas become wind proof using the following Separation Principles?

- *Segmentation?* An antenna that is telescopic, folding or dismantled in bad weather.
- *Taking out?* We could remove structural elements to leave only a thin, low drag wire remaining.
- *Universality?* Structural antennas that are built into tall, robust buildings.
- *Nested Doll?* A tall telescopic antenna that retracts in bad weather.
- *Prior Counteraction?* Mitigate drag with a low drag profile.
- *Prior Action?* Deploy the tall antenna only in low wind locations using weather prediction.
- *Cushion in Advance?* Mitigate poor weather conditions using weather prediction.
- *Spheroidality and Curvature?* A tall but curved and aerodynamic antenna.
- *Dynamics?* The antenna is curved because it flexes in the wind.
- *Partial or Excessive Action?* Construct a massively strong and very tall antenna.
- *Periodic Action?* A tall retractable antenna that only extends during transmission.
- *Rushing Through?* A rapid, momentary extension with burst transmission.
- *A Blessing in Disguise?* A tall, high drag antenna is pinned to the ground buy forces from high winds.
- *Disposable?* A tall antenna might be entirely replaced after wind damage.
- *Pneumatics and Hydraulics?* Lift a thin antenna wire with a balloon.
- *Flexible Membranes and Thin Films?* Lift a tall antenna with a kite.
- *Porous Materials?* A tall but porous, low drag antenna.
- *Rejecting and Regenerating?* A tall but low-cost disposable antenna that is replaced after wind damage.
- *Transform Properties?* A tall, stiff structure might be folded flat by high winds.
- *Inert Environment?* An orbital antenna can avoid bad weather.
- *Composite Materials?* Construct a high strength, high flexibility carbon fibre antenna.

How might mobile antennas become tall using the following Separation Principles?

- *Segmentation?* Assemble a large antenna from small, easily transported components.
- *Counterweight?* Lift a lightweight, mobile antenna with a balloon.
- *Prior Action?* Route planning could ensure mobility across high ground only.
- *Equipotentiality?* Choose only to move over high ground.
- *Spheroidality and Curvature?* Once more suggests orbit.
- *Dynamics?* Mobile antenna could be enlarged at the destination.
- *Rushing Through?* Rapidly lift a small, mobile antenna and offer short, burst transmission to minimise stationary time.
- *Blessing in Disguise?* A moving platform tows a kite or glider that carries a small, mobile antenna.
- *A Mediator?* Bounce a signal from a small antenna off the atmosphere.
- *Copying?* Remain static but gain coverage through multiple low-cost repeaters.
- *Replace a Mechanical System?* Bouncing the signal off the atmosphere.
- *Pneumatics and Hydraulics?* Lift a small mobile antenna with a balloon.
- *Flexible Membranes and Thin Films?* Transport a small antenna with a kite.
- *Rejecting and Regenerating?* Multiple small, mobile but disposable repeaters.
- *Inert Environment?* Once more sends a message repeater into orbit.

How might windproof antennas become tall using the following Separation Principles?

- *Copying?* Multiple, small, low-cost and windproof repeaters that can hop a message a long range.
- *Local Quality?* A small, windproof mountaintop antenna.
- *Nested Doll?* Once more offers an extendable antenna.
- *Counterweight?* Again, uses the wind to lift a small antenna to great height.
- *Partial or Excessive Action?* A gigantic, very strong windproof antenna.
- *Periodic Action?* A short, squat antenna that leaps into the air and transmits.
- *A Blessing in Disguise?* Again, offered by a kite that lifts a small low drag antenna.
- *A Mediator?* Bounce a signal from small antenna off atmosphere.
- *Copying?* Multiple small, squat, low drag, low-cost repeaters.
- *Disposable?* Multiple small, squat, low drag disposable repeaters.
- *Replacing a Mechanical System?* Bounce a signal off the atmosphere.
- *Pneumatics and Hydraulics?* An inflatable antenna. Inflated by the wind?
- *Flexible Membranes and Thin Films?* Again, a kite to lift a small antenna.
- And finally, *Porous Materials* suggest a low drag mesh antenna.

Note that this comprehensive treatment results in duplicate ideas that separate *different* contradictions. These repeating strategies are well worth identifying. If a single strategy can separate all of your contradictions, an elegant solution may emerge.

The 40 Separation Principles offer a large reservoir of inspiration to generate questions with which to query your workshop delegates. With these 40 principles to hand, your delegates are likely to run out of endurance long before you run out of questions to ask them.

76 STANDARDS CREATE A BRIDGE FROM PROBLEM TO SOLUTION

The use of Altshuller's Substance-Field and the 76 associated Standard Solutions to support a workshop requires a little care, as the flexibility of this tool can be limited by the complexity of the technique. The construction and modification of Substance-Fields can be a time-consuming activity that may be unsuitable for a short timescale collaborative activity unless delegates are skilled in the use of this technique. I have observed workshop delegates attempt to construct diagrams that describe system interactions. In my experience, to construct an effective Substance-Field schematic during the limited period of a workshop may not offer the utility desired.

Alternatively, the Substance-Field could be used as a framework for your discussion, much like the 9 boxes constrain and focus our thinking in time and scale. Prepare a suitable Substance-Field illustration before the workshop, and use this framework to talk delegates around the problem and to generate questions.

This leads us to a contradiction. Rather than separating contradictions, the Standard Solutions focus upon the blocking of harms or the improvement of insufficiencies. This technique is a useful tool for improving the operation of an existing system. If our customer discovery offers only a list of benefits desired, how can we construct a Substance-Field schematic of the solution before the problem has been resolved?

One might expect that to describe the interaction between benefits, insufficiencies and harms with a Substance-Field requires an incumbent solution to refer to. In fact, we need not construct a complete solution, but can suffice with an understanding of how the components of the system alluded to by the benefits desired might interact. In this example, we desire the following benefits.

- Communication between remote actors.
- Tall antennas for long range.
- Mobile antennas.
- Windproof antennas.

Scrutiny of these desires tell us that a solution is likely to contain at least the following components.

- A transmitting antenna,
- a receiver,
- a means to transport the antenna,
- and inclement weather.

To construct a Substance-Field diagram of the system that may arise from the benefits desired, we can cross reference the interaction of these components and determine whether they inflict harms upon one another or offer support. This cross reference can be observed in Figure 155. Beneficial interactions are indicated with a white background. Harmful interactions are indicated with a strike through.

The relationship between the transmitting antenna and the receiver is clearly beneficial. Note that the receiver does not change the transmitter unless we reverse their roles. The antenna is likely to encumber the mechanism that will transport it, and the antenna is likely to be buffeted by the wind.

What influence does this...	...have upon this?			
	ANTENNA$_1$	RECIEVER$_2$	TRANSPORT$_3$	WIND$_4$
ANTENNA$_1$		informs	~~stresses~~	~~blocks~~
RECIEVER$_2$			~~stresses~~	~~blocks~~
TRANSPORT$_3$	moves	moves		~~blocks~~
WIND$_4$	~~stresses~~	~~stresses~~	~~stresses~~	

Figure 155: Before constructing the Substance-Field, we must understand how each component influences every other.

With the interaction between components understood we are at liberty to choose how much of this system we wish to illustrate with the Substance-Field. Substance-Field diagrams can become very complex very quickly. The Substance-Field need only be as complex as it needs to be, and no more. In this example, as we are attempting to design a better transmitter, we shall ignore the influence of the receiving antenna upon the rest of the system and assume that any improvements we make to the transmitter will offer benefits if made to the receiver.

Reference to the matrix of influences offered by Figure 155 allows us to build each Substance-Field interaction of interest in isolation, illustrated in Figure 156.

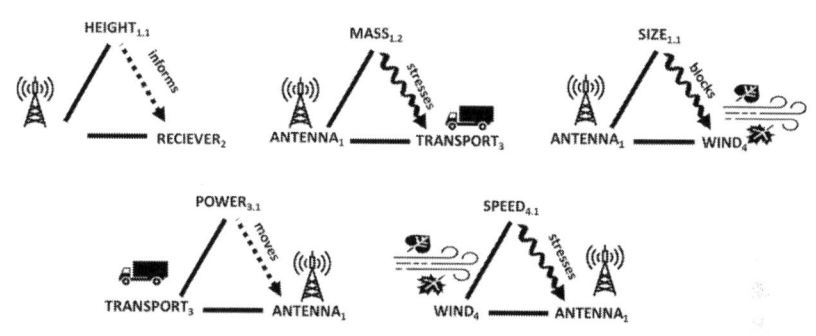

Figure 156: Build each Substance-Field in isolation.

These isolated Substance-Field interactions can them be assembled into a complete system, illustrated in Figure 157. This complete Substance-Field illustration offers a tool that you can present to workshop delegates, which which they can better understand the interaction of benefits, harms and insufficiencies in the system. Workshop delegates can scrutinise this illustration to better understand the problem. The Substance-Field offers a language with which to ask questions and propose means by which harms may be mitigated and insufficiencies improved.

By reference to this workshop tool, delegates can easily form a shared understanding of the problem.

- Large antenna demand that transport systems be powerful. As mass increases, the power of the transportation system may become insufficient to move it.
- Tall antennas will catch the wind. The taller the antenna the greater force imposed by the wind and the more stress is placed upon the structure.
- Long range demands large antennas. If we shrink the antenna the range will become insufficient.

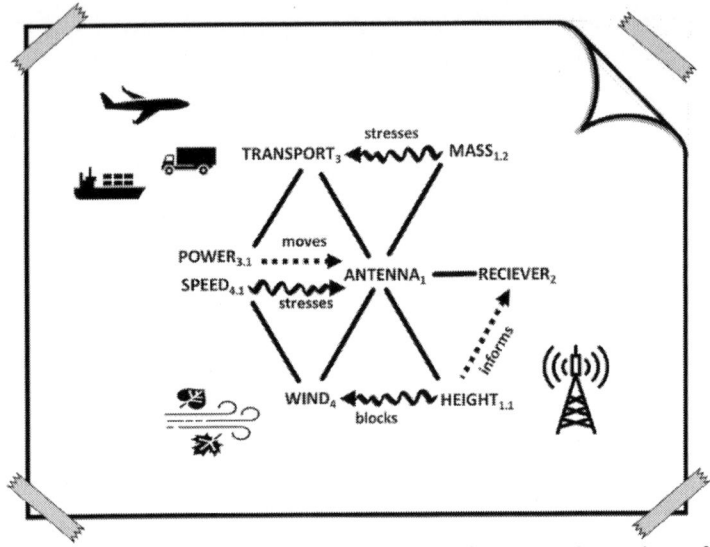

Figure 157: The desire for height and mobility introduces benefits, harms and insufficiencies

Clearly, if the antenna must be tall, we could construct a huge, strong structure that can be carried by large, powerful transportation. If we don't wish to exacerbate our harms by creating this behemoth, our alternative strategy must be to create an antenna that is both lightweight and low drag. This is obvious from simple inspection of the Substance-Field diagram. A more comprehensive resolution might be achieved by generating questions derived from the 76 Standard Solutions.

The Standard Solutions can be introduced to the workshop delegates in much the same manner as the Separation Principles. The facilitator could introduce solutions into the discussion when it seems appropriate. Cards that summarise each solution could be printed, shuffled and distributed manually. Games could be wrought with these cards, to contrast or compete for innovations. Using these Standard Solutions, the workshop delegates are encouraged to suggest modifications to the Substance-Field diagram. Harms should be diminished or blocked and insufficiencies should be strengthened.

Although the Substance-Field may help delegates understand the problem, how delegates unfamiliar with this technique express their ideas may require some finesse. A skilled delegate may very well offer a reformed Substance-Field. Others may simply express their ideas using more familiar language, perhaps recording their ideas on a sticky note attached to the appropriate part of the illustration.

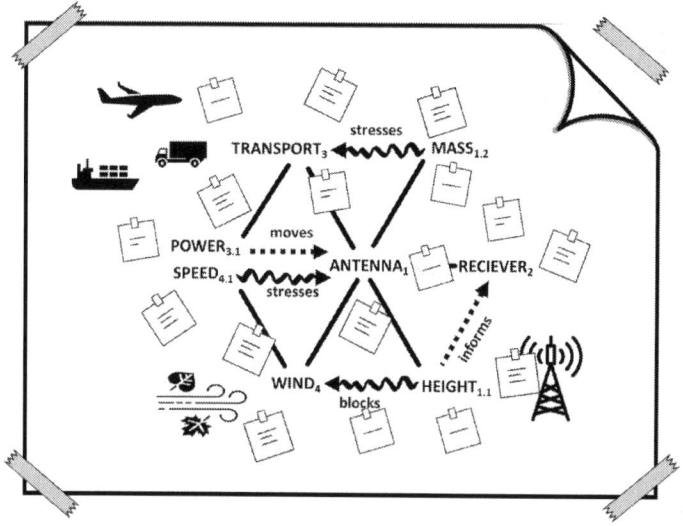

Figure 158: Delegates might simply offer their ideas in language familiar to them.

How delegates offer their ideas is very much up to you, and depends upon the skill of your delegates and your facilitators. We proceed by describing how the 76 Standard Solutions might be employed in a workshop to raise questions and resolve this problem. I offer two potential solutions.

Thin, porous, collapsible antennas?

We could start solving this problem anywhere on the Substance-Field diagram, so we will start with the wind buffeting our tall antenna structure. The relevant portion of the Substance-Field diagram is illustrated in Figure 159.

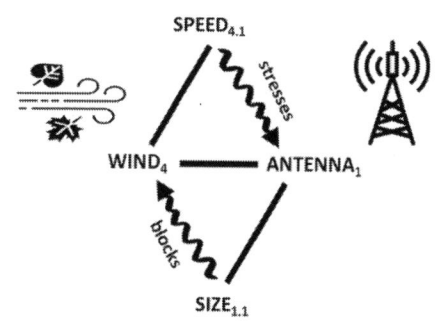

Figure 159: The tall antenna is buffeted by high winds.

As facilitator you might reach into your pool of Standard Solutions, and simply suggest to the delegates that these harms may somehow be blocked. This blocking of harms is suggested by Standard Solution 1.2.1, illustrated in Figure 160. Whether you explicitly show the delegates this symbology is up to you. However, translating this into more familiar language might be appropriate, depending upon the group. *How can we block the drag caused by the structure? How can we block the stresses caused by the wind?*

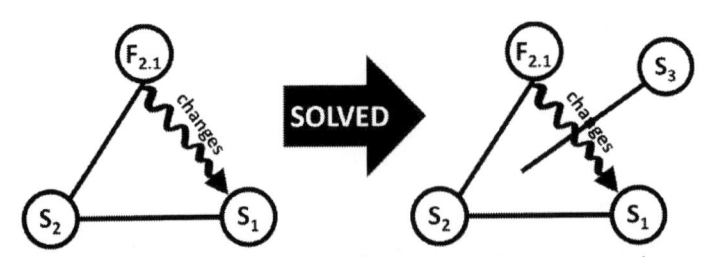

Figure 160: 1.2.1 Block the harm by introducing a new substance. Introduce the third substance between the given two substances. This third substance will remain unchanged.

This solution provokes a number of questions. *What substance could we introduce that will block the stresses imposed upon the antenna, or block the manner in which the antenna structure will catch the wind? If we introduce a new substance, do we not simply add more material to block this wind? How could we add a substance without adding more substance?* One of the Class 5 helper functions offers a clue.

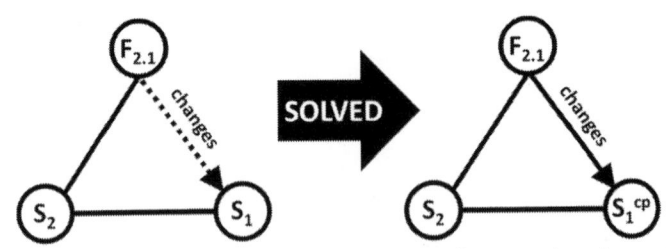

Figure 161: 5.1.1.1 Introduce substances under restricted conditions by introducing voids, fields, air, bubbles, foam. The 'cp' suffix suggests a transformation to a porous or capillary form.

Perhaps we could add <u>nothing</u>, rather than adding something, by introducing gaps or spaces? Could this addition of nothing block either of the harms in Figure 159? The formal Substance-Field illustrated of this application is offered in Figure 162. Unless delegates can think of a means to add voids into the wind, they may introduce these voids into the antenna. The antenna could be constructed from a thin porous mesh. Perhaps a wire mesh?

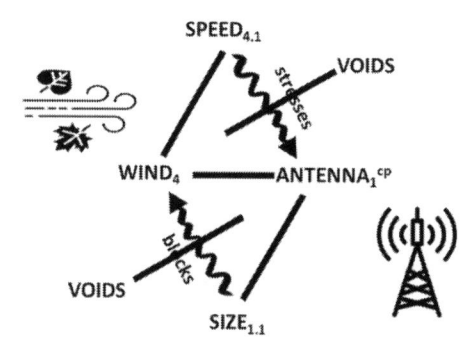

Figure 162: Voids or spaces in the antenna prevents the antenna from blocking the wind, and reduces the stress upon the antenna.

Next, you might direct the delegates' attention to consider the harms and insufficiencies observed in our effort to move the antenna, illustrated in Figure 163. The mass of a large antenna stresses the motive power of the transportation device. Consequently, the power available to move this large antenna becomes insufficient. How could we resolve this poor relationship?

To resolve the insufficiency of the transportation device provoked by the mass of the antenna, delegates could be directed to determine a means by which the power available from the transport may be increased, or the mass of the antenna might be reduced.

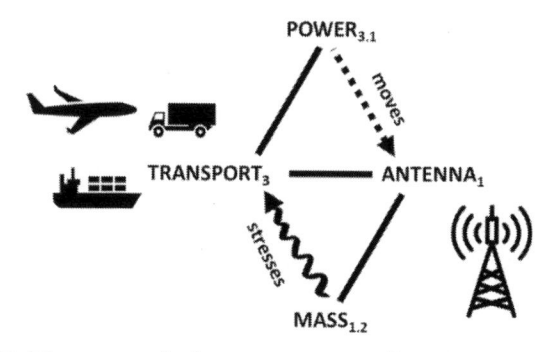

Figure 163: The mass of a large antenna will make transportation difficult.

A facilitator listening carefully will note that the group have already offered means to reduce the mass of the antenna, by introducing those drag reducing voids.

When proposing solutions, we are always keen to find repeating strategies that resolve multiple problems. As facilitator, if you observe the same solution strategies arising over and over, it is well worth pointing this out to the group.

Try to avoid solving the problem for the group. If a solution seems obvious, try to retain the facilitator role and couch this solution as a question. *Do those drag reducing voids help to solve the transportation problem?* After all, your primary purpose as facilitator is to provoke your delegates into having good ideas. For all you know, the above question could very well provoke not the obvious answer, but drive the group to a novel alternative. Perhaps the antenna is not simply lightened by the voids, but becomes a compressible foam to be crushed into a small container?

Once more, we can block the harm introduced by the antenna mass by introducing gaps, spaces or voids into the antenna to lighten the load.

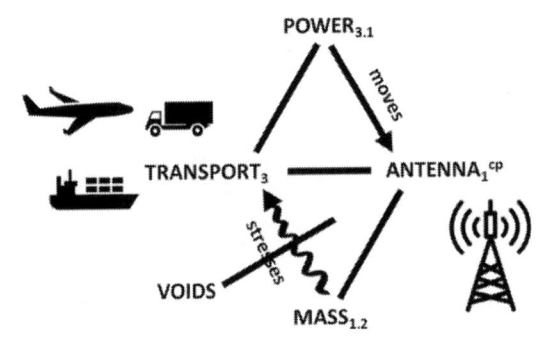

Figure 164: Introducing a mesh antenna lightens the load.

In this simple example, diminishing the cross section of the antenna to the wind will reduce the stresses upon the antenna. We could create an antenna that is full of holes, that leads us to consider a mesh, or a net. This strategy resolves both the wind load and the power required to transport this structure. If your Substance-Field is not too complex, you might encourage the delegates to make modifications to the workshop tool, as illustrated in Figure 165. However, be sure to carry spares should this line of enquiry prove fruitless.

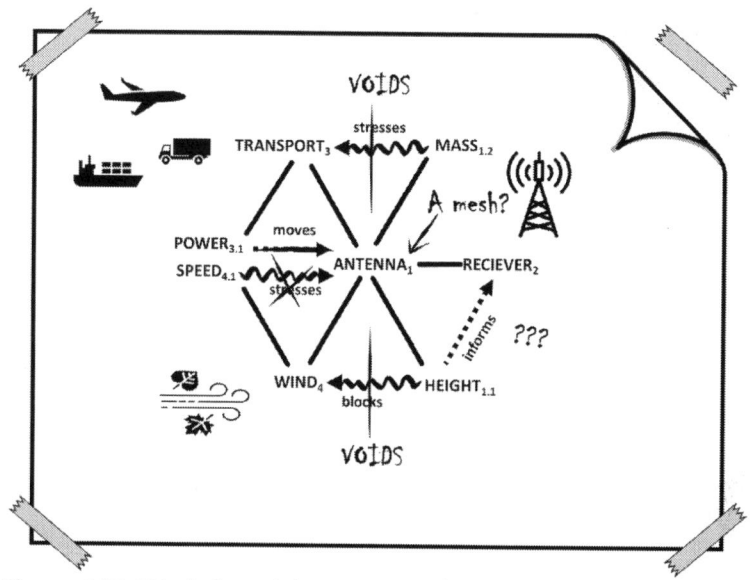

Figure 165: Workshop delegates may find it useful to append the illustration. If this is likely, be sure to carry spares.

As facilitator, once some solutions have been suggested you should introduce the idea of *Benefit Induced Harms*. Delegates may be so pleased with a new idea that they may neglect to identify new harms or insufficiencies that they have introduced with their genius. Unfortunately, it's up to you to dampen their spirits.

The Substance-Field illustrated in Figure 157 offers a means to introduce this new problem. As with the 9 boxes that help delegates to think in time and scale, the group's modification of the Substance-Field will show you which part of the system they have neglected, indicated in Figure 165 with some question marks.

We remind the delegates that this mesh antenna still needs to exhibit some height if the receiver is to be informed. *How can an antenna denuded of material reach the desired altitude?* We have introduced a Benefit Induced Harm. If full of holes the antenna may no longer support its own weight. With a little support from a skilled facilitator, perhaps our delegates could add this new harm to our new Substance-Field description of our wind proof antenna, illustrated in Figure 166. However, note how untidy this illustration may quickly become if modified during the workshop itself. Care must be taken when allowing delegates to modify a tool directly. This is where spare tools can come in very handy.

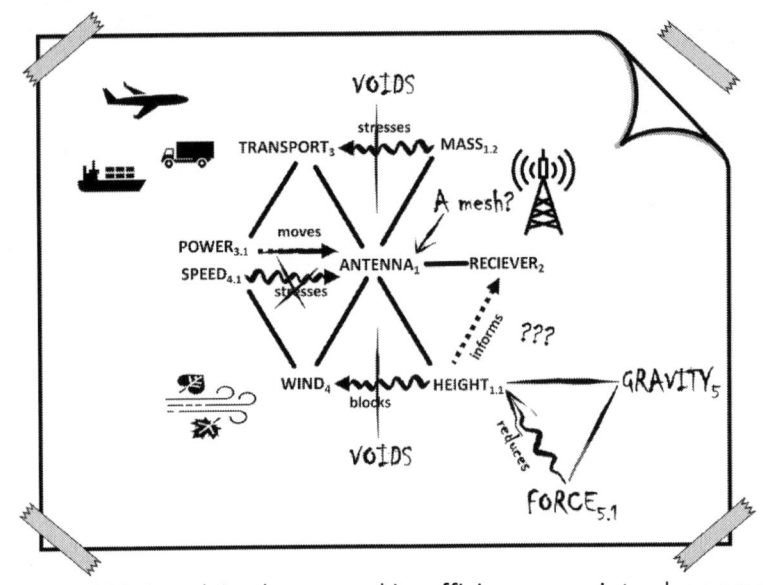

Figure 166: Resolving harms and insufficiency may introduce new harms into your system. Gravity pulls the flexible antenna to the ground.

How might we resolve this Benefit Induced Harm? We direct our delegates back to the 76 Standard Solutions. Solution 1.2.3 offers a suggestion, illustrated in Figure 167.

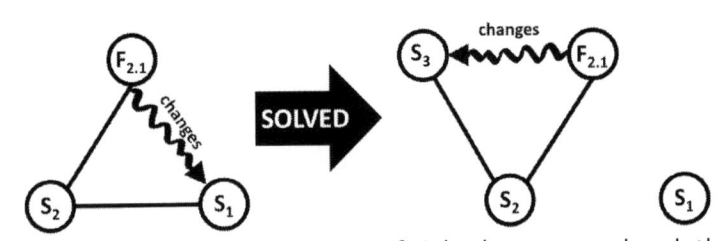

Figure 167: 1.2.3 Introduce a sacrificial substance to absorb the harm.

What type of substance might we add to our system to absorb the forces introduced by gravity that crush our delicate mesh antenna? A more ideal introduction of this hypothetical substance is suggested by 5.2.2. *Could we raise fields from substances that are present in the environment?* Employing substances already in the environment to raise a new, beneficial field encourages delegates to offer elegant solutions that are closer to the ideal. The Substance-Field allows us to work around the problem, asking the same question of each substance in the system. *Could we raise a field to absorb those gravity forces from the transportation mechanism? Or from the mass of the antenna? Or from the receiver? Or from the wind?*

As we facilitate this discussion, we need not solve the problem. We need only to raise questions assembled from our observations of the Substance-Field and our understanding of the Standard Solutions. The delegates will do the rest. Rather than modifying the Substance-Field itself, your delegates might be encouraged to draw simple schematics of the ideas that come to mind when provoked by your questions. Raising fields from the environment to counteract gravity's effect upon your flexible antenna may offer the sketches illustrated in Figure 168.

Figure 168: Could we raise a field to absorb those gravity forces from the transportation mechanism or the wind?

Delegates might imagine a thin, low drag cable lofted to high altitude by a buoyant balloon. Perhaps the motion of the wind itself could provide the force we need, lifting the antenna with a kite? If we experience no wind, perhaps the motion of the transportation itself could raise the field that provokes lifting forces, by towing a glider?

If we have a sufficiently simple Substance-Field, perhaps a short break may allow the facilitator to modify the Substance-Field diagram to ensure that no new harms of insufficiencies have been introduced. For more complex problems, perhaps a recess may be required for a new Substance-Field to be constructed and a new workshop scheduled. For the buoyant balloon sketched by delegates in Figure 168 this modification to the Substance-Field is illustrated in Figure 169. The antenna mass is transferred from the transportation mechanism to the balloon, where the atmospheric buoyancy counteracts this harm. The thin antenna still blocks the wind, but the stresses provoked are no longer harmful.

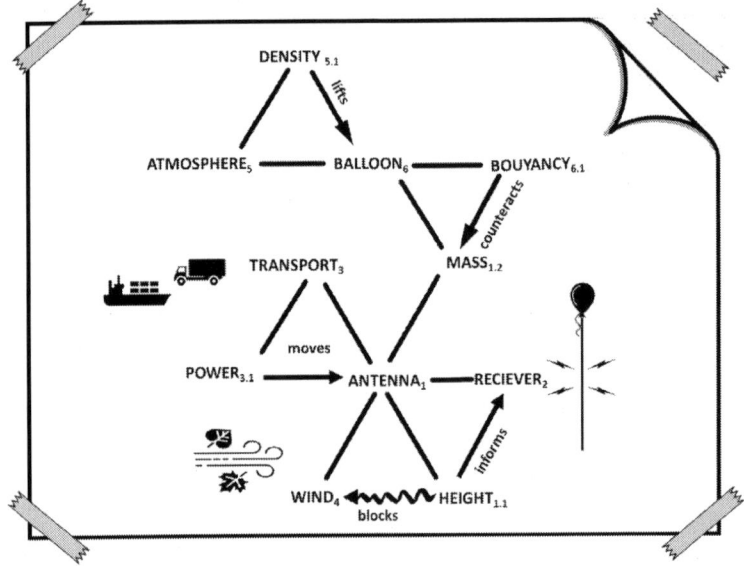

Figure 169: Add a balloon and a tall antenna can become low drag

Developing a Substance-Field to offer a new workshop tool may be unfeasible in a time limited event. The need for a new Substance-Field need not end your workshop. If you reach a conclusion that requires some preparation to progress, our formal framework allows us to return to the original question described by Figure 157 and encourage the workshop delegates to take an alternative path.

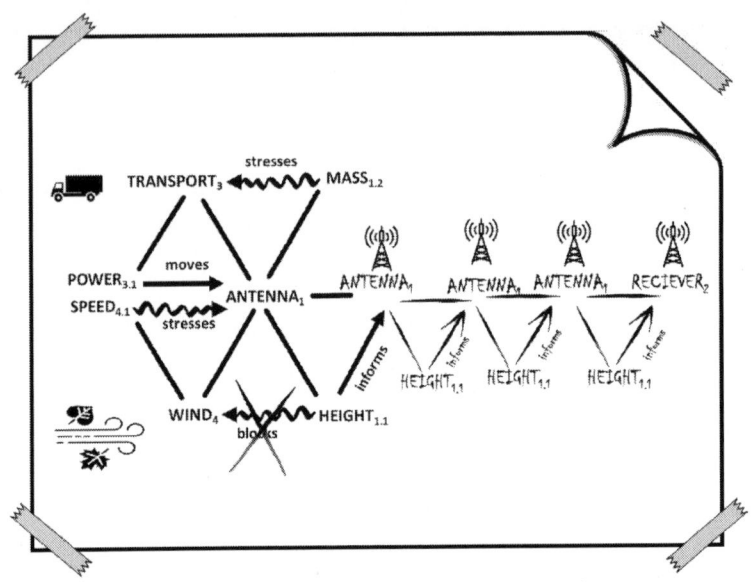

Figure 171: No transport, no height, no wind stresses.

Multiple ground level repeating stations seem to be a viable solution. The range of each would be short, and therefore limited by the near horizon. A new Benefit Induced Harm is discovered. This limitation is sure to raise yet more questions. *Can we do better with a more mobile system that emerges from a combination these two ideas?*

If we release our balloon lofted equipment up into the atmosphere, the altitude and transportation of this repeating station could both be offered by the buoyancy and wind forces from the atmosphere. The Substance-Field diagram of this modification is illustrated in Figure 172. Consequently, one of the solutions we can derive from a consideration of the 76 Standard Solutions involves multiple, balloon lofted, disposable repeater stations spanning the globe.

With this example we have observed multiple passes through the problem, starting from the same tool but taking different routes through the problem. Each route is guided by Thinking In Time and Scale, the Separation Principles or the Standard Solutions transformed into countless questions that we inflict upon our delegates. This iteration will squeeze as much information as possible from delegates. If your workshop attendees are not a little tired by the end of the session, they have more ideas to offer. Squeeze them some more.

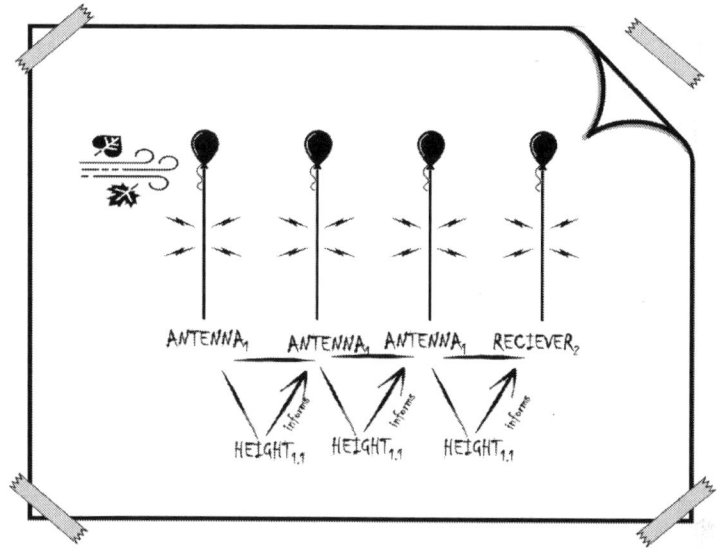

Figure 172: Lofting the repeater stations will offer more altitude and greater range.

This solution is by no means the only outcome of this exercise. Consideration of resources, prior art, the separation of contradictions, the mitigation or harms and the strengthening of insufficiencies can generate a great many solutions to a single problem.

This ability of Altshuller's work to create solutions in volume is of great utility to the innovator. Reis reminds us that having only a single good idea transforms one from a problem solver into a politician. With a single idea to your name, clutched to your chest, protected from others, you must now sell this idea to the stakeholder and fund managers to secure the finances you need to proceed.

With a large volume of solutions to choose from you now have the material that you need to begin a comprehensive campaign of customer experimentation, as described by Reis, Osterwalder, Blank and Dorf. Multiple proposals can be illustrated, mocked up, simulated, prototyped and costed to determine which features are most desirable to potential customers, and which miss the mark entirely. The simple workshop example presented in this chapter, and Figure 173, illustrates that Altshuller's frameworks can be embedded *inside* the Value Proposition Canvas. With Altshuller's work embedded inside the business building tools, innovation becomes a volume proposition.

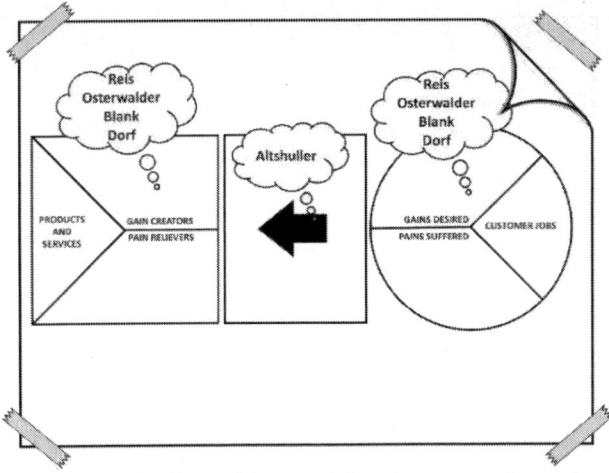

Figure 173: Altshuller's problem solving framework can be used to bridge our Value Proposition in volume.

Using this bridge, we ultimately reach the far side of Osterwalder's Value Proposition Canvas with a rational and staged framework that ensures that we have squeezed every last drop of creativity from our workshop delegates. Finish by summarising your ideas on the left side of the Value Proposition Canvas. The Value Proposition of our airborne repeaters might look as illustrated in Figure 174. As for your delegates, if they do not leave the workshop elated, energised but exhausted, then there are still more ideas within them.

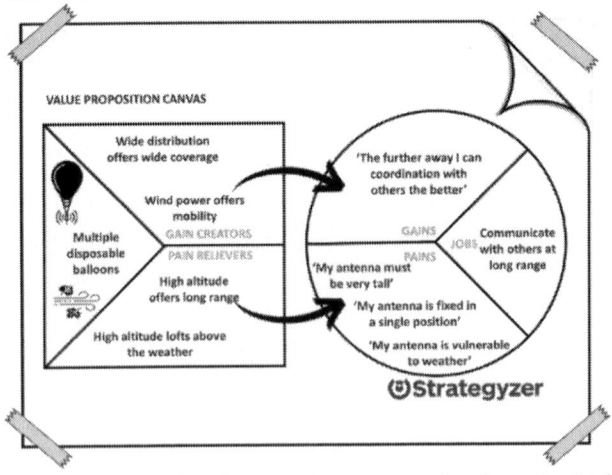

Figure 174: A single idea can be summarised on the Value Proposition Canvas.
(*The Value Proposition Canvas is copyright Strategyzer AG, strategyzer.com*).

15. CASE STUDY: STORMS, NORMS, PERFORMS.

The Soldier wearily heaved himself to his feet and took in his new surroundings. He was standing upon an entanglement of twisted tree branches, a mingling of structures from mighty boughs to tiny twigs that collaborated to produce a wide platform within the canopy of the world tree[117]. The older, slower man eventually emerged from beneath a rustle of dry leaves to take in the same sight.

The tree's simple but repeating nature surrounded the interlopers. Great boughs formed the main structure to create the huge platform beneath their feet, to curve upwards into a natural bowl, and inwards to form a dome over their heads. Smaller branches wove in and out of these primary trunks to form floor and ceiling and walls. The air was still, and silent, and sultry, as tiny twigs filled in remaining voids to offer a shelter from the winds that whipped by the canopy at this extreme altitude. Dry green leaves sprouted from every surface and an odour of wood and damp and the forces of nature permeated this horticultural cathedral.

The void was not absent of life, as the tree was home to a broad church of creatures. Small insects scurried to and fro amongst small flowers that dotted the interior. Worms slid amongst the detritus of the forest floor. Occasionally small birds could be spied as they chased the other denizens of the canopy, or pecked at the many strange fruits that sprouted from the branches of this massive tree.

High above, the boughs that formed this wooded dome did not quite reach at the summit. At this peak a huge hole remained that permitted a strong shaft of sunlight to cast a tangle of shadows amongst the twisted knots of wood.

Near one wall, some distance from the new arrivals, squatted a copy of this wooded dome, in miniature. This structure looked more recent than its larger companion, and the twisting of cracked and splintered branches seemed artificial, forced and extemporaneous. The soldiers made towards this small dwelling to investigate what may reside inside.

As they approached, the voids in this cage of wood revealed a single forlorn occupant sitting upon a hard bench improvised from twisted branches. This could only be one person. The old soldier recognised his Queen. Rushing to this cage and gripping its rough wooden bars in his

---

[117] Resolve a contradiction. A structure must be both light and strong. GA SP 40 *Composite Materials*. This environment is a composite structure composed of collaborating elements separated by scale.

burned hands the old soldier hissed carefully chosen words to both attract attention and prevent alarm[118].

The Queen turned and immediately recognised her old comrade. As part of her army they had fought together against the beast that now imprisoned her. The bold service of her army was a powerful source of gratitude and pride to the Queen, and the effort she had made to know each and every one had not been dulled by the long intervening years.

The Queen explained that the Last Dragon continued its search and would not return for many hours. The Soldier considered it safe to risk the sharp report of a tree's felling, and began to hack at the bars of the wooden cage. The sword, now returned to a passive state made short work of the barrier, and the soldier snuck inside the structure for fear of the dragon's return[119].

The Queen and her old guard embraced and began to talk at that chattering pace reserved for old, long separated friends[120]. The Queen's first thought was, of course, for her daughter, and the old soldier reassured the Queen that the Princess had indeed grown into a beautiful and capable young woman. The younger man remained unintroduced and stood apart, respectfully silent amongst the old friends. Whilst his Father talked of the Princess he inadvertently gestured to the young Soldier, and a mother's instinct for these things provoked an uncontrollable blush from the young man[121].

The Queen next asked after her King, and was crestfallen as the old man described the King's loss and his deep and endless sadness. The old soldier noted this turn, and quickly changed the subject to their exploits of old[122].

As he listened, the young Soldier noted the endless heroic exploits the pair had endured in their long-ago quest to rid the world of dragons. Great clashes had been fought in torrential rains and muddied

---

[118] Resolve a contradiction. We must be both quiet and audible. GA SP3 *Local Quality*. Speak at a volume only audible locally.
[119] Resolve a contradiction. We are trapped in the presence of a predator. We must be present and not present. GA SP7 *Nested Doll*. SP32 *Colour Change*. Enter cover to camouflage oneself from detection.
[120] Resolve a contradiction. We must transmit information, but have no time to do so. GA SP21 *Rushing Through*. Little time is available to catch up on long awaited news.
[121] Make a measurement. GA SS4.3.1, *Create a measurement system using natural phenomena*.
[122] Listen carefully.

battlefields against waves of winged demons. The bitter cold of mountain top snows had been endured to explore dank and frigid caves in their quest to drive the beast from their habitats and out to the edges of the world. These adventurers had pitched and rolled on stormy seas to reach the remote outposts to which the beasts retreated. Great war machines had been constructed to offer complex contraptions devised to match these giant monsters. The whole Kingdom was united and coordinated in their shared goal of ridding the world of dragons.

The young Soldier listened with interest, and reflected upon his own years of soldiering. He had been well trained and excelled in these soldierly duties. Until the Last Dragon had returned, he had fought in no wars, responded to no disasters, and defeated no great beasts. The young Soldier had diligently guarded a great many things that required little protection. As one year had rolled into the next it seemed that the heroic exploits of the Queen, the King and their brave army had indeed rid the world of danger to leave it safe for their children. The Kingdom had become secure, stable, static, stagnant and without challenge.

The old man completed his brief review of the intervening years, and politely enquired after the Queen herself. In particular, his curiosity focussed upon why the Queen was fashioning what seemed to be the introduction of new dragons into the world.

The Kingdom's campaign against these beasts had almost prevailed, but a single dragon remained. The very dragon who had abducted his Queen. With only a single dragon left in existence, this species had no means to create more of their kin. Only a human hand could fashion dragons from the earth itself. A suitable creator was to be found in a regal hand who knew dragons well. A hand who knew the ways of dragons, and their form, and their function. One who had pressed against their scaled hides, and gazed into their fanged jaws, and soaked in the roar of their very stink. Such a woman could be taught the necessary process to form a dragon from the earth itself.

This task was to be a long labour, as a dragon is a complex creature who must gestate for many years before emerging into the world. Ripped so suddenly from her beloved daughter, the Queen had acquiesced to her task in the hope that she might find freedom from her imprisonment at the top of this detestable tree.

The Queen had not always been trapped in this wooden dwelling within the canopy. For much of her time in the tree and on the island she had free reign to explore her surroundings. Imprisoned only by this canopy, the Queen had explored the very extent of its branches in the hope that they may ultimately extend over land, but encountered only an endless liquid horizon. As she laboured in the earth, the Queen had explored the subterranean network beneath the tree, and once had even found the moon pool. However, no escape could be found.

Through fear of a fiery end, the Queen laboured upon the task of undoing her life's work and building the population of dragons anew. Until one day from her towering perch she spied a single ship heading towards her new realm. In all her years of incarceration she had never seen a single ship pass anywhere near to the great tree, and feared that she may never again see such a sight.

She considered descending the tree and waving from the shore, but the ship was a tiny speck upon the horizon. She would never be spotted. So, with the dragon absent the Queen elected to venture out once more into the far canopy and hoped to attract the attention of these sailors. The mighty height of the tree would continue to offer her as a mere speck to this crew, so the Queen scooped up the nearest object to hand that she might drop from the heights and alert these potential rescuers.

With a single iron grey dragon's egg under one arm the Queen scrambled out onto the canopy and, after some considerable effort, managed to position herself above the presumed track of the approaching ship[123]. Far below she could see the assembled crew gazing in wonder at this magnificent tree. If the iron egg was dropped from such a height it would make a considerable splash[124]. The Queen would have to time the release carefully and drop this lure as close to her target as possible.

With her best judgement she released the iron ball and watched it rapidly shrink from view towards her rescuers. The ship crept ever closer to her aim point, whilst the Queen waited in anticipation for the huge splash that would draw their intention and usher in the beginning of her return home.

This beacon of hope never arrived, as the Queen's aim was too effective. She was, after all, a highly trained and experience warrior. The iron projectile in its fall from the canopy had reached a tremendous

---

[123] Resolve a contradiction. The egg is heavy. The target is moving. Aiming a heavy egg at a moving target will pose a challenge. GA SP10 *Prior Action*. Optimally locate the projectile in advance.

[124] Make a measurement. The egg is small and the range is large. It will be undetectable once it reaches its destination. GA SS4.4.1 *Create a measurement system by using a suitable detectable substance*. A large splash.

speed, and punched clean thought the deck of this rescue ship, through the decks below, straight through the hull and out into the depths of the great Southern sea blasting the guts of the vessel into the brine. Back broken, the ship twisted along its length and issued a low, mournful moan as timber scoured timber in the agony of its demise.

To the horror of the Queen the gravely holed and broken ship sank within minutes with all hands[125]. The Queen could only watch in impotence as the ship disappeared below the waters in a frothing broth of wreckage. She remained in the canopy extremity for some time, watching the surface of the Southern sea heal over this tragedy that she had provoked in her desperation to escape and return to her daughter.

The sailors' suffering has passed quickly, as the ship was lost with all hands. The Queen's own troubles did not stop there. There was no way to hide the Queen's theft of an egg. Dragons are intelligent creatures, and they can most certainly count. Upon its return the Last Dragon raged in fury at the loss of this precious egg. It roared with frustration and rage at the Queen who the Last Dragon both reviled and required to achieve its ends. Heaving aloft and diving for the deep water, the Last Dragon plunged into the sea to search the depths of the ocean for this lost prize, but to no avail.

Returning to the canopy the Last Dragon devised a suitable punishment. With its great strength it bent mighty boughs double to create a cage into which it forced the Queen, and within which she remained when otherwise not consumed by her dragon making duties.

Story complete, the Queen turned to practical matters. The dragon would slumber for long periods, and over the years she had learned to control her power to climb the tree. The Queen could wait for sleep to consume the dragon, descend the tree unaided, so they could return to the island, embark the boat the soldiers must have arrived in and escape the dragon before it awakened.

The two soldiers glanced at one another nervously, and the Queen understood immediately. This was no rescue team. These troops had been transported here just as she had, and here they all remained trapped. The Queen covered the embarrassment of her soldiers with a hasty change of plans.

They were trapped, but they were now three. They were now armed with sword and shield, offered the Soldier, hefting these tools in

---

[125] Not every great idea is a great idea. Protect yourself from the potential stinkers.

illustration[126]. Could they overpower the dragon? Unlikely, suggested the old man who had fought many dragons in his time[127]. Certainly not without some cunning strategy and careful preparation, added the Queen, and the only other resource to hand was the tree itself[128]. How could such a small band use such basic tools to defeat a powerful dragon? The Queen knew the dragon may return at any moment, and her mind raced to devise a plan. As she listened to her small army, she closed her eyes to concentrate.

Stop. Take a step back. To overpower the dragon is to offer a solution. What is the real problem to solve? A dead dragon? A trapped dragon? No dragon at all? All were solutions, not problems, and none transported them from the island. Ideally, we wish to leave the island. Ideally, we do not want the dragon to prevent or pursue us. Still this does not offer transport from their captivity. A boat may offer some means to escape. The only resource available is the tree from which a raft may be constructed, but this does not prevent the dragon from easily capturing them. The dragon must <u>want</u> us to leave, and there was only one resource remaining which may offer them the transport they need. The dragon itself...[129]

The Queen reached this inescapable conclusion with dismay, for she has been acquainted with this dragon for many years and knew of its foul malevolence and its intolerant prejudice towards Humankind. This was, after all, why she had attempted to slaughter every last one of its kind with sword and spear and fire and water and every ounce of her nation's will. This was a relationship surely beyond any negotiation[130].

The Queen quietened the soldiers with a raised hand, explained her impossible conclusion, and sank back to the hard bench that was her only comfort. There was no escape. Her old comrade joined her on the bench, wrapped a brotherly arm around her shoulders and attempted to lighten their fate with talk of a heroic last stand. To go down fighting. To never give up. A last hurrah against the malice of fate itself that her King and

---

[126] GA. List your resources to find elegant solutions.
[127] Innovation is often assumed to be monopolised by youth. However, experience is a valuable commodity. Just because a problem is new, does not mean that age and expertise have no foothold or perspective.
[128] Enhance a benefit. Elevate the function to the super system, or in this case, GA SS 1.1.4 *Use the environment*.
[129] All benefits. No harms. The dragon takes them home. The Ideal Final Machine.
[130] The problem may not have changed, but has the problem-solving team?

daughter would be proud of.

At the mention of his beloved the young Soldier rejected such terminal solutions to their current captivity. As he set his will to resolve the task before him, a darkness descended like a cloak. The group rushed outside the cage, but their worst fears were confirmed. High above, filling the aperture that offered the only light to this chamber, perched a huge, reptilian beast. The Last Dragon had returned.

There was no time to lose as the Dragon launched itself from its perch and dove for the group. The shield would not protect three, so the young Soldier ushered the Queen and his old Father back into the wooden dwelling, rushed some good paces from this improvised hideout[131], turned to the descending Dragon and stood his ground[132].

The Dragon swooped low over the Soldier, peering at him with a jaundiced eye. This parasite was familiar to the Dragon, and it elected to finally rid itself of this bothersome pest. Another low pass, a deep breath and a gout of scorching flame should offer the best disinfectant[133].

The Soldier raised the great dragon scale shield. A slug of flame slammed into this protection and boiled around him, pressing him backwards. Two further passes hammered into the Soldier, pressing him into a stumbling retreat.

The Soldier survived two more onslaughts, and the Dragon became convinced that a more sustained treatment was in demand[134]. With cracking of branches and a crackling of twigs the Dragon landed before the embattled Soldier, took a heaving breath, and blasted the Soldier with one long, endless, intolerable gout of red flame.

The Soldier dropped to one knee and pressed his shoulder into the shield as the inferno boiled around him, fighting for breath and all too aware of the heat leaking through the scale's protection. The Soldier had been pressed back up a rise in the forest floor, where the smallest twigs burst into flame, but the larger boughs blackened, scorched and held their strength[135].

The Soldier stood his ground on the very rim of a wide wooded basin,

---

[131] GA. A separation in space.

[132] Ultimately, you may simply have to work with what you have to hand.

[133] Block a harm. GA SS 5.3.1 *Change the phase of a substance*. Mitigate a harm by oxidising the material it is made from.

[134] Resolve a contradiction. GA SP20 *Continuity of Useful Action*. Continuous work at full capacity without a break.

[135] A resilient structure that employs properties from different system scales.

Multiple short range repeater stations?

Take a short break, produce a spare of your original workshop tool and present to your delegates a Standard Solution that may lead the group down a new path. For example, we might consider the Class 3 solutions. In particular, 3.1 improves systems by adding or copying elements. In particular we might copy elements already in the system, illustrated in Figure 170

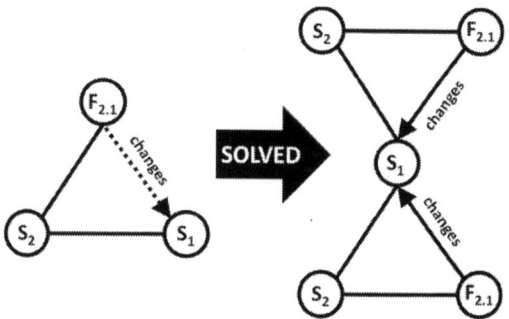

Figure 170: 3.1.1 Use multiple copies of components already present in the system. Note that Substance 2 is repeated.

Once more you employ the framework to raise questions for the delegates to consider. *Could copying elements improve our system? Which elements in our diagram could we copy? Multiple transportation mechanisms? Multiple transmitters? Multiple receivers? How might multiple copies of each component improve the system?*

Such questions may lead the delegates to propose a solution to long range communication offered on multiple occasions by the Separation Principles, and illustrated in Figure 171.

This second pass through the problem starts from the same rudimentary schematic, but arrives at a quite different solution. With this string of repeating stations discussed, perhaps we once more reach and impasse that may require an adjournment to reformat our Substance-Field. But once more we need not end our workshop, for once again we might return to our original tool. However, on this occasion the questions that arise do not consider new solutions, but combine solutions we have already discussed. To offer this sort of finesse to a workshop is a difficult task. It is for this reason that multiple facilitators are of great benefit. Whilst one hosts the ongoing effort, the other proposes the next steps. This is why we need multiple facilitators. This is why you can't have too few.

assailed by fire and in desperate need of a plan. Looking around for inspiration he noted behind the position he defended the rough rank and file of iron grey eggs. He was standing on the edge of a huge dragon's nest. Retreat into the Dragon's precious cache would surely stop the fiery torrent that threatened to engulf him[136].

For a moment this strategy worked. The Soldier scuttled back into the nest of iron, and provoked a pause in the Dragon's assault. The two combatants regarded one another with heated fury. In the Soldier's case quite literally, as smoke rose from his jerkin, trousers and boots. A pregnant pause in the conflict hung over the nest, and with a chuckle the cruel Dragon heaved another great breath to blast the Soldier to ashes.

The Soldier retreated once more behind the shield and considered his options as they shrivelled in the heat. All around him lay iron grey dragon's eggs that began to glow in the heat. Grey turned to a brazed bronze to a red hot molten red, to a searing white hot, to a magnificent electric blue.

Despite the heat, a cooling wind began to whip around the Soldier's smouldering feet. Leaves and ash were picked up in the maelstrom and electric blue began to dance between the white-hot eggs. Immersed in a deafening, blazing tumult, from behind the shield the Soldier endured a rumbling, roaring cry as flames impacted upon the surface of his protector. Not faint, like the cries of his Princess, but a cry so loud that it barely registered as a voice at all. A deafening rumble with so much fire and fury the individual words could barely be discerned from one another.

At this, the Soldier was reminded of his Father's old ear trumpet, and supporting the embattled shield with one hand and a shoulder, attempted a trick that he had employed only days before. The moment he put the trumpet to his ear the blasting roar only grew louder, to shatter the Soldier's senses with an incoherent scream. This trick was clearly not going to work twice.

The Dragon had only blasted the Soldier for a few moments, but to the target this felt like an eternity of hellish flaming torment. He needed to hear that cry, but the trumpet only amplified its thunderous shriek. The shield bucked and twisted in his hand as the torrent battered against its scales, which gave the Soldier an idea.

Pressing the wide-open end of the ear trumpet against the rear side

---

[136] GA. Force a contradiction upon his opponent.

of the smoking shield[137] the Soldier blocked the trumpet's only purpose[138]. Carefully placing his ear against the other end, the Soldier could now hear the shrieking cry transmitted through the thick, insulating shield. Words flooded through the shield in a torrent of pain.

I AM THE GREAT DRAGON OF CHAOS! I WAS HERE AT THE BEGINNING PREPARING THE WORLD FOR YOUR ARRIVAL I WAS HERE BEFORE HUMANKIND AND I SHALL REMAIN HERE AT YOUR END FOR I SHALL BE YOUR END I AM EXALTED AMONGST ALL OF CREATION FOR IT IS I WHO BRING ALL YOUR TRIALS AND TERRORS INTO THE WORLD I AM THE STORM DEMON I CONTROL THE WINDS FROM THE NORTH AND FROM THE SOUTH AND FROM THE EAST AND FROM THE WEST IT IS I WHO THRASHES AT THE SEAS AND DRAG SAILORS TO THEIR SUFFOCATING DOOM I WASH AWAY SCORES OF HUMANITY WITH FLOOD AND WITH FIRE AND WITH DISEASE I RAZE FOREST AND PLANE AND TOWN AND VILLAGE I AM THE FRENZIED PACK OF WOLVES WHO HUNT YOU TO EXHAUSTION I AM THE DARKEST NIGHT I AM THE COLD WHO LULLS YOU TO AN ENTERAL SLEEP MY GAZE IS THE WITHERING DROUGHT I AM THE HUNGER THAT GNAWS AT YOUR ENTRAILS MY BLOOD IS POISON I PROVOKE EVERY CONFLICT AND EVERY ATROCITY I AM SHARP OF TOOTH AND WILL NEVER SPARE THE FANG LOOK UPON ME AND PERISH ONE THOUSAND-FOLD PERISH BECOME BENUMBED WITH FEAR FROZEN WITH PAIN AND PERISH OR TELL ME WHAT I WISH TO KNOW ANSWER MY QUESTION! *WHERE IS MY CHILD!*

The inferno eventually penetrated the mighty shield, and the wooden beams that held together the scales of a long dead dragon began to smoke and crack. Swept by the wind, surrounded by the blue field of electric eggs, assailed by a torrent of fire the young Soldier eventually understood. The Soldier had a means to bargain. The Soldier had something to trade.

The young man bellowed into the firestorm, but his voice carried little in the roaring flames. He screamed his bargain again, but his words were consumed by the torrent of fire. Again, he tried until his voice grew

---

[137] Enhance a benefit. GA SS1.1.6 *Be excessive. If a small enough quantity of a substance cannot be applied. Add too much, and remove the excess.*
[138] Resolve a contradiction. The trumpet must both amplify and block the noise. GA SP13 *Do it in Reverse.* Implementing the opposite action. Block the trumpet.

hoarse, but his efforts to broker a deal were carried away on the blazing wind. He still grasped his Father's ear trumpet in his hand, and placing his mouth to the narrow end screamed what he knew into the horn and into the blaze[139].

The egg of a dragon was dropped by a queen and swallowed by a fish to be caught by a fisherman then stolen by a prince who commanded a girl to carry it to a King to be presented to a Princess as a gift to seal a marriage to win a Kingdom!

The flames extinguished and the canopy fell silent. The eggs tempered by a dragon's breath continued to glow the brightest, deepest blue within the nest around the Soldier's feet that crackled and smouldered. The Dragon peered at the Soldier with a yellow, sceptical eye and waited for the terms of this bargain. The Queen and the old soldier emerged from their refuge and waited pensively for the young Soldier's trade.

The Soldier wanted to return home. The Dragons listened, in silence. The Soldier wanted to rescue his Father. The Dragon listened, patiently. The Soldier wanted to rescue the Queen. At this demand, the Dragon resisted with a simple retort.

NO.

A pause in negotiations as the Soldier considered this riposte. Obviously, the Queen was required to finish her labours. In trade for the Queen, the Soldier must agree to dragons once more roaming the world. This was a bargain to which he could not consent. He made his case, and once more the Dragon refused.

NO.

A long pause. The Soldier was taken aback by this assertion. No one needed dragons, least of all the frail and peaceful people of a Kingdom that had long ago rid itself of the pain and suffering that dragons wrought, to live peaceful, happy, uneventful lives under clear blue skies that brought long quiet summers and a plentiful harvest. Why should anyone *want* dragons in the world?

The Dragon listened with interest to this plea. This brave young man

---

[139] Resolve a contradiction. GA SP13 *Do it in Reverse*. Implementing the opposite action. Use the ear trumpet to amplify not the voices of others, but one's own voice.

had risked everything for a hearing and had fought hard for his truth. Most importantly, he has asked the right question[140]. He had asked the question that no Human had ever asked of dragons. He had asked a question that no one would have ever even have asked another Human soul, for fear of retribution, alienation and isolation from a beleaguered Humanity. The pain that dragons wrought meant that no one had ever wanted to even consider such a question, and so no one had ever asked such a question[141].

With a tolerant sigh as if explaining the most obvious of facts to a small child, the Dragon's voice boomed around this canopy in the heights of the world tree.

I AM THE PRECOSMOGONIC CHAOS BEFORE PROBLEMS AND BEFORE SOLUTIONS I AM THE STORM AND THE WIND THAT WRECKS YOUR BOAT BLOWS YOUR SAILS AND DRIVES THE FISH INTO YOUR NETS I AM THE FILTH OF THE WORLD AND THE SEA SHORE FLOTSAM OF THE WINDFALL DISCOVERY I AM THE WRECK AND THE JETSAM THROWN OVERBOARD IN A DESPERATE STORM I AM THE WARMING FUR AND THE PREDATOR THAT CARRIED IT TO YOU I AM THE COLD THAT DEMANDS THE CAMP FIRE THAT BONDS AND THE POISON THAT DEMANDS AN ANTIDOTE I AM THE FLOODED RIVER AND THE LONG AWAITED AND WELCOME RAINS THE FIRE THAT DESTROYS AND CLEANSES AND PROVOKES NEW GROWTH I AM THE WAR AND THE PEACE THAT FOLLOWS TO FIGHT ME IS TO RISK DEATH TO AVOID MY WRATH WILL ENSURE YOUR DOOM I CREATE BOTH THE UNSOLVED AND THE SOLVED AND THE BOUNDARY INBETWEEN I AM THE SELF-CONSUMING SERPENT I AM THE ORBORUS AND I PROMISE ONLY ETERNAL TRANSFORMATION!

An even longer pause as the Soldier stood silently under this onslaught, under this truth. The Queen froze in horror, as this revealed truth banished the efforts of a lifetime and of a Kingdom. The Soldier's old Father accepted the truth, for the question that provoked it had come from his son's lips which could utter no a lie.

Preparations were made to return to their homes and to their loved ones. Preparations were made to release dragons back into the world.

---

[140] Ask the right question, and you'll get a valuable answer.
[141] If there is a question that you should *never* ask, this is the question to address.

DRAGON EGG

16. PRESENTATION

A clever solution to an important problem has little worth if you cannot communicate that value to a potential customer. This customer may be an external source of cash flow, or may be a funding body internal to your organisation. In both cases you must convince this customer that you have identified a valuable problem and a suitable solution if your project is to survive.

I believe that I have endured enough tedious presentations to offer some worthwhile opinions on how this persuasion should be achieved. The reader is likely to have endured similar experiences.

A valuable key to effective presentation can be found in the work of Dan Roam. Roam has produced a number of texts on the topic, and many of the techniques employed by Roam are developed from the same source observation. Your brain engages in a great deal of unconscious pre-processing of visual images before delivering this processed result for consideration by your conscious mind. The easier it is for this pre-processing to function, the more comfortable your audience will be. Consider the illustration of a monkey that I offered in the introduction to this book, and repeat in Figure 175.

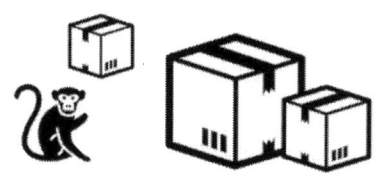

Figure 175: What's the story?

It is likely that in the few moments after you saw this image your mind had managed to determine the problem illustrated by this image and offered a narrative of how this problem might be resolved. In the context of this book, this single image contains a representation of every component of a problem-solving exercise. We see a customer represented by the monkey, and the presence of the bananas in the image suggests that he may be hungry. If so, there's a clear benefit that our simian customer desires - to eat the bananas. This customer is beset by a problem that can be described as a contradiction between the monkey's desired benefit and a clear harm. The monkey and the bananas reside at different heights. There are resources in this image that could help to resolve this contradiction. A variety of boxes are strewn around the environment. Your visual cortex will also attempt to solve this problem by composing a short narrative. If the boxes were stacked one upon the other, they might create a structure that the monkey could climb to reach the bananas[142]. The extremely fast, subconscious problem-solving processes of your brain can exercise all of the techniques described in this book in mere moments.

Alternatively, the smallest box could be thrown at the bananas to dislodge them from their suspension, but it seems that the visual cortex has learned to offer elegant solutions to this type of simple problem and will offer the stacking of boxes as a solution. This entire unconscious problem-solving capability bursts into operation with only a second's glance.

Roam demonstrates that the unconscious function of your visual cortex has developed not only to allow you to perceive the world, but also to solve simple problems very quickly. Over tens of thousands of years avoiding fangs, claws and venom spat from the dark, speed is of the essence in human decision making. This observation is echoed in Peterson's text. The environment is not perceived as a world of nouns to be observed and classified. Our perception plunges us into a universe of *verbs*. As we move through our environment our minds instantly and constantly classify the world around us in terms of its immediate function. To classify the surroundings by function your mind must also be adept at understanding the immediate problem each function solves. If the immediate problem changes, the perceived function of any object must change in sympathy.

Hence, we look at the plight of the monkey and immediately understand the problem, the function that each element of the scene could offer to achieve these ends, and at least one potential solution.

Roam notes that the problem-solving machine of the visual cortex has its limits. This processor trades complexity and familiarity to achieve its incredible speed. Roam offers a simple example to demonstrate this. As fast as you can, count the objects in Figure 176.

---

[142] Separation principle number 12. *Equipotentiality*. Removing the need to change the height of an object, or by using the environment to change its height.

Figure 176: How many?

Obviously, there are three. You probably achieved that numerical feat in mere moments. Let's try something harder. Count the objects in Figure 177.

Figure 177: How many?

I doubt you reached an accurate answer as quickly as the previous example. In fact, you may have resorted to counting each object manually. You may even have placed a finger on the page to do so. Roam proposes that you counted the second group using a different part of your brain. Your visual cortex can count at incredible speed, but can only count to about four or five. Beyond this it classifies the total as 'many' and dumps the problem into your conscious mind to labour over.

The ability to cope with complexity is traded away to achieve speed. Try another example. Count the objects in Figure 178.

Figure 178: How many?

You may have immediately jumped to three. You may also have sensed a little mental stutter. The question is a little ambiguous. Do we count all of the objects regardless of their classification? Or do we first classify each object and count two apples and one banana? You will probably have assembled both answers at high speed, but the clarification is left to your conscious actor to follow up.

The influence of this relationship between high speed, unconscious perception and your slower more complex conscious deliberation upon effective presentation can be illustrated if we return to our monkey. What happens if we remove a feature of this comprehensive problem description? In Figure 179 we have replaced the bananas with something else that you might expect to see hanging from the ceiling of the room – a lamp. How do you now react to this illustration?

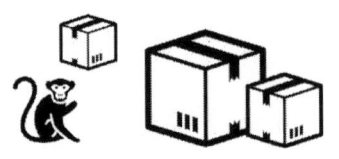

Figure 179: Now what's the story?

To me, this image has lost its immediacy. To me Figure 179 is an image of a monkey sitting amongst some boxes in well-lit room. There are no clear problems to resolve, and so the boxes and the monkey have no particular function in the scene. The image becomes boring. I know it has become boring because I begin to wonder what's in the boxes, whether the monkey will attempt to open them and what will happen to the monkey if it does. Without a clear narrative I cannot help but invent one. Eventually I decided that the monkey is trapped in an uncomfortable and harshly lit room, and then I considered how an escape may be made. Perhaps the boxes could be stacked to climb to an open window?

We can take this illustration a little further. Rather than bore our high-speed perception processes with little to grasp, let's overload them. In Figure 180 we now see one of the boxes hanging from the ceiling.

Figure 180: Now what's going on?

This might be a little incongruous. The best your high-speed processes might manage is to ask why is there a box hanging from the ceiling? It might wonder what it did when it last saw a box hanging from the ceiling? It's likely to dump all of these questions for conscious deliberation and return its attention to the more important task of detecting tigers, or bears, or other exciting threats. Roam's observation can be further illustrated with the simple narrative that results from the interaction between a chicken and a lion. Consider the story told by Figure 181.

Figure 181: What is their motivation?

A likely assumption is that the lion on the left is chasing the chicken on the right. This is, after all, what a lion is likely to do if it encounters a chicken. This narrative is likely to immediately accompany a mere glance at this image. The hungry lion is chasing the nervous chicken, and when the lion catches its prey the chicken will be consumed. Meanwhile, the nervous chicken runs for its life away from the hungry lion. The desires and motivations of each actor are obvious and instantly understood.

It does not take much to provoke your high-speed processing to abort altogether. We could simply reverse the images, illustrated in Figure 182

Figure 182: If we reverse the icons is the story as clear?

Now your high speed, subconscious processing may rush to construct a narrative that assumes that the chicken is chasing a lion. This is likely to provoke questions that this high-speed processor cannot answer. Chickens don't chase lions. Why is the chicken chasing the lion? Why is the lion running away? This doesn't make sense, so the whole narrative is dumped into your conscious processing for scrutiny. Perhaps they're running a race?

How is this related to good presentation? Roam recommends that the more information that can be processed by the audience's high-speed processor, and the less often this information is dumped into the conscious mind for scrutiny, the more comfortable the audience will be. The more comfortable the audience is the more likely the audience will accept your narrative. If your message is presented in such a way that it matches the instant assumptions made by the visual cortex, the more convincing your argument will be treated. Note that all of the problem-solving techniques offered in this text offer many simple visual cues.

To illustrate the influence of visual cues, consider the alternative. Imagine I wish to tell a story in only a couple of images. Let's return to the fruit theme. Perhaps you have noticed a problem with how fruit is stored in the cafeteria so assemble an audience and ask them to consider the rudimentary narrative in Figure 183. What's going on?

Figure 183: What narrative accompanies this image?

The visual cortex can make simple assumptions about how events may unfold in time. It's likely that the audience will immediately assume that some fruit that was sitting in a bowl has been removed from the bowl and now sits on the table next to it. The audience will be happy with this story, until you explain that they have misunderstood. They have it all wrong. What you're trying to illustrate is a problem when *replacing* consumed fruit. The fruit that was stored in a bowl has been removed and consumed. When fruit is replaced by a fresh supply people become lazy. The new fruit is not placed in the bowl but on the table next to it. This image clearly indicates this problem, doesn't it?

Your audience may be uncomfortable with this explanation as it does not match their initial assumption. In fact, they are going to have to go through the brief mental gymnastics required to re-parse what they are looking at and hold that in their heads whilst you continue to express your grievance. An uncomfortable audience attempting to parse this image in an unexpected way is an audience that is not listening to you as closely as they might.

Ultimately, how can we present our material whilst keeping as much of the cognitive effort of the audience within the high-speed, unconscious processing of their minds? A common approach is to simply write it down, but reading text takes mental effort. The modern trend that many seem to be taught is to assemble some slides that one can read from. This results in appalling presentations that force a choice upon the audience. They can either listen to the presentation, or they can read the information on the slide. They cannot do both. If you offer a text heavy slide, such as that presented in Figure 184, then you might as well put the slide up on the screen for the audience to read, and then remain silent so that you don't disturb them.

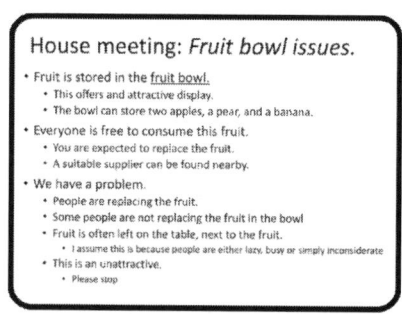

> House meeting: *Fruit bowl issues.*
> - Fruit is stored in the fruit bowl.
>   - This offers and attractive display.
>   - The bowl can store two apples, a pear, and a banana.
> - Everyone is free to consume this fruit.
>   - You are expected to replace the fruit.
>   - A suitable supplier can be found nearby.
> - We have a problem.
>   - People are replacing the fruit.
>   - Some people are not replacing the fruit in the bowl
>   - Fruit is often left on the table, next to the fruit.
>   - I assume this is because people are either lazy, busy or simply inconsiderate
>   - This is an unattractive.
>   - Please stop

Figure 184: Text filled slides are extremely dull.

If you must add words to your presentation, keep them simple and avoid full sentences. If removing words from your presentation now leaves you bereft of notes for you to read from, then practise so that you don't need any notes. Unless you are adept at public speaking then the presentation is not going to come together on the day. Rehearse. Rehearse again. Keep rehearsing until you are sick of rehearsing.

Now deliver the presentation backwards, and make it make sense on the fly. Now get a friend to interrupt you every 10 seconds whilst you power through the presentation. A very useful bit of advice I was given many years ago that works like a charm is to never give a presentation the same way twice. If you introduce small variations into the material every time you present it, this will distance you from the monotonous and robotic sounds that you will produce if you memorise your presentation verbatim.

Also, practise out loud. For me, to pick the correct word at the correct time requires my mouth to be engaged. The process of picking words using an internal mental dialogue seems to be quite different from that process that picks words for me to physically speak. I have practised presentations over an over with an internal, mental dialogue, only to have whole thing fall apart when I actually attempt to present it out loud.

A well-rehearsed presentation will sound easy, conversational and can cope with the inevitable shocks that arise when audience members interrupt and ask you questions.

Another modern habit that exacerbates this problem of word infested presentations is the lazy habit of storing the outcome of work in presentation formats. Different storage formats specialise in different types of presentation. The storage of a project's outcome for personal perusal by the customer is best achieved by a long document that contains words that form sentences that inhabit paragraphs accompanied by figures and tables, all referenced and identified with a contents page. The storage of visual cues that support a presentation in person is best achieved with a storage medium that breaks the material up into panels of work that can be projected on a screen as slides.

Too often we must endure a set of slides which the presenter is using as the long-term storage of their complete work. If you cannot spare the time to produce an appropriate and engaging presentation for your audience, then don't expect them to spare the time to attend and listen. No-one enjoys sitting through a long and tedious presentation, so think of an attractive and entertaining presentation as a *'thank you'* to the audience for turning up. There is nothing wrong with using the serious points in your serious presentation to energise and entertain your audience. Remember, innovation is funny, and an engaged audience will remember you and your work.

So, our presentation must support what we are saying by offering some visual cue that reflects the material. *But I can't draw*, most will respond. Roam disputes this, and asserts that anyone who can draw a circle, a square and a triangle can draw well enough to illustrate a presentation in an engaging manner. Roam is correct, and my own effort is illustrated in Figure 185.

Figure 185: With a little practise and a fat pen it is not so difficult to draw your own images.

I am very fond of this type of hand drawn icon. However, corporate settings can occasionally demand more digital outcomes in the rendering material, which is a shame.

If we are to offer a visual aid to our presentation then we need some means to offer this more processed result with little effort. Fortunately, in this digital age there are many options available to even the most inept operator of drawing software.

The simplest is to find a repository of icons that you can cut and paste onto your slides. Avoid launching into a comprehensive internet search for material, as much of this is likely to be under copyright. You have little permission to employ this material in a corporate setting, and little excuse if you are caught. Alternatively, find an online repository of icons. This is to your advantage for two reasons.

First, you can negotiate permission to use the material. Second, a central repository is likely to standardise the look of the icons offered. If you standardise the style of illustration you employ throughout your material this will always improve a presentation. A wide variety of mismatched material gathered from anywhere often looks quite amateurish.

The illustrations in this book are assembled from an online repository of icons that offers a standard size, shape and style to their material, and offers simple mechanisms to grant you permission for their use[143]. An example of an illustration assembled from these standard icons using a slide presentation editor is presented in Figure 186.

Figure 186: Icon repositories can help you quickly assemble images

If you want to transform your presentation material into something special then your next option is to venture into the employment of three-dimensional computer-aided design (CAD). The employment of CAD

---

[143] At the time of writing, this repository is called the *Noun Project*. It's a great site, so I hope it still exists by the time you read this book.

software used to be a specialist task. Some vendors have ventured into simplified versions of CAD tools that take little time for the non-specialist to master.

Those unfamiliar with CAD software may hesitate at the prospect of employing this type of tool. It is worth noting that these truncated CAD tools are designed for the inexpert user, and often come supplied with a secret weapon. User generated content. Many CAD tools are accompanied by a repository of CAD models developed by thousands of users. The content of these 3D CAD databases can be employed to very quickly assemble suitable dioramas to illustrate your point. Figure 187 took less than five minutes to create.

Figure 187: CAD software is not particularly difficult to exercise.

WHAT'S THE STORY?

Our presentation will employ visual tools to support our narrative, and we will hopefully have some means to create these images. How do we structure our presentation? Here we encounter the focus of Roam's *Show and Tell* [22]. Effective presentation can be hung upon a standard framework, much like the standard frameworks that support our problem-solving approach, or the standard frameworks employed by film, TV or music production. Roam offers a number of useful frameworks which I employ frequently. To avoid repeating Roam's work, in this text I present one of these frameworks to offer a taste of how they operate, and direct the reader to Roam's original work. Furthermore, I present Roam's presentation framework to illustrate how the material gathered during the problem-solving frameworks in this book supports the construction of a presentation structured using Roam's work.

We start with a presentational issue that may be obvious to those of a sales, marketing or business persuasion, but is less obvious to engineers like me. A common mistake made by those of a technical persuasion is the assumption that the audience may be as interested in the technical details of an innovation as its creator. When presenting work, engineers and scientists may often focus upon *how* a technology works rather than *why* it was developed in the first place. For example, I once endured twenty minutes of enthusiastic presentation from a young engineer who regaled me with pages of complex mathematics until I was eventually forced to ask, *what's it for?*

Roam's *pitching* framework offers a structure to convince fund holders to support a potential project. To this end, it does not force the audience to sit through technical material before we get to the point. Instead, this framework begins at the beginning, with the bottom line.

Roam recognises that as a presentation unfolds the audience are not passive spectators. As the material is revealed an engaged audience will scrutinise the logic of an argument, generate options and predict where the presentation will take them next. Roam illustrates his presentational structures using a graph that describes the relationship between the presentation timeline and the number of options the audience is provoked to consider. These axes are illustrated in Figure 188.

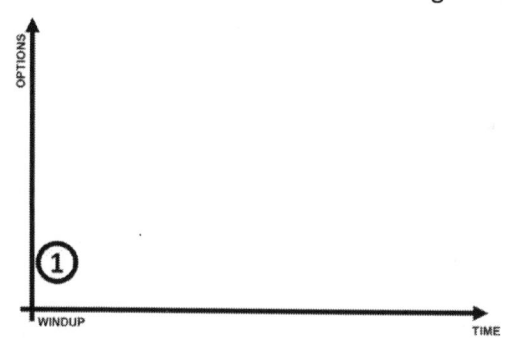

Figure 188: Roam's pitch compares time to the audience's perceived options. *(Dan Roam, SHOW & TELL, copyright 2020 all rights reserved)*

We start at 1, indicated in Figure 188. Roam describes this as is the *windup* that describes the situation before the problem is encountered. Here we wish to gain some consensus with the audience regarding the customer's roles, jobs and objectives. Here we can leverage material we gathered during our customer discovery exercise. If you are fortunate enough to have free access to this customer, this part of the presentation can be populated with material discovered during a comprehensive customer discovery campaign as described by Reis, Osterwalder, Blank and Dorf. At this stage of the presentation you want some nodding heads of agreement from the audience to assure you that you have accurately described the customer and the jobs they must do.

If you are presenting up your reporting chain it is likely that your audience may know the customer better than you. If you are unsure about the veracity of your information in the face of a more experienced audience, it is worth crafting a presentation that uses that audience to verify the quality of our information. The audience may agree, in which case you can proceed with the rest of your presentation. If they do not, you will face an uphill struggle if the rest of your presentation uses this erroneous customer discovery as a foundation. Under these circumstances it might be worth assembling back up material that transforms your presentation into a customer discovery exercise, using your audience to gather source material.

If you have indeed managed to achieve this consensus from the windup, your presentation will then summarise the problem itself. Roam describes this as the *hurdle*, which is illustrated at location 2 in Figure 189. Here the details we gathered using our problem-solving framework become extremely useful. By identifying our problem using formal means we have all the material that we need to clearly describe this hurdle. This hurdle will manifest as a contradiction between a benefit blocked by a harm or perhaps between two benefits that cannot coexist in the problem space.

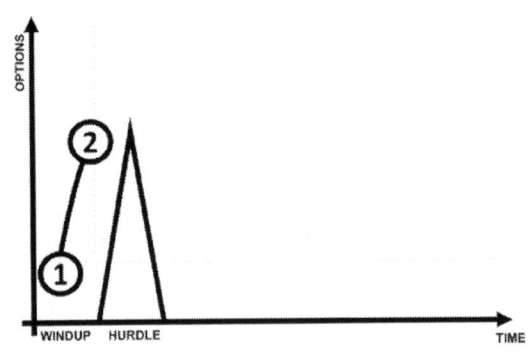

Figure 189: A hurdle over which the customer must climb is illustrated. This may be a difficult benefit to achieve, or a hurdle that spoils our objectives. *(Dan Roam, SHOW & TELL, copyright 2020 all rights reserved)*

With the customer's objectives understood and described, and the hurdle that must be overcome summarised, each audience member will commence a private, internal attempt to solve this problem. If you have offered a clear objective and an easily understood hurdle, they will be unable to avoid considering possible options, even subconsciously.

Figure 189 illustrates this private activity as a rise in potential solution options between your starting point and 1, and the hurdle at 2. If you have managed to engage your audience in this predictive exercise, you should have them engaged in your presentation.

A convincing pitch is not a mystery tour. We are not attempting to surprise anyone. In fact, we wish to achieve quite the opposite. If you have structured your presentation well the audience should be able to predict where you are going next. They should hopefully be forming an image in their mind of what your next slide may look like. Preferably, this image is assembled subconsciously. If their predictions match your material then they are going to understand your presentation. If you can achieve this, then you offer your audience the best chance to agree with your conclusions.

With the hurdle understood we move onto how we intend to solve this problem. Roam illustrates this at 3, in Figure 190. At this stage in the presentation we offer the audience a summary of our overall *vision* on how we might resolve this problem. We don't offer our particular solution. We offer a brief description of the type of functions we wish to create that will offer the benefits desired, resolve the harms provoked or separate the contradictions encountered. For example, we could describe the Ideal Outcome, or the Ideal Final Machine. We could offer some *subject-function-object* or Substance-Field interactions to describe how a function might resolve the problem, but without specifically referring to how this vision might be practically instantiated.

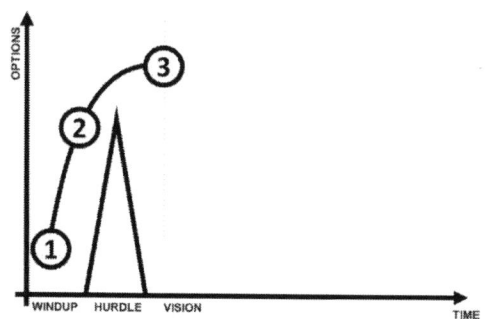

Figure 190: What vision will leap over this hurdle?
(*Dan Roam, SHOW & TELL, copyright 2020 all rights reserved*)

We constrain our audience to consider our personal vision on how this problem might be resolved. As a result, the number of options they might consider to solve the problem may begin to slow. With this vision to guide them the field narrows, but is still wide open. Every option is on the table. This is the apex of this trajectory, illustrating the point in the presentation where the audience may be considering the maximum number of possible options.

Now Roam begins to constrain the audience, much like we do when engaged in a structured problem-solving exercise. Ultimately, we want to narrow the options that they will consider to options we want them to choose. Cynically, one might think of it a little like *forcing a card* during a card trick. In stage magic, a *force* is a method of controlling a choice made by a spectator during a trick. Some forces are performed physically using sleight of hand, such as a trick where a spectator appears to select a random card from a deck but is instead handed a known card by the magician. Other forces use equivocation to create the illusion of a free decision in a situation where all choices lead to the same outcome.

Our presentation objective is not quite so cynical. We have accurately interviewed our customer, discovered a valuable problem and solved this problem. The option we are leading the audience towards is not merely forcing some arbitrary objective to serve our own ends, but assembling an argument to prove that we have arrived at the correct outcome.

With our vision clearly described we constrain the customer further by offering only *three* possible practical solutions, illustrated in Figure 191. Each *option* should be a valid solution to the problem described by the hurdle and a valid instantiation of the vision. This section of your presentation could draw upon the solution strategies considered during the problem-solving exercise. One could refer to Separation Principles considered in the effort to resolve a contradiction. One could demonstrate which Standard Solutions might block harms or enhance insufficient benefits. Perhaps even a Substance-Field diagram could be employed to demonstrate possible solution strategies. Finally, the incumbent solution could be offered, at the least to demonstrate why this current solution is inadequate.

Our intention is to demonstrate how each of these options do solve the problem. Despite this, we plan to reject two of them. We offer each option in turn, describe why it is a good potential solution, but reject two of them in favour of the third.

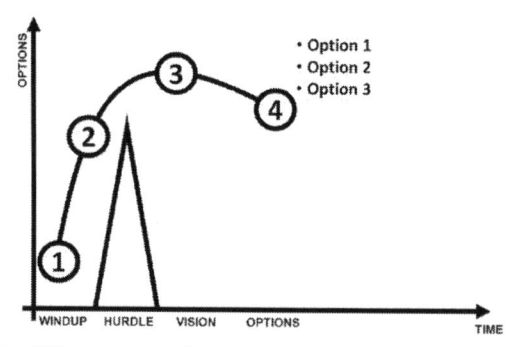

Figure 191: We narrow the audience options by offering three possible solutions.
(Dan Roam, SHOW & TELL, copyright 2020 all rights reserved)

One of these three solutions is the outcome we wish to offer to the customer. You do need to give the audience the opportunity to contrast your chosen solution with two acceptable alternatives. If the alternative options that you intend to reject are weak, this will make your preferred solution appear weak. In fact, the better the rejected solutions are, and the more convincing their rejection, the more willing your audience may be to accept your selected solution.

This trade leads us to location 5 illustrated in Figure 192. Roam describes this choice as the *close*, where we select the best option to resolve the hurdle, explain how this solution works and why it is the best solution. Here we want to show how this solution entirely separates contractions. Perhaps we want to who how this solution removes all harms from the system, or resolves all insufficient benefits. Perhaps we can illustrate how this solution offers the Ideal Outcome or the Ideal Final Machine.

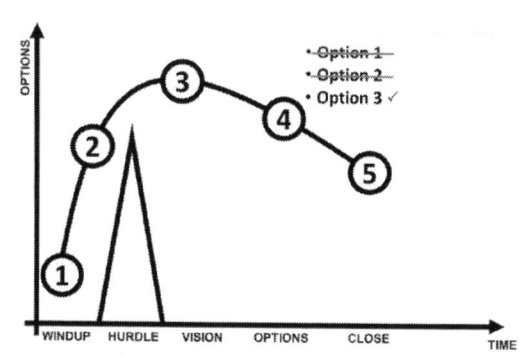

Figure 192: We close the pitch by choosing one of these options.
(Dan Roam, SHOW & TELL, copyright 2020 all rights reserved)

At this stage we should have presented to the audience a customer, a problem and led them to a suitable solution. If your argument is convincing, they should now be willing to sit through the technical or practical details of your proposal. This leads us to location 6, illustrated in Figure 193. Feel free to drill into the *Fine Print* of your proposal.

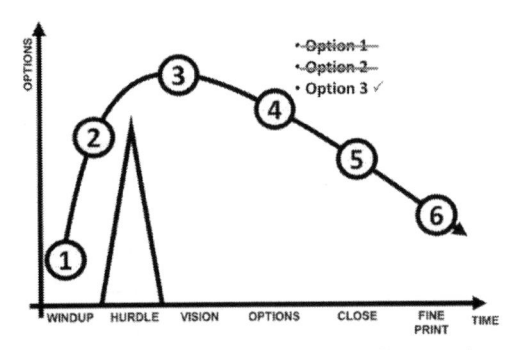

Figure 193: The audience should now be willing to listen to details.
(Dan Roam, SHOW & TELL, copyright 2020 all rights reserved)

Roam does not end here. Steps 1 to 6 in Figure 193 should constitute a complete argument. Roam suggests an encore. We don't want the audience to leave the presentation with a head full of fine print. We want them to leave them with some inspiring possibilities. We use the end of the presentation to generate some extra credit. To this end Roam recommends ending with a *Hook*, illustrated at location 7 of Figure 194.

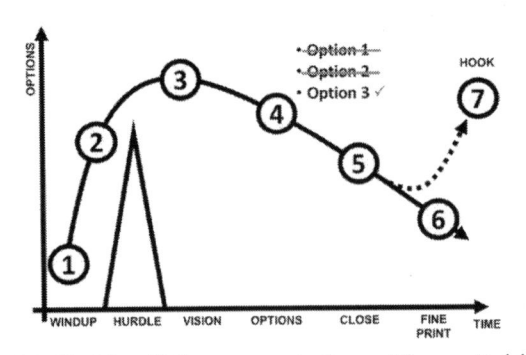

Figure 194: Finish off the presentation with a suitable hook.
(Dan Roam, SHOW & TELL, copyright 2020 all rights reserved)

This hook represents some additional benefit, or the resolution of some additional harm that is not explicitly addressed by your solution, or some function achieved without additional harm, or for free. These too can be drawn from your solution strategy. Perhaps you have managed to incorporate some multi-functionality into your solution to offer additional benefit? Perhaps additional functionality could be drawn from those secondary benefits that are not addressed by the problem-solving exercise? Perhaps the solution presents a growth path towards an alternative solution that you rejected as too expensive or complex?

The examples employed in this text are used to give an impression of how Roam's framework might translate into a presentation. Consider once more the *Mail Order Store of the Future*. How might we sell this service?

Windup. *'I think we can all agree that if we could deliver large payloads further and faster to the most inaccessible customers, the better we can compete in this market and the greater profits may become.'*

Hurdle. *'Unfortunately, the speed, range and altitude of delivery that our customers desire imposes considerable fuel costs and demand sophisticated and disposable vehicles. If we can deliver large payloads with both efficiency and high performance, competitiveness will be dramatically increased.'*

Vision. *'We propose to first lift the payload to a high altitude, to gain the benefits of low drag that will then allow us to efficiently drive each package to a high speed.'*

Option 1. *'We could lift the payload to orbit with a staged rocket. This is a tried and tested solution employed for many years'*

Option 2. *'We could loft the payload to high altitude using a balloon. This too employs well understood and well tested technology'*

DRAGON EGG

Option 3. *'Enormous payloads could be hoisted using an elevator that stretches from the ground all the way to orbit. Once in orbit the onward journey can be made at extremely high speeds'*

Reject option 1. *'Unfortunately, although the current solution solves the problem, it employs a very expensive but also disposable vehicle'*

Reject option 2. *'Lofting a payload with balloon will not lift it to a high enough altitude so also employs a very expensive but disposable vehicle'*

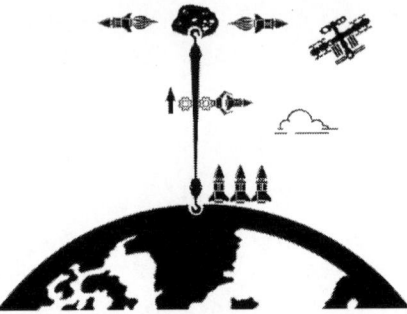

Close with option 3. *'A space elevator could loft enormous payloads to orbit. Once orbit is achieved the zero-drag environment could allow very small, low cost vehicles to boost payloads to high speeds. This project would be very expensive, but the primary component is not disposable and could offer a monopoly service for many, many years to come.'*

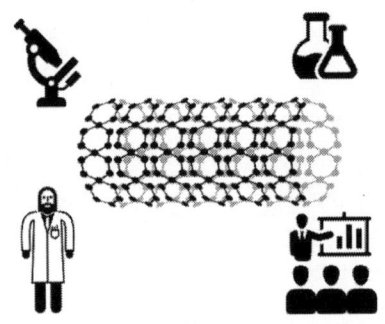

Offer some fine print. *'We will next offer a presentation on new materials technologies that will manufacture hundreds of miles of high strength material at low cost...'*

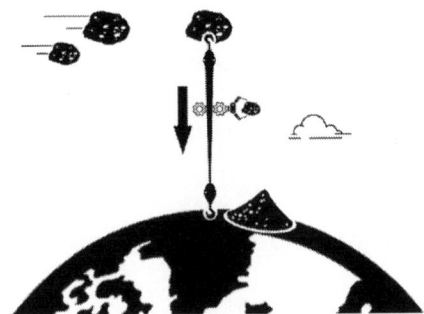

Offer a hook. *'A method that could elevate a large payload into orbit, could also deorbit large masses without the need for complex re-entry mechanisms.'*

Note that Roam's pitch offers a structure similar to the process with which the problem itself is solved. The pitch identifies the customer, focusses upon their primary problem, offers a strategy to resolve this problem, considers a number of means that this could be achieved, and selects a suitable candidate.

Roam offers effective presentation structures, and our problem-solving frameworks should offer suitable visual cues to support our message that are easy for the eye to understand and clearly illustrate what we are saying. Hopefully these images are infrequently drawn to the attention of the audience's conscious intellect for scrutiny. This should leave the audience comfortable and amenable to your message.

THE RISK OF EXCITEMENT

Here we encounter another error that may be obvious to those with a sales background but which may be opaque to those of an engineering or scientific persuasion. It can be quite difficult to secure funding at the early stages of a development. Technical evidence is scarce and the appetite for funding is very low. As a result, you may have to work hard to compete for funding that will allow you to take your first few steps.

If you are untrained or inexperience with selling an idea you may fall back on the sales environment in which we are all immersed every day. This is where I took my cues from, but it was a mistake to translate this into the effort to convince fund holders to support my proposals. After all, the sales to which I am exposed every day attempt to get me *excited* about that new car, holiday, phone or other gadget that will make my life simpler, easier or more fun. It was an almost unconscious motivation to parrot these promises of an exciting new future, and make my own proposals as exciting as I could. I didn't go quite as far as Figure 195 might suggest, but it does serve to illustrate my naive approach.

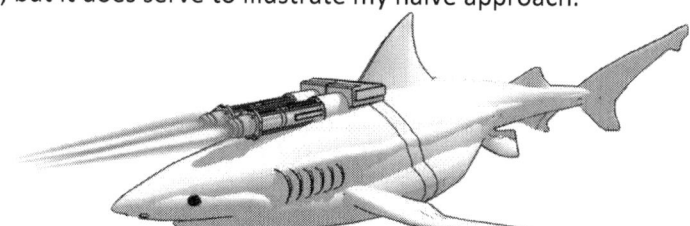

Figure 195: *A killer shark! With Lasers! It will be awesome! What could go wrong?*

It was some time and many sceptical audiences later when I eventually asked myself a simple question. If I am trying to excite audiences with my proposals, what else is exciting and how are they sold? Figure 196 illustrates my answer. Some people regard jumping out of a functioning aircraft with only a fabric sheet between them and a terminal meeting with the ground as exciting. Others seem to believe that climbing up sheer cliffs without a rope, with only the strength in their fingers to connect them to Mother Earth is exciting. What do these two activities have in common?

Figure 196: Why are skydiving and rock climbing exciting?

Sky diving, free rock climbing and other related activities are *risky*. Of course, the risk is managed to a level that the participant can bear, but these activities take them to the very edge of their performance where small mistakes can cost them dearly. If excitement and risk are related in the mind of my audience, is this the model that I should employ to convince fund holders to take a risk with my project proposal to deliver new solutions that employ immature technology?

Obviously not, and the work of Reis, Blank, Dorf and Osterwalder all offer very clear guidance towards the proper approach. The *build-measure-learn* cycle described by Reis offers a model where experiments make careful measurement of the customer's reaction to an emerging product. Blank and Dorf offer a clear and risk managed path to building a business, from zero to world domination. Osterwalder offers visual tools and a step by step approach to discovering a customer, understanding their problems and delivering your solution. All of these business modelling frameworks assemble the evidence that you need to demonstrate to fund holders that your proposal is a safe investment.

If you take an evidence-based approach to the risk management of a proposal mined from an uncertain environment, you are going to spoil all of this hard work if you present the idea as an exciting roller coaster ride for your investors to enjoy.

Alternatively, to remove the perception of risk we should perhaps not rely upon our extreme sports metaphor to sell our ideas, but should transform our inspiration into the more mundane but potentially more successful activity described by Figure 197.

Figure 197: A proposal for investors should propose an easy, risk free journey to the summit.

Our presentation to convince fund holders to invest should draw from our problem-solving framework to show the risk managed and staged progress to reach the objectives desired. Carving steps into the side of a mountain may be a less exciting way to reach the summit, even if your objective is a killer shark with lasers, but it will calm the audience's fears that they may be about to throw their money off that cliff.

It is hoped that the problem-solving frameworks presented in this text support this effort to contribute to the structured business modelling offered by the authors referenced. Investors are unlikely to be comfortable with your engineer's hunch, your scientific authority or that you can feel in your bones that your solution is viable. Investors will be comfortable with a clearly identified customer, a valuable problem and evidence that your solution can bridge the divide between the customer and the benefits that they ultimately desire. A structured and well documented approach to problem solving will allow you to assemble the evidence that you need to step the audience from the customer need to your proposed solution. This should be possible without intuitive leaps or the need for the customer to trust your technical expertise without supporting evidence. If the investors can make that journey from customer to solution themselves, the more comfortable they will be by the end of your presentation.

How do you know that you have succeeded? An audience that rejects your proposal is easy to spot. Furrowed brows, folded arm, shaking heads, probing questions that do more to illustrate the questioner's disapproval than simply their search for answers. Much harder to spot is an audience that will leave your presentation and take no action. The main reason for this may be that they haven't decided yet.

If you are selling an idea for potential funding, it's likely that this sale does not take place during the presentation. For example, if you are pitching an idea at the very beginning of a development exercise, the internal or external customer is unlikely to send their most senior asset to a presentation about an untried, untested, immature idea. You are likely to be presenting to their subordinate.

The objective of this subordinate is not to make a decision, but to report back to the real decision maker. Here we discover the most important reason for offering a presentation that is highly visual, evidence based, offers clear links from one point to the next, does not demand intuitive leaps of faith and does not demand considerable intellectual effort to follow. *The actual sale may take place <u>within</u> the customer's organisation.*

Consider the role with which this subordinate has been tasked. They must attend your presentation, understand your pitch and then report it back to their boss, perhaps some days later. Ultimately, your audience must deliver your presentation, without rehearsal, potentially without your presentation material, and without the mountain of experience that you assembled in your effort to reach your conclusions.

Present your work to a colleague. Ask them to present it back, *without* your presentation material. See how much they remember.

17. CASE STUDY: A BOLD PROPOSAL.

A solemn scene unfolded in the wide atrium of branches in the canopy of the World Tree. The Queen held a single blue glowing dragon's egg in both hands before her chest. Static raised the hairs on the nape of her neck, and her hands burned with pain where her palms met the cool surface of the egg. The Queen betrayed no emotion as she supported the egg. She had long learned to endure the pain of creation, as now her daughter must if they were all to return home.

The Soldier stood before the Queen and peered with concern into its deep blue void. A blue so deep he could have been gazing into the depths of an ocean. The old soldier stood a respectful distance away, shifting nervously alongside his old foe whilst the Dragon observed proceedings with curiosity. An odd audience, considering their history.

The stage was set for the young Soldier's experiment. Drowning in the depths of an electric blue ocean the Soldier called out his beloved's name and waited for a response. Nothing but the blue void swam before him. Again, he called, a little more urgently, and waited patiently.

As anticipated, from the depths of the abyss swam his love. Eyes black as night and long hair swept and tangled by the maelstrom of wind that surrounded her. Lighting flashed within the jewel, but the Princess's howling scream was stifled as if she was trapped within the suffocating deep.

The Soldier called out once more to his Princess, and finally attracted her attention away from her suffering. Her black eyes softened as she gazed into the jewel clutched to her breast. Within its depths she found her brave Soldier who she had worried about so desperately ever since his dramatic departure off the castle battlements.

'I have someone here that I'd like you to meet', the Soldier said tenderly.

The back eyes of the Princess scanned around the borders of the jewel in search of her new acquaintance. The glowing jewel was lifted by the Queen to gaze into its depths. Not a word was exchanged as both the Queen and the Princess broke into wide tearful smiles at the sight of their long-lost connection. Reunited with her Mother, the Princess flitted with joy inside the confines of the jewel, as a moth might inside a jar.

The Queen continued to gaze into the jewel, and the winds that assailed the Princess died, her eyes lost their dark void and the pair fell into a wordless reverie through the union granted by the Dragon's egg.

The Soldier patiently observed this silent communion between Mother and Daughter, punctuated for a moment as this Mother's gaze flitted momentarily towards the Soldier, and a wry smile creased her face. The young man flustered at these secret words, but stood his ground.

After a long but silent discussion with her daughter, the Queen lowered the egg to the atrium floor and released it with relief. She rubbed her seared palms together to relieve the discomfort. Everything now rested upon the Princess and her ability to persuade her Father, the King.

*

The Princess carefully placed her own egg onto a large, soft cushion that lay on the floor of her dungeon residence. Now that she well knew what she handled, she was powerfully motivated to take ever more care of this marvel. The Princess clutched her raw palms together, and formed a plan. Her Mother had passed on a great deal to consider, and the Princess had work to do. How was she to convince a King that had devoted his life to the defeat of dragons to introduce them back into the lives of his subjects? The Queen had forbidden the use of her own survival as a means to persuade the King as a cruel extortion upon a man who had his subjects to consider above all else. This negotiation must rest upon its own merits.

The Queen had assured her daughter that they were in no danger and that they were unlikely to receive any further visits from the Dragon, so the Princess had a little time to think. It was upon one of her frequent strolls through the town that inspiration struck. She immediately made for the throne room, and found her Father upon his seat of power as she always had. Slumped upon the throne the King carried out his regal responsibilities as he always did, with a resigned sense of duty that ever seemed accompanied by an air of endless sadness that only lifted as the Princess entered the great hall.

The Princess adopted her most girlish manner which she had learned over the years was most likely to wrap her Father around the smallest of his daughter's fingers. She would like her Father to join her in a walk. A walk through the town amongst the townsfolk.

Any particular danger to the royal pair from this request was of little consequence to the King, for it was not he who had reigned over the people for many years, but simple peace and prosperity. There was little to be feared by this regal procession walking unprotected in the open.

The King and his daughter strolled through the town and entered the busy marketplace. People greeted the pair enthusiastically as they strolled by. The Kingdom had been safe and secure and happy for a great many years. A monarch like the King had no fear of walking amongst his subjects for they seemed pleased with his rule. The King had strolled amongst his subjects many times over the years and this journey outside the castle walls was like any other. Happy smiling people greeting their beloved monarch.

The Princess grasped her Father's hand and ducked down a nearby alley. A clothing merchant at the end of this alleyway had been selected, and the Princess spent some time selecting suitable items and dressing her Father as if he were some overstuffed mannequin. The Princess had been given this idea by a play she had read, and planned to walk her Father around the town incognito[144]. The King, now dressed as a butcher in a dull smock covered by a brown leather apron, stepped out into the street. The King saw the world through new eyes[145].

After all, when the townsfolk looked at the King they saw a crown, and fine robes, his regal stature and his magnificent beard. They didn't really see his sad eyes, or the slump of his defeated shoulders, or the vulnerability of a man who had lost the focus of his Kingdom many years previously in a battle that he would happily have lost simply to retain his Queen.

The Princess retained the role as her father's daughter. Now suitably dressed, she adopted the role that any other young girl of the town might as she accompanied her hard-working father on his daily duties. As they strolled back out into the market square the Princess impulsively snatched a meat cleaver from a nearby ironmonger and tossed the startled merchant the appropriate payment. As the King surveyed his new Kingdom his daughter slipped the cleaver into his hand to complete his new ensemble[146]. Startled at this addition, the King hefted the weapon in his hand and regarded it with curiosity, as if feeling the familiar weight of such a tool for the first time.

The pair started their tour perusing the wares on sale in the market

---

[144] Resolve a contradiction. A King is highly recognisable, but must be invisible. GA SP32 *Colour Change*.

[145] If you could spend the day as your customer, what would you learn?

[146] What butcher walks around town wearing his apron and actually *carrying* his cleaver? Do you really understand your customer, or are you simply imagining a cliché? Get out of the building and paint your impressions from first-hand experience.

square[147]. They strolled through the busy streets amongst the bustling townsfolk. They enjoyed a refreshing drink outside a local inn, and watched their subjects as they went about their daily lives. They laughed as they dodged the soldiers they would occasionally encounter, as surely the castle guard would recognise the pair.

The market was packed with goods. The townsfolk laboured in the fields, but the labour did not seem particularly arduous for the harvests were always bountiful. Fish were drawn from a quiet sea. Game was easily encountered within forests that burst with bounty. It seemed to take little effort to gather enough to feed everyone over the mild winter months.

The Kingdom was by no means an eternal paradise. Death would only occasionally visit the Kingdom, but only after a soul had lived to a ripe old age. Consequently, funerals these days were surprisingly upbeat affairs were the bereaved would offer speeches about a long and happy life, and how the deceased had likely enjoyed a jolly good innings.

As the weather was always mild, even the flimsiest of structures would last, so little maintenance was required. Youngsters inherited the homes of their parents and their grandparents as land and property were passed down through the generations. The older generation had no desire to change their ways and traditions, and the younger generation had no reason. No-one wanted for anything, and as a result no-one needed to worry nor care about the welfare of others.

After a short walk, the pair watched a game on the village green. The teams passed a leather ball from one to another as they raced across the well-kept pitch. The King was pleased that the youngsters would compete in healthy sporting endeavour, but the tackles did on occasion seem a little egregious, and the competition did on occasion break its banks to spill out into open hostility. It was only a game, after all, and the Princess had to lay a hand upon her father's arm to stop him striding across the field to remind the youngsters of this fact.

They watched the young men and young women flirt near the great fountain at the centre of the town where all the roads met, like the hub of a great cobbled wheel. The boys strove for attention from the girls. The girls jockeyed for attention from the boys. As expected, in such a setting argument would break out, but these affairs were on occasion more vicious than such a cheerful occasion might demand. Recriminations would be cast to and fro, as adversaries would stomp to the edges of the

---

[147] SB. *Get out of the building.*

far side of the fountain to sulk, in the hope that they'd be cajoled back into the group by concerned friends.

The Princess urged her father to look closer. The youngsters jockeyed for position in their improvised social hierarchy, and the means by which they valued one another was built upon petty disagreements and foolish notions. Despite their high spirits and dramatic games, these youngsters were bored and retreated to trivial entertainments and distractions. They had little meaning in their safe and secure lives, because their lives had little challenge. With few challenges to face they had invented challenges to overcome, and these inventions were often trivial in nature and provoked unkindness towards one another.

A temporary stage had been set up near the corn exchange to host an afternoon's entertainment. The King did enjoy the theatre, for the tales reminded him of his youth, and the youngsters enjoyed hearing about the heroic exploits of their parents and their grandparents and respected their efforts to create such a secure and happy life. Poetry was written, even if the poetry was not about the poets. Songs were sung in a family's name, but the songs were infrequently of the singer's own exploits.

There were no needs that demanded solutions. No problems to overcome. No boundaries to break. The King was aghast at the difference between the lives of these youngsters and the early adventures of his own generation. How could he offer meaning to those so happy and secure? The King could not control the weather nor the seasons. He was certainly not going to start a conflict with his neighbours. On the contrary, his efforts to seal an alliance with the impending marriage was to achieve the precise opposite. What was he to do? How could he offer meaning to the lives of his subjects if they had no challenge to overcome?

Then a single clear voice rang out from the stage and the young crowd hushed into silence. A girl sang alone on the stage to sing a tale that had become popular in recent times. She sung of a dragon that now terrorised the land. She sung of a foul wind whipped up by its arrival, and how the seas thrashed and boiled as it flew overhead. She sung of the fishermen flung from their boats, and how the young townsfolk gathered ropes to tie themselves into a chain. She sung of the bravest who swam out in the maelstrom to fish the stricken sailors from the sea, whilst those who remained on shore took the strain upon the ropes to avoid losing these young heroes to the deep and to haul them to land once they had hooked those lost from their boats. She sang of the barn that was crushed, and the desperate search amongst the wreckage for survivors throughout a night lit only with lanterns and torches. She sang of the destruction of the grain silo and the fears for a lean winter, and the efforts made to gather as much from the fields as they could to recover the deficit. She sang of the army barracks that was destroyed, and a young girl who risked everything to rush into the building to warn the troops of the approaching monster so that everyone escaped with only moments to spare.

The youngsters had found a new meaning to their lives without the King's help, and they had found it in a new and terrible threat to the Kingdom. The King's solution required no solution at all[148]. He had killed the dragons nearly to their last, and in turn had killed the spirit of those young people of the town with kindness. However, this was clearly not a spirit that could stay dead for long.

---

[148] Altshuller's Ideal Final Machine. Elevate your required function to the super system, to the environment.

18. LETTING GO.

Consider the events that unfold when you fund a creative individual to innovate. For example, you fund a talented scientist or engineer to develop new technology from some recently discovered scientific principle. This technologist will consume your resource to mature this technology. The maturity of technology is often described using a standard scale called the *Technology Readiness Level*, or TRL.

The TRL scale was developed by NASA in the 1980s, and has been widely used to describe the maturity of technology ever since. This description of technical maturity was standardised by the International Organization for Standardization under ISO16290 in 2013 with a 9-point scale.

1. Basic principles observed and reported.
2. Technology concept and/or application formulated.
3. Analytical and experimental critical function and/or characteristic proof-of-concept.
4. Component and/or breadboard functional verification in a laboratory environment.
5. Component and/or breadboard critical function verification in a relevant environment.
6. Model demonstrating the critical functions of the element in a relevant environment.
7. Model demonstrating the element performance for the operational environment.
8. Actual system completed and accepted for flight ("flight qualified").
9. Actual system flight-proven through successful mission operations.

With funding in hand our technologist begins this journey at TRL1, with the basic scientific principles observed and reported, illustrated in Figure 198.

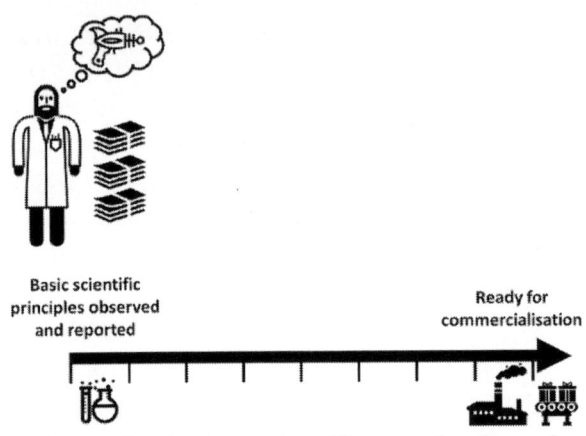

Figure 198: Our technologist starts with some funds, and a great idea.

The desire to manage the risk of this experimental development will firmly fix the timescale and budget exposure whilst allowing the scope to flex as the experiment unfolds. A technologist may expend all of these resources to mature this technology, but will only get so far. Typically, the technologist will reach TRL 3 or 4. The technologist will burn through the cash and a proof of concept or a laboratory demonstration will be produced, illustrated in Figure 199.

Figure 199: The funds may lead to a spectacular demonstration at TRL 3 or 4.

A technologist may expect that the success of this laboratory demonstration is sufficient to sustain further funding. They also may be very much mistaken, and may wonder why no-one has adopted this technology despite an amazing technological display. Large corporations must be mausoleums of clever laboratory demonstrations.

Those who are in control of funds that finance this demonstration may not be technologists, or may not consider technological performance as their primary interest in the early days of an innovation. Fund holders are likely to the business focused. *What problem does your technology solve? How does it solve this problem? Who is the customer? Who has this problem? Do they experience this problem frequently? How many of these customers are there in the world? Is there an alternative solution? Why is this solution better? Do we have competition? Can this technology be patented?*

Note that much of the material from our problem-solving framework can be employed to answer these questions. The techniques required to identify a customer, discover their problem, formulate a solution and determine how that solution can be realised serve a dual purpose. This information supports effective problem-solving, and also assembles the material that you will need to convince fund holders that you may possess a valuable idea. Your problem-solving framework helps to increase the appetite for further funding, so it is well worth taking comprehensive notes as your solution unfolds. These notes will act as material to assemble a narrative to these fund holders at a later date.

Not all fund holders may share the same appetite for your science experiment. We could illustrate this with an additional axis for our technologist to climb, shown in Figure 200.

Figure 200: Not all fund holders share the same appetite for innovation.

If you develop technology maturity without embedding this into some valuable context, then the project may not maintain enough attention to attract continued funding. Similarly, if you develop attractive concepts without a proven technological foundation then fund holders may not believe your claims. To ensure that the project survives, the technologist must expend resources to not only increase the technical maturity of the work, but must also expend some of those resources to increase the appetite for further funding. Our technologist must consider both technical maturity and also market fit for the project to survive the next round of funding, illustrated in Figure 201.

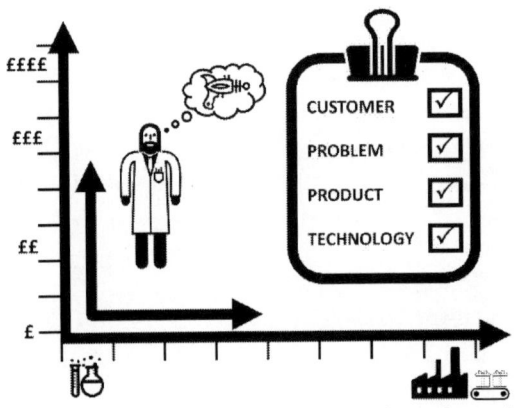

Figure 201: Our boffin needs to consider both technical maturity and the appetite for funding.

Funding opportunities tend to be matched to the maturity of the innovation and the exposure that the organisation is willing to endure to realise these plans. It is unlikely that your wild idea is going to attract all of the funding that it needs to become a fully-fledged product without proof, no matter how much passion you exhibit for the project. To manage the development risk, that proof tends to be assembled using staged funding.

Figure 202 illustrates that novel technologies which exhibit a low maturity tend to attract small funding opportunities that are designed to discover whether the scientific principle may be of use, or to trawl for technology to serve a particular end. The early stages of an innovation will inhabit a region on the bottom left of this illustration. The source of funding tends to be labelled to reflect its function. Early funding opportunities may be labelled something like *'Technology Discovery'*, or another fitting moniker.

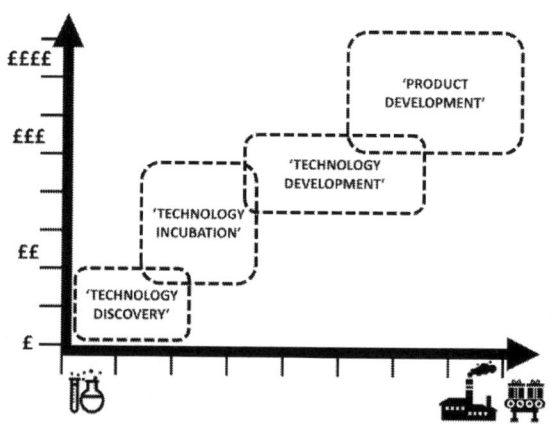

Figure 202: Funding opportunities tend to match the development stage.

The objective of our technologist is not to swim in this small pond forever, but to leap from this small pool of resources to a larger opportunity waiting further up the relationship between technological maturity and the appetite for funding.

This next funding opportunity might permit technology that is supported with some evidence to attract the attention of greater funds. This larger funding opportunity may be identified with a label something similar to *'Technology Incubation'*. Here the organisation may be willing to endure a greater financial exposure to develop technology that has been proved to show a practical potential to solve a real problem.

The relationship between two disparate funding opportunities is another of the significant, but very obvious, lessons I have eventually learned in my time working with innovation. This is the sort of lesson that is obvious to those of an entrepreneurial persuasion. For those of us with a scientific or technological focus this may need to be explained very clearly indeed. If you are an experienced innovator or entrepreneur please bear with me as I spell this out to those who may have trodden the same science and technology path as me. If you are a boffin, like me, read the following carefully and repeat it often enough so that you don't forget it.

The purpose of funding is not to develop technology.
The purpose of funding is to <u>attract more funding</u>.

If you are in the early stages of technology development, you are not going to use your meagre funds to provoke a fully-fledged product into existence. To illustrate using Figure 203, your task as innovator is to first secure a small quantity of funding from the *Technology Discovery* fund. With these funds your task is to leap into the *Technology Incubation* fund. To achieve this, you must simultaneously increase the maturity of technology *and* the appetite to fund you further.

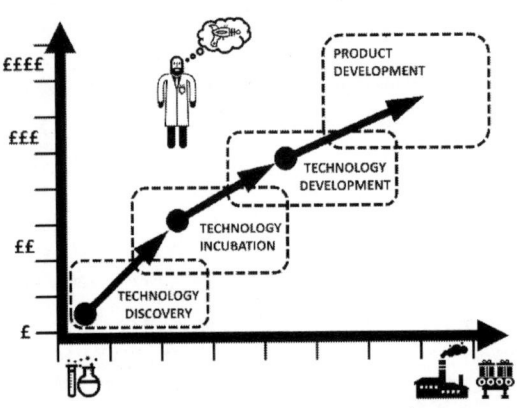

Figure 203: Funding opportunities create a stairway you must climb.

Similarly, once you have reached the *Technology Incubation* fund, the purpose of those funds is to reach *Technology Development.* Finally, in this example, the *Technology Development* fund is there to propel you into a full-fledged *Product Development* programme. The funding opportunities we each face in our disparate organisations will vary. This illustration describes a funding stairway which we all must climb to simultaneously increase technical maturity and our understanding of the customer, their problems and the effectiveness of our solution.

Figure 204 illustrates that if you mature the technology without addressing the market demand, your fund holders may see no reason to fund you further and your project may die. Alternatively, if you offer the most exciting and eloquent reason for pursuing this business opportunity without offering any evidence that your proposal will work, then no one is going to believe that you offer a practical proposal and your project may die. To those familiar with the work of Reis this stairway is an alternative means to illustrate the benefits of an iterative *build-measure-learn* cycle employed by the *Lean Start-up* [5]. I refer the reader to Reis for details of this product development cycle.

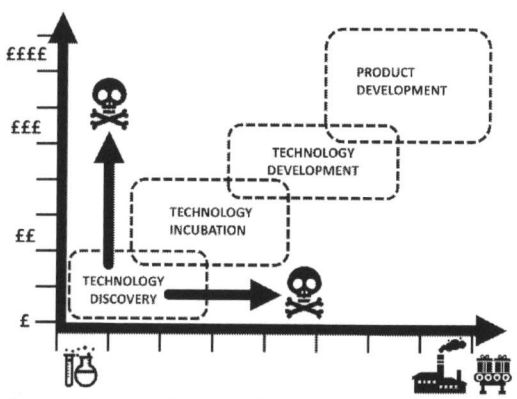

Figure 204: If you do not aim carefully you may miss the next funding opportunity

This illustration can also serve to show how those who can afford to ignore this staged, risk management approach may achieve a successful result. Everyone can think of at least one example of a highly influential entrepreneur with enormous credibility that arises from a long track record of success. Do investors need to limit their exposure as this superstar innovator climbs from crazy concept to product success? This business cliché would suggest not. Figure 205 illustrates that a *Rockstar Entrepreneur* could exploit an enormous quantity of credibility to dash up the appetite for funding, quickly gather a large investment that then permits a drive to technical maturity. An alternative business cliché might describe a *Technical Genius*, who can ignore the business fundamentals and drive technical maturity using raw talent alone with little investment until a near complete product lands upon the desk of a potential investor.

Unfortunately, for the rest of us mere Humans in the real world, a staged campaign that manages risk by balancing the technical maturation and funding appetite is perhaps our best and only option.

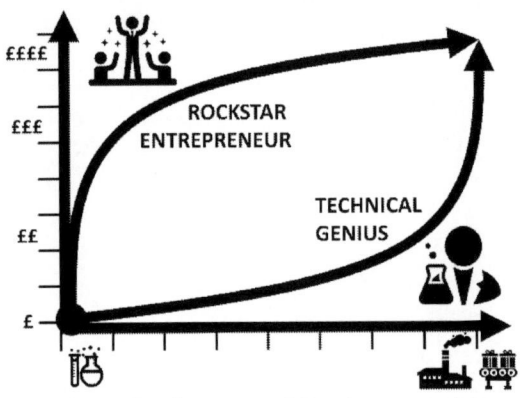

Figure 205: Perhaps Rockstars and Geniuses could monopolise a single axis?

As you climb this funding stairway your project will transform from an immature concept into formal product development. McKinsey[149] offers a framework that describes how a company will treat the different stages of a product or business development, and splits these behaviours into three *Horizons*. Blank extends this Horizons framework and describes each, as follows[150].

Horizon 1 is the core business. This horizon contains those well-established activities that a company carries out to provide the greatest profits and cash flow. Horizon 1 encompasses all that the company executives manage and worry about most of the time. Blank extends McKinsey's description of Horizon 1 by explaining that under this grouping we know who the customers are, what features the customers want and who the competitors are. The manufacturing and delivery of products will be treated as a low risk activity. In this horizon the management build repeatable and scalable processes, procedures, incentives and performance indicators to execute and measure the business model. Within Horizon 1 innovation and improvements occur

---

[149] McKinsey & Company is an American management consulting firm. It conducts qualitative and quantitative analysis to evaluate management decisions across public and private sectors. McKinsey was founded in 1926 by James O. McKinsey to apply accounting principles to management. McKinsey died in 1937, and the firm was restructured several times, with the modern-day McKinsey & Company emerging in 1939.

[150] The description that follows is drawn from an online CXO Talk presentation by Steve Blank at www.cxotalk.com

within processes, procedures and costs.

Horizon 2 encompasses rapidly growing business or emerging opportunities that might offer future profits but require more time and investment to realise. Blank extends McKinsey's description by describing this horizon as not the execution of the core business model, but instead looks for new opportunities within that existing business model. For example, one might sell the existing product via a different channel, or use the same technology by pursue a different customer, or sell new products to existing customers. Horizon 2 will flex the known features of one's existing business model and the manufacturing and delivery of products will be treated as a moderate risk activity. Management will use performance indicators, processes and procedures to experiment inside this established business model.

Horizon 3 contains the crazy things. This horizon will encompass emerging businesses. This horizon contains those things that you might want to invest in, or are under experimentation by a small research and development group. Blank describes Horizon 3 as the place that companies put their crazy entrepreneurs and contains all the people you might want to strangle or fire, but don't because you worry that outside your own company they may become be the CEO of a start-up that will compete with you. These innovators want to create new and disruptive business models. Here the parent company is incubating a start-up, so the company will exercise Horizon 3 with speed and urgency to find new, repeatable and scalable business models.

Blank describes a need for Horizon 3 groups to be physically separated from the parent company in a corporate incubator or their own facility. Such groups will develop their own plans, procedures and processes that are likely to be different from those employed in Horizon 1. It seems likely that Horizon 3 is where both the barnstorming entrepreneurs and the diagnostic problem solvers are safely contained.

These horizons could be superimposed upon our funding stairway as illustrated in Figure 206. At some point on this journey you may need to make a decision. What kind of innovator are you? Are you interested in exercising the current business model? Do you wish to innovate with the processes, procedures and costs? Alternatively, are you better suited to work with the crazy ideas and experiment with emerging, disruptive business models, products and services?

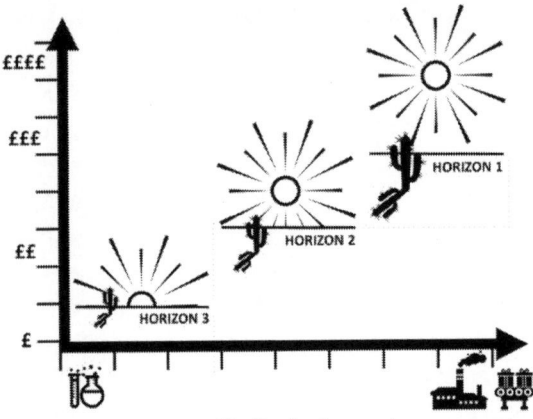

Figure 206: An innovation will climb through our product Horizons.

Further orientation can be achieved if the risk management strategies of these horizons are considered. As illustrated in Figure 207, in the early stages of an innovation exposure will be minimised by fixing the time scales and costs and flexing the scope, such as the customer, the product and potential solutions. Once an innovation becomes a fully-fledged product line, this scope will become frozen and fixed, with negotiation focussed upon finance and timescales. The risk mitigation strategy employed must transform from one strategy to the other as it transforms from research study to product line.

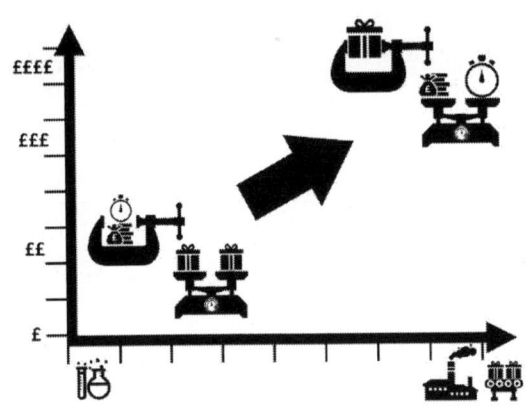

Figure 207: At some point on this journey the risk management strategy must change.

Which risk management strategy are you suited to? Do you prefer to experiment with customer and product under extreme uncertainty, tight budgets short timescales? Alternatively, is negotiating through the planning, timescales and budgets of a firmly understood business model your preference?

The innovation required to solve tricky problems and develop new products is supported by the entrepreneurship required to build a successful business. Just because you are adept at one, does not mean you will exhibit skills in the other. The ability to exercise the problem-solving techniques described in this book do not mean that you will exhibit the core skills and *chutzpah* required to build a successful business. The two are so often conflated that many make the assumption that they can be found in a single person.

If you are very creative you may not possess the conscientious attention to detail required to build a successful business. If you possess a conscientious attention to detail this may allow you to construct a business with ease, but may not offer the flexibility you might need to consider the novel possibilities.

Personally, I reside very firmly in Horizon 3 and probably lack the necessary acumen, motivation or stamina to build a stable business. I describe in the introduction to the book that I am not particularly entrepreneurial. I work with innovation, but reside at the early stages of development where we determine the customer, their problems and potential solutions under extreme uncertainty. This exercise is perhaps better described as *diagnostic* rather the entrepreneurial as I would surely cross the *i* and dot the *t*, just to see what happens.

Those that do possess this entrepreneurial spirit are extremely valuable to the diagnostic problem solver. Without them your project is going nowhere. Within a large, established company an equivalent to this entrepreneur might be a skilled project manager who can adopt your idea and transform it into a vehicle that will drive your proposal all the way up the funding stairway.

Don't be fooled into thinking that the person with the ideas offers the most value to your project. This is a lesson I learned at almost the moment I graduated from the University of Glasgow with my brand-new Aerospace Engineering degree in hand.

My first employment after graduating was offered by a steel engineering firm on the banks of the river Clyde. This was a family run business managed by a director who was literally born to the job and taught me my first and most important lesson in business. During a tea break the boss enquired about my Aerospace Design degree and offered some advice on the topic of designers.

Designers have no value.

I will admit I was a little crestfallen by this unexpected advice, so the boss elaborated. He enquired how much it might cost me to design an aircraft? How much risk would I endure when designing an aircraft? What materials do I need to achieve this?

I guess he did have a point. Beyond the costs of my own time, a pencil, some paper, a good calculator and my copy of Stinton's *The Design of the Aeroplane* [23] I could make a rough stab at some dimensions that afternoon.

Those who take the risk deserve the rewards, the boss declared, and waved an arm to broadly indicate the extent of the family business as evidence of a risk well taken. Those who gathered the investment, purchased the materials, hired the staff and placed their bets upon a valuable match between customer and product take the risks. Those who risk pencil and paper risk little.

You may believe that your ideas are valuable. You may even work in *stealth mode* to hide your work and protect those ideas from those who might steal them. Reis offers an exercise to demonstrate how valuable your ideas might be. Find your competitor and *try* to encourage them to steal your idea [1]. Your counterpart will have enough to deal with already, and a large backlog of ideas to work through.

Your idea will have little value until you have climbed some way up the funding stairway and proved its technical viability and the customer interest. This climb is offered by your entrepreneurial partners. Competitiveness is to be found in the *implementation* of your ideas and the associated lessons learned on that journey as you climb the funding stairway.

If you only possess a single good idea Reis proposes that you become a politician. With your single idea clutched in your hand, you must find a way to negotiate this idea to the top of the funding stairway. The entrepreneur does not want a single idea to husband into existence. Those building business propositions need multiple solutions to the customer's problems to contrast and compare. An entrepreneur following the *Lean Startup* wants material from which to construct Minimum Viable Products (MVP) and experiment upon this customer.

MVP are similar to prototypes, but offer a quite different experiment to that offered by a prototype. A prototype offers an early technical instantiation of a product. With the prototype we experiment on whether or not the science and technology deployed will safely and reliable offer the function desired. A Minimum Viable Product is an early instantiation of the product, but it is an analogue to a *product*. This early product is employed to experiment upon the technology and also employed to experiment upon the customer. *Does the MVP offer the functions that the customer desires? Does the customers like the MVP? What would we change about the MVP to make it more desirable?*

Under these circumstances, to offer true value the diagnostic problem solver must offer a volume proposition. If an entrepreneur needs material from which to fashion experiments upon the product and the customer, the diagnostic problem solver should be in a position to offer that material, in bulk.

To this end the problem-solving techniques presented in this book do not lead you to that singular perfect solution, but instead offer you techniques the create a volume of solutions. The problem definition tools allow you to identify multiple contradictions amongst the customer's desires. The Substance-Field analysis allows you to illustrate the system and describe how those contradictions interact. Thinking In Space and Time extends your reach up into the resources of the surrounding environment and down into the resources offered by tiny subcomponents. The cross referencing of benefits and harms will generate multiple potential solutions that can be combined. The 40 Separation Principles offer numerous ways to resolve each contradiction. The 76 Standard Solutions present abundant means to block harms or enhance insufficient benefits. The Evolution of Technical Trends predicts a whole future of solution development.

The problem-solving techniques described in this book allow you to approach problem solving as a volume proposition. This volume of ideas created by those diagnostic problem solvers allow the more entrepreneurial to experiment upon these ideas and upon the customer to determine which will offer a desirable and profitable product.

If you are of a diagnostic disposition, then it is worth regarding the task of business building as a complex and specialist skill better left to those entrepreneurs who can construct a working business from scratch. If you do not specialise in these skills, then at some point you must hand your project over to one of these business experts. When does this handover take place, and how?

I was once given some straightforward advice from a project manager who could indeed transform an innovation into a viable and successful programme of work. We were discussing what he needed from me to take a project on. His advice was simple.

Please don't dump onto my desk a pile of junk from your science experiment.

This seems fair, and sticks with me as it is indeed just the sort of thing I might do once I have become bored with an idea, once the excitement of exploring a complex and alluring new problem has waned. The problem-solving techniques described in this text hopefully help you to generate the material that you need to avoid this outcome.

A possible entry point into the problem-solving process for a project manager is illustrated in Figure 208. A project manager will need to determine the scope of the intended project, the time scale in which the project can be completed and the resources required to fund the task. This triangle represents the balance that a skilled project manager must attempt to create between the scope, schedule and resources. Change one, and the others must also be adjusted to maintain this balance. For example, if you increase the scope, then the time and resources required to achieve this must also increase. Restrict the resources available and we can achieve less and must spend less time doing so. Contract the schedule, and our scope will have to drop, or we may have to pump more resources into the project to get the job done on time.

Figure 208: A possible starting gate for the Project Manager.

This triangle represents a possible entry point to dive into a text on project management, which is a specialist skill that I do not possess. So, I have no intention of describing this particular skill any further than briefly describing this starting gate that a problem solver may eventually encounter once they reach the end of their current problem-solving cycle. So, you have journeyed through the unknown, faced an uncertain problem and an uncertain future, braved the storms of a comprehensive solution process and arrived at the gates of the project manager, illustrated in Figure 209. You must consider carefully what it's going to cost to pass through these gates and provoke a fully-fledged and well-funded programme manager to realise your solution.

Figure 209: What is the price for entry?

Beyond this point lies an entirely new world, and you may need a skilled entrepreneur or project manager to help you navigate this environment. What must you possess to permit passage? How much information do you have already to offer to the project manager to allow an effective plan to unfold?

To pass an idea on, at the very least you must offer the recipient a complete argument. We know what the customer wants, so we can offer some idea of the scope of a development programme that will create a potential solution. We may know the value of this solution to the customer, so may be able to contribute to a discussion on the resources worth burning in the effort to create a solution. We may understand the urgency of a problem and when the customer will need this solution, so perhaps we can offer some information to describe a suitable schedule of work.

Most importantly, you should offer a customer. A *real* customer. Not some imaginary beneficiary, but a real person who suffers a real problem for which they will pay real money to resolve. You should offer a detailed description of the problem that they endure. You should prove that this is a problem that occurs so frequently or is so influential that this customer would be willing to offer a significant sacrifice for its solution.

You should demonstrate how you can bridge the gap between the customer's needs and a viable product with a volume of potential solution strategies, and you should clearly indicate to what extent each solution resolves the contradictions amongst the customer's desires.

This can be a difficult hurdle to overcome, particularly if the gatekeeper is good at their job. They'll understand the risks the organisation must take to pursue your ideas. They'll understand the resources available to realise these plans. They will understand the other demands upon the organisation's resources and the other ideas that are competing for the same resources that you are pursuing. Passage will demand that you build a good relationship with these gate keepers. Passage will take negotiation, and will demand that you trust the judgement of your entrepreneurial counterpart.

Hopefully the problem-solving framework offered in this book will arm you with the material that you need to make your case. Don't be too disheartened if you don't succeed every time you approach this transition from discovery to programme. Under the circumstances, if you manage to get only 1 in 10 of your ideas through this gate, then you're doing okay.

19. CASE STUDY: LETTING GO.

Father and daughter walked out into the broad central courtyard of the castle, unaccompanied by guards, advisors, or any court functionaries. Together, they were alone. The courtyard was deserted.

After enduring repeated attacks from the Last Dragon, a hiatus in this terror had descended upon the Kingdom. This welcome relief was marked with a joyous celebration in the town square, so the palace guard had been granted the day off to join the festivities.

The pair stopped before the huge wooden doors of the castle's great grain store and scanned the skies. A bargain was to be struck, and this was a bargain that the King both despised and desired. The spirit of his Kingdom was dying from a lack of challenge and meaning. As the father of this nation, the King recoiled at becoming the cause of any future pain. He had risked his life and those of his subjects to achieve a safe and secure world, and now must relinquish this hard-won prize.

How his daughter had brokered this agreement, the King had no idea. The glowing blue gem that she continued to clutch and never left her possession seemed surely to be the cause. The Princess frequently gazed into the gem, to see the tiny growing dragon within call out to its parent. The Princess knew that the time of reckoning had arrived.

Without thunder or lightning or roar or bluster the enormous beast slipped lithely between the clouds and amongst the battlements with a grace that such a monster surely could not possess. A dragon's roar is for show. The gale force beat of its wings is for effect. A dragon can slip into your life without a ripple, and wreak havoc before you even know it's there. A dragon is both the titanic storm that sinks your boat, and the single missing nail in the horseshoe that loses a Kingdom.

No one but the Princess and the King were aware of this encounter, and this was how it must remain if the townsfolk were not to feel betrayed by their protector. The Dragon landed gently upon the cobbles of the courtyard, and waited. The King and the Last Dragon eyed one another with hostility and suspicion. The King had not yet been presented with the terms of their bargain, and feared the outcome of this fateful day. Tensions rose.

This standoff was broken by a proud young voice that hailed from atop the Dragon's broad head. The Dragon lowered its huge head, and the King was aghast to note not one but two of his finest soldiers dismount from this fearsome beast. Things were developing fast, and the King struggled to retain an impassive, regal demeanour as he moved to welcome his troops from such a clearly hazardous mission.

The Princess, on the other hand, rushed past her father to the Soldier, to be swept into the arms of the young man in fits of laughter. The electric blue dragon's egg caught between them sizzled angrily against the Soldier, who ignored the discomfort as he lifted his love from her feet and swung her in a joyous orbit around this shared nucleus. The joyous pair rather reminded the King of his long romance with his Queen and noted, after all, that his headstrong daughter will not many any prince after all.

Recovering their decorum, the Princess and her Soldier turned to the serious task of negotiating the return of dragons to the Kingdom. Noting the conclusion of their reunion, to this end the Last Dragon swept aside a huge leathery wing to dramatically reveal to the King his long lost and beloved Queen.

The King was stunned, but only for a moment. Was this to be the terms of the negotiation? To recover his beloved, and return to the fight against their shared foe? To return to the challenges of their youth? The King was but a man. His regal responsibility was forgotten for a moment. He would agree to this bargain in a heartbeat.

Before the looming shadow of the Last Dragon, the Princess approached her Mother with trepidation, and placed the bright blue glowing egg into her hands. The Queen turned and returned the egg to the Last Dragon and with a rush of wind a great scaly wing swept the egg from the Queen's hands with a desperate hunger for this offspring.

The Queen turned back to her family. The Princess stepped aside, and the Queen approached her King with a solemn grace. Stopping before him, the pair so deeply entwined required a mere glance to recover their long acquaintance.

The Queen leaned towards the King as if to place a kiss upon his cheek, but she had a bargain to deliver. An unexpected bargain. Some minutes passed as the Queen whispered into the ear of the King everything he must know for this contract to be sealed.

The effect upon the King was clear. A frozen figure, in denial. A clenching of the fists in anger. Clutching the Queen's hands, in negotiation. Upon a sympathetic shake of the Queen's head, a stoop of the shoulders, in submission. A raise of the chin in acceptance. The pair parted, and with a nod the King was ready to pay the price demanded to recover his Queen. Lifting the crown from his head, he prepared to pass it onto his successor.

And with a thunderous crash the huge wooden doors of the great grain silo flew open. Standing at their centre the Prince proudly stood in victory. Hands on hips, feet spread in heroic stance, cloak billowing from the dramatic division of the great swinging doors. The party in the courtyard froze and all eyes turned to the Prince and to the arrow head of the great iron bow that loomed over his head.

The huffing, puffing men who had manoeuvred the weapon into position had long departed for the town's celebrations, as the Prince had at last predicted the destination of this fearsome dragon and was hiding in wait. All seemed to rest upon the Princess and it was her movements that allowed him to predict the Dragon's next assault. The Prince pulled taut the thick rope that connected his plan to the trigger of the giant mechanism.

A beat. A pause. All looked to the Prince, whilst the Prince looked to the golden crown that hung slackly in the hands of a bewildered King. The Prince's eyes then turned to the Princess, and finally to the Last Dragon itself at whom the great bow was aimed directly. The Prince's own bargain was clear. The Prince gulped nervously, and pulled the rope ever more taut. The Last Dragon heaved a huge breath.

Generations hence would tell tales of the Prince's heroic exploits on that fateful day in his efforts to defeat the terrible dragon that had returned to the land. How he valiantly attempted to rescue the King as the Last Dragon swept him away to his terrible fate. Poems were written in his name. Songs were sung. A monument was made of the burned and blacked iron bow he had devised to save the Kingdom, to which his relatives on occasion made tearful pilgrimage to read the golden plaque screwed to its frame. *'From a grateful neighbour, in thanks for your son's heroic sacrifice'.*

The only tales of the Prince's end that were true were told some years later by the Princess to her young children when they were naughty. Misbehave or the dragons will get you, and you'll go the same way as that Prince. The children giggled with feigned fear, and wrinkled their noses in cheeky disgust at the caricature of that day described by a playful Princess. The Soldier disapproved of this bedtime tale, as the rest of the party in that courtyard on that day remembered the event in rather more gruesome detail and never again even mentioned it to one another.

A billow of dry ash was swept aside by the draught whipped up by a scaly wing as the Last Dragon enfolded the Queen back into its care. The beast heaved itself into the air, and after a hurried farewell the King was snatched into the air by great iron claws. At this rapid departure the golden crown was snatched from his hands to land with a clunk on the courtyard cobbles. The young Soldier reacted quickly, and tossed his sword and the great dragon scale shield into the King's now empty hands.

The crow rung as it clattered around upon its edge, to eventually rest silently upon the stones. The Princess reached for the crown as the Old King was lofted into the air, above the courtyard, above the castle, and high above the town and his erstwhile Kingdom. Time to put on a show.

A great roar suspended the merrymaking of the townsfolk in the market square. Looking to the sky, the last these subjects saw of their King he was engaged in single combat with his mortal foe. High above the Kingdom, clutched in the claws of a fearsome monster, their King fought with sword and shield to free their land from this terrible enemy.

The lost King and his lost Queen returned to the great World Tree, and together they introduced dragons back into the world.

*

Night had fallen on a long and arduous day. A well-established gale furiously lashed heavy raindrops at the castle windows, rattling the leaded glass against the iron casement. A fire roared in the grate, and within the warmth of the castle the new Queen and the new King looked out over their realm, watching the rain run in brooks and tributaries down the window pane and across the land. Despite his elevated position, the new King felt no less a soldier than before, and wrapped a protective arm around his shivering Queen. Both were wet through to the skin.

Timing had not been on their side, and a nasty turn in the weather had taken the whole town by surprise. The novel liquid stone of the newly constructed damn had not yet hardened to rock before the torrents of water had threatened to collapse this new structure. The new King had spent the afternoon with his troops up to his waist in the frothing river water, shoring up the structure with broad tree trunks hewn by others from the nearby forest.

The new Queen strode with purpose back and forth along the mud sodden river bank in the pouring rain, passionately directing men, women and materials to support the collective efforts of the submerged soldiers. The new-fangled steam ploughs had redirected the river for a short time, which had bought the town's people the respite they needed to save the dam, and save the fishery. The King looked up to the river bank to his beloved Queen as she rallied the town. Despite his labours in the muddied river, the King remained distracted that his Princess should be out in this horrendous weather in her current condition. This Queen was no more likely to slow than the Princess before her, nor the Queen that she replaced.

Dragons had returned to the land, and with them all the struggles that beset Humankind. Winters were sometimes harsh. Long hot summers could lead to drought. Crops could fail. Winds could destroy homes. Floods could flash through the town. Problems would arise, but solutions would be found. Ingenuity would transform the troubles of the world into victories to be shared. The youngsters believed once more in dragons and appreciated the ordeals endured by their forebears. They avidly consumed tales of trial and triumph with a relish that spurred their own efforts to make the world a better place for everyone.

Dragons had returned to the world, and with them followed problems. In response, the townsfolk had discovered all manner of ingenious device and artifice in response. Machines were constructed. Homes were heated in cold times. Food was preserved for the lean times. Home comforts were shared in the grim times. In their cosy dwellings the townsfolk found the health, happiness, fellowship and solidarity in the problems shared and the solutions devised.

The King and Queen looked out over the rain lashed land towards the river to spy a tiny orange speck that glowed in the dark. Despite the torrential rain and howling wind the entire community had spent their difficult day protecting this luminous speck. Paddle wheels, coils of metal and rocks that attract like a dragon's egg had wrought a spark through a glass bulb that cast a weak light across the river. Everyone agreed that it was still early days for this mechanical spectre, but this contraption most definitely was the future. Without dragons there would be no progress. Dragons had returned to assail Humanity, and despite the endless difficulties of being only Human in this unforgiving but bountiful world, they all lived happily ever after.

DRAGON EGG

20. THE LAST WORD

There is a magic to problem solving. To release that magic, you must take practical steps to prepare. You must peel and dice the problem. You discard the loose ends and state the problem clearly. You then feed your carefully prepared problem to the creativity of human minds, who will digest the problem to a warm glow.

Consider life clinging to a rocky cliff face before a thrashing sea. The turbulent waters generate moving mountains of new information to dash against the weathered rocks. The outcrop of land to which this life clings offers structure and order to protect and conserve any information that might offer some small advantage to this evolution brewing amongst the windswept crevices between the land and the sea. With a ready supply of new information, and a secure structure upon which to grow, this life may slowly become more complex and encounter new problems as it grows.

Two distinct characters inhabit the world of problem solving, who together offer a complete diagnostic whole.

The *chaotic creative* generates material in large quantities for others to consider. This inquisitive character will ask countless questions, and roam freely across the problem landscape picking things up, moving them around, looking under rocks and stones. This character is the boiling sea that tosses information this way and that to generate for just a moment volatile new forms and fleeting structures. This character is helpless without its counterpart.

The *conscientious curator* is just as creative as its partner, but adopts a more ordered approach. New information that is dashed against this character will be classified, catalogued and arranged into some suitable framework. This editor will employ structured frameworks to contain an exuberance of ideas and harness a chaotic power. This curator structures information to define action. It is the curator who takes this information and gives it *meaning*. The curator is the cliff face to which innovation can cling and grow.

A balanced team will disagree well. Opposed, but balanced, they will struggle against one another. The dark, cold, creative chaos draws information from the unknown. The light imposes structure, creates order, identifies the known and fixes it in place. Each the genesis of the other. Too much chaos breeds desire for order. Too much order breeds the desire for novelty, as antidote to stultifying predictability [7]. As the negotiation unfolds, ideas are created and ideas are destroyed in pursuit of the elusive Ideal, whilst the truth snakes along a sinuous boundary between the two. Ultimately, the idea gains life, clinging to that cliff face between the chaotic crashing ocean and the secure, stable land.

Then, you must squeeze. And squeeze. You squeeze that collective creativity until the pressure builds to ignite a spark amongst those minds. If you carefully fan that ember you will build an inferno that will burn your problem to the ground.

There is a *magic* to problem solving, and that magic comes from dragons.

21. THE 76 STANDARD SOLUTIONS

Class 1 Building and destruction of fields

1.1 Building or completing fields.

1.1.1 Complete the SU field. Determine if the system is missing any substances or fields, and add them where necessary.

1.1.2 Transition to an internal complex SU Field. Introduce an internal additive to the system to enhance an insufficient benefit.

1.1.3 Add something outside the substance. Introduce an external additive to enhance an insufficient benefit.

1.1.4 Use the environment. Introduce an additive from the environment to enhance an insufficient benefit.

1.1.5 Add something to the environment. Add something to the environment to enhance an insufficient benefit.

1.1.6 Be excessive. If a small enough quantity of a substance cannot be applied. Add too much, and remove the excess.

1.1.7 If a field is excessive, protect the substance by putting the full required force elsewhere. Add an intermediate that will absorb this excess field, and pass the required quantity on.

1.1.8.1 Maximum field, but not everywhere. A field may introduce harms whilst also offering benefits. Introduce a substance to block the harm.

1.1.8.2 Minimum field enhanced where required. A field may introduce harms whilst also offering benefits. Reduce the field until it no longer presents harm. Make the subject more sensitive to the diminished beneficial field.

1.2 Destruction of fields

1.2.1 Block the harm by introducing a new substance. Introduce the third substance between the given two substances. This third substance will remain unchanged.

1.2.2 We cannot introduce a new substance. Block the harm by introducing a substance made from substances already in the system.

1.2.3 Introduce a sacrificial substance to absorb the harm. This sacrificial substance will be transformed by the field absorbed.

1.2.4 A field presents both benefit and harm. Introduce a new field that counteracts the harm, whilst leaving the beneficial field. The useful effect is therefore provided by the existing field.

1.2.5 Use an opposing field to remove or counteract a magnetic harm.

Class 2 Development of Substance field models

2.1 Make things more complex, to deliver benefits more efficiently.

2.1.1 Chain substances together. Add an intermediate substance to amplify the influence of an insufficient field.

2.1.2 Create a double field. Use the field of one substance to enhance the field of an insufficient benefit.

2.2 Evolution of models.

2.2.1 Replace an uncontrolled or poorly controlled field with an easily controlled field. Escalate the type of field from gravitational, to mechanical, to acoustic, to thermal, to chemical, to magnetic, to electrical, and finally to the most controllable field, the electromagnetic.

2.2.2 Segment substances into particles, grains or powders.

2.2.3 Change the object from solid to a porous or capillary material that will allow gas or liquid to pass through.

2.2.4 Make the system more flexible, adaptable or dynamic. Make the characteristics of a substance vary in time.

2.2.5 Change from a uniform or uncontrolled field to a field with predetermined patterns. Transform a field from an unstructured or uncontrolled action into a more structured, periodic, pulsed, or resonant action.

2.2.6 Change substances from a uniform or uncontrolled structure to a non-uniform substance with a predetermined spatial structure.

2.3 Coordinate fields.
> 2.3.1 Match or mismatch the natural frequency of the field with the natural frequency of the substance that creates the field or the substance the field acts upon.
> 2.3.2 Match or mismatch the frequencies of the different fields employed.
> 2.3.3 When we have two incompatible actions, perform one action whilst the other is inactive.

2.4 Models using magnetic and electrical forces.
> 2.4.1 Use ferromagnetic materials or magnetic fields to add functions.
> 2.4.2 Segment ferromagnetic substances into particles, grains or powders.
> 2.4.3 Use magnetic ferro-fluids to provide the desired functions.
> 2.4.4 Use capillary structures that contain magnetic particles or liquid.
> 2.4.5 Introduce magnetic additives into one of the substances.
> 2.4.6 Introduce ferromagnetic materials into the external environment.
> 2.4.7 Control ferromagnetic system with physical effects. Add a field that modifies the properties of a ferromagnetic substance.
> 2.4.8 Dynamize a magnetic field. Enhance a ferromagnetic field by moving it. Make a magnetic field pulsed, periodic or modulated.
> 2.4.9 Shape a substance by introducing magnetic particles and applying a structured magnetic field.
> 2.4.10 Match the rhythms in ferromagnetic fields. Match the rhythm of a magnetic field with the substance against which it acts.
> 2.4.11 Use an electric current to create magnetic fields.
> 2.4.12 Use electro-rheological fluids where viscosity is controlled by an electric field.

Class 3 Transition to the super system and sub system

3.1 Improving systems by adding or copying elements.

3.1.1 Use multiple copies of components already present in the system.

3.1.2 Improve the links between copied system elements. Make the copied elements interact with one another.

3.1.3 Transform the functions that copied components offer to increase the differences between their functions, to opposites if required.

3.1.4 System simplification. Achieve all functions but reduce/trim components. Integrate several components into one but still deliver all the functions desired.

3.1.5 If two desirable functions cannot coexist, or counter one another's actions, deliver opposite incompatible functions at different system levels.

3.2 System transition to the micro level.

3.2.1 Transition function delivery to the micro level.

Class 4 Solutions for detection and measurement

4.1 Indirect methods of measurement.

4.1.1 Change the systems so that there is no need for detection or measurement.

4.1.2 Measure a copy or an image of a substance.

4.1.3 Transform the problem into detection of consecutive successive changes.

4.2 Create or build a measurement system.

4.2.1 We need to measure something, but cannot do it directly. Measure a substance that is connected to the substance measured.

4.2.2 We need to measure something, but cannot do it directly. Measure a field that is connected to the substance measured.

4.2.3 We need to measure something, but cannot do it directly. We cannot add anything to the system. Introduce an additive to the surrounding environment which reacts to changes in the system.

4.2.4 If substances cannot be added to the system or the environment, create a measurement system by changing the state of something in the environment.

4.3 Improving, enhancing measurement systems through fields
    4.3.1 Create a measurement system using natural phenomena.
    4.3.2 If changes to the system cannot be measured, measure the excited resonant frequency of the entire system.
    4.3.3 If a measurement system cannot be created from the resonant frequency of the entire system, measure the resonance of a joined object or the environment.

4.4 Use external substances and fields to help measurements
    4.4.1 Create a measurement system by using a suitable detectable substance, such as ferromagnetism.
    4.4.2 Create a measurement system by adding detectable ferromagnetic particles to the system.
    4.4.3 If detectable particles cannot be added to the system, or a substance cannot be replaced by detectable particles, create a complex system by putting detectable particles into the substance.
    4.4.4 Make a measurement system by putting detectable additives into the environment.
    4.4.5 Measure the effect of phenomena associated with magnetism. Create a measurement system using the Curie point, Hopkins and Barkhausen, etc.

4.5 Evolution of the measurement systems
    4.5.1 Use more than one measurement system to get a more accurate result
    4.5.2 Measurement systems evolve towards indirect measurement of features or derivatives of the functions being measured.

Class 5 Support to create more ideal systems.

5.1 Methods for introducing substances under restricted conditions.
    5.1.1 Indirect methods.
        5.1.1.1 Introduce voids, fields, air, bubbles, foam.
        5.1.1.2 Use a field instead a substance.
        5.1.1.3 Use an external additive instead of an internal additive.

5.1.1.4 Use a small amount of a very concentrated or active additive.
5.1.1.5 Concentrate an additive at a specific location.
5.1.1.6 Introduce an additive temporarily.
5.1.1.7 Use a copy or model of the object in which additives can be used.
5.1.1.8 When no new substances can be permanently added to a system, introduce a chemical compound which can be later decomposed.
5.1.1.9 When no new substances can be permanently added to a system, create an additive from the decomposition of either the environment or the object itself.

5.1.2 Segmentation. The new substance could be created by divide the object into smaller units.

5.1.3 Introduce a substance that disappears after carrying out its work or becomes identical to substances already in the system or environment

5.1.4 When we need large amounts but must use nothing. Use voids, foams, inflatable structures, etc.

5.2 Introducing fields under restricted conditions.

5.2.1 Use fields present in the system to cause the creation of another field.
5.2.2 Use fields that are present in the environment.
5.2.3 If we cannot create new fields, use fields that substances already present in the system can generate.

5.3 Phase transitions.

5.3.1 Improve the function of a substance by changing the phase of the substance.
5.3.2 Multiple properties can be obtained from a substance by converting the substance from one phase to another.
5.3.3 Use a phenomenon which accompanies a phase change, such as a change of volume, viscosity, etc.
5.3.4 Dual properties can be obtained by replacing a single phase state with dual phase state – a substance that can exhibit two different states simultaneously.
5.3.5 Dual properties can be obtained by replacing a

single phase state with dual phase state which can be improved by creating an interaction between the two phases of the substance.

5.4 Clever use of natural phenomena.

    5.4.1 If a substance must change its state, use substances that can control themselves. A substance should transition from one state to the other by itself using reversible transformations.

    5.4.2 From a weak input field produce a strong output field. Drive a substance to a near critical state, then drive the transition with a weak input signal.

5.5 Generating higher or lower forms of substances

    5.5.1 Obtain the required substance by decomposing a more complex substance.

    5.5.2 Obtain the required substance by combining particles of simpler substances.

    5.5.3 If a substance of a high structural level has to be decomposed the easiest way is to decompose the nearest higher element. When decomposing particles of a lower structural level, the easiest way is to complete the nearest lower level.

DRAGON EGG

22. WORKS CITED

[1] E. Reis, The Startup Way: How Entrepreneurial Management Transforms Culture and Drives Growth.

[2] S. Blank, The Four Steps to the Epiphany: Successful Strategies for Products That Win, 2013.

[3] G. B. A. S. T. P. Alexander Osterwalder Yves Pigneur, Value Proposition Design: How to Create Products and Services Customers Want (Strategyzer), 2014.

[4] B. D. Steve Blank, The Startup Owner's Manual: The Step-By-Step Guide for Building a Great Company, 2012.

[5] E. Ries, The Lean Startup: How Constant Innovation Creates Radically Successful Businesses, 2011.

[6] F. Capra, The Tao of Physics: An Exploration of the Parallels Between Modern Physics and Eastern Mysticism, 1976.

[7] J. B. Peterson, Maps of Meaning: The Architecture of Belief, 1999.

[8] J. Campbell., The Hero with a Thousand Faces, 1949.

[9] S. Levy, ARTIFICIAL LIFE, 2008.

[10] U. K. L. Guin, Lau Tzu Tao Te Ching, 1998.

[11] B. Lee, The Tao of Jeet Kun Do., 1975.

[12] S. Field, Screenplay, 2005.

[13] G. Altshuller, Innovation Algorithm, 1999.

[14] L. Haines-Gadd, TRIZ For Dummies, 2016.

[15] G. Altshuller, Creativity As an Exact Science, 1984.

[16] M. Lewis, Moneyball, 2003.

[17] K. Gadd, TRIZ for Engineers: Enabling Inventive Problem Solving, 2011.

[18] K. Tsiolkovsky, Speculations about Earth and Sky and on Vesta., 1895.

[19] C. M. Christensen, The Innovator's Dilemma: When New Technologies Cause Great Firms to Fail, 2013.

[20] Y. P. Alexander Osterwalder, Business Model Generation: A Handbook for Visionaries, Game Changers, and Challengers, 2010.

[21] D. Roam, Unfolding the Napkin: The Hands-On Method for Solving Complex Problems with Simple Pictures, 2009.

[22] D. Roam, Show and Tell: How Everybody Can Make Extraordinary Presentations, 2014.

[23] D. Stinton, The Design of the Aeroplane, 1985.

[24] G. Altshuller, And suddenly the inventor appeared, 1996.

[25] T. F. Giff Constable, Talking to Humans: Success starts with understanding your customers, 2014.

Printed in Great Britain
by Amazon